GET IN

Also by Patrick Maguire and Gabriel Pogrund

Left Out: The Inside Story of Labour Under Corbyn

GET IN

The Inside Story of Labour Under Starmer

PATRICK MAGUIRE &
GABRIEL POGRUND

BH

THE BODLEY HEAD
LONDON

1 3 5 7 9 10 8 6 4 2

The Bodley Head, an imprint of Vintage, is part of the
Penguin Random House group of companies

Vintage, Penguin Random House UK, One Embassy Gardens,
8 Viaduct Gardens, London SW11 7BW

penguin.co.uk/vintage
global.penguinrandomhouse.com

Penguin
Random House
UK

First published by The Bodley Head in 2025

Typeset in 11.5/14pt Dante MT Std by Jouve (UK), Milton Keynes
Printed and bound in Great Britain by Clays Ltd, Elcograf S.p.A.

The authorised representative in the EEA is Penguin Random House Ireland,
Morrison Chambers, 32 Nassau Street, Dublin D02 YH68

A CIP catalogue record for this book is available from the British Library

ISBN 9781847928375

Penguin Random House is committed to a sustainable future
for our business, our readers and our planet. This book is made
from Forest Stewardship Council® certified paper.

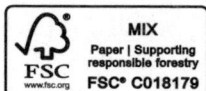

MIX
Paper | Supporting
responsible forestry
FSC
www.fsc.org
FSC® C018179

'Greater love hath no man than this, that he
lay down his friends for his life.'

Jeremy Thorpe after John 15:13

Contents

PART V: RESOLUTION

Prologue

Enough. She's heard this conversation before. Beating himself up again. Wanting more – needing more. Whenever her husband is alone with him it's like this. Obsessive, never satisfied. Usually he hates talking about politics, but these conversations are an exception. All he wants to do is win. Tonight he has, but still, somehow, it doesn't seem good enough.

Victoria Starmer is watching them going up, the two boys together at last after six weeks apart, heading to the party they always wanted. It's being thrown in her husband's honour and yet now, just as it's real, he's talking like there's nothing to celebrate. Parties like this don't happen often. When this journey began, seven years ago, the smart money was on a party like this never happening again. But when he steps out of the lift on the sixth floor of Tate Modern, hundreds of people will cheer him.

Because it's happened. He's going to be prime minister. Only six other leaders of the Labour Party have ever known that feeling, only three have known this one: to win an election from opposition, everything changing at 10 p.m. on polling day, the impotence giving way to the power and the glory the left so seldom knows in Britain. Only he knows how it feels to win like this. Four years ago, when he took this job, they told him he'd never be here – the colleagues who looked upon him with pity and condescension. There was no party in 2019, when Labour lost nearly as badly as the Conservatives just have. There were times, too, when Keir Starmer told himself he'd never do it.

Now he has, but he can't enjoy it. As they're going up and up, Starmer turns to Morgan McSweeney. He always does, because this Irishman always has the answers. He's asked McSweeney questions like this so many times – about the numbers he doesn't quite understand. Tonight looks a little different. McSweeney's in a suit: that's new. There's a faint smell of cigar smoke. In victory Labour's campaign director looks like a different man, dressed like he works for winners.

A few hours earlier they'd been apart, awaiting the same moment with their arms around family. Just before 10 p.m., Starmer was in Covent Garden, over the Thames, in a penthouse loaned to him for the campaign, holding his wife and children tightly. McSweeney had been in Labour headquarters, not far away from where they are now, almost inconspicuous in a dense crowd of young advisers who worshipped him like a god. When the hour came they both heard the BBC tell them that the Labour Party had won, and won big, with a landslide majority of 170 seats. Both had wanted more.

They know it's real now, and that's a problem. 'I think we can get a few more seats,' McSweeney says, his voice and the fading red hair betraying where this journey really started, in a small town in West Cork. 'But I don't think we'll get to 1997 numbers.' That's the year they've both been thinking of – the last year a Labour leader, Tony Blair, felt what they're feeling. But Blair felt something more. His majority was bigger – 179 seats. Starmer doesn't like that. People often ask what he really believes. He sometimes struggles to answer. Those who know him have a simple answer. He wants to win. He needs to be the best.

Tonight Starmer has fallen short. It's a small failure, perceptible only to him. But he can't resist. He and McSweeney start moaning. Victoria Starmer has heard enough. She tells them to stop, just as she's had to before, when they spent the night at a friend's wedding talking endlessly about politics. 'You're bringing the mood down,' she says. So they stop, and soon the lift stops too. The doors open onto a room that's waiting for Keir Starmer – a gathering so few people in Britain thought would ever come to pass. Before he takes his first steps into this new reality, Starmer turns again to McSweeney.

'Come and walk through with me.'

'No,' the Irishman says. 'I'm not doing that.'

Starmer walks in, alone. All around him are the people who helped make the unthinkable happen: a sea of smiling faces who for so long, when Labour was still losing, had so little to be happy about. Nobody says it – not tonight – but they spent the first years of his leadership frowning, too. When he became leader, in the months after Labour's worst election defeat since 1935, more of these people than he could ever know doubted whether he would lead them to its greatest victory since 1997. For now that doesn't matter. There's a deafening cheer.

Starmer makes his way to the middle of the crowd. Before long he realises something is missing. He can't do this by himself. Not now, after everything they've done together. It wouldn't be right. It has to end like it started. He turns back and he grabs McSweeney, bashful now, and drags him exactly where he doesn't want to be. Now everyone is cheering both of the men who made it happen. Before long McSweeney slips away, alone, back into the obscurity he knows he'll never enjoy again.

*

The twisting, implausible story of British politics in the twenty-first century has been told mostly in cliché and hyperbole. In Westminster, a place addicted to instability, what is unsurprising is breathlessly recounted as shocking or astonishing. Recurring and predictable events are described as unprecedented. Forgettable disagreements over unremarkable issues are cast as civil wars. To organise is to plot, and mild dissent is revolutionary insurrection. The truth – inconvenient though it is for political journalists – is that little of what happens in Parliament or to politicians really merits its billing as high drama.

The recent history of the Labour Party is a rare exception. To study the party's troubled, 124-year life is to categorise different kinds of failure, punctuated intermittently by successes containing failures of their own. In 2020, when Keir Starmer succeeded Jeremy Corbyn as leader of the opposition – the highest honour most of their predecessors ever knew – conventional wisdom dictated that he, too, would fail. This judgement was at once the hardy perennial of British politics, for Labour leaders seldom win, and also a reflection of time and place.

Over the preceding four years, Labour had done things differently. Under Corbyn it was transformed. Its answer to a new age of economic and geopolitical uncertainty was an old gospel of left populism, powered by a mass membership of half a million. Proudly socialist, anti-imperialist, at one with the idealistic activists to whom Labour

leaders had only ever been a disappointment and at odds with the
corporate interests to which most mainstream politicians paid loyal
obeisance: this was not the sort of opposition Britain had ever known
before. Fleetingly, at the general election of 2017, Corbyn looked as if
he might remake the country as he had his party. But for a few thousand votes in a few dozen constituencies he might have been prime
minister.

He never was. When Britain came to vote again, in 2019, Brexit and
accusations of antisemitism against Corbyn had broken the left of the
Labour Party. A political project defined for so long by its unbreakable solidarity was shattered by events and the questions it could not
answer. Its leader, once a man whose moral clarity seemed to speak for
a lost generation, struggled to speak for himself. When Labour lost to
Boris Johnson's Conservatives that year it seemed to herald a permanent realignment of British politics. Voters in the very seats the Labour
Party had been founded to represent – the old industrial towns of the
north and Midlands – instead gave a historic mandate to the party they
had once blamed for making them poor. The English suburbs that had
once voted for Blair and New Labour had long since turned blue. Scotland, too, seemed lost to nationalism. As McSweeney would say later to
friends at a south London dinner table, 'There's something very stubborn about these voters. They're going to be very hard to get back.'

In the aftermath of that defeat, Starmer did not tell Labour members
that he would be different. His promise was predictability. To the left,
this former human rights barrister said he would preserve the radical
spirit of Corbynism. He spoke an idealistic language they understood
and he had, after all, served dutifully as Jeremy's shadow Brexit secretary and marched with them as they tried and failed to overturn
the result of the EU referendum. To the party's activists he made Ten
Pledges, each a commitment to a consensus the British public had
rejected: higher taxes on the wealthy, a dovish foreign policy, and a liberal immigration regime.

Labour's establishment – the Blairites and hard-nosed right-wingers
the unclubbable Starmer did not know – did not much like that. But
Starmer was at least recognisable to these people, too. As a former director of public prosecutions he was, at least, a serious person. It was
possible to imagine this square-jawed man of indeterminate middle
age addressing the country from outside 10 Downing Street. But really

they expected that Keir Starmer – the prime minister – would stay there, in their imagination, to be replaced in time with a leader who spoke with the self-confidence and fluency this stopgap option could never quite summon.

What they did not imagine was what happened. For this they could hardly be blamed, for so much of what brought it about was withheld from all but two men and their intimates. Even the chosen, secretive few did not dare to dream of the minutes after 10 p.m. on 4 July 2024, when McSweeney stepped out onto the balcony of Labour's headquarters in Southwark. He took a long drag on a cigar and called the man who had asked him, in the summer of 2019, to help make him leader of the Labour Party.

'Congratulations,' McSweeney said to Starmer. 'You're prime minister.'

That night those words had come naturally. Nobody working in British politics in 2019 might have predicted that Labour would win 411 seats to the Conservatives' 121 come the next election. But in a single night Starmer reversed electoral trends that had ossified into the laws of British politics. His Labour Party won in urban England and rural England; in counties that had long since turned true blue, like Essex, Kent, Norfolk, Suffolk, Cornwall, Devon and Dorset; and it once again became the largest party in Scotland. All of this he managed with only 33.7 per cent of the total votes cast, fewer than any winning prime minister in the history of the United Kingdom, and with collapsing support among Labour's old core voters on the liberal left and in British Muslim communities.

By 2024 three Conservative leaders had so spectacularly failed to fulfil the promise of Johnson's mandate – a booming Britain whose poor provinces were levelled up with its wealthy capital – that their defeat seemed all but inevitable. That, however, was never how it had felt to Starmer. Nor McSweeney, who, having come to London as a seventeen-year-old slacker, applied himself with almost deranged intensity to changing a Labour Party whose failures he experienced first-hand. At first a young and unremarkable organiser, sent out by New Labour into a country that was rapidly falling out of love with Blair, a series of historic victories came to bear his fingerprints. What each had in common was the understanding that candidates who did not listen to their voters were doomed to lose.

It was just as unlikely, too, that Angela Rayner should ever know this feeling. That night the deputy leader of the Labour Party was nearly 200 miles away, awaiting her re-election as an MP in Greater Manchester. Having begun life as the child of a broken home on a Stockport council estate, once mistakenly fed dog food by her illiterate mother, in mere weeks she would be dining with the King at Balmoral as deputy prime minister. Belittled by her own party, maligned by the press, here she was nonetheless, on the cusp of power people like her were never supposed to know – ready, like only a handful of working-class women before her, to change the country at the helm of a Labour government.

So too Sue Gray, the chief of staff who had left school at sixteen for a career cleaning up after the gilded sons of Britain's Civil Service. Now, at last, she had the chance to run a government that did things differently, just as Starmer wanted – planning for the long term, for the public good, pursuing five missions in the national interest, not merely chasing headlines and the affirmation of the press who had made these past few years a misery. This victory was her vindication, too. Only two years earlier she had been hated by Conservative ministers as she investigated their misdeeds, and was pursued by shadowy figures on her own street. Starmer alone seemed to understand and respect her – to want her at his side. Now she held the power in the land that she had watched, resentfully, being wielded by well-heeled men who all seemed to look and sound the same. This government would be *her* government. She had written its script and auditioned its cast of ministers. Here was her chance to prove them wrong. That, at least, was how it felt that night.

Did McSweeney always tell voters the truth about his mission? Did Starmer? For four years that question recurred, asked repeatedly by the politicians and colleagues never invited into the tight and tiny circle of trust that remade the Labour Party and discarded Starmer's principles, so many of which were casually abandoned by the leader they once trusted. The Keir Starmer of 5 July 2024 was not the man who had become Labour leader on 4 April 2020, when he embodied the values of the activist left that had been his making as a lawyer. His utopian promise was that another future was possible. The future he and McSweeney offered was one in which the leader of the Labour Party defined himself against its very identity.

The prime minister's favourite band is the Wedding Present, the indie rockers he came to know when he was at Leeds University in the 1980s. In 'Brassneck', one of their better-known singles, they sing of asking 'if the end was worth the means / Was there really no in between?' The many people whose careers have come to a brutal end at Starmer's remorseless hand ask the same question, and the British public may in time come to ask it too.

★

This book is the first full account of how these two journeys became one, and returned the Labour Party to power after fourteen years in opposition. Much of this story has necessarily been untold until now. Starmer himself tells a bowdlerised version in which, having reckoned with the electorate's comprehensive rejection of Corbyn's Labour by the electorate in 2019, he concluded that his party needed to change and made sure it did – even if that meant expelling Corbyn, the leader he had once called a friend.

McSweeney, who is one of many people to have advised Starmer but is without question the most significant, has never spoken publicly of his work for the man who became prime minister. But there is now an accepted and all but authorised version of his story, too: of the Labour organiser who spent the Corbyn years polling a party membership thought to have been lost to the hard left, concluded Keir Starmer was the man to win them over, and proceeded to execute a seamless strategy to transform their party and make him prime minister in a single term.

Tony Blair tells one version of the Starmer story like this: 'I think he realised pretty early on that the Labour Party was just in a fundamentally bad position, needed to be shifted, and then he started to do it. It's possible that his journey isn't like Neil Kinnock's, where you start on the left and then you move right. I don't think he really started anywhere except vaguely progressive. And then, very unusually, only when he was leader did he really start to think about politics in a different way.' It is at once a faithful retelling of the official history and a glimpse into the private doubts of the politicians who now make up Britain's government. Many of the current cabinet begin this story at a degree's remove from the Starmer project, refusing to endorse him for the leadership and nurturing doubts that still endure about what, if anything, his politics represent – and whether, even now, they truly wish for him to lead the Labour Party and the country.

Political histories are written by victors, even in the Labour Party, and in doing so they elide the inconvenient events and people that once stood in the way of their ending. Gambling is recast as strategic genius. Doubters and dissenters, however well reasoned their arguments may have sounded at the time, are maligned as cranks. Tensions evaporate and the most awkward questions that recurred in private go unasked. It is precisely because of the nature of Starmer's victory – its implausibility, the fragility of his electoral mandate, and the sharpness of the contrast between the Labour leader he promised to be in 2020 and the Labour prime minister who went on to govern Britain – that the full story of his leadership to date deserves to be told.

That story, at its heart, is the story of his relationship with McSweeney – and its defining question is whether the man who became prime minister can truly be described as its primary author. So much of what has unfolded under Starmer's leadership departs so dramatically from what he has said publicly and privately at any given point in these five years that even the people who have worked at his right hand in opposition and government question whether he can truly be described as a leader. The prime minister has already contributed extensively to a fine biography by Tom Baldwin. This book does not attempt to retell comprehensively the life story of Starmer the man. Instead it seeks to decode the mystery of Starmer the politician, which by turns deepens and dissipates as one speaks to the many people who have known him professionally throughout his rise to power, and place him in his proper context.

On the morning of that Labour landslide on 5 July, the most fundamental questions about the party's candidate remained unanswered. How did Starmer do what most Labour leaders so singularly fail to do – not only win, but win so convincingly? Why did he do it? How many of the discombobulating changes Labour made under his leadership – how it looked, what it said, who it sought to represent – can really be said to have anything to do with him? These are unusual questions to ask of a leader. For better or worse, the politics of the Labour Party usually bear the imprint of their personality and philosophy. But then Starmer is unusual, because more often than not he projects neither – and often quite deliberately. The only consistent answer shared by the many interviewees whose testimonies inform this book is that he wants, more than anything, to win. 'He is a completely hard bastard,' says Martin Plaut, a friend from Kentish Town who has watched Starmer on the football pitch as well as the doorstep. 'He plays to the edge of the rules, really hard.'

Having promised unity with the left, he proceeded to purge the Labour Party with unprecedented vigour. Every principle he said he held dear in 2020 has been ritually disavowed. That year Doreen Lawrence, the Labour peer who channelled her sorrow at the 1993 racist murder of her son Stephen into a campaign for justice championed by Starmer, launched his campaign for the Labour leadership. By 2024 she was complaining: 'I wish Keir listened to me. There are gatekeepers who stop things from happening.' Did Britain elect the leader of the Labour Party, or the people leading him? As one senior government adviser said in the first months of Starmer's premiership: 'It's impossible to work out whether Keir realises he is a pawn in a chess game. Or does he like being a pawn in a chess game, provided it makes him powerful?'

★

This account is the product of a year of interviews and contemporaneous conversations with more than a hundred people who played their own part in Labour's return to government – the advisers closest to Starmer and those who left, his personal friends, members of his shadow cabinet and cabinet, Labour MPs, trade union leaders, and his avowed opponents on the hard left and at the commanding heights of Conservative politics. It draws not only on their recollections as recounted in formal interviews with the authors, and the candid assessments they offered at the time of events, but also their emails, text messages, and other contemporaneous written records that were never intended to be published but reveal far more of the complicated truth of the past five years than any public statement ever will. Memories are often fallible or selective. Conflicting interpretations of the same words or moments abound, even among close friends – all of which are reflected and recorded alongside the facts of this history. Written words, particularly those transmitted digitally, are not so vulnerable to revisionism.

The story unfolds primarily in Westminster, Starmer's home turf of Kentish Town, and the various corners of central London where

Labour has been headquartered since 2019 – with forays out into the rest of the UK, Ireland, Europe and the Middle East. It will be for others to offer academic analysis of the 2024 result, provide an exhaustive account of the Covid pandemic that so disrupted the first years of Starmer's leadership, and trace in full the revival of the Scottish Labour Party. The dinner tables of private homes feature more frequently in these pages than the streets of individual constituencies. This, to borrow from the high Tory historian Maurice Cowling, is instead the story of fifty or sixty politicians and advisers in conscious tension with one another. Some win, many more lose: all of their experiences are recorded here.

The events described do not amount to a comprehensive record of British politics during this period, but instead are those the Labour leadership, its servants and its adversaries now recall as formative. Many of these stories have never been told before and in some cases considerable effort has been expended in preventing them from being reported. They have been told as they are told privately, complete with the expletives that illustrate the ferocity of feeling only Labour politics can inspire. Together they record more of the truth of how Morgan McSweeney and many others made Keir Starmer prime minister than has been told before, and how close that story came to ending long before July 2024. This is the story the people who now run Britain tell themselves about their rise to power. As the country makes its uneasy adjustments to a new era of Labour government, it also reveals how its rulers will exercise it – and who those rulers really are.

PART I: ORIGINS

I

The Irishman

It's late afternoon on 2 April 2019 and Jeremy Corbyn is about to come face to face with the conspiracy that will one day destroy him.

He waits in the office of the leader of the opposition – his office – a room that looks nothing like the average Briton's vision of politics. To reach its doors, visitors have to walk away from the chamber of the House of Commons, turn their back on the statues, ministerial cars – on Parliament itself – and instead walk away from history, go underground, up escalators, through cigarette smoke. Once they arrive before the fading red bricks of Norman Shaw Buildings, looming over the Thames like a Victorian sanatorium, they must climb a winding stair to the fifth floor. On this afternoon an Irishman climbs the stairs to that room where Jeremy Corbyn, now in his fourth year as leader of the Labour Party, is waiting for him.

Corbyn does not know him, nor his intentions. Had his staff googled the name they would have read of a baseball pitcher for the reserve team of the Baltimore Orioles. Nor will the visitor reveal those intentions. If he does, his plan is doomed.

Since 2015 almost everybody in the Labour Party has tried to destroy Jeremy Corbyn, the socialist whose politics they dismissed as dangerous and mad. No – everyone in Westminster has tried to destroy Jeremy Corbyn. In 2016 Labour MPs tried to destroy him by demanding his resignation, and he said no. They staged a leadership challenge, and the activists of the Labour Party said no. In 2017 the Conservatives tried to destroy him at the ballot box, and the country said no. By April 2019 dissent against Corbyn seems pointless, self-defeating. The Labour Party now belongs to him, the quiet old man alone at the boardroom table, surrounded by empty cans of Diet Coke. But his visitor today, a man named Morgan McSweeney, thinks otherwise.

In fact, he knows otherwise. He says he's here to tell Corbyn about something called Labour Together. It sounds unthreatening. *Labour Together*. That's the kind of ethos Jeremy likes. In the press, and in the parliamentary bars, they call him a Stalinist. But really he hates conflict. He can't bear to hear his critics accuse him of antisemitism, or read of himself villainised as a friend of terrorists by the newspapers. So when Morgan McSweeney arrives to tell him about Labour Together, he has nothing to fear. McSweeney looks like a whippet in denim, and speaks softly – nothing like the bruisers of the Parliamentary Labour Party (PLP) who make Corbyn's life a constant misery. He talks the leader through some polling, the most detailed ever conducted on the half a million grass-roots members that are Jeremy's pride and joy. Labour Together knows what they think of Europe, of economic policy, of Corbyn himself, and they're happy to let him have the data for free.

It's a generous gesture. Corbyn likes the sound of Labour Together. He listens for a while and endorses their work. Soon he's chatting idly about the Italian Marxist philosopher and politician Antonio Gramsci. He thinks he's in the company of people who respect him, unlike so many others in the Labour Party. It will be eighteen months before he realises he was wrong. Because Morgan McSweeney is not there to help Jeremy. He's there to destroy his politics. And, like everyone else, Jeremy hasn't noticed a thing.

Beside McSweeney sits an aide to Corbyn who scrolls through Jeremy's Facebook page as the discussion rambles aimlessly on. He basks in the affirmation. Like. Like. Like. Labour activists love Jeremy. This is why they'll never be beaten.

Within a year, Corbynism is defeated. Six months later, Corbyn is humiliated: suspended from the party he had led into two elections, never to return.

His guest that day in April 2019, the man from West Cork, was the mastermind of a deception without precedent in British politics. Even the name of Labour Together was a lie. Its mission was division, the inverse of the old prayer of St Francis of Assisi so often invoked in Westminster. Where there was harmony between the Labour Party and its leader, it would bring discord. Where there was truth, it would bring error. Where there was faith, it would bring doubt. Where there was hope, it would bring despair. McSweeney would convince the left-wingers of the Labour membership, who had waited lifetimes to hear a leader speak with the moral clarity of Jeremy Corbyn, to abandon Corbynism without them ever realising. And he would convince them to make Sir Keir Starmer, the human rights lawyer from north London, the Labour leader who buried the left.

Starmer had become a Labour MP because he wanted to be prime minister. He never knew how to defeat the Corbynites. Nobody did: Starmer had been forced to work with them – as their spokesman on Brexit – instead. He had gritted his teeth as they rowed over the future of Britain in Europe and examined his conscience. 'They're just *bastards*, aren't they?' his wife, Victoria, would say in unguarded moments. But they were bastards that her husband did not know how to beat.

Until he met Morgan McSweeney.

★

The journey that would eventually take Sir Keir Starmer to 10 Downing Street began twenty-five years before McSweeney's meeting with Jeremy Corbyn.

It was a heady summer to be young in Ireland in 1994. Jack Charlton had taken a team full of Englishmen in green jerseys across the Atlantic to the World Cup. One afternoon, a seventeen-year-old set out from Cork in the opposite direction. He boarded a Slatterys coach to London, destined for the Fulham home of an aunt. Thirty-six hours later he arrived in a city whose political class was ill at ease with itself. John Smith, the leader of the Labour Party, had died suddenly of a heart attack. He was a Scotsman of both the old and Enlightenment schools: hard-living, quick-witted, deep-thinking. His young disciples, Tony Blair and Gordon Brown, watched him less with awe and reverence than fear and anxiety. Not of the scale of the challenge before them should Labour return to government under Smith, but the fear that he was not equipped to meet it. That they would lose again, that for all the conciliatory gestures in City boardrooms he was really Old Labour's last hurrah. On the evening of 11 May, drawn and exhausted, Smith rose to his feet before an audience of donors on Park Lane. 'The opportunity to serve our country. That is all we ask.' Twelve hours later, he was dead on the linoleum floor of his Barbican flat. In the weeks that followed, Blair and Brown agonised over who might replace him. It was the younger man who would win, and pull his unwilling party towards the Third Way and a new Labour: furling the red flag, abandoning its old shibboleths, courting the Conservative press. Neither knew that in those weeks another new chapter in the contested, troubled history of the Labour Party had begun, far away, with the tentative steps of a lazy boy at a bus station.

Had anyone in Cork been told, they would not have believed it. Morgan McSweeney was a slacker. He hated school. He had little time for the political obsessions of his parents, an accountant and a clerical worker. Only the most conscientious student of Irish geography might know Macroom, his home town, site of the fiercest fighting in the Irish Civil War. Tens of thousands of Irishmen without prospects had taken the same journey. None would think their destiny was to change the politics or the history of a country to which they did not belong, just as Blair would soon do. Not the eldest son of Tim and Carmel McSweeney, anyway. The boy Morgan seldom joined them as they canvassed for Fine Gael, the party of Ireland's petit bourgeois. The Blueshirts had been his birthright. In a country run by Fianna Fáil's 'gombeen men' – practitioners of petty, parish-pump corruption – it was not a happy one. Usually they lost: not only elections but the public appointments, money, power.

But the McSweeneys had no choice. Family lore stated that Morgan's grandfather had been an IRA courier as Michael Collins led the fight for independence, bearing messages from Dublin to Cork, evading the Black and Tans. When Collins was martyred after proposing compromise with the British, he stayed loyal. Subterfuge ran in the family. So would politics. As his cousins ran from house to house spreading the gospel of Garret FitzGerald, the short-lived Taoiseach who broke bread with Margaret Thatcher, Morgan stood alone before the wall instead. In his hand was his hurl and sliotar, unloved by the other boys in Macroom, who played in his father's Gaelic football team. All alone he bounced the ball back and forth for hours, as other people made politics happen.

In London he worked on building sites. Winter came and he concluded that he did not much like labouring. He went to university instead. Within twelve months he had dropped out. All alone, he bounced back and forth again. First to California, to live in the presbytery of the church at which his uncle was priest. Then to Israel, adjusting uneasily to the free-market reforms of a young Benjamin Netanyahu, for three months on the kind of kibbutz that was passing into history. The old collectivist dream of socialism and workers' power was dying in this changing country, just as it had in Britain.

Yet in a factory built by Czech Jews at Sarid, nine miles from Nazareth, the lazy teenager learned to work. He built saw-cutters and grinding wheels. He returned to London not just with a tan but a work ethic. In 1998 aged twenty-one he enrolled at Middlesex University to study for the life he had always avoided in favour of the hurling pitch, the family sweetshop and Liverpool Football Club. As he began his degree in politics and marketing, Blair had been prime minister for just over a year. By then his government had already brokered peace in Northern Ireland.

Inspired, McSweeney joined the Labour Party. His were not the politics of so many of the Irishmen and Irishwomen who found a political home away from home on the British left. His family did not know he had politics at all. But by 2001 he would be working in its headquarters, in the Millbank Tower, on a university placement. Few would remember the skinny kid with the scissors and glue, all alone before a hulking computer called Excalibur. McSweeney's thankless task was to cut up the newspapers, glue their component parts to pieces of card, and feed them into the database built by Peter Mandelson, Blair's close ally and key architect of New Labour, to rebut Conservative attacks. Eventually he went home jobless and waited, alone and bored again, until the landline rang.

'What are you doing?' asked a man from Labour's headquarters in Millbank. It was days before the general election of 2001. Millbank's receptionist had dropped a vase on her foot. Quentin Padgett, Labour's head of facilities, told him that he was now gainfully employed by the Labour Party.

McSweeney manned the entrance through which the aristocracy of New Labour walked. They never said hello. Mandelson does not remember the boy behind the desk. Not once did he look at the young man who one day was to change Labour twice as fast and twice as hard as he had. Members of Blair's cabinet are still bewildered by McSweeney's rise. It would take them a long time to grasp that their former receptionist had bigger plans. One senior Blairite who met him in the Corbyn years said: 'I didn't realise that he was the big brains behind the whole thing. He's quite modest. He talks in numbers . . . he's an unprepossessing character. He's not Peter Mandelson. And he's not self-promoting.' Blair himself now laughs at the very thought of Mandelson ignoring McSweeney. 'He may have then. He doesn't now.'

Then, everybody did. No minister was to hire him as their special adviser. Nor did he join the golden generation of Young Turks who went on to run the country. He was no Miliband, Balls or Burnham. In Westminster, as in Macroom, other people made politics happen. After New Labour won its second landslide, the hapless Iain Duncan Smith was elected leader of the opposition. When the news reached Millbank, everybody cheered. They punched the air and jumped on their desks. They said the Tories would never win an election again. McSweeney watched, and walked out into the country that Labour would soon begin to lose.

*

McSweeney learned his politics street by street. He did not walk the corridors of power but the pavements of places the Blairites who ignored him took for granted. As an organiser, his thankless task was to win the elections whose results the golden generation took as read. First, in 2003, he went to North Wales, grinding votes from tiny towns like Abergele, Ruthin and Colwyn Bay, for a new parliament a hundred miles away in Cardiff. It was lonely work. Most of the people did not care.

He went back to London. He was there, organising the Labour campaign, when the Liberal Democrats struck the first blow against New Labour after the Iraq War in Brent East. There the people did care. Blair, who had a different politics and a different country, had not listened to them. Two years later he went to the people again. They told Blair he had been wrong. Labour lost. He took his punishment. He called it the masochism strategy. He never conceded the point. Blair thought the people were wrong: about Iraq, about the state of their hospitals and schools. In that campaign McSweeney went to Hammersmith, where they voted in a Conservative MP. But it was not enough to oust Labour from power. Blair returned to Downing Street, chastened but comfortable, with the last parliamentary majority any Labour leader would win for nineteen years.

By 2006, the voters wanted Blair to hurt. They took every opportunity to tell him so. On the night of 4 May, New Labour watched its power base crumble in the local elections – the last set of elections Blair ever fought. The Tories won council after council. In Downing Street they were disconsolate. Even the cabinet minister Tessa Jowell, the high priestess of Blairism, conceded that it was a 'bloody awful night'. When she picked up the phone to call Labour's leader of the opposition on Lambeth Council she knew she would hear yet more bad news. Instead, for the first and only time that night, she was told that Labour had won. Wherever the party had stood elsewhere in England, it had gone backwards. But in this pocket of south London they had advanced. 'Fucking hell,' said Jowell, in shock.

McSweeney had gone to south London earlier that year. Lambeth's streets should have been Labour streets: home to the disadvantaged, the Irish, the black. Others, home to young professionals in search of a lively life, were richer but should have been Labour too. Yet by 2006 they had turned against the only party they had ever trusted. For that McSweeney blamed Ted Knight, Labour's former leader of the council. For eight years under Margaret Thatcher the old Trotskyist had made Lambeth a citadel of righteousness. To McSweeney, Knight was the gombeen man of south London: corrupt, driven by vanity, but protected by his party's invincibility. Red Ted – as he was known by his many detractors – twinned his borough with Nicaragua. He refused to fly the Union Flag from the town hall, whose offices had been opened to the London Squatters' Union and School Kids Against the Nazis. He praised the IRA and declared the streets of Clapham and Stockwell a nuclear-free zone. When the Metropolitan Police came out to put down the Brixton riots he denounced them as an 'occupying army'. When Mrs Thatcher passed a law to restrict his spending he set an illegal budget. Neil Kinnock, who stood helpless before his unruly party and its waves of protest like Canute, said Knight had brought Labour into disrepute. Nevertheless, he persisted, even after his defiance of the Thatcher government saw him disqualified as a councillor. Knight and thirty-one of his comrades walked out of the town hall singing 'The Red Flag'. His successors urged their constituents to break the law and refuse to pay the poll tax. They opposed the Gulf War. This, said the newspapers, was the Loony Left. But every howl of establishment condemnation hardened their commitment to protest. Knight never listened to Kinnock or the young Lambeth councillors, like Peter Mandelson, who told him that a silent majority of voters did not like what

he did. His Labour Party existed as a red shield for the teeming mass
exposed to Thatcherism's hardest edge. To criticise was to collaborate
with the cold forces of capitalism that impoverished them.

For years it seemed that Lambeth agreed. But in the council's
children's homes his most vulnerable charges had no protection at
all. In this corner of Labour London, boys and girls, many of them
black, were abused by council employees. Years later an independent
inquiry would find that Knight's Lambeth had been so distracted by its
protests – the municipal equivalent of a disastrous foreign war – that
it had neglected the one responsibility it spoke so proudly and stridently of fulfilling. It had let its most vulnerable people down. Politics
infected everything. Corruption, fraud and bullying had been tolerated
in the name of a higher cause. Poor children had become 'pawns in a
toxic power game with Thatcher's government'. Lambeth had become
a 'vicious' place. Whistleblowers were ignored, monstered as collaborators with the enemy. By 2002 its basic services were among the worst
in the country, its taxes among the highest. The very name of the
borough had become a byword for corruption. So its voters elected a
council of Conservatives and Liberal Democrats to run what Knight
had once called the Socialist Republic of Lambeth.

How the business of local government could have become so dysfunctional that child abuse was allowed to happen, that inquiry said,
was 'difficult to comprehend'. Not for McSweeney. Lambeth was not
the only council to have overseen child abuse – Islington, led by Margaret Hodge, a woman later elevated to sainthood among Labour
moderates, had the same problem – but to the Irishman the answer
was simple. The hard left subjugated everything before ideology.
Purity mattered above all else. Children had not suffered because of
negligence or incompetence. They had been failed, quite deliberately,
by an ideological cult. The left valued only themselves, not the voters
they served. McSweeney's view was itself extreme by the standards
of the Labour mainstream. His, after all, was a party of collectivism
and cooperation: the broad church of misty-eyed cliché. Kinnock sung
'The Red Flag' too. This, McSweeney came to believe, was precisely
the problem. Too many of his colleagues put the cause before the
voter. Ironically, his world view had a certain fanaticism, paranoia and
moral certitude in common with Knight's.

Steve Reed, Labour's leader in Lambeth who would pick up the

phone to Tessa Jowell that May night in 2006, agreed. He had hired
McSweeney as his organiser. This former publisher, openly gay, might
have appeared to be the very image of the kind of cosmopolitan progressive who agreed with Knight. As a teenager, he had campaigned
alongside hard-left activists and was sympathetic to their world view.
Once he saw what they did in power he turned against them. He recalls
now: 'What really disabused me of ideological politics was being elected
as a Lambeth councillor in 1998. First I discovered voters weren't at all
interested in theoretical politics – they just wanted their streets cleaned
and bins emptied; then I got an insight into the absolute chaos that the
hard left had left behind at the council – massive debts, failing services,
corruption, and a legacy of child abuse.' For all his differences with the
left, Blair was not altogether immune from this critique. After Knight's
comrades had forfeited control of the council, the local Labour group
enjoyed a short-lived renaissance under the stewardship of the party's
right wing, regaining a majority in 1998. That result delighted the new
occupant of Downing Street. He described its architects as 'more New
Labour than New Labour'. Naturally, Blair had meant that as a compliment. The people of Lambeth would soon beg to differ. They rebelled
at the earliest opportunity against the party's slick communications
but underlying lack of delivery, for which the prime minister himself
had become a grim metaphor. By 2006, Reed was once again seeking
to return Labour to a majority locally. Blair appeared more consumed
by spin and his misadventures in the Middle East than ever. It was the
opposite of the unglamorous politics which Reed prized. When local
elections came that May, the party's national leader, just like Knight,
had given Lambeth's voters every reason to reject Labour. McSweeney
should have lost again. Yet despite everything, his campaign told
voters that Labour was 'on your side'. He spent hours going door
to door on the estates that politicians had forgotten. He asked what
worried them. They showed him graffiti, overgrown trees, blinking
street lights. He told them that Labour had noticed. In Lambeth its
messaging was tailored street by street. Rather than *telling* them that
they cared – on protests and on the airwaves – Labour now showed
them. Reed and his organiser reported burnt-out cars to the police. By
polling day each voter received a tailored postcard, emblazoned with
the single policy McSweeney knew would make the difference to their
difficult lives, whether saving the leisure centre on the end of the street

or funding repairs on their estate. Those in marginal wards received not only the most hyper-local literature, but the most unsavoury too. After discovering a Lib Dem councillor had sought to purchase a council home under right-to-buy but been rejected on the grounds she did not live there, he deluged addresses with a mock newspaper accusing her of criminality. The 'fraud special' was blown out with pictures of the woman's home and breathlessly accused her party of 'keeping quiet about fraud'. In tandem residents received 'Dear neighbour' leaflets, authored by McSweeney, alerting them to the supposed scandal. By appealing to people's hyper-local hopes and concerns, McSweeney and Reed gradually shifted the dial. And so when Jowell called late that night, Reed alone could tell her what no other Labour politician in Britain could.

'I think we've won.'

*

In the subsequent days, a brooding Blair sent a private note to Reed. 'You were a beacon of light on a dark night,' he wrote of Lambeth. New Labour's darkest hours were still to come. Only in Lambeth had its traditional voters come home. Twelve miles north-east, in Barking and Dagenham, they had sought solace in the open arms of the far right. There, where industrial east London bled into Essex, the British National Party had won eleven of the seats contested. This was Blair's opposition now. Nick Griffin, a telegenic Cambridge graduate who preferred to package his Holocaust denial with tailored suits and a side parting rather than the shaved heads and tattoos of his predecessors, had told the white men who built cars for Ford and the women who raised their children that New Labour was paying Africans to relocate to Essex. Thousands believed him.

McSweeney was troubled. The founding fathers of New Labour had boasted that the workers of England would never leave them, no matter their overtures to the middle class and moneyed, for they had 'nowhere else to go'. In fact, once those in Barking and Dagenham abandoned them, the Labour establishment struggled to find them again. Every warning from Margaret Hodge, the MP for Barking, that eight in ten of her voters would support the BNP without tougher measures on immigration seemed to remind those voters that they preferred the BNP.

Jon Cruddas, the member for Dagenham, fretted publicly that New Labour's obsessive focus on Middle England may have brought the far right to 'the verge of a major political breakthrough'. Griffin, by then a habitué of television studios, vowed to oust Hodge from Parliament. This was not an idle threat. By the time the BNP reached its high-water mark in Barking the Labour Party was bargaining with people who had stopped listening, and only condemning itself in the process. And so it sought help.

New Labour still ran the town hall in Barking and Dagenham, if not its streets and estates. Race-relations law obliged it to promote 'good relations between persons of different racial groups'. It interpreted that line of the statute book as a licence to spend public funds to beat the BNP. They paid a campaign consultancy run by David Evans, who had run party headquarters when the young McSweeney worked unnoticed by the other Blairites, to organise the fightback. He, in turn, approached the young man who had won back Lambeth. He arrived, again, on streets scarred by neglect. He walked them, dumbfounded, for months on end. Nothing made sense. Twenty-first-century politicians thought they knew the electorate. They studied every little difference between demographics. Voters were not merely targeted, they were 'segmented'. They determined their views and beliefs by salary, age, tone of skin, degrees of latitude and longitude. A poor black woman in Tottenham would vote Labour, a rich white man in Wiltshire was probably voting Conservative. New Labour tailored its messaging accordingly to the Mondeo Men and Worcester Women who held the key to electoral success.

Dagenham was different. The voters defied segmentation. McSweeney spoke to them on the Becontree estate, once the world's largest municipal housing project for Europe's largest car factory, meeting a new white face at each pebble-dashed semi. All around was squalor. The jobs had gone. Soiled mattresses lay in the street. Heaps of filth were piled high in front gardens. Graffiti lined the walls. Homes that had housed the same east London families for generations – many of whom took advantage of Thatcher's right-to-buy scheme – sank into disrepair, sold to absentee landlords and given over to outsiders they exploited. Places like Becontree had been built for solidarity. McSweeney instead found a nasty enclave of isolation and individualism. Some blamed the migrants who filled the dirty homes around them. They did not apologise for their racism, for before their eyes was the evidence that proved it to be credible and true. Once they had been Labour. Now they belonged to the BNP. Others spoke in sorrow, not anger. They loathed the party their neighbours lionised. From these doors they saw Griffin was a Nazi, and these voters knew what they thought of Nazis. 'My father fought against these people,' many said. Others were less dogmatic than curious. They spoke of their concerns that migrants were hoarding housing stock. Barking was changing faster than they liked. At least the BNP understood that. Perhaps, if another party did, they might be persuaded to vote for them.

These conflicting answers came from the same sorts of people on the same sorts of streets. Sometimes they would come from within the same family. No one segment could staunch New Labour's slow bleed. McSweeney would have to think again. He focused not on what the voters *believed*, but what they *valued*. To parrot beliefs was easy. It had every appearance of empathy. But in Barking, it had not worked. It was one thing, he thought, for Hodge to speak sympathetically of their beliefs – however contradictory they may have been. To convince them that New Labour and its liberal, internationalist prime minister shared their *values* was quite another. Whatever they believed, the men and women on the Becontree estate loved their country. They wanted security as it changed around them. Even if they did not believe what Nick Griffin believed, his party at least understood what they valued. To McSweeney, the councillors who spoke of resisting neo-Nazism, and the earnest young Labour activists who took the Tube to east London chanting the anti-fascist slogan '*No pasarán!*' – they shall not pass – in the faces of the voters, risked doing more harm than good. At best they were demonstrating that the left did not understand them. At worst they were advertising that they held them in contempt. Labour would have to learn to listen again – to think and talk like the people it had lost.

It was not easy. David Evans told McSweeney there were three kinds of voter: the pioneer, the prospector, and the settler. The pioneers lived a free life. They emphasised individuality. Their social networks were large and lively. 'Change' and 'diversity' were inherently good. The prospectors prized their self-esteem, and winning the esteem of others. They wanted status, success, money. They consumed conspicuously. The settlers wanted safety, security, belonging. They valued their home, their family and their immediate neighbourhood. 'Change' was not automatically a good thing. More often than not it was inflicted upon them by other people. Most lived in council houses. McSweeney saw that it was the settlers who felt most unsettled by New Labour. Its politicians were prospectors who struggled to understand why voters felt their way of life was under threat. And so he made them fly the flag, just as he and Steve Reed had done in Lambeth. Labour did not attack the migrants, nor give racism respectability – as Hodge had been accused of doing when she defended 'the legitimate sense of entitlement felt by the indigenous family'. It pursued the rich landlords instead. It cleared their eyesore gardens and charged them for the trouble. 'We know the people of Barking and Dagenham want us to take action on this,' said Liam Smith, the council leader who wore an England rugby shirt as he walked the streets with McSweeney, 'because they have told us it worries them.'

Nick Lowles, of the anti-fascist group Hope Not Hate, recalled: 'The one thing I thought Morgan learnt from that time was the importance of delivery – and delivery for local people, not the political class or activists.' By orienting the council towards people's values, and day-to-day needs, Labour neutered the far right's attacks on the party, creating the conditions for the broader left to mount one of the most successful campaigns in British political history. In 2010, even as Gordon Brown lost the general election, Labour beat the BNP in every ward in Barking and Dagenham.

★

McSweeney had won again. Elsewhere in England, Labour lost. Its people were poorer. Even if a global financial crisis had really been to blame, it was Gordon Brown they wanted to punish. New Labour's last prime minister told them he had saved the banks, and the world, just as their worlds, collapsed. His electorate did not thank him. Why would they? By then McSweeney was convinced that The Voter was never wrong. If Labour had lost power in 2010 because the middle ground of Blair's England moved to David Cameron's Conservatives, The Voter had been right. If they blamed Brown for the recession, thought New Labour too profligate – they could only be right. The Voter was always right.

But in Brown's place Labour had elected Ed Miliband, the archetypal pioneer: intellectually open, well-travelled, content to ride the cultural tides of a changing world. He broke with New Labour and moved his party to the left. Try though he did, he could never reach The Voter. He tried to remake the centre left from on high but beneath him the ground of politics was shifting. Ukip's Nigel Farage spoke for the settler class, pushing relentlessly for tougher measures on migration and speaking a language that Labour's old voters understood. The Conservatives pilloried Miliband as Red Ed. To his left, new movements assailed him for prevaricating on austerity. His flunkies tried to hide the contradictions behind prime ministerial lecterns but The Voter would not be fooled.

McSweeney had spent those years in the foothills of British democracy. At Reed's suggestion he had gone to work for the Local Government Association, imparting his lessons to the leaders of Labour councils. They knew the settlers. Some *were* the settlers. The story of Becontree was playing out in inner cities and small towns in every part of Britain: places fractured, made redundant and changed utterly by globalisation. In 2010, Miliband had briefly flirted with a new movement that sought to recast the Labour Party in the image of the voters it had lost: Blue Labour. Socially conservative, it embraced faith and flag, and said what London liberals did not like to hear on migration and crime. Its economics were interventionist and its exponents attacked billionaires and 'fat-cat bosses'. They were eccentric. The movement's philosopher-king, Maurice Glasman, was the chain-smoking son of a toymaker from a Jewish home in east London. His assistant, an academic called John Clarke, was another Irishman: the son of republicans who had grown up beside a lead mine in County Meath. Labour never swallowed their medicine. In 2015 it lost again.

McSweeney flirted with Blue Labour. He knew Glasman and Clarke. In Dagenham, he had worked with its parliamentary flagbearer, Jon Cruddas, who later joined him during the deputation to Corbyn's office. Still, he was realistic about its appeal to the activists whose instinctive, self-regarding liberalism he had come to know all too well in Lambeth and Barking. When Labour came to elect its next leader he went to manage the doomed campaign of Liz Kendall, a Blairite shadow minister with no public profile to speak of. She was briefly Blue Labour's great hope, and quietly outsourced her campaign preparations to Glasman's Dalston office.

But Corbyn knew Labour activists even better than McSweeney – who they were, what they believed – because he was one of them. He travelled the country saying what he thought. He did not understand the sterile vernacular of compromise that had become Labour's official language. He railed against austerity and foreign wars with a moral clarity that had been throttled out of politics by New Labour. And those who would choose Miliband's successor – the activists, the trade unionists, the interested public who paid £3 for a vote – loved him for it. Blair had told Kendall to ignore the members. 'She should go over their heads,' he told her team. 'When she does, the members will see that she's appealing to the voters, and they'll vote for her.' To that the Irishman said: 'That's horse shit. Who's ever run a campaign and not talked to the people who have the vote?' Kendall did. And Kendall lost. Corbyn won 60 per cent of Labour members to her 4.5 per cent.

McSweeney was shaken. He had forgotten what it was to lose. In his mind Corbyn's politics were not just wrong. They were evil. The man who had served as Ted Knight's election agent was now leader of the Labour Party. To Corbyn, Knight was not the man whose ideological indulgence had led to the abuse of children. He was 'legendary'. Red Ted was still alive to vote his old friend in, loudly and proudly. Lambeth leftism would become the official alternative offered by Britain's opposition. This was not the politics of place and country McSweeney had taken to the estates of Brixton and Barking. It was the politics of anti-war marches and *Guardian* columnists. It was everything he hated. He was sure that voters would hate it too. He again retreated from Westminster, and looked askance at the Labour MPs who struggled through the stages of political grief. Some bargained with those who had given them Corbyn. 'He's not the Messiah,' said Sir Keir Starmer MP, elected for the first time that summer, of his new leader. 'He would be the first to say he doesn't have all the answers, and if you touch Jeremy you are not healed.' Most of his colleagues could not move beyond denial. They told themselves it would be over by Christmas. But McSweeney knew otherwise. On the Becontree estate he had learned that The Voter could not be wrong. Politicians could not browbeat them into wisdom. Those who tried were doomed to lose again and again.

The more Labour MPs tried to talk the membership out of their love of Corbyn, the more they lost the argument. A year later they tried to oust Corbyn in a coup. Owen Smith, the cocksure Welshman who was their chosen challenger, called McSweeney. Like the rest of the shadow cabinet, he had resigned after the EU referendum. They did not blame David Cameron, the prime minister who called the referendum, nor did they blame Boris Johnson, Michael Gove or Nigel Farage, who had led the campaign for Brexit. They blamed Corbyn, who could never disguise his Euroscepticism even as he appealed to Labour voters to back Remain. Smith asked McSweeney, who had spent the final days of the referendum campaign at his wife's side in a maternity ward, for advice. McSweeney recoiled. It was all wrong. He had learned from the Kendall disaster. To ignore a Labour membership still loyal to a leader who had given voice to their values, who *embodied* them, was to be destroyed. McSweeney told Smith, whose career as a special adviser to New Labour and lobbyist for the pharmaceutical industry could never endear him to the Corbynites, that he was like a teenager jostling in line for an exclusive nightclub. 'You can queue if you want to,' he said. 'But if you don't have any money, any ID, or the right shoes, then you're going to get to the front and they'll bounce you out the door.' It was not enough that Smith *wanted* to be leader or *thought* he could be leader. To run against the values of the members was a waste of money and a waste of time. Smith ignored him. He stood anyway. He likened Corbyn's supporters to a 'parasite' corrupting their 'host body'. Like Kendall, he was beaten badly. Corbyn won 61 per cent of the vote. Grief-stricken, MPs resigned themselves to his invincibility.

*

McSweeney thought otherwise. Before long he was drawn to a new project. Labour for the Common Good had been set up by John Clarke, the Blue Labour man from Meath, in 2015. Soon it would be renamed Labour Together, a name that so appealed to Corbyn's dislike of confrontation he embraced the group. 'I welcome Labour Together as a new initiative that explores a new kind of way to do politics,' he said. He did not realise they saw him as the enemy. With Corbyn – the candidate of the activist left, of the young idealists, of the metropolitan minorities and middle class – in the ascendant, Clarke knew that Blue Labour's brand was spent. Even those sympathetic to it – like McSweeney's mentors Steve Reed and Jon Cruddas, and the young Wigan MP Lisa Nandy – knew they would not beat the left with politics of hard borders and English flags. One involved described Labour Together as 'Blue Labour without the accidental incel vibe, and the side order of racism'. Bernard Donoughue, who wrote policy for Harold Wilson and James Callaghan in Downing Street, was its first donor.

Their brief was in the name that Corbyn misunderstood: to hold together a party fractured in an instant by his politics. Its money came from two men with lots of it. The first was Sir Trevor Chinn, a multimillionaire Jewish philanthropist who had made his fortune from the sale of the Royal Automobile Club and grew to love the trade union shop stewards who worked for him. To Chinn, politics was about people. But he feared Corbyn. Chinn had once been targeted for assassination by Al Qaeda. He had great concerns about the election of an outspoken opponent of the Jewish state as Labour leader. The second was Martin Taylor. He had grown up in a poor house in Greenwich, the son of a Labour councillor, and became a hedge fund manager whose computers expended so much energy in making money that he would work dressed in cycling gear, to better withstand the heat. Where Chinn literally embraced politicians, Taylor did his politics from a distance, via cheque. Only a tiny circle of people knew the extent of his tribal loyalties. Privately, he spoke of his 'West Ham' test, where people in politics were judged less on their love of the game and more their fealty to the club, the cause, the badge – that is, to Labour. Both men wanted to save their party from a politics they feared would make it unelectable.

They sent for McSweeney. At first he refused to join them. Labour had become a basket case. From the offices of the Local Government Association, the political equivalent of a birdwatcher's hide, he could wait and see as the contagion of Corbynism seeped through the roots of the party in the country. Obsessed, he read their tweets and watched them organise. But he needed security for his wife and baby. In a paper written for Labour Together in December 2016, after Corbyn had

won his second leadership election, McSweeney made no secret of
the group's potential: 'You want it to be a project that not only points
the Labour Party back towards the road to government, but drives
it there.' Yet he doubted that Labour Together was ready to play 'a
covert but leading organisational role' in opposing the hard left. Too
many people in the Labour Party had reconciled themselves to a 'grad-
ual decline'. 'Many MPs and councillors,' McSweeney complained,
were 'approaching the crisis the party is in as an era that needs to be
endured and which will eventually pass'. He regarded that as a dangerous mindset. Nor could McSweeney run Labour Together – which
possessed not even an office – until it decided whether it was a think
tank, which held no interest for him, or a resistance movement, willing
to disguise its true aims and allies.

But in 2017, McSweeney was ready. He had already proven that the
party was not entirely lost to Corbynism. He knew it existed beyond
Westminster as a matryoshka doll of boards and committees, all
elected by activists. Blair and Brown had ignored them. Power had
been wielded from Downing Street. Now, deep in the wilderness of
opposition, every vote mattered. Every committee in every constituency party, no matter how small; every delegate to every conference,
no matter how obscure; every activist seeking election at every level
of the Labour Party was now conscripted into its civil war. By 2016, as
MPs collapsed into nervous exhaustion, those who cared to look could
already see that Corbyn was neither omnipotent nor omnipresent in
the committee rooms and working men's clubs in which the democratic battles for the party's future would really be won. That summer
McSweeney pushed his friends on the party's ruling National Executive Committee to hold elections to the board of the London Labour
Party before the members who had joined to vote for Jeremy would
be eligible. These polls were not usually seen by their participants as a
generational struggle for the soul of the British centre left. But this was
a committee that the Corbynites were yet to win. If they did, then they
would control the selection of candidates for the capital's local councils
in May 2017. McSweeney feared this would open the door not just to
another Ted Knight, but 'twenty militant Lambeths' controlled by the
hard left. Corbynites would also adjudicate on questions of internal
discipline and propriety. In November, the results were announced to

little fanfare. Nobody really noticed, but by the narrowest of margins McSweeney's moderates won.

There would be no time to dwell on that result and what it meant. In 2017 came an unexpected general election. Theresa May, the Conservative prime minister, called it early, hoping to annihilate Corbyn. In the week before polling day the cover of Labour's house journal, the *New Statesman*, showed Jeremy Corbyn, John McDonnell and Diane Abbott cowering beneath an asteroid. Having run on a manifesto of big-statism that harked back to the 1970s, soon they and their Project would be ground into dust. Or so Westminster thought. May ran an abysmal campaign and Corbyn gained seats, denying the Tories a majority on his own terms. Soon he might be prime minister on his own terms. Those who had spent two years opposing him seemed to have little option but to agree to those terms. When Corbyn first addressed his parliamentary party in the hot, heady hours after polling day, his destroyers were made supplicants. Chuka Umunna, who had spent the preceding weeks planning his leadership campaign, told reporters: 'Government is the watchword – unity is the aim!'

McSweeney wanted neither – not under Corbyn. Before the shock of the election result he had finally agreed to take the helm of Labour Together, whose MPs were determined to unite what would remain of a post-apocalyptic party after Corbyn's inevitable annihilation behind a candidate who might return it to some version of normality, and turn once more to the voters it had lost. Their motives were constructive. Now, in a changed world, McSweeney would devote himself to destruction. As he left the Local Government Association his colleagues inquired as to his plans.

'I've got a job at Labour Together,' he said.

'What are they?' asked a friend.

'We're going to renew the Labour Party.'

'But it's already renewed,' said another, revealing the Corbynite sympathies that few could resist in the wake of Jeremy's great vindication.

McSweeney was baffled. However impressive the Corbyn surge, Labour had lost again. It had won millions of votes from the middle classes but, almost unnoticed, had lost pockets of support in the old industrial towns that backed Brexit to the Conservatives. It was a portent of what was to come in 2019. The Voter, the angry man McSweeney had met on the Becontree estate in Barking, was closing his door to Corbyn's Labour. His answer now was not to wait, nor let Jeremy fail on his own terms. It was to use any means necessary to delegitimise and destroy him. And so the Irishman turned to deception.

The ruthlessness with which he set about hoodwinking the Labour Party shocked even his closest colleagues. As one MP on the Labour Together board said: 'I remember thinking that he needed to speak a bit more loudly. I couldn't hear him. I asked him to repeat himself a few times. He looks very nice, very agreeable, very softly spoken. Probably hard as nails underneath.'

*

On Tuesday 20 June, as Corbyn packed his bags to address hundreds of thousands of adoring fans at Glastonbury later that week, McSweeney assembled the board of Labour Together in Steve Reed's parliamentary office. Before him sat Jon Cruddas, Lisa Nandy, and Sir Trevor Chinn, who paid his wages. McSweeney told them hard truths. While Corbyn had not won the election, he had won control over his own fate and would only leave office on his own terms. The next general election was his to lose. That was an outcome none of them could control. They could, however, control the aftermath – and help to ensure he lost badly.

Reed, at his old assistant's instruction, had printed copies of a strategy paper for those assembled. Authored by McSweeney, it was to be the order of service at Corbynism's long funeral. The mission: 'Move the Labour Party from the hard left when JC steps down as leader and to reconnect the Labour Party with the country, build a sustainable winning electoral coalition, based on a vision that is radical and relevant and protects the labour interest.' The imperative: don't get caught.

McSweeney described his first strategic objective as evading 'the threat of attacks of disloyalty by supporters of the leader'. The Corbynites – be they 'from online organisations, from the media or from official party bodies' – could not be allowed to learn that Labour Together existed to eradicate them. Progress, the Blairite think tank controlled by Peter Mandelson, was cited as a cautionary tale. To the left it was 'the enemy within'. Petulant and pugnacious, its leaders had argued themselves into bankruptcy and irrelevance. Labour Together

could not afford to become 'a new internal enemy' for 'JC supporters'. MPs, wrote McSweeney, were similarly dangerous. Those invited
into their confidence 'may publicly attack the leader or privately brief
that we are their leadership campaign or the leadership campaign of a
potential rival'.

The risks were considerable – and potentially fatal. The solution was
subterfuge.

Anything that might provoke hostility or even cursory interest from
the Corbynites would have to be disguised. Labour Together would
be elaborately costumed to appear at one with the party's new order.
It would brand itself like Greenpeace and campaign as if it were any
one of the countless leftish pressure groups doing earnest work on the
fringes of the Labour Party. They would say so explicitly to Corbyn's
face. Through subterfuge they would 'build an official relationship
with at least one trade union'. When Corbyn fought elections, they
would support him and they would build official relationships with
'bona fide JC supporters'. If Blairite backbenchers tried to take control, Labour Together would 'robustly defend ourselves from MPs
co-opting us'. As he stood before a cartoonish slideshow, McSweeney
called his strategy Operation Red Shield. Emphasising the point, he
presented the room with an image of Roman legionnaires forming a
phalanx. Labour Together's soldiers would need to hide beneath their
red shields too.

Once the Corbynites had been lulled into disinterest and ignorance,
McSweeney would pursue his second strategic goal: 'Win the battle of
ideas.' As he had learned in Barking, Labour was 'increasingly discon-
nected from its traditional electoral base'. The Voter knew that Corbyn
did not share their values, or even understand them. That word again:
values. 'The key to reconnecting,' the paper declared, 'is to develop a
political vision that is relevant to voters' concerns in a rapidly changing
world and reflect their values.'

The self-confident language belied the difficulties they faced. The
election had now confirmed Corbynism's hold on the party. Whatever
policies they presented would have to be seen as harmonious with it:
'the New Testament to Corbyn's Old Testament'. And they would be
forced to address and convince the activists who worshipped at his
altar. 'Labour Party members credit our relative success in the general
election to the manifesto and the leadership of Jeremy Corbyn,' he

said. 'Since our immediate audience is party members, whose support
we need to gain traction, we need to present our work as building on
what they already consider to have been successful.' But *how*?

Corbyn's supporters lived online. The fallen rulers of the Labour
Party had failed utterly to understand 'how digital media has transformed the rules of political debate'. The members had little time for
the mainstream media. Instead they read 'insurgent propaganda sites',
most notably the *Canary*, a blog that supported Corbyn in the manner
of a football fanzine. Its editor, Kerry-Anne Mendoza, was an Occupy
protester who lived far away from Westminster, in the Welsh Valleys.
She had started with nothing – neither the resources nor the brand
prestige of the legacy newspaper – but in railing against austerity and
revelling in condemnation of the Conservatives – a slur it applied as
readily to Labour MPs as to the Tory government – she had gamed
the algorithms of social media and now commanded 8.5 million hits
a month. That, McSweeney told his co-conspirators, was nearly twice
the audience of the *New Statesman*.

Other populist blogs fluent in the confrontational language of the
digital left included the *Skwawkbox, Evolve Politics, Another Angry Voice*.
This was the newsstand of the Labour Party in 2017. 'These alt-left sites
have grown dramatically,' McSweeney warned, 'and pump out stories that often go unchallenged by the mainstream and are therefore
accepted uncritically by their committed readers.' Without breaking
this unlikely cartel of media influencers, there was no way any attempt
to wrest the Labour Party from the left's control would succeed.
Labour Together, which barely existed beyond the room in which its
leadership spoke, would have to build 'a rival infrastructure to communicate our politics'. Like *Endeavour*, the leftist literary magazine secretly
funded by the CIA to undermine the British intelligentsia's support
for the Soviets, McSweeney would cultivate 'seemingly independent
voices to generate and share content to build up a political narrative
and challenge fake news and political extremism'. The *Guardian* might
help. Ditto LabourList, the blog devoted to the minutiae of party business, Hope Not Hate, the anti-fascist campaign group he had worked
alongside in Dagenham, and Reg Race, a former MP who had turned
his back on his old comrades like Tony Benn and ran a Facebook page
called Saving Labour.

All that was missing was a leader. 'Ultimately,' McSweeney concluded, 'we will need a candidate to win a future leadership election on the political platform we are developing. There is no need to identify a candidate at this stage, but we will proceed on the assumption that our organisation must be able to generate a successful leadership campaign operation when required.' Lisa Nandy, sitting expectantly across from McSweeney, believed it would be her. Whoever it was would need to win a membership with little desire to renounce its faith in St Jeremy. And to secure that new leader's hold on the party, 'We need to make sure the party's organisation is not used by the hard left to conduct political purges against our supporters.'

There was every chance Labour Together was doomed to fail. McSweeney's final slide listed the threats it faced: its true identity being uncovered by the *Canary*, denunciations by a trade union, a hijacking by a self-serving MP. Graver than all of them was the unthinkable: 'A Labour government.' However unlikely they believed it to be, Corbyn's victory would be their permanent defeat. Still McSweeney was undeterred. In the style of Dominic Cummings, the eccentric, single-minded strategist who had delivered Brexit and broken the Tory establishment, he concluded with a quote from Sun Tzu. 'To not prepare is the greatest of crimes; to be prepared beforehand for any contingency is the greatest of virtues.' So began the great deception that would destroy a movement.

2

The Candidate

McSweeney worked on Black Prince Road, a long street in Lambeth with a longer history. It took its name from Edward of Woodstock, the Plantagenet heir to the English throne whose palace had once stood nearby. The Black Prince was the great knight of his age. He psychologically crushed his enemies with the *chevauchée*: small units of mounted soldiers who stampeded and pillaged their way through villages whose rulers and riches never recovered. With Trevor Chinn's money he hired space in China Works, a fashionable hot-desking space in an old ceramics factory. Room 216, the sparsely furnished headquarters of his conspiracy, was undecorated save for the skull and crossbones of a pirate's Jolly Roger, pinned clumsily to the white walls a little while later. McSweeney was intoxicated by the arguments of *Be More Pirate: Or How to Take On the World and Win*, a book that presented the lawless behaviour of Captain Kidd and Blackbeard as rulebreaking for the greater good. Alone with his laptop, he had a view across the Thames to the citadel he one day hoped to retake.

For anyone to learn of Labour Together's true intentions would be fatal. Few beyond the staffers it employed, Hannah O'Rourke and Will Prescott, were welcomed into Room 216. Only one outsider was allowed to sit beside McSweeney: Imran Ahmed, the eldest of seven children from a poor Pakistani family in Manchester, who looked and sounded like the investment banker he had once been. McSweeney was shy and shifty, disorganised and dishevelled: old colleagues recalled him as the man who would arrive late for meetings, jeans caked in mud. Yet the two men were of one mind. As an adviser to Hilary Benn, the shadow foreign secretary, Ahmed had helped draft Benn's Commons speech in which he defied Corbyn to demand airstrikes on Syria. Like McSweeney, he believed the pages of the *Canary* and the Facebook groups of the left were incubators of extremism where prejudice and misinformation metastasised into conspiracy theory. Ahmed, traumatised by the assassination in June 2016 of the Labour MP Jo Cox, an old friend, had come to China Works to set up the Center for Countering Digital Hate. He appointed McSweeney his co-director.

They studied their subject closely. McSweeney and Ahmed joined Facebook groups full of thousands of Corbyn fans, including the leader's own staff. The pair found their members were consumed with rage. They hated the media. They hated Labour MPs. They hated the Rothschilds. They hated Israel. One of the most voluble posters, Ian Love, an organiser for the Corbynite campaign group Momentum, declared that Tony Blair was 'Jewish to the core'. Here, in full view of the leadership of the Labour Party, the left spoke the conspiratorial, hateful language of the far right. This was the army McSweeney would have to overcome.

McSweeney commissioned YouGov to poll members of the two biggest groups: We Support Jeremy Corbyn, and Labour Party Supporter. It revealed more about their minds than any Labour MP knew. Corbynism's most devout, fanatical adherents believed the left's political project was sustained by champagne socialists in north London. Nearly half were working class. 33 per cent were older than sixty, 65 per cent over forty. 56 per cent said they were dissatisfied with their standard of living – twice as many as Britain at large. Half said they found it hard to sleep at night. A quarter agreed that 'sometimes I let people walk all over me'. They were paranoid and pessimistic, with nearly half agreeing that the world was controlled by a secretive elite. Nearly two thirds said the media could not be trusted to report the truth. Political violence did not shock them. When asked for their view on George Osborne's vow to chop up Theresa May and store her remains in his freezer, 55 per cent described it as light-hearted banter. Their views were markedly more extreme than those of the population at large – and of the paid-up party members who had twice voted for Corbyn alongside them.

McSweeney ensured the most disturbing examples found their way to the *Sunday Times*. It reported his findings on its front page on 1 April 2018, underneath a screaming headline: 'Exposed: Jeremy Corbyn's hate factory'. Members of the groups were quoted praising Hitler, advocating for the murder of the prime minister, and dismissing the Holocaust as a 'big lie.' Activist Ian Love defended his comments to

reporters: 'The Rothschilds control all the money in the world.' The
BBC emblazoned the news across its website.

It could have been a crisis for Corbyn but instead it hardened the
left's resolve. The Labour Party's spokespeople called the story a
smear. Its members reappropriated the headline as a badge of honour.
They ridiculed the media under the hashtag #armyofhate. The experiment had failed, succeeding only in persuading the Corbyn supporters
who did not share the extremism of those quoted that there really was
a conspiracy arrayed against their leader. Labour Together needed to
persuade these people, not demonise them. Every member who felt
unjustly accused of racism was a member more likely to reject overtures from outside Corbyn's circle of trust.

McSweeney concluded that that was exactly what they had done. The
YouGov polling paid for by Chinn and Taylor had confirmed his long-
held thesis that the Labour membership was not overrun by Trotskyites
and racists. If the research had proved anything, it was that they were
in the minority – albeit a noisy and influential one. But to challenge
them – as he had done via the *Sunday Times* – was to reinforce their conspiratorial world view. It was to prove the *Canary* right. Anyone who
wished to break the hard left would first have to jam its feedback loop.

Perhaps the answer was to shout louder. In the 1980s, dismayed
by the monopoly power of populist tabloids like the *Sun* and *Daily
Mirror*, left-wing activists briefly printed their own red-top: the *News
on Sunday*. It failed, just as McSweeney's attempt to disrupt a new eco-
system of digital media would too. *Tribune*, the venerable old weekly
once edited by Nye Bevan and Michael Foot, had collapsed into insol-
vency. McSweeney tried to buy it. The hard left did instead. A bid for
LabourList, the party's parish noticeboard, went nowhere fast. So did
Changing Politics, a podcast hosted by the comedian Gráinne Maguire
and journalist Marie Le Conte. Nobody listened, and for many months
nobody was paid. Maguire later recalled that every episode was scripted
by McSweeney. After six episodes, McSweeney's brief foray into audio
production was over. If he was to clip the *Canary*'s wings and concrete
over its 'cesspit of antisemitism', he concluded that his only option was
to kill it entirely.

He foresaw no end of opportunity in its death. Without its online
Pravda, the hard left would lose in an instant its ability to manipulate
the narrative to which its angry audience was so receptive, and which

held disproportionate influence over the membership at large. Corbyn's allies, too, would lose one of the only media outlets willing to report uncritically on its political project. Even veterans of the movement like Len McCluskey, the general secretary of Unite, consumed and amplified its agitprop: he repeated live on BBC television its baseless suggestion that the lobbying firm Portland Communications was at the heart of a conspiracy to oust the Labour leader.

The real conspiracy against Corbynism, meanwhile, sought celebrity backing. Rachel Riley, the co-presenter of *Countdown* on Channel 4, was an implausible fellow traveller for the political odd couple of McSweeney and Ahmed. As a Jew who had been moved to frequent and occasionally foul-mouthed criticism of the hard left, however, she was in search of a productive outlet for her anger. Corbynites derided her as a dilettante and publicity junkie. One of the leader's aides dismissed Riley publicly: 'She's as dangerous as she is stupid.' In February 2019 she came to China Works accompanied by Adam Langleben, a Jewish Labour Movement activist convinced his party had been poisoned by racism. McSweeney and Ahmed made a modest proposal. Might Riley be the public face of a campaign to defund the *Canary*? She agreed with alacrity.

Branded, like Labour Together, in the idealistic language of the liberal left, Stop Funding Fake News was born. It did its job. Once alerted to the *Canary*'s combative and conspiratorial content by Ahmed, the FTSE 100 firms and corporate multinationals whose adverts appeared on its pages soon shut off their spigots of cash. Already weakened by a change to Facebook's algorithms, which served users fewer news articles, within months the bird had been caged, and its staff cut by two thirds. Riley crowed on Twitter: 'Bye bye birdie!!!' The *Canary* blamed 'political Zionists' for the demise of its business model. They did not know what McSweeney had done.

★

For four years Corbyn had refused to be defined by the dreary old saws that pass for political commentary in Westminster. But by the summer of 2019 he was living Hemingway's old cliché on bankruptcy: gradually, then suddenly, his project fell apart. Brexit, still unresolved, had shattered Labour's old electoral coalition. Its interminable, tedious parliamentary debates kept Corbyn chained to the despatch box, bored and restless. And when Britons elected their final Members of the European Parliament that May, Labour finished a distant third behind the Brexit Party and the Liberal Democrats, whose leaders were unafraid to speak the political languages Corbyn could never learn.

Meanwhile, accusations of antisemitism inflicted deeper wounds on his very sense of self. Jeremy Corbyn was an anti-racist. That was the very essence of his being. MPs, the media, the commanding heights of Britain's Jewish community: all told him otherwise. Ancient comments on Israel and Zionism were disinterred by his prosecutors and accepted by his opponents as evidence that Jeremy Corbyn was not an anti-racist but an antisemite. He withdrew into himself. When he dared defend his record, he was cantankerous, unapologetic. He could no longer speak to the country. He could no longer bring himself to leave the house.

McSweeney revelled in Corbyn's misery – and did all he could to exacerbate it. Ahead of a planned trip by Corbyn to address students at the University of Warwick that February, McSweeney had urged Patrick Heneghan – an election strategist who had been exiled from Labour HQ under Corbyn – to send young Remainers to harangue him. 'Morgan wanted to get twenty People's Vote volunteers to have a go at him,' a co-conspirator recalled. On 28 May, the Equality and Human Rights Commission announced it would investigate Labour's handling of antisemitism complaints – just as it had once investigated the racist membership policies of the BNP. Armed with 10,000 leaked emails supplied by Corbyn-sceptic staff, Ahmed disseminated some of their most shocking contents to political journalists. Meanwhile, in secret meetings in Room 216 of China Works, McSweeney and Adam Langleben 'mapped out people inside the party who might want to come forward' with witness statements attesting that the leader's aides had interfered in racism complaints – among them the embattled and unnoticed Labour councillors McSweeney knew from his work at the Local Government Association. The dossier of evidence they amassed would one day secure a verdict of unlawful discrimination by Jeremy Corbyn's Labour Party against Jews.

McSweeney's friends saw him as smilingly compliant with Corbynism. MPs such as the acid-tongued Brownite Chris Leslie told him they wanted to challenge Corbyn again. Two years earlier, over lunch at

Leslie's Nottingham home, McSweeney had urged caution, telling Leslie: 'We're giving up a party that had a bad leader for two years. This is a 125-year-old party. This is insane.' In 2019, Leslie was no longer in any mood to listen. In February, along with six other Labour MPs he set up the Independent Group, later Change UK – the first official split in the Labour party in thirty-eight years.

Change UK crashed and burned but others continued undeterred. Tony Blair was chief among them. He told friends that Labour had become 'too weak to win, but too strong to die'. He dreamt of a new party, a British answer to Emmanuel Macron's En Marche!, unburdened by a membership that was at odds with the electorate. It could at last exorcise the division that had haunted progressives since the 1900s and unite Labourism and Liberalism under one banner. Jonathan Powell, Blair's former chief of staff, went from boardroom to boardroom, seeking converts among Labour donors. He distributed glossy brochures that promised a party that could transcend the old divisions of class, geography and education. One fell into McSweeney's hands. He told the donors – among whom he spoke frankly of his intentions – that it would never work, for he would never let it. If people like Blair and Powell were allowed to abandon the Labour Party, it would forever belong to Corbyn. He spoke to the donors as if they were idiots. 'We're trying to take back the ship. You're funding the lifeboat,' he told them. 'As soon as you give me money, I'm going to blow up the lifeboat. I can't let them escape.' Not least because the shore had at last hove into view. With Boris Johnson installed as prime minister and the Conservatives remorselessly focused on Brexit above all else, the reckoning loomed: a general election.

McSweeney was in no doubt: it was an election that Corbyn would lose. It was time to find his candidate. As he had told Labour Together's board in 2017, he was agnostic as to who it might be. Several MPs sought his counsel. Their motivations were too transparent, their ambition too unsubtle. The more obvious their aspirations to leadership and hostility to Corbynism, the less plausible they would appear to the members. For two years he had imagined a silhouette, its exact profile as yet indistinct. They would need to be known by the members but they could not be a Corbynite. At the same time, they could not be a rebel. Above all they could not be honest about their ambition to replace the incumbent leader until the very moment of release. One

July afternoon in 2019 the profile's features at last resolved into clear view. The candidate was Keir Starmer.

★

Keir Starmer wanted to be Labour leader – and a Labour prime minister – long before he met McSweeney, and long before his arrival in Westminster. He did not say so; his actions spoke for him.

Gordon Brown tried first. As he prepared to take power as prime minister he had dispatched Jonathan Ashworth, his long-suffering Man Friday, to invite Starmer to join his future Government of All the Talents. One day in 2006 he met Starmer in the Treasury canteen and asked if he would like to become an MP. Starmer was interested in principle. He said he was interested in environmental law, and then demurred. He would soon begin a five-year term as director of public prosecutions. Parliament would have to wait. When his term ended, in November 2013, Ed Miliband was looking to use his powers of patronage to install a friendly barrister in the House of Lords. He called Charlie Falconer, the QC and former Lord Chancellor to Tony Blair, for his recommendations.

Starmer was a man of the left. Falconer did not know him intimately. Occasionally he had offered his younger colleague counsel. Starmer had sought his advice when, after two decades banging on the door of the big state as a human rights barrister, agitating against power from the outside, he applied to work within its ramparts and run the Crown Prosecution Service. It surprised only those who could not sense Starmer's vaulting ambition. Falconer did. Even after five years as the apex predator of the English bar it still burned, unfulfilled.

'Obviously,' Falconer told Miliband, 'the standout candidate would be Keir, by a million miles.'

'No, no, no,' the Labour leader said, with all the impatient insistence of a man who had been disappointed before. 'I know Keir. I've discussed this with Keir. I suggested it to him, and he said no. Keir is determined to get a seat.' Like his namesake, Keir Hardie, and every Labour leader since, he knew that only from the Commons could he change the country he wished to rule.

He coveted the safe seat in which he lived, Holborn and St Pancras: a long, thin wedge of London, from Primrose Hill to Covent Garden. Neil Kinnock, whose war against the left as Labour leader Starmer would one day wage again, recalls meeting him at a party fundraiser for Frank Dobson, the bluff old Yorkshireman who was then the local MP, in a Camden Cypriot restaurant in 2008. 'He was a straight-up guy,' says Kinnock now. Six years later he was selected to succeed Dobson in a contest that had been deliberately delayed by Miliband – aspirant Labour MPs were required to be members for six months before standing, and Starmer had been obliged by public service to resign his party affiliation until 2013. He applied himself to the select contest with the same single-minded rigour he had brought to countless complex cases. Though he betrayed little of his politics, he won comfortably. Martin Plaut, a local activist who later became a firm friend of the Starmers, recalls how the would-be candidate walked through sleet and snow to lobby members in their own homes. 'He said: "Can I come and have a coffee?" I said sure. So we met him in our house in Kentish Town. I can honestly say, within ten minutes, I thought . . . he could be a gift to the Labour Party . . . there was something about him . . . What he did to us, he did to the whole of our Labour Party. Three months off, and he went door to door, knocking on every single Labour Party member.'

Holborn and St Pancras would be his for as long as he wanted it. If – when – Miliband won, so too would high office. In the Labour government that would take power after 2015 he was to be attorney general or justice secretary.

Starmer did not admit his ambition, but nor could he disguise it. He did not deny that his ultimate aim was to become prime minister in interviews with the legal press. When Miliband lost the general election and a traumatised and enfeebled Labour Party debated the succession, columnists urged the newly elected MP for Holborn and St Pancras to run. He told them their suggestion had come too soon. Not that it was ridiculous – merely that it had come too soon. Instead he supported Andy Burnham, the former cabinet minister who by 2015 spoke more stridently, and sold himself as New Labour's prodigal son. Of course, the party members bought Corbyn instead. Starmer, an MP for only two and a half months, took a seat on his front bench as shadow immigration minister.

But Starmer longed for higher office, for real power, and needed help to get there. Friendless and unfamiliar in the byzantine, backstabbing world of Labour factionalism and intimidated by Westminster's arcane insularity, he knew what he did not know. That October he turned to Chris Ward, the career bag-carrier with a cowlick and wide smile. Ward had arrived in Parliament in June 2007, the very month that Labour's last election winner, Tony Blair, had retired from the fray. He had written a PhD on Marxism and the ballot box and wondered whether mainstream social democracy was as doomed as communism. In their first conversation Starmer told Ward of his ambition.

'The Labour Party doesn't win very often. It only wins when it faces the future. It's only won three times in the past. I don't think Jeremy could win. There needs to be someone who takes that through. I think it'd be an interesting project to work on . . . to try and see if that's something I could do.'

Starmer employed Ward to manage his office. They devoted spare hours and afternoons to furtive preparations for a job interview that would not be advertised for another five years: the acting lessons, the amateur dramatics of pretend Prime Minister's Questions, the torturous evenings spent poring over old budget documents. Like the Corbynites, they called it the Project. 'Is this a regular conversation,' Ward would ask Starmer knowingly, if he made some request or other, 'or a Project conversation?'

His tutee approached every task with the same masochistic, methodical obsession for detail that had been the hallmark of his unflashy manner as a barrister. He listed the demands of political leadership that he could not meet and worked through them one by one. Starmer took acting lessons from Leonie Mellinger, who had once appeared alongside Rik Mayall in *The New Statesman*. With every chaotic week that passed under Corbyn, Starmer's conviction grew. By the spring of 2016 he believed that a leadership election could come any day, that the left's brief experiment with power would soon collapse under the weight of its own contradictions and the opposition of the Labour establishment. He wanted to be ready.

Starmer was wrong. Corbyn crushed the revolution his MPs launched after the Brexit referendum that June. As if already conscious of the need to preserve his reputation among the Labour members who would one day choose Corbyn's successor, Starmer had joined the rebellion late, and almost apologetically. Twenty-four hours after almost all of his colleagues had resigned from the front bench, he quit in sorrow, not anger. Not for him the melodramatic assessments of Corbyn's moral failings as a leader and human being. 'I have never spoken out publicly against you,' he wrote to Corbyn, 'and I do not intend to now.'

Three months later, when the leader's aides gathered at Lambeth's Novotel hotel to appoint a new shadow cabinet, they suspected Starmer would be among the few willing to return to active service. Perhaps he could be shadow home secretary, or lead Labour's response to Brexit. Seumas Milne, the Marxist polemicist now locked in an uneasy dance with Fleet Street as Corbyn's head of communications, strongly advised against the latter. To appoint a man who had proven himself disloyal to their cause and empower him to set Labour's policy on the defining issue of the day was 'dangerous'. He preferred Emily Thornberry, the shadow foreign secretary and Corbyn's constituency neighbour in Islington.

Karie Murphy, the leader's combative chief of staff, took the same view. The Glaswegian nurse and trade union lifer was already disinclined to trust Londoners in smart suits. Starmer was no exception. The only cross words she had ever exchanged with her close friend Amy Jackson, Corbyn's political secretary, had been in an argument over Starmer's true intentions.

'You don't know him,' Jackson had told her. 'He's actually quite left wing.'

'Is he *fuck*,' said Murphy, enraged by the suggestion that she might share common cause with the man who had prosecuted the London rioters in 2011. Starmer would betray Corbyn, she insisted, as he had betrayed those disadvantaged youths.

Murphy and Milne nonetheless conceded, reluctantly, that Starmer could be appointed shadow home secretary. While Corbyn's old friend Diane Abbott clearly coveted the role, they preferred her to serve as shadow foreign secretary: better a true believer to spread the left's gospel on nuclear disarmament and peace in the Middle East. Abbott disagreed. She claimed – a little speciously, her comrades thought – that her son's role as a Foreign Office diplomat in Rome amounted to an intolerable conflict of interest. Corbyn agreed. Murphy was left with little option but to accept that Keir Starmer would be shadow Brexit secretary. John McDonnell, the shadow chancellor who knew that their radicalism needed some semblance of establishment credibility, had made a spirited case for Starmer. Later that evening, standing on the balcony of the leader's office, the Thames churning beneath her,

Murphy made the call to Starmer that Corbyn was by then too tired to contemplate.

A foreign dialling tone rang out. She reached Starmer in Taiwan, where he was campaigning against the death penalty. Here, from the unlikeliest of callers, came his political reprieve. Murphy told him that he was to be shadow Brexit secretary, sharing his responsibilities with Thornberry.

'Are there other options?' he asked.

'You're not in a position to negotiate,' Murphy replied. The left were the masters now.

★

Over the three long years that followed, Starmer proved Murphy wrong. For the Corbynites, Brexit was to become one long negotiation with their own spokesman, the lawyer reborn at the despatch box. The Commons was the court, Theresa May's government the defendant. As he had as a barrister, he performed emotionlessly, methodically: detail was his cudgel. He resisted every call to set out Labour's preferred outcome from Blairite Remainers on the back benches and Bennite Eurosceptics in the leader's office. Starmer subordinated every vexed question to New Labour's guiding mantra: 'What matters is what works.' Under his watch, the opposition voted against every possible Brexit deal. In Westminster politics ground to a halt. The country longed for release.

So did Starmer. He had his reservations about Corbyn. But Labour activists loved Jeremy, and hated those who defied him. Time and time again Starmer had kept his counsel at moments of maximum peril for the leadership. Twice in 2018 he had written letters of resignation – over Corbyn's response to the Salisbury poisonings, and accusations of antisemitism against the party machine – and twice he had stayed, a good and faithful servant of the Project. In shadow cabinet meetings he criticised Corbyn but in public he was curiously reticent. 'He was literally absent on the antisemitism stuff despite having a wife of Jewish heritage,' said one moderate MP who later became a secretary of state in Starmer's government. Yet his reasons were obvious. He coveted the leadership and could not be seen as seditious. 'He kept his skin very clean for this exact reason, and therefore was the only viable show in town.' He had spent long evenings travelling to small towns to address the activists who would one day vote for him, and glad-handing the MPs who would one day nominate him: sharing beer and Colombian food at World Cup parties hosted by his friend Jenny Chapman that summer, held specifically so that they might get to know the man they did not know was planning to lead them.

He defied Corbyn only once: to prove to the members that he was one of them.

Labour's activists, like its MPs, agitated furiously for Corbyn to back another referendum. As they gathered in Liverpool for Labour's annual conference in September 2018 their campaign overshadowed everything. Seumas Milne moaned that the foot soldiers of the left had switched their allegiance to the 'Republic of Remainia'. Even Alastair Campbell, the New Labour spin doctor whose name had long been mud to the left, had been reborn as its folk hero for his willingness to say to the grass roots what Corbyn could not: Brexit must be stopped. Starmer, who knew he would one day need their votes in a leadership election, watched carefully. It was he who would have to address them on Europe – and perhaps disappoint them.

In the week before conference he lunched with Tom Kibasi, the director of the Institute for Public Policy Research. Kibasi urged Starmer to use his speech to endorse a referendum that gave Britain the option to vote Remain and cancel Brexit altogether. He knew of his friend's ambitions to win the hearts and minds of members, and knew that to say so was almost certainly to fulfil them. Starmer refused. The price of such brazen sedition was too high. Like any good barrister he intended to respect the brief that had been given to him. Instead, on the eve of his speech he spent five hours negotiating with trade unionists and party members over the wording of a Brexit policy that might reconcile their conflicting demands. It was not easy: their discussions were so disputatious that even the meaning of the word 'consensus' was debated at length. But at 1 a.m. on Sunday 23 September, he emerged with a delicate formula for party unity. 'If we cannot get a general election Labour must support all options remaining on the table, including campaigning for a public vote on the terms of Brexit.' He believed that Remain would be on the ballot paper.

The next morning, John McDonnell said otherwise. Arriving at the BBC tired, alone and badly briefed, he told the Today programme:

'We'll be arguing that it should be a vote on the deal itself and then enable us to go back and do the negotiations.' Stopping Brexit would not be an option. As he listened, Starmer snapped. He raged to his advisers, salting his invective with the sort of profanity they seldom heard pass his lips: 'What the fuck have they done? I've worked my arse off for them, for hours and hours, and they fucked it up.' He felt his own honour had been besmirched. He loathed the thought that the members who had put their faith in him – the members who might soon be required to vote for him – would think him a liar. Journalists harried him as he walked the conference floor, asking if McDonnell was right. His clarification was to come on the biggest stage of all.

As Kibasi had suggested, Starmer would tell members what they wanted to hear. It was at once a question of high principle and low politics. His honour was at stake, yes, but so too the future he had laboured to build. To disappoint the members was to become the one thing he told himself the next leader could not be: a traitor to their cause. Hundreds and hundreds of hours had been spent in pursuit of his future. All would be wasted if he did not defy the leader. Europe scrambled the reliable signal that once came from the membership. They loved Corbyn but hated Brexit. Silence was no longer a fail-safe option for a politician who wished to inspire them. Starmer had no option but to speak. 'You can do it,' warned Ben Nunn, his spokesman. 'But we've got to get clearance . . . because that is a big story.' He declined to seek permission from Team Corbyn. Instead, as he rose to address conference on Tuesday morning, he scribbled eight words onto a Post-it note and appended it to his speech. 'It's right that Parliament has the first say. But if we need to break the impasse, our options must include campaigning for a public vote, and *nobody is ruling out Remain as an option.*'

The hall erupted. So too did the Corbynites. The frown on the face of eighty-six-year-old Dennis Skinner, the cantankerous old pitman who embodied the Eurosceptic soul of the old left, ran as deep as a seam of Derbyshire coal. As he was confronted by Amy Jackson in the wings, Starmer stressed he had merely intended to state the obvious. Whatever McDonnell had said, the letter of the party's policy did not rule out Remain as an option. He was sticking to the script, not seeking to rewrite it. Murphy disagreed, as did the Conservative Party, which tweeted: 'CONFIRMED. Labour will not respect the result of the referendum.'

'What have you done?' asked Jackson.

'John had said Remain won't be on the ballot,' Starmer replied, indignantly. 'I had to correct it. What did you want me to do?'

What Jackson and Murphy wanted was to sack him. They thought of doing so on the spot. But the ovation for Starmer proved that this would make him a martyr for the membership. Starmer was unassailable. Like Barack Obama at the Democratic National Convention in 2004, Starmer had elevated himself to a higher plane in an instant. He had succeeded not only in securing his own future, but in binding Corbyn's hands behind his back.

Thanks to Starmer, Corbyn's dislocation from his natural supporters in the membership quickened into an avalanche of disaffection. Above all else they wanted to stop Brexit. Simultaneously, Leave voters in what had once been Labour's traditional heartlands wondered what had become of the party that had been made for them. With every twist of Starmer's ratchet, the Corbyn project edged away from the politics and the people that had served them so well in 2017.

Simultaneously, at Starmer's command, the two sides of the Brexit debate had become so entrenched that the prospect of May's hung parliament agreeing on *anything* was receding into the realms of fantasy. It was plausible, if not likely, that Corbyn would lose the general election required to break the deadlock – however divided the Conservatives appeared at the time. It was plausible, too, that he might not make it to polling day. Comrades whispered of the leader's failing health and darkening moods. Starmer sensed that the moment he had for four years prepared for, and almost unconsciously willed into existence from the despatch box, would soon be at hand. His leadership campaign, for four years conducted via nods and winks, would now begin.

3

The Leadership

One evening in February 2019 Keir Starmer summoned Chris Ward and Ben Nunn to the Admiralty, a tourist trap of a pub on Trafalgar Square, with interior inspired by Nelson's flagship HMS *Victory*. He made explicit the ambition that had until then been implicitly understood, but never straightforwardly said. Ward, the office manager, knew of his ambition. It had been his job to make it achievable, and keep it a secret. Nunn had assumed this day would come – had *hoped* this day would come – but had never dared ask. Starmer was now prepared to tempt fate.

Nursing his pint, he told his aides: 'I've spoken to Vic about this. If Jeremy steps down, pre or after the election, I'm going to put my name forward. I want to be ready.' He went on: 'It's very febrile within the PLP. There's a lot of unease, there's a feeling something might happen soon, there's a problem coming along.' He was confident that the parties and dinners hosted by Jenny Chapman would pay dividends: 'Lots of people are going to ask me to stand.'

As tourists chatted obliviously around them, Starmer turned to Ward. 'We've talked for a while about how this might happen. But I want to have a proper conversation with the two of you.' The three men sat just five minutes from Downing Street but it was by no means inevitable that they – or any other Labour leader – would ever arrive there.

Starmer was undeterred. 'My feeling is that I should go with it,' he said. 'I don't want to unless you two are with me. And that we are fully committed to what that means.'

His advisers immediately agreed. Said Ward: 'Obviously, we are with you. But if you're going to do it, you need to do it properly. We need to have a plan, a proper strategy.'

The party's MPs were not the answer. Starmer had watched, horrified, as their kamikaze campaign against Corbyn radicalised an
embattled left against the PLP in 2016. Nunn, indeed, had worked on
Owen Smith's ill-planned campaign, and was now embarrassed to have
done so. That leadership challenge was an emotional spasm: Starmer's
would have to be the opposite.

The lawyer's long deliberations were over. As was his wont when at
last convinced by the evidence before him, he was ready to press on,
hard, to the next phase of his political career. At Starmer's insistence
the trio now met with Chapman, who had urged him to stand a year
earlier. She had grown impatient with organising on behalf of a candidate who would not confirm his intentions. Her role as convenor
for the undeclared campaign – the World Cup barbecues, the dinner
hosted by Lord Falconer for Starmer and other Labour lawyers – had
its uses, but was no substitute for formal planning. Just as she had for
the social occasions whose political purposes were never revealed to
her invited guests, she made her home available as headquarters. So
it was that weeks after his drink at the Admiralty, one Monday morning in March 2019, Starmer arrived for the first formal meeting of a
leadership campaign that would not be revealed to the public – or the
colleagues who had been unwittingly invited to its earlier gatherings –
for another nine months. They met not in Westminster but in Camden
Town, in Chapman's house on Arlington Road.

Around her kitchen table sat the trusted few who called themselves,
elliptically but unimaginatively, the Arlington Group. Ward, Nunn,
Nick Smith, Chapman's Labour MP husband, and Tom Kibasi, the
think-tanker who had urged Starmer to make his fateful intervention
at Labour conference the previous year. All were sworn to secrecy. If
the mere fact of the meeting became known – with a general election
looming, Corbyn secure in his position, and Starmer publicly loyal –
his reputation among members would be destroyed in an instant. A
strange pall descended on the room. There was none of the excitement or intrigue one might expect, secrecy being the very stuff of
politics. Instead the atmosphere was almost funereal. It was almost as
if he himself could not bear the weight of his own ambition.

He was not ready. His friends had gathered at his insistence, to make
him Labour leader and prime minister, yet Starmer was overcome by

diffidence. He declined to chair his own meeting, deferring instead to Smith. Starmer contributed tentatively to the discussions as if he was an invited guest and not their instigator. When he did speak he spoke not of his political vision but of tedious bureaucratic process. 'He made sure that notes were kept,' recalled one person present. 'He wanted action points, for people to be accountable for what they said they'd do.' He did not say *why* he wished to lead the Labour Party, or *what* he wished to do with power, but preoccupied himself with the tedious minutiae of the *how*. 'He wanted to be involved in things like trade union rules, the financial reporting rules, and what the election rules were going to be.'

His friends accepted he was half right. Running for the leadership – winning the leadership – would be hard work. In an organisation with such byzantine internal structures as the Labour Party, the arcane questions of law and process Starmer raised were not unimportant. But it seemed bizarre, even to his greatest admirers in Westminster, that he should be the one asking them. *They* ought to be responsible for the process, their candidate for the politics. If Starmer knew what those politics were, then he kept them secret even in his safest of spaces.

Every Monday morning, as the Brexit deadlock in Parliament tightened, the confidants gathered at Arlington Road, honing their strategy, assessing their chances. Eventually Starmer took the chair, as his aides updated him on their work to win over donors, the unions, MPs, members and the media. Once each meeting adjourned, they would leave in turn for Westminster, to evade capture: first Starmer, then Ward and Nunn, and finally Chapman and Smith. It was some months before their circle widened. Yasmeen Sebbana, Starmer's diary secretary, was invited after she queried exactly why she had blocked out every Monday morning and found herself alone in the office.

In public, Starmer began to carry himself with a new seriousness. Nunn, who preferred to distil his theories of communications into Post-it notes rather than rambling memoranda, had stuck to his desk a three-word strategy: 'Attack. Leader. Depth.' He urged his boss to do the things which, by then, even Corbyn's trusted comrades accepted were beyond the leader, so often visibly bored by the parliamentary process and demoralised by Brexit. Labour members wanted blood sport – or at least the closest thing permissible to it under the rules of *Erskine May*, the bible of Commons procedure. At Nunn's behest, Starmer strived to show he 'really knew how to use Parliament', 'to haul a minister in front of it', to 'skewer them'. In December 2018 he had forced a vote which found the government in contempt of Parliament and reduced Geoffrey Cox, May's blimpish attorney general, to tears. It was catnip for activists who defined their politics in almost Manichean terms. 'The membership don't really care if you're on the left of the Labour Party, or the right of the Labour Party,' a source familiar with the discussions recalled, 'as long as you beat the Tories. So we had to show that Keir was very good at Tory attack.'

Outside of the chamber, however, Starmer consciously withdrew from the limelight. It was a counterintuitive strategy. Emily Thornberry and Lisa Nandy, his rivals for the leadership, were omnipresent on the airwaves. Yet the Arlington Group dismissed them as commentators, not leaders. Not for Starmer the rent-a-quote life of a talking head. He would not take the flak for Corbyn on morning media rounds. He was to be a 'ten past eight' politician – accepting only the 8.10 a.m. interview on the *Today* programme, reserved for cabinet ministers – not a 'ten to seven' politician. He would only speak, be it from behind a microphone or a lectern, if he had something to say – and if it advanced his leadership bid.

Depth proved more elusive, more difficult. *Why* had he left the law for politics? *Who* was Sir Keir Starmer, really? Transcending his lawyerly persona, so useful for his Brexit brief, at first seemed beyond him. Having endured a difficult youth, with a distant father, ill mother, crowded home and straitened finances, he jealously guarded his private life. He was never demonstrative. To speak in the first person seemed almost alien to him. Stories of childhood penury were the lingua franca of the Labour Party, but Starmer refused to speak it. Aides urged him to tell the world that, behind the clipped vowels and knighthood, was a working-class boy done good. He thought it absurd. '*You* don't go around telling everyone you're middle class,' he told Nunn. He could not bear to tell the story of Rodney Starmer, the toolmaker. At one meeting, Nick Smith had asked precisely what a toolmaker did. Unwilling to disinter his buried trauma, Starmer refused to elaborate. 'Most people don't know what a lathe is, Keir,' Smith snapped back. 'So you're going to have to explain.' For months Starmer refused, before eventually agreeing to provide bowdlerised versions of his life story to podcasts with Matt Forde, the Labour adviser turned comedian, and Nick Robinson of the BBC.

Their preparations soon assumed a new urgency. Six weeks after the Arlington Group first convened, May resigned. Having finished fifth in the European elections of May 2019 – a historic humiliation – she was replaced by Boris Johnson, who pledged to unite the right and get Brexit done. Spooked by polling from the anti-racism group Hope Not Hate that suggested Labour would be wiped out even in its new heartlands in the cities and university towns if it gave effect to Brexit, John McDonnell and Diane Abbott finally agreed with Starmer: Labour would have to back a second referendum. Corbyn himself, however, could never bring himself to say so with the clarity they demanded. By the time Parliament dissolved for its summer recess on Thursday 25 July 2019, the day after Johnson became prime minister, Corbyn's electoral reckoning was a question of when, not if.

As MPs returned to face their restive constituents, Starmer went to see Steve Reed in the basement restaurant of the Royal Court theatre on Sloane Square. He preferred to speak in the dark. Reed asked him two questions. Would he run for the Labour leadership when the vacancy arose? If so, would he like Labour Together's help? Starmer said yes, and yes again. He invited Reed to join the Arlington Group. Three days later, he did. Reed was the first outsider to take a seat at Chapman's kitchen table. He knew immediately that another would have to join.

'What you need is Morgan.'

*

McSweeney came to Camden. Those who knew Starmer best were wary. But they did not know what their new recruit had achieved. In their eyes, he was an emissary from a failed state. Blairites like Liz Kendall, whose disastrous leadership campaign McSweeney had run, had blown their chance to change the Labour Party. Nor was he loyal, as they were, to their friend. McSweeney and Starmer had met only once before, fleetingly, at a Labour Together dinner. What could McSweeney teach them that they did not know?

By the end of their meeting they were converted. 'Bloody hell,' Nick Smith told himself. 'A gift from heaven.' As they walked together to catch the Tube at Mornington Crescent, Starmer flashed a grin at Chris Ward. 'I told you he was good.'

McSweeney made an offer that the Arlington Group could not refuse. Over three years he had spent hundreds of thousands of pounds on YouGov polling: more than both Labour and the Conservative Party combined. Their ignorance was excusable. McSweeney had failed to declare the donations that funded his work to the Electoral Commission. Much later the group would be found guilty of twenty breaches of the law over its secrecy. The oversight ultimately served its strategic interests. It kept the secret. But it was also informed by a desire to protect Trevor Chinn, Labour Together's great benefactor and a lightning rod for antisemitism. The explanation they eventually offered in public had the advantage of ringing true to anyone who had worked with McSweeney: that he was simply too disorganised to have known what to declare and when.

The result was that nobody caught him amassing the data he used to understand and destroy Corbynism. By 2019 his reams of spreadsheets and focus group reports had cohered into a grand unified theory of the Labour grass roots. While the hard left was loud and poisonous – exerting malign influence on Facebook groups and via new media outlets like the *Canary*, controlling the party's National Executive Committee and its regional boards – they accounted for only 25 per cent of the party membership. McSweeney called them the 'ideologues'. Their politics were black and white, conspiratorial, suspicious of the strictures of parliamentary democracy. Sir Keir Starmer would never win them over.

But there were just as many 'instrumentalists' – what the media called the moderates. This 25 per cent self-identified as pragmatic. They believed in compromise for the sake of power. Here were members who would support Starmer in a heartbeat. Of course, their support alone was not enough. The road to victory instead ran through the 'idealists'. This 50 per cent had lost faith in the technocratic, televisual culture of New Labour. They wanted honesty. They yearned for radicalism. McSweeney explained: 'They are pro-Corbyn, but not hard left.' Idealists were willing to compromise. They did not like Brexit, nor were they comfortable with antisemitism. While they had voted for Corbyn twice over, there was no guarantee that they would support his anointed successor. It was an analysis that cut sharply across the received wisdom which the PLP and their friends in the media accepted as unarguable.

It was not an exact science. But McSweeney believed he knew how to win, just as he had in Dagenham. That word came up again: *values*. Starmer could convince the idealists he was one of them. The question was not what he did or did not wish to nationalise, or whether he subscribed to every dot and comma of Corbynite proposals on internal party reform, but whether he was at one with the members. Did his heart bleed at the injustice of austerity? Had he marched on the same protests against Thatcher? Was he committed to a different world? Was he motivated by social justice, not self-advancement? If he could show the idealists that the answer was yes, yes, and yes again, then he might convince them that he was the man to prosecute their shared goals and return Labour to government. If he could transcend factionalism and resist the crude binaries into which candidates would be divided in the contest to come – Blairite versus Corbynite, power versus principle, state versus private – then Starmer would win. Unity would be his watchword: a moral and political necessity. He would promise to heal the Labour Party and return it to power to enact the values of its members.

Whether Starmer truly believed what he was about to say was immaterial. McSweeney knew the left could be divided against itself. Labour Together had run campaigns like his before. That spring he had helped Liam Byrne, a Blairite languishing on the back benches, secure the Labour candidacy for the West Midlands mayoralty. Byrne was steeped in New Labour. His final act as a cabinet minister under Gordon Brown was to write its epitaph on Treasury notepaper as he left office in 2010: 'I'm afraid there is no money.' And yet, with the help of McSweeney and Shabana Mahmood, a hard-nosed Birmingham MP who sat on the board of Labour Together, he had sold himself to members with as anodyne a message as it was possible to send. Byrne didn't like homelessness. Byrne didn't want people to go hungry. Byrne blamed Tory austerity for both. In 2017, McSweeney had pulled off the same trick in Lewisham, convincing local activists to back a young moderate called Damien Egan – the least left wing of five candidates – with the promise of party unity. It was all a lie. His true objective was to restore the favoured sons and daughters of New Labour to their rightful place in positions of power. In the West Midlands, the confidence trick was so successful that even John McDonnell endorsed Byrne.

Starmer would be next. The machine had found its candidate. The candidate had found its machine.

★

It would be months before the campaign acknowledged its own existence. Its script was written but its reluctant lead still struggled to read his lines. Starmer remained ungainly, awkward. He still flinched when asked to tell the story of being the toolmaker's son. He settled on another narrative: of the left-wing lawyer who had opposed the Iraq War, who watched police horses charge striking printworkers outside Rupert Murdoch's Wapping headquarters, who won justice for the pitmen of Arthur Scargill's National Union of Mineworkers, who had helped secure justice for the family of Stephen Lawrence, the black teenager murdered by racist thugs. Yet still he struggled to say so. His team took matters into their own hands, inviting Starmer to speak at the annual Trades Union Congress commemoration of Nye Bevan's birth in Smith's constituency in the South Wales valleys on 7 July. He read words written for him, attacking Boris Johnson as a 'scruffy incendiary bomb' and paying misty-eyed homage to Labour's history. As he spoke, all the right people were clapping.

They clapped all summer. For that, Starmer had Johnson to thank. On 14 August the prime minister threatened to prorogue Parliament to foreclose all opposition to his strategy. He denounced MPs organising with Starmer to stop a no-deal Brexit as 'terrible collaborators' with Brussels. Along with the rest of the shadow cabinet, Starmer took to the streets to accuse Johnson of plotting a coup. He spoke with the confidence that eluded him at Chapman's kitchen table. Throngs of protesters cheered him. He posed holding an EU flag. By then the Corbynites knew the game he was playing, but had no grounds for appeal. In pursuing a no-deal Brexit, Johnson had embraced the outcome Corbyn had already rejected. It gave Starmer the political space to restate his demands for a referendum, and he did so without the ambiguity and lawyerly restraint that had once been the hallmarks of his rhetoric.

By the time Labour gathered in Brighton for its 2019 conference, he was fluent in the native tongue of the membership: 'If you want a referendum – vote Labour. If you want a final say on Brexit – vote Labour. If you want to fight for Remain – vote Labour.' The next day he sat down with Tom Kibasi on the conference fringe, for an 'in conversation' event hosted by the Institute for Public Policy Research. To the man who was secretly advising his leadership campaign Starmer offered seemingly spontaneous reflections on his life and socialist credentials. His rivals did not know that every utterance was part of a script written in secret. With every panel, rally and stump speech, Starmer was stealing their votes three months before a leadership election had been called.

*

The stalemate at Westminster could not hold. Johnson called his 'Get Brexit Done' election on 31 October. Corbyn would lose. Having staunched the bleed of middle-class votes to parties of Remain, his team scrambled to win back the country of Brexit. It was a campaign in which Starmer would play no part. 'They locked him in a cupboard,' one of his aides recalled. He appeared only once alongside the leader. That suited him. His own future was far more important. He would have six weeks to prepare himself for the election that really mattered: for Corbyn's successor.

Events obliged him to dispense with secrecy. As defeat loomed, he told outsiders of his intentions for the first time. Three weeks into the campaign he texted Simon Fletcher, a former adviser to Corbyn and Ed Miliband, and invited him for coffee. Fletcher, who dressed like a mod and spoke like a sociology lecturer, was nothing if not one of McSweeney's idealists. He had made his name as Ken Livingstone's chief of staff in London's City Hall, having run his successful independent campaign for the mayoralty in 2000. While a man of the left, he knew their project was nothing without power. Indeed, it was Fletcher who Starmer had to thank for his parliamentary career. From Miliband's office he had helped engineer Starmer's selection in Holborn and St Pancras in 2014. The next summer, he oversaw Corbyn's first landslide victory among the membership. Any candidate to succeed

Jeremy would want him – indeed, four of the eventual five asked him. But it was Starmer who *needed* him in order to prove he was above the petty splittism that so dismayed the idealists.

The two men met on Camden High Street, a short walk from the house in which the strategy to which Fletcher would soon become an unwitting accessory had been planned. Their conversation was warm but purposeless. Fletcher sensed their meandering catch-up was really a preamble to something more transactional. Eventually the question came. As they parted, Starmer affected a naivete that belied the years he had spent preparing for moments such as this. He remarked casually that 'some people' had told him to consider standing for the leadership if Labour lost. 'What do you think?' he asked.

Fletcher was non-committal. On balance, he said, it was a good idea. But he knew immediately that this was no passing fancy. Starmer was not his friend, or his comrade. They did not speak regularly. That he had invited Fletcher to meet at all suggested that the question was rhetorical.

Nick Brown knew it too. Labour's chief whip, the squinting Sphinx who had served three party leaders, received the same invitation. Starmer would be in Darlington, not far from Brown's seat in Newcastle, canvassing for Jenny Chapman. Could they meet? Intrigue was the chief whip's vocation. The reason for the rendezvous was obvious. Brown later joked that he arrived at Chapman's constituency home appropriately inconspicuous in a baseball cap, his coat collar turned up. Over coffee, Starmer did not tell Brown that he *would* run. He asked, innocently enough, for his thoughts on the prospect of a leadership election. The chief whip dispensed with the pretence. He knew Labour MPs better than they knew themselves. He knew Chapman had told any colleague who would listen that it had to be Keir. 'Go for it,' he told Starmer. 'They were meeting in secret in Darlington, during the election campaign. Nick had made the effort to go down there. Keir was already campaigning. They all knew what they were doing,' a friend of Brown says now.

Starmer and his team engaged only cursorily with the Labour Party in the country. The campaign that really mattered was their own. The Irishman was busy assembling a team. Chapman and Reed would secure endorsements from MPs. McSweeney planned to win the members. To reach the final ballot, candidates needed nominations not only from 10 per cent of MPs, but from three trade unions or at least 5 per cent of Constituency Labour Parties (CLPs) too. Starmer would win the support of his colleagues and the unions easily enough. But McSweeney wanted to win on all three fronts. Racking up nominations from CLPs would give the impression of unstoppable momentum, and lock potential challengers out of the contest too.

In early November, more than a month before the date of the general election, McSweeney met the man who would win them for him. Matt Pound, a banjo player with a jet-black beard, had spent the Corbyn years working for Labour First, the embattled campaign group of the party's old right, struggling – and sometimes succeeding – to out-organise Momentum. Over a Mexican dinner at Wahaca in Waterloo, McSweeney told him: 'Corbyn is going to lose the election. I am going to run Keir's campaign to be leader, and I want you to join.' Pound immediately agreed to enact McSweeney's plan to marshal members in each constituency to nominate Starmer.

No other candidate was thinking so hard, or planning so extensively, for the campaign to come. Starmer left nothing to chance. He sought and secured a donation of £100,000 from his old colleague from his days at Doughty Street Chambers, the judge Robert Latham, to be deposited at will. His slogan, a deliberate echo of words once uttered by John McDonnell, was ready to print on posters and placards: 'Another Future Is Possible'. His first interview, and interviewer – the pro-Corbyn, anti-Brexit *Guardian* columnist Zoe Williams – was already planned. In the days after the election he would tell her that he was 'seriously considering' a bid for the leadership. Tony Blair would get in touch to complain he didn't like the interview, nor the tributes to Corbyn it contained. Starmer could not have cared less. He knew it would help him win.

★

The night of the general election of 12 December 2019 was cold and wet. Starmer waited at home in Kentish Town with his wife, Vic. Their two children were away. His team would join him behind another closed door. Five minutes before the 10 p.m. exit poll, Chris Ward and Ben Nunn arrived, fortified by pints from the Pineapple, the pub their godless boss called 'my church'. Tom Kibasi arrived later. So did McSweeney. He had returned to Dagenham to save Jon Cruddas, who had been at his side in Corbyn's office and in the fight against the BNP. Chapman was in Darlington, awaiting the end of one political career and the beginning of another.

They heard the BBC's Huw Edwards say: 'Our exit poll is suggesting that there will be a Conservative majority.' The numbers on the screen spelt Armageddon. CON 368. LAB 191.

'Oh my God,' said Starmer. 'This is worse than I thought.' He knew Chapman had lost, and dozens of MPs who might have supported him would drown in the deluge with her.

'This is really bad. A lot of colleagues are going to lose their seats.'

Ward turned to Vic. 'You know what this means, don't you?'

'Yeah,' she said, matter-of-factly. 'There's going to be a contest.' She knew her husband must run. As a friend of the family recalls: 'Her gut reaction was: he needs to do this. I think she was less reluctant than Keir. I think she saw the point that he needed to do this.'

In the early hours Starmer received a text from Carolyn Harris, the Swansea MP with purple hair who had poked him in the back on his first day in the Commons and said she would make him leader of the Labour Party.

'No arguments, you've got to do it,' she said.

'I'll think about it,' he replied.

'You've got to stop thinking and you've got to start doing and you cannot allow this. You can't allow us to continue like this. We know Corbyn's going. You have got to put yourself forward.'

With Ward and Nunn, Starmer went to face the music. He knew, as he took to the stage at Somers Town Sports Centre to hear his own result declared, that he had to put himself forward. The time for thinking had already passed. He knew too that he would soon reveal his hand. But not yet. He permitted himself only one comment to the media, telling the *Camden New Journal*, his local newspaper, that it had been a 'devastating night for the Labour Party'. As Starmer waited for the result, Corbyn resigned the party leadership. Ward imparted the news with a whisper. He nodded impassively. 'We'll talk about this later,' he said.

The next morning his team again convened in secret, away from the cameras, at Nunn's Camden home. Their rivals for the party leadership

stood no chance. As the dust settled on the ruins of Labour's old England, McSweeney took a call from Ian Warren, a friend of Labour
Together's Lisa Nandy.

'Lisa's going to run,' Warren said. Would McSweeney join them?

'It's too late,' McSweeney said. 'This is a mistake.' He told Nandy,
too: 'I'm already committed. Sorry, you're too late.'

Emily Thornberry, who as shadow foreign secretary had been
Starmer's steadfast ally in the shadow cabinet, made the same uncomfortable discovery soon afterwards. In the days after the election she
met with him at the German Gymnasium, a restaurant in King's Cross,
to discuss who was best placed to win over the Remainers in Labour's
membership. Thornberry had first met Starmer three decades earlier as a fellow barrister giving legal advice to sacked P&O employees
in Dover. They drank coffee and chatted awkwardly. Starmer would
not budge. Thanks to Labour Together's data, he knew he was the
answer. Mahmood, an MP on its board who had long suspected that
McSweeney was using the group as a Trojan Horse for Starmer's leadership campaign, had told him so. 'You can thank Labour Together for
the polling later,' she said.

It was too late: for Nandy, Thornberry and everyone else. The race
had begun long ago, its starting pistol audible only to Starmer and
McSweeney. Theirs was a plot without precedent in Labour history.
Tony Blair had quietly coveted the leadership, then seized it. Gordon
Brown demanded it, again and again, enduring years of torment before
destiny came too late. Ed Miliband chanced upon it, winning unexpectedly. Jeremy Corbyn stumbled into it, unwilling and unwitting. But
McSweeney fixed it for Starmer, and Starmer fixed it for McSweeney:
methodically, clinically, secretly.

Victory was easier than McSweeney had ever foreseen. The hard left
had no plan. There was no sabotage. On a WhatsApp group populated
by lawyers who would have cost hundreds of thousands of pounds to
hire – including Richard Hermer, the QC who later became attorney general in Starmer's first cabinet – Team Starmer had considered
every possible wrecking tactic the left might deploy to keep him off
the ballot. But there was no conspiracy by the unions and Momentum to crown Corbyn's chosen heir, Rebecca Long-Bailey. Starmer
soon knew he had won. His landslide was as definitive as Johnson's.
His 275,780 votes were more than double those of Long-Bailey, the

candidate of continuity. They amounted to more than Corbyn himself had won in 2015.

McSweeney's prophecy was fulfilled. 'Ultimately,' he had told Labour
Together in 2017, 'we will need a candidate to win a future leadership
election on the political platform we are developing.'

He had found his candidate. And his candidate had won.

PART II: UNITY

4

'Everything is broken'

On 4 April 2020 Sir Keir Starmer and Morgan McSweeney walked into a world they did not recognise. The room where Jeremy Corbyn had waited for the Irishman just twelve months earlier now belonged to them. The Labour Party did not – not yet: the offices of the leader of the opposition were still littered with the debris of Corbynism, like a family home abandoned before the arrival of an enemy army. The shredder was jammed, the scriptures of the old religion only half destroyed. A birthday card from a senior adviser's lover stood alone on the mantelpiece. On a flipchart was the unfinished plan for the election Corbyn had lost. 'Day 1: GE called; Day 2: Brexit/ position speech; Day 3: Landmark policy anno—' Propped up against the wall was a reminder of *why* he had lost. During the campaign, Remain activists had gone to Archway, the northern frontier of Corbyn country, and asked voters to place stickers of his face in one of two columns: *Support People's Vote now!* or *Oppose People's Vote.* Under the first phrase the people of Islington had stuck Corbyn, over and over again.

Starmer could not bear the mess. The handful of staff permitted to be present under the lockdown restrictions of the coronavirus pandemic swept up the flotsam and jetsam into bin liners and envelopes, locked it into cupboards, and made appeals to its presumed owners. Nobody came, and a little while later what the left had left behind was thrown away. It was as if the Corbynites wanted every trace of themselves to be erased from the Labour Party. Eight months later, Corbyn himself would be thrown away too: suspended, disgraced, never to return to the ranks of Labour MPs he had led for four years. The new leader of the Labour Party had promised unity, to stay true to the radical course set by his predecessor. He had never spoken ill of Corbyn in

public, nor acceded to the demands of television interviewers to rate
him out of 10. Jeremy was a colleague, and a friend. But by October
the project was defined by division, and Corbyn was gone. 'Jeremy put
me in an impossible position,' Starmer later told Len McCluskey. 'I had
no choice.'

★

To govern is to choose, so it was just as well that Starmer was to lead
the Labour Party in opposition. The rituals of professional politics
that came effortlessly to colleagues – reshuffles, parliamentary games
and courting MPs – instead irritated and confused him. Said his friend
Martin Plaut who was in and out of Starmer's parliamentary office
in his first year as a Labour MP: 'He wasn't very clubbable. He didn't
go around speaking to people. He was the least "shake hands, have a
beer with the guys" person I met.' On the eve of his victory Starmer
had stood behind a lectern in his living room, the wooden shutters of
its window closed as a foil to waiting photographers. Ben Nunn and
his videographer wife Florence Wilkinson stood awkwardly before
him, and recorded the acceptance speech he by then knew would be
needed. These were not the circumstances in which he had hoped to
meet the country. Indeed, he was unable to meet most of the party's
staff. Ordinary life had stopped, and with it ordinary politics. In the
preceding weeks, before the virus had spread across Britain, Starmer's
advisers had planned to redesign Labour's logo: a new emblem for
a new leadership. But April 2020, with public attention diverted to
matters of life and death, was not the time for anything but the
briefest of introductions.

Much of Starmer's first speech as Labour leader was written by
a man he had never met. Jonathan Rutherford, an academic whose
kindly mien belied the intensity of his distaste for the liberal left,
was confined to his home two miles away from Starmer, in Jeremy
Corbyn's constituency. Rutherford had been among the founders of
Labour Together. He knew McSweeney, but not Starmer. It was the
latter who called, seeking help with his victory speech. Rutherford
thought the task was for Starmer to define himself as a politician and
man. Who was he? What did he believe? What made him different to
Jeremy Corbyn, to Ed Miliband?

Starmer recoiled. He refused to distil his political philosophy and biography into neat little lines for the next day's newspapers. In his vernacular, the gravest insult that one man could level against another was the word 'glib'. That was the problem with Westminster, and the Labour Party. Starmer did not share its obsessions over small differences and contested histories. He seemed to resent Rutherford's assumption that he would have a distinct political philosophy at all, as the journalist Paul Mason had learned when he asked Starmer time and again to explain why he wished to be Labour leader in 2019. He did not see himself as factional: 'nobody's -ite', as Ed Miliband would later say. Rutherford's approach would lead to a trap Starmer wished to avoid. To label was to divide. He believed in competence. Professionalism was his philosophy. He was in the business of bringing the Labour Party together.

And so the speech was a paean to the 'unifying spirit' of his campaign, the 'friendship and support' of his vanquished opponents, Rebecca Long-Bailey and Lisa Nandy, and his other, older 'friend', Jeremy Corbyn, who 'energised our movement'. Indeed he had, as McSweeney well knew. Only once, as he read the words Rutherford had written, did Starmer betray any appetite for confrontation. 'Antisemitism has been a stain on our party,' he said. 'I have seen the grief that it's brought to so many Jewish communities.' Even then he did not reveal the difficult conversations he had endured at synagogue services with his wife and children. 'On behalf of the Labour Party, I am sorry. And I will tear out this poison by its roots and judge success by the return of Jewish members and those who felt that they could no longer support us.' While Starmer would go on to break many of the promises he made that year, that internal measure of his project's success and respectability would remain – as Corbyn would learn to his fatal cost.

★

Starmer's first day in the leader's office was an exercise in self-contradiction. He at once sought to unite the Labour Party behind him and divide himself definitively from its immediate past. Starmer telephoned each of his predecessors in turn. He had refused to meet with Labour's last election winner at all during the leadership campaign for fear of discrediting himself among the left. Now they could safely communicate, if only for a few minutes. Only Corbyn failed to answer the call. It would not be the only time they rued his pacifist's instinct for disengagement from political battle that year.

Jennie Formby did pick up. The former Unite official, a close friend of Karie Murphy and Len McCluskey – with whom Formby had a child – was still Labour's general secretary, despite Starmer's victory. For two years she had managed the party bureaucracy, coordinating its work via flurries of emails on her commute from Brighton. To McCluskey, Formby was the embodiment of a party that now paid the unions it had for so long treated as embarrassing uncles their due respect. To the idealistic new left, the young men and women of Momentum, she was an unloved enforcer of machine politics. To the right – and McSweeney in particular – she bore responsibility for Labour's failure to deal with antisemitism, something her closest colleagues vigorously denied, and could not be allowed to turn Labour headquarters into the last castle of Corbynite dignity. Whatever she was, she would not be general secretary for much longer. As the inevitability of his victory had made itself clear to the Corbynites in the preceding weeks, she had been paranoid about her future. But unity was what Starmer had promised and so Formby answered in good spirits. Breezily, she congratulated him on his victory.

'What are we going to do?' she asked, expectantly. 'How are we going to restructure, Keir?'

His response, unambiguous and direct, was all that she had feared. 'I have no confidence in you. I want you to resign as general secretary.'

To begin his tenure with the revenge killing the Labour right had long dreamt of was, his critics said, a funny kind of unity gesture for a leader who claimed to abhor factionalism. Indeed, Starmer knew that he would be indicted before the court of Corbynite opinion on that very charge. But in his mind he drew a distinction between the *ideological* continuity he had promised in his leadership campaign and the *institutional* continuity that position might have implied. His politics were purist on only one question: competence. It was a standard he believed Corbyn and his team had failed to meet. Fairly or not, he also blamed Formby for the party's failures on antisemitism. It was under her watch the party had been referred to the Equalities and Human Rights Commission (EHRC), whose investigation into Labour was still ongoing. McSweeney's own paranoia about the hard left had also influenced his thinking. From the outset of the leadership election he had warned – baselessly, it would turn out – that Formby would use and abuse her power as general secretary to wreck Starmer's candidacy and disqualify him from the ballot. McSweeney had even retained the services of a legal team in anticipation of a court battle. It never came, but his conviction that Starmer needed to clear the stables of the Labour HQ at Southside never faltered. The two men, improbable as it seemed in the bleak aftermath of Labour's worst election defeat since 1935, had resolved to return their party to power within five years. That would prove impossible unless McSweeney could assume total control. Formby was an impediment to it, as were the countless party staff employed under Corbyn on permanent contracts that made them extremely difficult to dismiss. In time they would be ostracised too. But first he would train his crosshairs on Seumas Milne, the brain of Corbynism, and Karie Murphy, the brawn – both of whom were still employed by the Labour Party.

Yet the counter-revolution would have to wait. Just as McSweeney had predicted, Starmer's victory in the leadership election had been clear and decisive. But it was far from total. The unreconciled and irreconcilable party bureaucracy, as unenthusiastic of his leadership as New Labour's apparatchiks had been of Miliband and Corbyn, was one thing. His lack of a stable majority on the party's National Executive Committee – where the unions, Corbynite activists and unreliable representatives of the soft left held sway – was another. Demoralised though they were, the fall of Corbyn had left his disciples with an inheritance of unprecedented riches after decades of political penury. With a lacklustre candidate they had won 32 per cent of the leadership vote. They still had jobs in Labour HQ and could, if they so wished, wage a war of attrition against Starmer on the NEC. For now McSweeney could not afford to pursue the cleansing confrontation he so longed for – not least because Covid had frozen the Labour Party in March 2020. His leader did not yet understand what was necessary either. Starmer had won a mandate for unity and expected the left to honour it, just as he intended to. As one member of his inner circle explains: 'Keir's view of unity was: I'm the leader and you back me. When Keir was in the shadow cabinet, we never briefed against Corbyn, Keir didn't agitate. I think Keir assumed people would get behind him.' And so to

others on the Corbynite left he extended a hand of friendship, unaware
that it would soon clench into a fist.

Len McCluskey, general secretary of Unite, came first. On the eve
of the leadership result he and Starmer spoke for ninety minutes, a
much longer audience than even Tony Blair would receive the following day. 'I've told my team that I have a good relationship with you,'
Starmer told McCluskey. 'I want unity, Len, more than anything.' It
was sincerely meant, but really he had little choice. To declare war on
Labour's most generous donor – and the spiritual leader of the organised hard left – would plunge an already disorganised and divided party
into bankruptcy, or worse. Yet McCluskey was in a conciliatory mood.
The man the tabloids derided as Red Len knew Corbyn had ultimately
been the victim of his own inadequacies as leader, rather than the
malign establishment conspiracies of which he often warned. In 2015
his private preference had been for Andy Burnham to lead from the
soft left. In Starmer he saw a man with whom Unite might do business.

'Well, look, Keir,' McCluskey said. 'You're in a fortunate position,
because you will get unity.'

McCluskey approached their conversation as he had countless negotiations with shipowners and bosses on the Liverpool docks. He sought
assurances that the left would not be made redundant, and asked who
Starmer might appoint as shadow chancellor. That would be the ultimate test of every tribute the leader had paid to the radicalism of his
predecessor.

'No, Len, of course I'm not saying. I'll need to speak to the person
first,' Starmer replied.

McCluskey persisted. 'You do know,' he said, in equal parts suggest-
ive and threatening. 'This will define to a great extent the direction
you're interested in taking the party.'

'I'm not going to tell you.'

McCluskey did not know what Starmer knew: that McCluskey would
be perfectly satisfied with the new shadow chancellor. Nor did Starmer
know that McCluskey suspected he might appoint Rachel Reeves,
the Leeds West MP who had for five years conscientiously objected
to serving in any front-bench role under Corbyn's leadership. The left
loathed Reeves with a special and furious intensity. As Ed Miliband's
shadow work and pensions secretary she had said that Labour was not
the party of benefit claimants. If Corbynism had meant anything it

was to have rid the Labour Party of precisely that attitude. In early
2020, Starmer still insisted that it had. As if inviting his own betrayal,
McCluskey had assumed – without evidence – that the new leader
would nonetheless appoint the folk villain of the Labour membership
to rewrite John McDonnell's economic policy in Thatcherite language.
Starmer did not do so. Yet, just as McCluskey feared, in the days before
his victory Starmer was enthused and beguiled by Reeves, whom he
first met at a private breakfast two weeks before the announcement of
the result.

'I want her in the shadow cabinet, and I want her in a senior role,'
Starmer told his team upon his return. 'She's great.'

Trevor Chinn, the donor whose generosity was funding the leadership campaign just as it had sustained Labour Together before it,
agreed. A few weeks earlier he had urged Starmer and McSweeney
to appoint Reeves, a former Bank of England economist who had
whiled away the Corbyn years as chairwoman of Parliament's business select committee, as shadow chancellor. Wes Streeting, another
willing exile from shadow ministerial office under Corbyn, told
McSweeney: 'You've got to have Rachel as shadow chancellor. Absolutely
the most important appointment you're going to make is the shadow
chancellor.' From the left came the same argument in reverse – but
expressed just as sharply. Within Starmer's campaign headquarters,
Simon Fletcher made clear his opposition to her appointment. Owen
Jones, the *Guardian* columnist, told his old friend Chris Ward much
the same. Despite Starmer's enthusiasm, their warnings were heeded;
the left's veto duly exercised. As an early member of Labour Together,
Reeves had influential friends at the very apex of the new regime. Yet
it was weaker than its margin of victory implied. For McSweeney, the
realpolitik of managing a divided party within whose finely balanced
bureaucracy the left still wielded considerable influence made her promotion impossible. Nor did Starmer himself wish to breach the terms
of his contract with the Corbynites. To appoint Reeves would provoke,
not unify. Her endorsement of Jess Phillips's doomed candidacy did
not aid her cause either. 'The thing we were most conscious of,' recalls
a senior aide involved in those torturous discussions, 'was not over-
promoting people from the right of the party who had been outside
of the campaign.'

That left those who *had* been aboard the bandwagon. Ed Miliband, who envied the unselfconscious clarity of Corbyn's critique of capit-alism, was briefly considered. He let it be known to Starmer: 'If you want me to be your shadow chancellor, I'll be your shadow chancellor.' His offer was not accepted, nor was it ever taken especially seriously. Having witnessed at first hand the death throes of the New Labour ascendancy of which Miliband – for all of his born-again radicalism – was indelibly part, Starmer had no desire to resurrect a generation that had blown its chance at leadership. He did not even bother calling once and future cabinet ministers and leadership contenders like Yvette Cooper. As the aide explained: 'We didn't want to be seen as simply returning to continuity Miliband, putting the shadow cabinet of 2015 back together. We didn't want to be seen as continuity Corbyn either. We wanted to have fresh people . . . and that's why we end up with people who aren't as well known.'

Few could rival Anneliese Dodds for obscurity. Like Reeves, the softly spoken Scot was a trained economist. Unlike Reeves – or, indeed, Miliband and Cooper – she was little known even within Westmin-ster, had been elected to the Commons in 2017, and served loyally as a shadow Treasury minister under Corbyn. Starmer had not been close to her. Theirs would not be a partnership forged by the personal and political intimacy, nor the unbreakable feeling of shared destiny, of Blair and Brown, Miliband and Balls, Corbyn and McDonnell, and Cameron and Osborne. Starmer and Dodds had had their first serious conversation only weeks before her appointment, as he sat exhausted in the passenger seat of her car. As Dodds drove him from her Oxford constituency to the TSSA union's hustings in Loughborough, they exchanged their thoughts on the future as he ate a packed lunch. To Starmer she seemed intellectually gifted, diligent, unburdened by fac-tional baggage: all qualities he was proud of possessing himself. Dodds did not rush to speak when a moment or two of thought might yield a considered answer.

For Starmer, that was enough. Once the deal was done he called McCluskey. 'Well there you go, Len,' he said. 'What do you think of that?'

'Oh, very good, Keir,' the old Liverpudlian purred. Starmer had passed this first test. Friends of Reeves were unimpressed if unsur-prised that he should play down to their lowest expectations. 'I did not think that appointing someone from John McDonnell's shadow

Treasury team to be shadow chancellor was credible,' reflects one of her closest allies in Parliament now.

Things indeed seemed very good for the left. In the leanest years of the Socialist Campaign Group, the Bennite caucus mocked and marginalised by New Labour, John McDonnell dreamt that just one of its members might be appointed as a shadow minister. Now they were everywhere, even if the leading clerics of Corbynism were abruptly defrocked. McDonnell retired hurt. Ian Lavery, the rumbustious former president of the National Union of Mineworkers who bellowed the case for Corbynism as party chairman, was sacked, as was Jon Trickett, the gentle giant who had watched in vain as the working-class voters of his native Yorkshire abandoned the left. With self-deprecating mischief Trickett had told Starmer that he would be the first Labour leader since John Smith who had not retained his services: 'I worked for Blair, I worked for Brown, I worked for Ed.' His new leader was content to depart from tradition, and signed off impassively: 'Keep in touch.' A cursory look at the rest of the front bench made it sound sincere. Rebecca Long-Bailey was appointed shadow education secretary. Andy McDonald, a mainstay of Corbyn's shadow cabinets, kept his seat at the top table and with it responsibility for party policy on employment rights. Dan Carden, McCluskey's former bag-carrier, became a shadow Treasury minister. Lloyd Russell-Moyle, so zealous a Corbynite that he had once branded opponents of the former leader 'cunts', would sit on the front bench too. In the new leader's office itself, Simon Fletcher remained in place as a campaign adviser.

The other great offices of state went not to the prodigal sons and daughters of Blairism and Brownism but to 'clean skins', whose primary qualification was the novelty of their presence. Nick Thomas-Symonds, a barrister and historian who was born in the same Welsh Valley as Roy Jenkins and had been Starmer's first true friend in the Commons, was made shadow home secretary; Lisa Nandy was to be shadow foreign secretary. They were joined by stalwarts of the Labour mainstream who had persevered in shadow office under Corbyn's leadership – like John Healey, the Brownite warhorse who became Starmer's shadow defence secretary. Telegenic right-wingers who had waited patiently for the day the left ceded control of the Parliamentary Labour Party had to content themselves with junior posts of little significance. Pat McFadden and Wes Streeting, both reduced

to supporting roles in Dodds's Treasury team, were told they were
the Blairite 'ballast' to counterbalance a soft-left chancellor and Dan
Carden. These were the politicians who had always looked askance at
Starmer's tolerance for Corbyn. To moderate eyes these first appointments confirmed everything that had led them to vote against him.
'I looked at the shadow cabinet,' said one disappointed recruit, 'and I
thought: this is just not serious.'

*

But unity was all that Starmer knew. Forced to live alongside the left,
it was all he *could* know. His next most significant appointment to the
shadow cabinet had been made for him, by the same members who
had picked him to lead the Labour Party. At his right side as deputy
would be Angela Rayner. If Sir Keir Rodney Starmer QC had an
opposite, it was the freewheeling single mother who had left school
pregnant aged sixteen. Both had arrived in Parliament in 2015, dutifully
nominating Andy Burnham for the leadership. Both had a hinterland
beyond party politics: Rayner as a union representative for her fellow
carers, Starmer as a barrister. Both ascended to Corbyn's shadow
cabinet almost by accident. Rayner was drafted in as shadow education secretary only once everybody else had resigned. But she revelled
in the limelight; Starmer hated it. In public the former trade union
official spoke of her politics and troubled youth with the candour and
flair that even in private Starmer struggled to summon. From the force
of her personality and arguments the newspapers inferred her politics
were Corbynite. The Corbynites did not trust her. She eulogised Blair,
whose Sure Start nurseries had given her children the start to life she
had been denied by circumstance. In reality she was closer to Barbara
Castle than Tony Benn: her leftism was pragmatic and plain-speaking.
It did not matter to the members, who loved her. Rayner was the very
reason the Labour Party existed. When she declared her candidacy
for deputy there was no question that she would win.

In another universe she might have become leader. As Corbynism
disintegrated, some in McSweeney's orbit wondered whether Rayner
might be the candidate to unite the idealists and instrumentalists of
the grass roots, as Starmer eventually did, but unlock the ideologues
of the hard left too. As a former shop steward, she was the darling of

the unions. Labour Together's tame intellectual, Jonathan Rutherford, believed she might reproduce the insurgent energy of Corbyn's leadership campaigns. One day in 2019 Rayner was invited to Rutherford's Finsbury Park home with McSweeney, to discuss her options. According to two people present, there ensued what one aide called a 'coded' conversation about the leadership, as she refused to make the implicit explicit. From his corner table in Brown's, the Mayfair hotel that served as his court, Trevor Chinn also told Rayner to think big. There were no limits to the ambition of her admirers. She, however, was happy to settle for less. They never persuaded her to stand for leader. Protective of her private life, and her three boys, she told McSweeney that she was not ready. Nor did she wish to betray Long-Bailey, her fellow Mancunian and flatmate, when it became clear that she would accede to John McDonnell's fatherly entreaties to run. For a few weeks they contested the election on a joint ticket, but their alliance fell apart. Rayner had been assured by McDonnell that she would not be outflanked on the left. Within days, he had endorsed Richard Burgon, whose campaign pledge to set up a university named after Tony Benn said all that needed to be said about his politics. It would not matter. Rayner won easily, and arrived as unenamoured with the hard core of the hard left as Starmer. Her chief of staff, Nick Parrott, held furtive discussions with Starmer's team on the margins of each leadership debate, and later in the offices of Unison, the trade union that had endorsed them both. Rayner too wanted unity across the Labour Party, for it had served her well. She drank with MPs that the leader did not know in bars he did not visit: the personal was political. Unlike Starmer, she did not need McSweeney to guide her like a sherpa over the treacherous terrain of internal Labour politics: it was her life. It was, as Rayner herself would later admit, an arranged marriage for an odd couple.

Both bride and groom were determined to make it work. Over breakfast with Trevor Chinn, Rayner had confided that she wished to be made party chairwoman alongside her role as deputy: to hit the road and run Labour's election campaigns, and take its message to the country as Starmer applied lawyerly scrutiny to the Tories in Westminster. It would also give her the meaningful influence she craved. Parrott had urged her not to accept any position that left her as 'the Labour Party equivalent of the Queen' – exalted and all-powerful in theory, but in practice reduced to cutting ribbons and smiling politely at official functions. Once confirmed in post, Starmer obliged – just as Chinn told her he would. 'You've got it,' he had said. 'That's what they want you to do.' At first they spoke to the members as one, thanking them for 'putting your trust in *us* to lead the Labour Party'. Tom Watson, the last deputy, had kept an office beside the parliamentary press gallery – the ideal location for a den of sedition. Rayner installed herself in the side room beside Starmer's office, once occupied by the Corbynite brains trust of Seumas Milne and Andrew Fisher, repainting its dirty walls as the Labour NEC held long meetings via Zoom. She believed the leadership of the Labour Party would be a joint enterprise.

★

Rayner was right, but not in the way she imagined. Long before the official shadow cabinet had been assembled, another had been convened in a Georgian terrace in Cleaver Square, in Lambeth. Labour's strategy was really written by the kitchen cabinet of Morgan McSweeney, which met in secret on Sunday evenings at the Kennington home of Roger Liddle, a Labour peer and old friend of Peter Mandelson from their days as councillors under Ted Knight. Save for Liddle's doomed foray into the breakaway Social Democratic Party, the two men had grown up together. Together they had written pamphlets that had refined and codified Blair's political philosophy. Now they would help McSweeney refine his.

Around Liddle's table sat New Labour's past and future. Alongside McSweeney was Wes Streeting, the smooth talker all present hoped would one day lead the party, and his partner Joe Dancey, who in his twenties had advised Mandelson, Blair's friend and favourite. They were invariably joined by three men called Matt: Matthew Doyle, who had worked for Blair as spokesman in and out of Downing Street; Matt Pound, who led the guerilla resistance to Corbynism at Labour First; and Matthew Faulding, a baby-faced organiser who had cut his political teeth at Progress, the struggling Blairite fan club. Its director, the tattooed Welshman Nathan Yeowell, was also at McSweeney's side – as he had been in ill-tempered Labour meetings in Lambeth, and in the offices of the Local Government Association. James Asser, a stalwart of the right-wing minority on the NEC who had once been upbraided by Karie Murphy for refusing to give Corbyn a standing ovation at Labour conference, completed the set.

Once these ageing princelings of New Labour had ruled their party. Under Corbyn they had been exiled, but as Starmer had edged closer to the leader's office they dared to dream again. The Irishman warned them it would not be easy. Among friends he could speak frankly, and set out his vision for the party he would soon run with striking clarity. Over dinner on 8 March, just under a month before he became chief of staff to the leader of the Labour Party, McSweeney spoke of its members contemptuously. Their politics were performative. Half of them wanted a leader who thought like them, looked like them. Winning elections was desirable, but not essential. The result? First Miliband, then Corbyn. The red wall of Labour seats that wound its way through the north and Midlands had been 'crumbling and behaving differently for many years', McSweeney said. Labour had no hope in towns like Darlington, Bolton and Bury. Worse still, there was 'no path to victory' that did not run through Scotland – where their party had been reduced to a single MP and was led by Richard Leonard, a tubthumping Yorkshireman whose appearance and politics were stuck somewhere in the early 1970s. McSweeney proposed a course of shock therapy. Absurd, if not offensive though his words may have sounded to a room full of liberal Londoners and two peers of the realm, he asked: 'Are we always going to be for the judges? Are we always going to be for the BBC? Why should Gary Lineker be paid £2 million a year?' Labour's instincts had become conservative, elitist, too willing to defend failure provided those failing were its friends: lawyers, activists, columnists. For all its sentimental claims of iconoclasm and people power, it was really a 'party of the status quo', an echo chamber for the received wisdom of metropolitan England that its traditional voters despised. None embodied it better than Lisa Nandy, whose thinking McSweeney described with a devastating tricolon: 'No gender, no borders, no Queen.' Boris Johnson understood as much. He had plundered Labour's working-class votes.

Why, McSweeney asked, had Labour sat by and watched its voters flee as if driven by some unstoppable force of nature? Decline was not inevitable, no matter what the commentators who spoke so confidently of a permanent realignment in British politics were writing at the time. His solution sounded familiar. As his friends enjoyed Liddle's vintage wines and roast lamb, he declared – like Blair had before him – that Starmer's Labour must become 'the political arm of the British people' once again. It would have to look and sound like them too. Evocative though his words may have been, their author had ceased to believe them. Blair had told friends that what energy and dynamism now existed in politics was channelled through the right. 'The people who are *really* getting things done in the world,' he told an intimate, 'are Trump and Bibi [Netanyahu].' McSweeney had been a Blairite once, but no longer. He disagreed, but to prove Blair wrong, he knew he would have to reinvent the Labour Party.

There could be no compromises: not with the Corbynites, nor with the party's mushy middle. Under the hard left, McSweeney said, Labour had become 'an antisemitic, racist party'. The new leader would have to defeat the old order: sack Jennie Formby and 'all senior directors' who had worked for Corbyn, most importantly Murphy and Seumas Milne. 'Get them out,' McSweeney explained, 'and maybe the others will follow.' Maybe. He admitted they would never be eliminated entirely. A minority would linger, 'always there in the swamp . . . impossible to drain'. He argued that the so-called soft left held the party back, indulged its moralistic instincts and dismissed entreaties to an electorate concerned by immigration as 'chasing white racist voters'. They had stood by while the Corbynites ascended to positions of power and influence. Only by demoralising and discrediting the hard left could the soft left be shaken into sense. 'It's okay as long as they're not in control,' McSweeney said. 'The key is the soft left not falling in behind them.' Some in the room wondered whether he was talking about Starmer. They doubted that this north London lawyer could ever reconcile himself to the 'progressive platform' McSweeney described with all the furious certainty of a televangelist urging sinners to repent. But he believed. Starmer, by then only days from victory, was 'smart, capable, ambitious, non-ideological and non-factional'. He was not a 'nerd' like Ed Miliband, nor 'crazy', like Corbyn. His politics were made for the moment. McSweeney described them with an almost damning simplicity: 'Let's all be friends.'

Starmer would be forced to move quickly. McSweeney suspected he had only 'six months' to build a party that could credibly fight elections. He was hamstrung by circumstance. The shadow cabinet would need to reflect the unity platform Labour Together had built. Nor could elected politicians achieve *anything* without a stable majority on the NEC, whose elections would be held that November. Those present, led by Yeowell, would have to cobble together an uncontroversial band of candidates the new leader could rely on – camouflaged by their 'embrace' of the soft left. At the same time, Starmer would need something to say to the country. McSweeney believed his CV – specifically his five years as director of public prosecutions – made him a natural spokesman for the politics he wished to sell to the country, just as his allergy to factionalism had made him the perfect candidate for the idealists. 'What we want,' McSweeney told the table, 'is for Keir to go out straight away on crime, policing and social care. Corbyn sided with terrorists, whereas Keir locked them up.' Despite what he had told members as a leadership candidate, he would have to stop dangling 'bribes' before the voters – like the abolition of university tuition fees. 'Cultural and economic protection' would instead become his lodestar. Every chance to show that Labour had changed would be seized. The final report of the Equalities and Human Rights Commission into the party's handling of antisemitism was to be Starmer's 'Clause IV moment' – as decisive a rejection of its past as Blair's deletion of its commitment to nationalising the commanding heights of British industry had been in 1994. Any parliamentary vote on Johnson's Brexit deal would be another such 'opportunity'. Starmer, once the patron saint of Remainers, could demonstrate without equivocation that he stood on the side of the Brexiteers who had abandoned Labour in 2019.

★

'Just know,' Charlie Falconer said, hours after the election of Keir Starmer as Labour leader, as he stood at the door of the room that had just been vacated by Jeremy Corbyn, 'this is the best it's going to get. It's all downhill from here.' It was an old joke from an old cynic. But like all old jokes, it alluded to a truth that none present could bear to confront.

Starmer's first hours and days followed beat for beat the script McSweeney had written: the vow to root out racism, the summary execution of the general secretary, the rainbow coalition as shadow cabinet (including Falconer as its attorney general). Before long the two men found themselves confronted with unknown unknowns that only sharpened McSweeney's conviction that the Corbynites could not be tolerated. Eight days into his tenure, on 12 April, Sky News was leaked an 860-page report – written for submission to the EHRC by an undisclosed author at Labour HQ in the death throes of Corbyn's leadership – which described in unflinching detail the dysfunctionality of the party machine, and the toxicity of its factional culture. McSweeney had helped engineer the EHRC's investigation in the hope that it would expose the administrative incompetence and moral bankruptcy he had diagnosed on the left. The contents of the leaked report showed something else. Upon Corbyn's election as leader he had found himself trapped by Labour officials who loathed all he stood for. Tens of thousands of private messages between Corbynsceptic staff that were accidentally saved on the party's servers were reproduced as a morality play: the fifth column versus the democratically elected socialists. Seumas Milne was 'Dracula'; Karie Murphy 'Medusa', a 'crazy woman', and 'a bitch-faced cow'; Diane Abbott 'repulsive', her whereabouts leaked to hostile journalists. In one conversation a party staffer confessed their hopes that one young left-winger would 'die in a fire'. In others, Labour's leading officials conspired to divert resources to safe seats held by Corbyn's opponents, Rachel Reeves among them. Readers were invited to conclude that the old leadership stood no chance of doing what needed to be done to expel racists from the membership with such irreconcilable and obstructive staff.

McSweeney watched as these selective quotations were reproduced on the websites he had fought to destroy: the *Canary*, the *Skwawkbox*. Here, he thought, was the left's baseless stab-in-the-back myth written to rescue Corbyn from the condescension of posterity, and convince his followers that he had not committed the sins of which he was now accused. It posed an immediate threat to Starmer. How could he unify the Labour Party if left-wing members now had reason to believe their new comrades had tried to kill them in their sleep? Nor did it help that, however defamatory or partial its presentation, the central contention of the report was essentially true. Many of those who had unwillingly worked in Labour HQ for Corbyn *had* disliked, even hated, his politics. Some had even left Labour altogether. They were proud to have been vindicated by Boris Johnson's landslide. Paradoxically, McSweeney believed that nothing made the Corbynites happier. They *wanted* to be betrayed. A. J. P. Taylor, the great historian of interwar England, had once written that the fabricated Zinoviev Letter that alleged a Labour government would lay the groundwork for Communist revolution on the eve of the 1924 general election – which Ramsay MacDonald duly lost – had convinced generation after generation on the British left that conspiracy was to blame for its electoral failures. McSweeney thought the same of the leaked report. It would be easier for the left to blame their factional enemies and the media for defeat than themselves. Having been humbled by Starmer, their leading lights could once again engage in a display of political machismo – having ceded control for barely more than a week, McSweeney sensed the hard left was determined to take it back. They could demand unity on their terms, not Starmer's, now their internal opponents had been exposed: the new leader would have no choice but to change course, abandon the Blairites, and build a project as reliant on the unions as Corbyn's had been. Right on cue, Len McCluskey condemned the 'rancid and very cruel behaviour' documented in the report, which he declared to be credible and true.

McSweeney resolved to resist, even though the social media networks that sustained the left were ablaze with criticism. He took a call from a distraught staffer named in the report. Panicking, they asked whether their career was over. 'No one's getting sacked,' he said. Yet Starmer was forced to take a different approach to that which the Irishman believed to be right. The left-wing activists he had courted were furious. On this evidence their party was a cesspit of racism, bullying and misogyny. They demanded action. Were Starmer's promises of unity a fig leaf, or a philosophy? For now it was the latter. Within twenty-four hours of the leak he had launched a 'swift' and independent inquiry. Even that was complicated by factionalism. If the investigation was to have legitimacy and funding, it would require the imprimatur of the NEC – whose hard-left officers were technically the legal custodians of the party. The leader's choice of chair, his fellow QC Martin Forde – one of Britain's most senior black barristers – was uncontroversial enough. Several of those recruited to assist his inquiries, however, did not pass the factional test to which Starmer had unthinkingly subjected himself. Alf Dubs, the Jewish peer who had escaped Czechoslovakia on the *Kindertransport*, was vetoed by a vote of the

NEC – including the leader – after the left decreed his endorsement of Starmer's campaign to succeed Corbyn undermined his impartiality. Even then the left briefed its websites that others on Forde's panel were unsuitable on the same grounds. They dismissed the inquiry they had asked for as a 'stitch-up'.

McSweeney thought it all absurd. The left were as recalcitrant and irredeemable as he had imagined. Labour's leader was so besieged by his detractors that he could not exercise his authority. He said as much when Liddle's supper club next met – by then virtually, given the coronavirus lockdown – on 4 May. McSweeney had long suspected that Labour's internal organisation was rickety at best. Now he knew it was 'rotten to the core', its processes 'corrupt', its most important committees still 'in hard left control'. The leaked report had 'solidified the left', cauterising in an instant the gaping wounds that had been inflicted by its divisions over Europe. Launching the counterinsurgency he wished to lead would have been difficult in ordinary times. The pandemic ensured it was impossible. McSweeney found that Corbynites who might have otherwise left of their own accord preferred instead to remain on the party payroll and wait for the crisis to abate. Murphy and Milne in particular would not be easily dislodged. Deftly, they had appointed themselves executive directors of the party, with contracts that did not expire upon Corbyn's departure – as was usually the case. They had named their price, and the new regime could not bring itself to pay it: advance sight of the EHRC report and consultation on Labour's response.

Having promised that another future was possible, Starmer was haunted by ghosts of Labour past. McCluskey, too, had dispensed with the niceties that had sweetened their first conversations. He demanded concessions and expected control. He even presumed to tell the lawyer who now led the Labour Party whether to take a case to court. Starmer had committed to settle a defamation case brought by seven former officials whose testimonies formed the basis for an explosive *Panorama* documentary on antisemitism the previous summer. When Corbyn's spokesman described them as 'disaffected former staff' with 'personal and political axes to grind', they sued. Starmer believed they deserved an apology, and compensation. McCluskey believed they should be pursued to the steps of the High Court. To settle with the whistle-blowers would be to concede that Labour under Corbyn had indeed been institutionally antisemitic. 'My lawyers say we can win it,' he told McSweeney, who preferred to take his legal advice from Falconer, a former justice secretary, and Starmer, the former DPP. When McSweeney's phone rang it was invariably McCluskey or Howard Beckett, Unite's obstreperous lawyer, making demands and giving orders. Settle the *Panorama* case. Agree a severance deal with Seumas. Put Karie in the House of Lords, just as Corbyn promised. To McSweeney it was as if McCluskey was not acting as the general secretary of Unite, but the personal shop steward of his closest friends. Alone they were powerless over Starmer. They could no longer shape his response to the EHRC, nor ensure he fought the whistleblowers in court – both of which would in due course dent their reputations and their livelihoods. But they still had Len, and Len still had power, and money, both of which he flaunted. Starmer was by turns deferential, exasperated and disgusted. Although he had been a trade union lawyer in his youth, he struggled to stomach a politics so raw. When McCluskey suggested that Murphy might receive her peerage as a quid pro quo for resigning from Labour HQ, Starmer told his staff: 'Absolutely no one's getting peerages. You can't negotiate that. I'm not having that.'

It was just as well that that month's local elections had been postponed, for Starmer's party was now in an 'absolutely dreadful state'. McSweeney told his friends: 'Not just the worst election defeat, but in absolutely every respect. The brand is battered in every sort of seat.' At his lowest moments, standing alone in his garden as Beckett ranted down the telephone, McSweeney wondered whether the leadership might have been a pyrrhic victory. He wondered whether Starmer was the wrong man in the wrong job at the wrong time. On one walk across Clapham Common with his Lambeth mentor Steve Reed, by then shadow housing secretary, he confided his frustrations. The Corbynites had not only broken the party: they had 'crashed it, set it on fire, and then gone back and shit over the ashes'.

'Literally everything is broken,' he said.

If negotiating with Unite was a precondition for party unity, then it was the unity of the hostage and his captor – and, if it united to fight the NEC elections on a joint slate, the left might hold them prisoner forever, the longed-for reunion with the voters deferred indefinitely. But even the Irishman conceded that winning *anything* was already a forlorn hope. Once impregnable citadels of Labourism, like Mansfield – the

Nottinghamshire mining town now held by the Tories – were 'all but beyond reach'. His plan to take Starmer to Downing Street within a single parliamentary term would require Labour to make 'the largest leap any party has ever had to make to win' at a moment when it was barely capable of standing unassisted.

5

'I just need this'

McSweeney said Labour must pass four tests for power. First 'fix the culture of the party' and build 'the moral foundations for credibility', then 'reverse the decline of working-class voters' in England and 'rob the SNP of their majority' in Scotland. When the official shadow cabinet had met for the first time via Zoom the previous month, it had been expressed even more pithily by the YouGov pollster Marcus Roberts, a towering Taylor Swift fan who was McSweeney's closest friend in politics. He told the call: 'We have to win everywhere. We have to win everyone. We have to be ahead on the economy and on immigration and on defence. And if we do that in one term, we will win.' Another attendee recalled: 'There was no guarantee it could be done in two terms. You'd have to have been nuts to believe the members wouldn't have swung back to someone who was more extreme.'

What else was nuts, according to McSweeney, was attempting to adopt those positions while allowing the left to have any control over the party machinery. To his sceptical dining partners he posed a difficult question: 'How *do* we show demonstrable change?' Victory should have allowed Starmer to 'set a very clear direction', and break with the past, but he was hidebound by that dread word: *unity*. What progress he *had* made seemed almost immaterial. It was true that Starmer's poised response to the Covid crisis and policy of 'constructive opposition' in Parliament impressed the opinion pollsters. Media interest was minimal, but what little there was he exploited ruthlessly: after Boris Johnson told the nation of his plans to loosen lockdown restrictions, Ben Nunn invoked an obscure clause in the BBC Charter last exploited by Hugh Gaitskell at the height of the Suez crisis, and secured a well-received right of reply.

When the crisis subsided, however, mere competence would not be enough.

★

The Irishman worked like a navvy to smooth Starmer's hard path. The job was ugly and attritional. He did not detain Starmer with every detail of his days, for Starmer did not ask. 'Keir is only interested in the outcome,' says one person present throughout those difficult days in early 2020. 'It's important never to forget that.' Starmer's object was to become prime minister. McSweeney's method was to change the Labour Party, and break the left.

He could not do so alone. Jennie Formby's defenestration had left a vacancy in the eighth-floor office of Labour's general secretary. Administratively and legally, it was a role second only in import- ance to the leader himself: they controlled the money, the rulebook, conference and campaigns. Whoever succeeded Formby would also administer the party's response to the EHRC report, whenever it came. McSweeney – and Starmer – would have to trust them implicitly. Ed Miliband, whose favoured general secretary was humiliatingly rejected by the NEC in 2011, had learned that lesson to his cost. So the chief bur- eaucrat of Starmer's Labour Party could not be aligned too closely to the Corbynite government in exile, nor Rayner.

That made Anneliese Midgley, the political director of Unite, a curious choice. Like Simon Fletcher, the gregarious Liverpudlian had worked for Ken Livingstone and Jeremy Corbyn. She was none- theless admired across the PLP's factional divide, having engineered their selections and spent the union's money on their campaigns. For a leader nominally committed to unity she would be an uncontrover- sial pick. On 4 May, the *New Statesman* anointed her as 'the candidate Labour MPs want to succeed Jennie Formby'. After one of his regu- lar phone calls with Starmer, McCluskey, her boss, was left with the unmistakable impression that the most powerful Labour MP of all wanted her too. 'I wouldn't stand in Anneliese's way,' McCluskey said, with studied magnanimity. One Unite official out, one Unite official in. Fair exchange was no robbery.

McSweeney did not do *fair*. That was another weasel word from the soft-left vernacular of niceness, the politics he had ascribed to Starmer:

'Let's all be friends.' His general secretary would not be in office to make friends, but know their enemy. McSweeney wanted David Evans, a big man of small indulgences: Chester Football Club, bottles of 7up Zero Sugar, the bottle of Tabasco he carried everywhere he went. He had joined Labour to stand up for the little guy, having watched as his disabled brother was abused on the streets as a teenager, but his gentle demeanour belied the coarseness of his politics – which brooked no compromise with the activist left. In the Blair years he had worked at the right hand of Margaret McDonagh, the platonic ideal of a New Labour general secretary, and proposed a total overhaul of local party branches. By the dog days of the 2000s his consultancy, The Campaign Company, was retained to advise the beleaguered Labour council in Barking and Dagenham. For that job, Evans had hired a young organiser called Morgan McSweeney.

Now his protégé wished to return the favour. When he met Steve Reed on Clapham Common both had agreed that Evans was the man for the hard road ahead. Shortly before the 26 May meeting at which the NEC would cast their votes, McSweeney told Starmer of his choice. As Miliband had discovered, the leader's imprimatur was no guarantee of a foregone conclusion. Midgley would be bought off and appointed to a senior role in the leader's office, but the left abhorred a vacuum. Byron Taylor, a lifelong trade unionist who had earned his place in socialist history when he urged Jeremy Corbyn to stand for the leadership in 2015, emerged in Midgley's place.

Here was the left's opportunity to arrest the rightward march of Starmerism before it had even begun. The leader of Unite stood furious at the head of their barricade. When he learned of Midgley's withdrawal he reached again for the telephone. Bosses did not rat on deals they had agreed with Len McCluskey.

'Keir,' he said. 'That's outrageous, changing like this. I've already told Anneliese, you know.'

'We'd like very much to make her an executive director,' Starmer said, dividing and ruling the left against itself. McCluskey, *primus inter pares* among the union leaders whose loyal servants could swing any vote on the NEC, vowed to beat him.

On the eve of the decision Byron Taylor took a call from Marcus Roberts, McSweeney's steadfast friend. Roberts knew all too well what happened when a Labour leader found himself at odds with his general secretary. Together he and Taylor had organised to install Iain McNicol over Ed Miliband's head. 'Byron,' he said, 'we both know when it does work, and we both know when it doesn't. I'm here to tell you that this is one of those times when it does work. Dave is going to win, it's not going to be you. Would you like to be part of—'

Taylor was undeterred. He believed he could go all the way.

Roberts, whose polling had informed every decision McSweeney had taken to destabilise and destroy the Corbynites at Labour Together, reminded his old friend that he knew how to count votes.

Taylor still believed he could do it.

By then he could not, for Starmer had intervened. Only at moments of maximum danger did McSweeney demand the leader dirty his own hands, to borrow and beg for the individual votes of NEC members he did not know. This was one such moment, an inflection point in what may have transpired to be the short history of his leadership. One by one he canvassed the committee, seeking a coalition of the willing. Alice Perry, the diehard moderate from Islington Council, was cycling along the promenade in Southend when – for the first time – she received a call from Starmer.

'Alice. I need you to vote for David Evans.'

But why? Starmer spoke as if Labour politics was his second language. 'You know, I just need someone I can run up and down the pitch with. I need someone I can rely on. I just need this.'

Football, with its brute meritocracy of technical skill and physical fitness, was a game he understood. Politics was not, not yet. Perry cycled on, faintly bemused. She needed no convincing. As an old friend of McSweeney she would be with the leadership whatever.

'I'm going to vote for him, don't worry,' she said. 'Whatever you need.'

That was Keir Starmer's vision of unity. He had been democratically elected leader of the Labour Party. He would work hard and ask, politely, for colleagues to work with him. They would give him whatever he needed, for they were all on the same side. *Let's all be friends.* To that the left said: let's not. Evans was a Blair man. By definition his candidacy could not be a friendly gesture. Matt Wrack, the leader of the Fire Brigades Union, denounced him as an 'extremely divisive' and 'factional figure'. Ian Hodson, of the Bakers' Union, accurately described him as 'Margaret McDonagh's right-hand man', and said:

'Our movement will never vote for one of the key figures involved in our isolation under New Labour.' The leaked report and its 'explosive revelations' made an unanswerable case for 'a unifying figure, who can bring our party together and command confidence across our broad church'.

McSweeney was a dissenter, uninterested in ecumenism. He needed this. Like the left, he understood the stakes were existential. Without Evans, whom he trusted implicitly, nothing could be done as he saw fit. Starmer would play supplicant to the very people McSweeney and his network had done everything to marginalise, asking permission to lead. Together they stared impotence in the face and turned to Angela Rayner to make another future possible. She was a native of the world Starmer did not know: of union organisers and bartered votes. She knew what he did not know, and privately delighted in his ignorance. It suited her to be the bridge between the leader's office, high above the Thames at Westminster, and the movement at the grass roots. She hoped to be the one to tell Starmer what he did not wish to hear about the inconvenient truths of Labour politics. To lead without her was to lose. And as the NEC prepared to cast its votes on David Evans and Byron Taylor, Starmer knew that to be true.

'I need this,' he told Rayner. After a little reflection, she obliged. The angry men who hoped to defeat the leader were not really her friends either.

In turn she told her supporters on the NEC: 'I need you to back me on this.'

Byron Taylor won sixteen votes. David Evans won twenty. At last they had what they needed.

★

Many months passed before Starmer knew how it felt to exercise control over the Labour Party. In Westminster, however, the rituals of leadership came naturally.

Under Jeremy Corbyn meetings of the shadow cabinet and NEC had been long and difficult. These were not the meetings Starmer liked to chair. MPs who had mastered the art of the monologue were now told to speak for two minutes at most. As director of public prosecutions Starmer's modus operandi had been efficiency. Professionalism was a political end in itself. The discursive, rambling conversations that Corbyn was happy to initiate *anywhere* – even on the opposition front bench – about *anything* but the affairs of state – his allotment, jam-making, the unreliable form of Arsenal Football Club – enraged his successor. Punctuality assumed extreme importance, particularly when the relaxation of lockdown restrictions allowed the shadow cabinet to meet in person. When Emily Thornberry arrived late for one meeting, Starmer performatively tapped his watch. He was an impatient man of exacting standards. The warmth his friends knew in private dissipated when his colleagues did not meet them. Visibly struggling with a bad cold, the shadow mental health minister Rosena Allin-Khan staggered through the door with a cup of Lemsip some thirty seconds late. 'This meeting starts at 9.30 a.m.,' Starmer said. 'I don't want you coming in two minutes later, clutching your coffee.'

Order was everything. He sought refuge in routine. Colleagues who spoke for longer than he would like to listen were told to 'move through the gears'. Every day his private secretary would deliver the same lunch to his desk: a tuna sandwich, salt and vinegar crisps, and a bottle of water. Convention, no matter how dreary it seemed to others, offered Starmer his own kind of liberation after the chaos of Corbynism and the insecurity of his childhood: the domineering father, chronically ill mother and ramshackle home. At the despatch box he was lawyerly and restrained, the register that permitted him the maximum of confidence and comfort: his inner team had taken a self-denying ordinance against partisan attacks on the Conservatives at a time of national emergency, much to the frustration of Labour pugilists who itched to criticise their failures.

But these moments of stability passed as soon as they came. The leader Starmer wished to be made only intermittent cameos in the day-to-day work of the Labour Party. Even with David Evans in place, instability reigned. For this, Starmer could not solely blame an intransigent left. In promising a future without faction, he had unwittingly created a Darwinian struggle for political dominance between Labour's constituent tribes – all of whom were represented in the leader's office. His speeches and interviews during the leadership election had said one thing: *unity*. 'We are not going to trash the last Labour government,' he had said, 'nor are we going to trash the last four years.' Yet the choices he had made once elected implied otherwise.

To the Corbynites this was a brazen breach of contract. On 11 February, Starmer had codified those values with Ten Pledges to the membership: each a totemic left-wing policy that could easily have been lifted from either of Corbyn's election manifestos. Income tax on the wealthiest 5 per cent of society would increase. Rail, mail, energy and water would be taken into public ownership. Tuition fees and Universal Credit were to be abolished. MPs would be given a parliamentary veto on overseas military interventions by British forces. Starmer would not only 'unite our party', but 'promote pluralism'. Chris Ward and Simon Fletcher, the aides responsible for their wording, foresaw no problems with the exercise. Starmer, after all, had made all of these commitments – and more – in his speeches, in televised debates, and in written submissions to the trade unions whose endorsements he had courted. Their candidate was in no position to subject them to detailed scrutiny, having lost his mother-in-law, Barbara, only seventy-two hours earlier. But he disagreed with only one word in the Ten Pledges: their opposition to 'illegal' wars. The correct term, he later told Ward, was 'unlawful'. He was otherwise content to approve the down payment he made to a wary left.

McSweeney was not. Having resisted every invitation to sign up to the demands of various campaign groups – most notably the Labour Campaign for Trans Rights – he too had been indisposed on the day the Pledges were agreed. A few weeks later, over dinner at Roger Liddle's on 8 March, he described the tuition fees pledge as a 'bribe', and said more broadly of the policies: they might well have been individually popular, he told friends, but together they were 'collectively incredible'. He did not believe it would be responsible for a Labour Party that wished to win a general election to keep these promises. Matt Pound, the faction fighter from Labour First, wondered why Starmer had made such extensive commitments in writing when the data he had amassed from local parties suggested he had already clinched the leadership. Steve Reed privately accused Simon Fletcher of having forced the Pledges past a grief-stricken Starmer, in the hope of lashing him tightly to the left. As is often the case with conspiracy theories, however, the truth was altogether more prosaic – and more difficult for opponents of the Pledges to confront. Ward and Fletcher had simply written on paper the things Starmer had already told the Labour Party

he believed. They would never be unsaid, or unheard, even as he began
to speak of a different politics.

★

Unity was impossible. Starmer soon found that the Labour Party
could not be timetabled into post-factional harmony. The profound
differences that existed within it – within his own office – could not
be professionalised out of existence. His coalition was so broad, his
promises so sweeping, that its component parts could not be reconciled
with themselves. The anti-Corbynites in his orbit willed something to
give. In the heat of a lockdown summer, it did.

The sunshine of May and June 2020 exposed the contradictions in
Starmerism's theory and practice. Some weeks he was a patriot of the
suburban school, an establishment man of impeccable small-c conservatism. The achievement his inner team remembers most proudly
from those early, troubled months of his leadership – during which
they had little to be proud of – is the front page of the *Daily Telegraph*
of 8 May, the seventy-fifth anniversary of the end of the Second World
War in Europe. Its splash headline read: 'Starmer: We owe it to VE
Day generation to protect them from virus in care homes.' The words
and their placement said much about how the likes of Ben Nunn and
Morgan McSweeney saw the Starmer project, and how they wished it
to be seen. At a moment of national crisis, the newspaper that had long
employed Boris Johnson was presenting his opponent – and the Labour
Party – as a champion of military veterans and a credible critic of a
government it otherwise loved. Corbyn's advisers had toiled vainly for
four years to be taken seriously as an opposition, to dispel the reflexive
and often baseless critique that they simply hated Britain. It had taken
their successors little more than four weeks.

Its internal audience – the party staff, MPs and activists who viewed
the new leadership with suspicion – was rather less receptive. They
had not joined the Labour Party to beg for the benediction of Middle
England and its right-wing tastemakers, but to fight for economic,
social and racial justice. Not all had believed Starmer when he spoke of
making the 'moral case for socialism' outlined in the Ten Pledges. But
the promise had been made and they demanded it was kept. It was a
murder on a street 4,000 miles from Westminster that led both sides to

ask themselves whether it could be. Confined to their homes, gazing at screens, the world watched in horror as a white police officer knelt for nine minutes on the neck of George Floyd, an African American, on a Minneapolis street on 25 May. As bystanders attempted in vain to intervene, Floyd told the officer that he could not breathe. He called out for his mother, and then he died. Protests against police brutality and anti-black racism sprung up immediately across America, and soon people of all races were marching to prove that Black Lives Mattered in Britain, too. The demonstrations were largely peaceful but isolated incidents of vandalism and civil disobedience posed an immediate challenge to a political class that had initially sought to put itself on the right side of history. On 7 June, Parliament Square's monument to Sir Winston Churchill was defaced with the spray-painted words: 'was a racist'. On the same day in Bristol, jubilant crowds toppled a statue of Edward Colston – the seventeenth-century slaver whose riches had left their controversial and hitherto indelible mark on the city's civic life – and dumped it in the River Avon.

Starmer, meanwhile, found himself at the crossroads of protest and power. Submerged in the lukewarm Corbynism of the Ten Pledges had been a promise to 'never lose sight of the votes "lent" to the Tories in 2019'. By and large, these were older white men in the north and Midlands who had not been through further education, and who had voted for Brexit and wanted punitive policies on law and order. Advisers like McSweeney made the snap judgement that Labour could not afford to side with those who had broken the law, however popular or morally justified their cause. These, however, were searching questions for Keir Starmer: the man, the lawyer, and the politician. In the past, his liberal instincts on racial justice had dovetailed with his work as prosecutor: as DPP he had ordered the retrial of the white thugs who murdered the black teenager Stephen Lawrence. His critics claimed the two were irreconcilable: Karie Murphy's conviction that Starmer was a rabid right-winger at heart was born of his prosecutions of young, black Londoners for individually trivial offences during the riots of 2011. Either way, as Labour leader Starmer sought deliberately to emphasise that for five years he had earned his living by locking up dangerous criminals. If voters who had abandoned Labour for Johnson in 2019 suspected that Corbyn might have cheered on the defacement of Churchill's statue as an act of righteous defiance, McSweeney – who loathed nothing more than the 'performative politics' of marches and pickets – wanted to present Starmer as the man who would have prosecuted him for incitement to riot.

Colston's statue had been underwater for less than twenty-four hours when Starmer was asked to pass judgement in a radio interview on LBC. Without hesitation, he said its removal had been 'completely wrong'. In the Commons, his shadow home secretary Nick Thomas-Symonds made the same political calculation: 'I do not condone an act of criminal damage to remove it, but I will not miss a public statue of a slave trader.' To the Corbynite left these carefully weighed words were at best underwhelming and at worst insidious. Labour, as Starmer's own Ten Pledges had reminded the members who had chosen him as leader, was a progressive party that existed to champion Britain's minorities. If it was not willing to defend their right to protest now, with the eyes of the western world for once open to racial injustice, what was the point? Nadia Whittome, the twenty-three-year-old MP for Nottingham East, spoke for many on the left when she celebrated Colston's fall as an 'act of resistance'. Diane Abbott, who knew all too well what racism meant, warned that Starmer must be 'careful not to sound as if we care more about vandalism than the horrors of the Atlantic slave trade'. Among the ugliest exposures in the leaked report into factionalism at Labour HQ was the casual viciousness with which some white staff spoke of black MPs on the left. That, of course, was a large part of the reason Starmer had asked a QC of colour to investigate its contents. Of Abbott the staff quoted in the report had said: 'She truly makes me sick.' Of Clive Lewis, the MP of Grenadian and English parentage who had briefly been the sixth candidate in that year's leadership election: 'The biggest cunt out of the lot.' Of the appointment of Dawn Butler, the first black woman to have served as a government minister and a persistent critic of alleged racism within the party, to the shadow cabinet: 'Good grief.' Just as the leadership had begun its work to rid Labour of the taint of antisemitism, it faced new allegations of anti-black racism from the party's own members.

In turning so decisively to face the electorate, had Starmer turned his back on the black men and women of the Labour Party? That, suddenly, was the accusation levelled against him with righteous indignation. At 11 a.m. on 9 June, a day after Starmer's ill-received interview on LBC, the Streatham MP Bell Ribeiro-Addy – a former

adviser to Abbott – asked the leader's private secretary Yasmeen Sebbana whether the entire Parliamentary Labour Party could be pictured
taking the knee, the silent gesture of protest that had united Britain's
sportsmen but divided its politicians. Only one Conservative MP
would ever kneel. Dominic Raab, Boris Johnson's foreign secretary,
pithily summarised the prevailing attitude on the right when he said:
'I'll take the knee for two people: the Queen, and the missus when I
asked her to marry me.' The left, as ever, was divided. Another circu-
lar debate began in Starmer's divided office. Ben Nunn and his deputy
director of communications, Paul Ovenden, wrestled with the competing demands of party management and political positioning. 'We
need to show willing,' Ovenden said, 'but I think we can stop it happening because of Covid guidance.' As Labour MPs gathered in New
Palace Yard, beneath Big Ben, it was decreed that their leader would
not join them due to Covid guidelines. This, itself, was a risk. It was
argued that Starmer's absence might vindicate every criticism that
had been made in the preceding twenty-four hours. A week earlier
it had been proposed that Starmer take the knee on the floor of his
own office, a suggestion vetoed on aesthetic grounds. Now it reared its
head again. Ovenden texted colleagues to say it was 'fine' if their boss
wished to show his solidarity by taking the knee – after all, the England
footballers he so admired were doing so too – 'but not Keir doing one
in his office on his own because it will look weird'. At 12.30 p.m. the
official photographer of the House of Commons was invited to take
a picture of Keir Starmer and Angela Rayner taking the knee in their
office, on their own.

'This,' one adviser to Starmer reflects now, 'was an absolutely classic
example of that first year. Knowing something was a bad or silly idea,
but not feeling able to stop it properly. Kicking yourself that you didn't
do more, or speak up properly. And working from home during Covid
meaning you could never get a grip on something properly. Stuff just
"happened".'

Jealously guarding their new electorate in the red wall, Tory MPs
now accused Starmer of siding with the vandals. In taking the knee he
had not merely endorsed the unarguable principle of opposing racism –
as the Conservative prime minister had himself done – but the most
radical demands of Black Lives Matter protesters too. Was the proud
prosecutor now in favour of defunding the police? Three weeks after

he had taken the knee, on 30 June, Starmer was impelled to mount the case for the defence – of the hurt felt by well-meaning people protesting racism who now found themselves maligned as rabble-rousing yobs and Marxist agitators, and himself. 'Nobody should be saying anything about defunding the police,' he told the BBC. As DPP for five years 'I worked with police forces across England and Wales, bringing thousands of people to court. So, erm, my support for the police is very, very strong . . . There's a broader issue here. The Black Lives Matter movement, or *moment*, if you like, internationally, is about reflecting something completely different, and it's reflecting on what happened dreadfully in America just a few weeks ago.' Again, he satisfied nobody. That word – *moment* – was interpreted by a distrustful left as a callous dismissal of the cause. For good measure, Nigel Farage salted the wound, tweeting: 'Heartily agree with @Keir_Starmer's condemnation of the Black Lives Matter organisation.'

In the days that followed Starmer seemed to prove Aneurin Bevan's old adage that Labour politicians who stood in the middle of the road were inevitably run over. His party wished to hear one thing, his team believed the country needed to hear another. The result was an incoherence that endeared him to nobody. By 2 July he had apologised for his description of Black Lives Matter as a 'moment'. He told LBC: 'What I was saying last week is that Black Lives Matter needs to be a moment, and I meant a defining moment and a turning point. I didn't mean a fleeting moment.' Four days later he had publicly promised to undertake unconscious bias training as penance for his lapse, and on 8 July he sought the forgiveness of Labour's black staff in a private Zoom. One staffer told him that they were no longer able to say they worked for an anti-racist party and promptly leaked the entire discussion to the *New Statesman*, before issuing a further demand that Starmer make an intervention condemning the 'misogynoir' experienced by black women in Parliament like Abbott and Butler.

What Starmer did not say was that his inner team thought this debilitating cycle was mad and maddening: an initial gesture to Labour's target voters followed inevitably by a long process of self-flagellation for the benefit of the activists they blamed for losing those voters in the first place. To the extent that a public contending with the otherworldly trauma of a global pandemic was listening to the leader of the opposition at all, all they heard was apologies and equivocation, often

for previous apologies. McSweeney in particular believed that identity politics was an electoral dead end for a Labour Party that wished
to win elections. It forced the party's politicians to speak the argot of
activism, a language supposedly impenetrable to the voters that truly
mattered. He had privately despaired when, as Starmer appointed his
front bench, shadow cabinet ministers demanded the appointment of
an ethnic minority MP to each of their teams. Over dinner at Roger
Liddle's his circle had bemoaned the supposed co-option of racial politics by the Corbynite left. This was not a vision of politics shared at
Labour HQ, whose mistake was to believe that all of Starmer's promises had been created equal – or, for that matter, within the leader's
own team. Far from uniting the Labour Party, he had exposed that it no
longer agreed with itself on the existential question of who or what it
was for. McSweeney's lament to Steve Reed replayed in countless conversations: *Literally everything is broken.* Starmer would soon be forced
to choose his side of the road.

6

'Keir will suspend him!'

Every Labour leadership has its foundational texts. For Blair it was the political philosophy of Anthony Giddens. For Attlee it was Keynes and Beveridge. Ed Miliband studied the work of Michael Sandel on the moral limits of the market economy. For Starmer, it would be an interview in the *Independent* with the actor Maxine Peake.

Labour politicians loved Peake. Born to working-class parents in Bolton, she was a rare thing in the rarefied world of British performing arts. She in turn had acclaimed Corbynism with just as much enthusiasm as the critics acclaimed her performances on stage and screen. So it was unsurprising that Rebecca Long-Bailey, herself the product of a comprehensive school in the industrial north-west, saw fit to tweet a profile of the left's favourite thespian at 10.02 a.m. on 25 June. 'Maxine Peake is an absolute diamond,' wrote the shadow education secretary. Buried within the text, which bore all the hallmarks of Peake's strong socialist sympathies, was an extraordinary allegation. Peake contended that the police officer who had killed George Floyd had learned the lethal technique of kneeling on his neck 'from seminars taught by Israeli secret services'. Her words appeared alongside a denial from the government of Israel. Whether she had read the piece in its entirety or not, Long-Bailey undeniably appeared to have endorsed the suggestion that the Jewish state bore responsibility for the racist brutality of police in the American Midwest.

As Long-Bailey typed the tweet that would end her career in frontline politics, Starmer was on a train to Stevenage. This, despite the glamourless destination, was a thrilling prospect for a Labour leader who had been denied for nearly three months any meaningful opportunity to leave the confines of his office and speak to voters directly. The great unlocking had begun. The first indication that he would instead spend another long day speaking to the Labour Party came from Jenny Chapman, who had graduated from her informal role as convenor for his leadership plot to the post of political secretary – the emissary from the leader's office to Labour MPs. She texted her travelling colleagues a little sheepishly: 'This has come up.' Starmer was possessed of acute and sudden outrage. He and Long-Bailey had come together from opposing ends of the party. That much he accepted. Unity, after all, was the guiding philosophy of his leadership – so much so that he had been prepared to stomach their ongoing disagreements over the reopening of schools. But Starmer read the tweet – and its implicit endorsement of an anti-Israel conspiracy theory – not as a question of left and right, but right and wrong. It posed a risk: not of an unseemly row with the Corbynite left, but to Labour's uneasy reconciliation with the Jewish community organisations to whom he had apologised repeatedly. One of the first phone calls he had made as leader was to Ephraim Mirvis, the chief rabbi; the first letter he had sent, itself drafted by the Board of Deputies of British Jews, had been a plea to Mirvis for a second chance. These had been difficult and demoralising conversations; all could now come to an abrupt end without action.

The shadow cabinet was just about the only constituent part of the Labour Party over which its leader had undisputed control. Starmer at once decided to wield it. He told his aides to demand the tweet's deletion. Back in Westminster, his deputy chief of staff Chris Ward demanded answers from Long-Bailey. Ward called: the phone rang out. Still phlegmatic, he turned to her staff. 'This is not a massive problem,' he said, 'but I can see a mistake has been made. You just need to take it down, though – tell Becky to deal with it, apologise. We'll move on.' By lunchtime Starmer was incandescent. He had a thinner skin and quicker temper than his stolid, emotionless public persona implied. 'It's been three hours since I spoke to you last,' he told Ward. '*Why* is this not coming down? I've told you this has *got* to come down. You've got to talk to me, got to tell her this, it's got to stop, *she's got to sort this out.*' Then the inevitable ultimatum came: 'I'm in a meeting for the next hour and a half. Tell her if it's not down in an hour and a half, she's going to get a phone call from me, and it's going to go badly.'

Ward and Chapman called and called. No answer came. When it did, Long-Bailey was rather more relaxed than either aide expected. 'I want to talk to Keir and explain,' she told her team. The tweet was 'fine'. She believed her leader had overreacted. She did not know this was not a problem Starmer was prepared to have explained away. His ninety-minute deadline came and went without the requested deletion. He emerged from his meeting onto a conference call, by which point his team had concluded that only one outcome was likely. Uncharacteristically, it was McSweeney who betrayed the greatest anxiety. Any move against Long-Bailey, who had inherited the moral and political leadership of the Corbynite left, would inspire an equal and opposite reaction from the likes of Len McCluskey. McSweeney told Ward: 'This is going to cause big problems. What you're doing is right. What we're doing is right . . . but it's going to cause big problems.'

Starmer, by contrast, had no doubts. 'Has she taken it down?' he asked Ward.

'No.'

'Has she answered your calls?'

'No.'

'Have you told her that she needs to?'

'Yes.'

'She's getting a call from me in five minutes,' Starmer concluded. 'She needs to take it.' At 3.11 p.m. it was announced that he had sacked Rebecca Long-Bailey as shadow secretary of state for education. By the time she spoke publicly, insisting that she had not endorsed every one of Peake's comments and had tweeted only to pay tribute to her 'significant achievements' and clarion call for left-wingers to remain in the Labour Party, she did so from the back benches.

The aftermath was indeed problematic, just as McSweeney had predicted. With appropriately dramatic timing, Len McCluskey condemned the 'unnecessary overreaction to a confected row', and warned portentously: 'Unity is too important to be risked like this.' John McDonnell, to whom Long-Bailey was 'my Becky', said: 'Throughout discussion of antisemitism it's always been said criticism of the practices of the Israeli state is not antisemitic. I don't believe therefore that this article is or that Rebecca Long-Bailey should've been sacked. I stand in solidarity with her.' As surely as night followed day, Starmer was again reduced to explaining himself to an implacable left through a webcam. The next morning he spent an hour calming the anxious minds of the Socialist Campaign Group, reassuring MPs including

Corbyn, who appeared on screen wearing a football shirt sponsored by the Communication Workers Union, that he had no wish to declare civil war.

'It's not an attack on the left,' Starmer said, repeatedly, as McDonnell wrung his hands and lamented the born-again factionalism of the unity candidate. 'It's about antisemitism and personal conduct.' In turn each left-winger accused him of abolishing their right to free speech on foreign affairs. 'I want to be clear,' one MP said, 'if there's something going on in Israel and Palestine, I'm allowed to speak out on Israel.'

'What are you talking about?' said Starmer. 'Somebody's put up a tweet that was clearly a mistake. I asked them, for five hours, to take it down. They refused to do so. I told them that if they didn't, I'd fire them. This is not about Israel and Palestine. What's wrong?'

What *was* it about? Long-Bailey's friends struggled to comprehend what she had done. Angela Rayner, her flatmate, was irritated by Starmer's failure to involve her in negotiations and believed she could have been the trusted interlocutor to defuse the row. In the tense hours before her sacking, Simon Fletcher – Team Starmer's house interpreter of Corbynism – had confessed to colleagues in the leader's office: 'I don't know what she is doing.' After weeks of needling disagreements over schools – a debate which had seen Long-Bailey and the teachers' unions at odds with the leadership – some suspected she had deliberately committed 'suicide by cop'.

It was certainly true that her political passing would go unmourned by most of the Parliamentary Labour Party. As one shadow cabinet minister said: 'I was horrified that Rebecca Long-Bailey had been made shadow education secretary . . . I was like: "What are we saying about our commitment to education?" We put a lunatic in charge.'

Others, like Ward, diagnosed a more embarrassing pathology than insanity: naivete. Whatever she imagined Starmer might do in response to her insubordination, it was surely not *that*. If unity meant anything – if unity meant Len McCluskey dictating terms to the leader of the Labour Party – then Starmer would not, could not, sack the woman who had won the votes of 135,218 members, having run a low-wattage, disorganised campaign. By historical standards the Labour left was as strong as it had ever been. Surely, they told themselves, Starmer could not afford to create a martyr.

They misunderstood him. As he had impatiently explained to

Corbyn and McDonnell, the sacking was not the first stage in a factional masterplan. The personal and political had collided at speed.
Allegations of antisemitism against the Labour Party induced nausea
and rage. Starmer's father-in-law, Bernard, was Jewish, and he would
recite the prayers as the family marked Shabbat with Friday-night
dinner. The custom and ritual of Judaism – however loosely it was
followed – offered Starmer the rootedness and warmth he had been
denied in his unhappy childhood home. He was an honorary member
of a community that had deserted the Labour Party en masse. On his
occasional visits to the liberal synagogue in St John's Wood he had seen
at first hand the visceral disgust of many British Jews. But Long-Bailey
was more than a victim of moral outrage. Those who knew Starmer
best did not believe his fury and revulsion were purely personal. If
anything he was more bewildered, more offended, by her disrespect
for the administrative structures of accountability on which his politics were built. The shadow education secretary had been given clear
instructions by the leader of the Labour Party and ignored them, even
when the matter at hand was foundational to his political project. That
was Long-Bailey's cardinal sin.

★

McSweeney had always known that he would not – *could* not – unite
with the left. Day by day, week by week, events led Starmer to the
same conclusion. They led the left away from the leadership, too.
Shortly after the Commons broke for its summer recess, in July, the
Johnson government brought forward legislation that held a mirror
to the face of the human rights lawyer who now led the Labour
Party, and dared him to say that he now saw a different man in its
reflection. The Covert Human Intelligence Sources Bill would grant
MI5 and the police formal powers to allow their undercover agents to
commit crimes in the course of their duties. They had always done so,
of course, but now the threat of legal action against the government
impelled ministers to write a licence to kill into the statute book. When
the left read the bill they were disgusted. Here was a Conservative
government giving the deep state the right to ignore the law, whatever
the baleful human cost. Amnesty International, the trade unions, the
Greens, the Scottish National Party, Sinn Féin: all opposed it in the

name of human rights and the rule of law. Undercover officers – the 'spycops' Starmer's old colleagues at the Bar had campaigned against for years – had lied and deceived their way onto the protests and into the beds of countless activists. They fathered their children under false identities, ruined their lives, and facilitated the civil disobedience and crime they had been employed to prevent.

The Corbynites thought it was a moral outrage. Shami Chakrabarti, the barrister and human rights campaigner who had served in the left's shadow cabinet and remained its moral conscience, said the bill blurred the line between agent and agitator. When the division bell rang there was no question that dozens of her comrades in the Commons would vote against it. At first Starmer wondered aloud whether he might unburden them from the strictures of the whip, grant them a free vote, allow them their protest against state power. He, after all, had spent year after year on the wrong side of courtrooms, struggling vainly to constrain the excesses of the police. When autumn came he turned against his younger self. He told Nick Thomas-Symonds, his shadow home secretary: 'I don't want anyone to be a part of my government who doesn't understand the importance of this.' Starmer no longer wished to lead a protest against the deep state. Under his leadership, Labour would *become* the deep state. Advising the police in Northern Ireland and leading the Crown Prosecution Service, he tasted the power that belonged to other people. He worked with the officers and spies he had pursued through the courts. 'I came better to understand how you can change by being inside and getting the trust of people,' he had said during the leadership campaign. He had tired of the thankless life of 'a human rights lawyer, railing against the system from the outside'. Another future may have been possible, but another present was not. Starmer believed he saw the world as it was. Undercover agents existed. How best to manage them? On 15 October, when the legislation came before the Commons, he told his MPs to abstain.

Corbynite MPs posed another question, its own logic just as powerful. Nobody on the left was comfortable with what the spycops had done to the miners, the environmental activists, the trade unionists whose struggles Starmer had co-opted as his own. It was illegal. How could their leader stand by as it became their constitutional right? Unite and Momentum, the two great bulwarks of the old politics, told Starmer that he 'must oppose the bill'. The din of opposition rose to intolerable volumes. Outside the Commons chamber Emily Thornberry turned to Thomas-Symonds, and said knowingly: 'Told you this was going to get rocky.' Starmer stood firm. Thirty-four MPs rebelled and six frontbenchers quit, among them Dan Carden, the protégé of Len McCluskey who now found himself surrounded by Blairites in the shadow Treasury team. Starmer's team believed the left had taken itself off the pitch. One shadow cabinet minister recalls that, in the first six months of his leadership, 'party management was a higher priority than ultimately it could be if we were to win'. The left was unignorable: its own covert agents embedded in Labour HQ, its parliamentary representatives occupying roles of prestige and import. By resigning they had clarified Starmer's vision of unity: he would demand support for the positions he deemed necessary, and expected to receive it. Without doubters on the front bench, it would be much easier to realise. Angela Rayner knew as much, too. She feared what it may mean for their partnership. More than thirty-four may have rebelled had she not intervened personally, assuring them that she had asked Starmer to make clear to the rebels that he would continue to defend the rights of trade unions against the long arm of the law. He did no such thing. His aides briefed the *Guardian* that none of the left-wingers who remained had been offered a single promise or concession.

The leader and the left were locked in an awkward waltz. Neither trusted the other. Neither was willing to make the declaration of war that both sides knew, instinctively, would one day come. McSweeney and McCluskey both had too much to lose: one their project, the other their influence. Within weeks, that would change permanently.

*

In the six months since his resignation, Jeremy Corbyn had almost disappeared from view, but his presence still loomed over the Labour Party, ambiguous and unresolved: marooned, with Starmer, between past and future. On 29 October both men broke free, cast in opposite directions. The new leader's old credo – 'Let's all be friends' – would give way to enmity.

At 10 a.m. the Equality and Human Rights Commission published the results of its eighteen-month inquiry into Labour's handling of antisemitism complaints under Corbyn. For so long the question had been bitterly contested, the left battered by claim and counterclaim, Corbyn's every step stalked by the media he loathed. The EHRC would draw a line. It would rule either that Labour had unlawfully discriminated against Jews, or it had not. Starmer knew its conclusion would not be the last word in a debate that had led countless voters to abandon his party. But it would at least be an authoritative one. He hoped there might now be some closure to the unseemly era in which allegations of racism against his colleagues had been headline news. *Did* Corbyn have a problem with Jews? Did the Labour Party?

Warring factions had often considered these questions as binaries. In reality it was not so easy. When the EHRC had last investigated a political party – the BNP – its adjudications had been straightforward. Nick Griffin, the leader McSweeney had helped destroy in Barking, was a convicted Holocaust denier. His party's constitution decreed that only 'indigenous Caucasians' were eligible for membership. In Labour's case there was no such smoking gun. Corbyn defined himself by his opposition to racism. So too did his advisers, who maintained that they had done as much as possible to use their power to discipline antisemites – only to be thwarted by right-wingers who wished to see them ruined.

The EHRC concerned itself with questions of legality, not morality. It had never proposed to conduct an inquiry into Corbyn's mind and soul. Its investigation was technical, focused narrowly on the question of whether Labour as a party had discharged its legal duty to protect its Jewish members from harassment and racism. Yet arguably there was no such thing as *the* Labour Party, as Starmer himself was discovering. Really there were at least two: the party of Jeremy Corbyn, who believed they were the victims of smears and sabotage, and the party of Tom Watson, his deputy. Watson had been so disgusted by antisemitism – and so convinced that Corbynism would destroy the party to which he had devoted his entire adult life – that he had promised Trevor Chinn, the Jewish donor, that he would lead a mass resignation of Labour MPs if they found themselves able to form a government after the 2019 election.

The leaked report had been prepared to emphasise this very point. The Corbynites believed *their* Labour Party had tried its best, only to be obstructed and undermined by their enemies – themselves no strangers to casual racism. When their lawyers told them the watchdog was unlikely to listen to that case, they told the press instead.

The Corbynsceptics had prepared their case, too. After the EHRC announced its inquiry, Shabana Mahmood – the Muslim MP and NEC member whose other faith was the politics of the Labour right – approached Charlie Falconer for legal counsel. If Labour *was* found guilty of racial discrimination, could she be held personally responsible? If she had broken her fiduciary duties, could she be sued by victims claiming damages, or be financially liable if the party was bankrupted? They spoke for three hours and concluded that in all likelihood no such scenario would come to pass. Falconer nonetheless advised Mahmood to lay a paper trail documenting their contributions to discussions on antisemitism. That way she might one day present evidence to a court that proved they had mounted a lonely stand against the Corbynites and their failure to protect Jewish members.

The notion that there was one Labour Party was a legal fiction. And the EHRC report was a legal exercise. No matter how intensely left and right loathed and attacked one another, their party *was* a single entity, governed as one by the same obligations and laws. Starmer would feel the pain of any finding of statutory discrimination as acutely as the charge of antisemitism itself. As a barrister, he had used human rights legislation as a cudgel against unaccountable power, entrenching progressivism in public life. Now the weight of the legal order he had helped create crashed upon him. The Labour Party – *his* Labour Party – would be punished for failures he had observed from his privileged position at the shadow cabinet table. Earlier in 2020, at a leadership debate in Dewsbury, Lisa Nandy had told him he had been wrong to work under a leadership that had not done enough to combat antisemitism. 'I spoke out publicly,' she said, 'and I left and I didn't return.' She turned to Starmer: 'There is a serious question of judgement here.' Privately, he was furious. He never forgave Nandy for her assault on his character. Yet Nandy did not know that he had considered resigning on several occasions, before concluding that only persistence could win him the leadership. Starmer told himself that, in victory, he would be the man to close the book on this troubled era in Labour history.

Six months into his tenure, the EHRC gave him the opportunity to do just that. McSweeney, whose work with the Jewish Labour Movement (JLM) had helped engineer the inquiry, was of the same mind. On 8 March, he had told his audience at Roger Liddle's supper club that the watchdog's ruling would be Starmer's Clause IV moment – the definitive, irreversible break from the past. Not only a break with the shame of Corbynism, but the ambiguity that had necessarily charac- terised Starmer's own early days as leader. Those who had challenged Starmer on antisemitism were wearied by his homilies to unity and professionalism. In private, he had told Peter Mason and Adam Lan- gleben, the leaders of the JLM: 'I understand the process. I'm a lawyer. I understand the situation. We need to fix it. We will fix it.' Both left dissatisfied. Like many others in their community – on their wing of the Labour Party – they did not share Starmer's analysis. He needed a permanent rupture with Corbyn and Corbynism, not a bureaucratic fix. Judicious edits to the small print of the party's complaints proce- dures would not inoculate Labour against the virus of antisemitism. 'You do know,' Mason told Starmer, 'that this is going to be a fight to the death?'

Starmer did not. Nor did Corbyn. By October the Corbyn of old emerged again onto the Seven Sisters Road: the constituency MP untroubled by the demands of high office, or any responsibility to the pressmen or politicians who hated all he stood for. In Parliament – on the Covert Human Intelligence Sources Bill just a couple of weeks earlier – he rebelled against Starmer as he had rebelled against Neil Kin- nock, John Smith, Tony Blair, Gordon Brown and Ed Miliband, with the quiet resolve of a man who knew his own mind. Everyone reverted to type. On 1 October he had been photographed – in contravention of Covid restrictions – at a table of nine people, dining indoors to com- memorate the life of their friend David Graeber, a leftist philosopher. When Jenny Chapman called from the leader's office to establish the facts, she found herself in conversation with the backbencher of old: courteous, gently defiant. He apologised and the new regime reacted with placid indifference. That was Jeremy. One could only shrug and ignore him. Nobody seemed to mind.

But whatever liberation he felt would soon pass. Corbyn felt the EHRC's reckoning loom closer. Only after the judgement could he build an organisation to preserve the spirit of his triumphs – 2015, 2016, 2017. Like his mentor and hero, Tony Benn, he wanted to retire from Westminster triviality and spend more time on politics. The wait was extended again and again, the sheer quantity of evidence delaying the prompt resolution all sides wanted. As long as the regulator's work continued, Corbyn would have to proceed with caution.

With his future at stake, Corbyn could trust only five people. From April, six months before the report's publication, they were in daily contact. In their preparations for the day of judgement, Milne and Murphy were joined by James Schneider, his former communications aide. Schneider, like Milne, was an old boy of Winchester College and Oxford, and had graduated from both institutions with a similar distaste for the British establishment. Jennie Formby, the departed general secretary, was the fourth member of this justifiably anxious inner circle. Having fought their successors in Labour HQ for the right to examine the report before its publication, the EHRC rescinded the offer during the summer. That much did not surprise them. Helene Reardon-Bond, the senior civil servant who briefly ran Corbyn's office in the last days of his leadership and survived under the new regime, confided to colleagues that the EHRC was 'a joke'. Her stint as director of the Government Equalities Office had convinced her that the watchdog was in fact a lapdog, 'completely' under the control of the ministers of the day, who would interfere in its operations as a matter of course. The Corbynites shared her analysis, and suspected the EHRC – New Labour's pride and joy – did not share its world view. Only after protracted negotiations did the commission allow Corbyn sight of a draft of the report ahead of its publication.

His friends were appalled by much of what they read. It was 'awful' and 'totally inaccurate in lots of ways', one said. What it did not do, however, was apportion blame to named individuals even as it identified breaches of equality law. Even a politician as hostile to criticism as Corbyn could live with that. His advisers had never denied that Labour had failed in its duties, but instead disputed both the scale of those failures and the question of culpability. As long as the EHRC had not blamed Corbyn himself, his team allowed themselves to believe that he would escape censure from his successor too. The summary execution of Rebecca Long-Bailey had opened their eyes to Starmer's ruthlessness, but she had arguably been the author of her own downfall. They would not be so careless. Starmer had begun his leadership with homilies to his old friend Corbyn, due solemnity on antisemitism, and the promise of unity. Jeremy's friends told themselves that Starmer would not politicise the report with another factional assassination. This, after all, was an investigation into the Labour Party – not its past or present leaders.

Only the fifth member of Corbyn's kitchen cabinet dissented. Laura Alvarez, Jeremy's third wife, defended her husband with a furious devotion that discomforted even his closest aides. She hated what the Labour Party had done to him. She hated the media. Their never-ending accusations of racism had changed the man she loved. Gone was the witty, wry, ebullient man she had met two decades earlier, when she had travelled to England from Mexico in search of her abducted niece. After an introduction brokered by Tony Benn, Jeremy had helped locate the lost child. Jeremy would always be her hero, no matter what his critics said. Laura did not believe that Labour had a problem with antisemitism. She believed the powerful had a problem with her husband. They had smeared and defamed him so that they might destroy his politics. Worse still, his supposed comrades accepted the libel as legitimate. When they suggested he might apologise for some mistake or other, she protested. At Jeremy's lowest moments she would always be on hand with articles from the *Canary*, vindicating her thesis, exposing to the world that it was all a malicious hoax.

Like Cassandra, Laura foresaw disaster, and nobody believed her. One of the inner circle recalls: 'She always said: "These people are going to get my husband! Keir will suspend him! Keir will suspend him!"' It was inevitable, she thought, that Starmer would use the report as a pretext to purge Corbyn. For a Latin American socialist, it was a simple fact of political life. A confidant of the couple explains her thinking: 'When you're in power, you have everything. And when you're out of power, you're in prison or exile.' Laura feared that Jeremy would end up like Lula, the left-wing Brazilian president imprisoned for corruption. Labour's own judiciary would be arrayed against her husband.

But there would be no summary execution and no kangaroo court – only a difficult forty-eight hours after the report was published. Just how difficult depended on what Corbyn said upon its release. The principles at stake were clear. Corbyn had a legacy to defend. He had an apology to make, even if he did not believe – and the EHRC did not say – he had done anything wrong personally. There would be no escape from a damning verdict on how the party had functioned under his leadership, but he would at least have an opportunity to take ownership of the past on his own terms. Once the date of publication had been disclosed, however, his advisers struggled to persuade him to engage at all.

As his leadership collapsed in 2019, Corbyn had become so traumatised and paranoid that the mere mention of antisemitism rendered
him mute. Milne's attempts to rouse him out of his depressive stu-
pors always failed. When another hostile headline came, he would tell
Corbyn: 'They don't know you, Jeremy.' Milne compared him to John
Lennon and Paul McCartney, blank canvases for the hopes and dreams
of teenagers at the height of Beatlemania. Their fans did not know
them, just as Jeremy's detractors did not know him. The antisemite
written about in the newspapers was an avatar: a parody of a man
most journalists did not know and would never meet. Once faintly
amused by the adulation of his supporters and the venom of his critics,
he now sought refuge in love as he was battered by hate. Even in the
safety of his garden, where his political business was now invariably
done, he could barely muster the strength to discuss antisemitism, or
assert himself as Laura wished he would.

For his long-suffering aides it was less than ideal that old friends
of Corbyn were encouraging him to say nothing at all. To say nothing was to invite the media to commence a game of cat-and-mouse,
harrying Corbyn on his doorstep – the intrusion he hated more than
anything – goading him into saying something he would immediately
regret. That was the very outcome they were desperate to avoid. However painful, he would have to reckon with reality and say something.
For once Laura agreed with them. She wanted Jeremy to say something too. That something, an aide involved in their discussions says,
was: 'This is about Palestine!'

Her suggestion was about as helpful as the constant missives
Corbyn received from Jewish socialists in his constituency. They told
him not to back down – to stick it to the Zionists, to Trump, to Benjamin Netanyahu, to stop saying sorry. Said one adviser to Jeremy: 'They
were saying: we're apologising all the time. This is actually encouraging the attacks. You have to stop apologising.' Murphy complained to
friends that she had argued about antisemitism with the Labour left
more often than the Labour right. It was obvious to her that Corbyn
would have to apologise. Milne, who had been deeply disturbed by
news coverage of Jews attesting to their fears of a Labour government
in 2019, agreed: that any minority could have sincerely believed they
were in danger under a Corbyn government had been a profound failing on Labour's behalf. Both knew, however, that Jeremy felt he had

apologised enough. They had watched, mortified, as he refused thirteen times to say sorry to British Jews during a BBC interview with
Andrew Neil in the days before the general election. In its aftermath,
miserable in the green room, he had struggled to speak at all.

Eventually, Corbyn agreed to issue a statement that would split the
difference between the defiance he shared with his wife and the desire
of his advisers to limit the damage they knew he might do if left unsu-
pervised. It would offer the apology he had been instructed to give,
and the self-justification that better reflected his emotional state. James
Schneider, himself Jewish, held the pen. His challenge was to write
something that offended neither his socialism nor his *Yiddishkeit* – or
sense of Jewishness. If he could manage that, then he had probably
struck the right balance. His preference was to include the word 'sorry',
but he knew that Corbyn would not tell the world in those terms. Schneider settled on an alternative construction, so that Corbyn could at
once acknowledge that there had been antisemitism on the left and
insist he had done his best to address it: 'I regret that it took longer to
deliver that change than it should.' Milne and Schneider considered
this compromise acceptable, if not ideal. Neither gave much thought
to a subsequent line that sought to provide another layer of context.
It argued that antisemitism, real though it was, had nonetheless been
amplified by Corbyn's opponents in a way that stoked the fears and
anxieties of the Jewish community – misleading and terrifying the kind
of people Milne had watched on his television. 'One antisemite is one
too many,' it read, 'but the scale of the problem was also dramatically
overstated for political reasons by our opponents inside and outside
the party, as well as by much of the media.' To say so seemed little
more than a statement of the obvious. Nobody knew that it would
become one of the most consequential sentences in the history of the
British left.

*

Starmer did not equivocate over his own apology, hoping it would
contrast with what Corbyn had said – or had failed to say – before.
Anything less would betray the already waning trust of Jewish leaders
within and without the Labour Party, who still doubted his resolve.
Did his promise of unity really amount to little more than forgiveness

for the people who had caused their community so much pain, so much grief? Starmer was determined to show them otherwise: that, yes, he would work with the left, but not if they denied that their party had a problem.

But what was the problem? Nobody – not even the most fanatical Blairites – was arguing that Corbyn was a Holocaust denier or violent racist. Starmer's team instead believed that his denials that there was any link between his socialist project and believers in the socialism of fools had given succour to those who did. Chris Ward, who wrote most of the words Starmer spoke, expressed that sentiment with striking clarity in the first draft of the speech the leader gave on 29 October: 'Let me be very clear: those who seek to blame others or downplay what happened in our party are, themselves, part of the problem, and we will have zero patience or tolerance of that.' Those words set a deliberately high standard that pleased Morgan McSweeney. He believed denialism was hardwired into the mindset of the Labour Party. In Rotherham, the government had seized control of a Labour-run council not because it denied the existence of a child sex abuse scandal involving the Pakistani community, but because it had denied the scandal's extent: an official report found 70 per cent of councillors in some way disputed an inquiry into what had happened, seeing external scrutiny as an attack on them or their politics. So McSweeney, who had come of age in Lambeth – a Labour council whose leaders had also turned a blind eye to child sex abuse – agreed with Ward's sentiment. But he was concerned about its implications. From his study of Corbynite Facebook pages he believed he had diagnosed the pathology of the hard left: a reflexive belief that any attack on Jeremy was a conspiracy cooked up by Blairites, lobbyists or the Israeli embassy. If denying the existence or scale of antisemitism was now a capital offence for Labour members, then countless activists would face disciplinary action. McSweeney called Ward: 'If you say this, you're going to take action against people. So can we make sure he's very comfortable with that?' Starmer insisted he was.

Had he deliberately laid a tripwire for Corbyn? The words set a test that the former leader, so publicly resentful of the suggestion that Labour had been overridden by antisemites under his leadership, was bound to fail. As one shadow cabinet minister close to Starmer said: 'We did attempt to create a hurdle that we thought he might not cross . . . we essentially set a trap that he leapt into. That's the truth of it.' Yet if that *was* Starmer's plan, he did not tell anybody. McSweeney anticipated the consequences, but was more concerned by the likely indiscretions of left-wingers on the NEC and within the trade unions – who still wielded power within his Labour Party – than Corbyn, who did not. Ben Nunn, who had choreographed the speech and press conference at which Starmer would deliver his message, was alone in grasping the significance of what the leader would say. The Corbynites did not like Nunn. To Karie Murphy and Amy Jackson, her loyal deputy, he had been 'the right-wing pad'. He reciprocated. Before his boss was elected to the leadership he had been ashamed to work for the Labour Party. At parties he had told strangers he was an account-ant employed by his father: the implied combination of tedium and nepotism killed conversation in an instant. Unlike Starmer, who had married into a Jewish family, or McSweeney, who, in his days as a kibbutznik, had lived in Israel, Nunn had no connection to the Jewish people. What he did have was the conviction that Corbyn himself was the problem, embodying as he did the hard left's conspiratorial mindset. Given the opportunity to obfuscate, deny, blame others, or otherwise 'say something stupid' Jeremy would seize it. On the eve of the report's publication Nunn told colleagues: 'There is a 70 per cent chance Jeremy is not in the Labour Party tomorrow.'

Like the Corbynites, however, Starmer had no desire for pyro-technics. This was a day of shame and atonement, for apologising to British Jews – not factional reprisals. Much of the preceding twenty-four hours had been spent reassuring the left of their intentions. At 10 a.m. on 28 October he had received and digested the final report. He repeated the message he had sought to impart to them after the sacking of Rebecca Long-Bailey: *this is not an attack on the left.* Cor-bynism itself was not a problem. Insubordination and indiscipline was. His position, as described by an adviser involved in discussions, was conciliatory rather than confrontational: 'Look, we don't want to over-personalise this – but Keir is absolutely going to go with the report, he's going to absolutely accept it in full, and he's going to implement it.' McSweeney, as so often, played emissary to the court of the Cor-bynites. He contacted John McDonnell, Len McCluskey, and Unite's lawyer, Howard Beckett. In turn he told them: 'This is what's going to happen. We're going to accept the report and implement all of its findings, but we're not going to blame individuals. Anyone who comes out and challenges it – their feet won't touch the floor.'

None disagreed, but Corbyn was blindfolded. He had read only an early draft of the EHRC's findings, not the final verdict. Nor did he know what Starmer would say in response. Would he damn his predecessor, just as everyone else had? Would he pin the blame on Jeremy Corbyn alone? Would he denounce the left as racists and expel them from his new model Labour Party? Corbyn tormented himself with each question in turn. By the time he spoke to Starmer on the evening of 28 October, he was desperate for clarity. Over the course of his brief and awkward phone conversation with his successor he believed Starmer would not attack him personally, nor cast him as singularly culpable for Labour's collective failures. Starmer praised an article Murphy had written for the *Guardian* two days earlier, in which she had put forward the Corbynite case for the defence: antisemitism and all it had done to damage Labour's relationship with British Jewry had 'deeply' saddened her, but they had not failed for want of trying. Instead they had been too slow to appreciate its scale, and had fallen victim to a 'highly politicised media campaign'. If Starmer was pleased to read Murphy saying so, then Corbyn could surely repeat the charge himself. That, at least, is what Corbyn allowed himself to believe. Even better: Starmer agreed to share the text of the speech he would give the following morning.

As with any diplomatic negotiation, the groundwork had been laid by officials. Milne was Corbyn's sherpa. Angela Rayner led Starmer's deputation. While distrusted by both sides – by the Corbynites for her abandonment of Long-Bailey, and the Starmerites for her cultivation of a loyal clique of supporters in Parliament and the unions – she was the natural interlocutor. Neither knew that she had already chosen a side. Years earlier, she had told Trevor Chinn: 'I don't mind if I get rid of 100,000 antisemitic members of the Labour Party to kill the antisemitism.'

At 6.30 p.m., shortly after Starmer's call with Corbyn, she telephoned Milne, who ended their conversation content that Starmer would not blame his predecessor, and that the new leadership wished to say the same thing as the old. He relayed Corbyn's belief that he had been promised a copy of Starmer's words. Would Rayner make sure that script was indeed sent? She would. Their exchanges were warm and comradely. At 6.55 Milne texted her his good wishes: 'good chat right now and [to] hear your voice', and he hoped their paths would cross before long. Rayner replied: 'Will do and yes, it'd be good to see you. I miss you guys in the world before COVID. Never thought I'd say it but sucks all this social distancing from what we had before. It's like going from 200 mph to 20.' She added: 'I'll get Ben Nunn to drop you notes ASAP and keep you looped in.'

Nunn, however, had not consented to her promise. If Starmer's promises of a new beginning for Labour and the Jewish community were to mean anything, then he could have 'absolutely nothing to do' with backroom horse-trading. His colleagues still maintain that the leader himself made no such undertaking either, whatever inference Corbyn may have drawn from their call. When Rayner came calling, they shrugged off the request. For that was all it had been: a request. One person present recalls now: 'She'd said she would ask for it, and she did.' It was in their gift to say no, and they did. Another aide now argues that it was Corbyn, not Starmer, who ought to have offered advance sight of their statement: his successor had no obligation to share a sensitive document with the man who had bequeathed him such a disastrous political inheritance. McSweeney was of the same view: that Corbyn had always had 'agency' and could not be allowed to outsource his political judgement to Starmer. There was nothing to stop him drafting a reasonable statement without outside assistance. The Irishman told colleagues that a politician of Corbyn's standing would surely know what was likely to pose problems for the party he had led, or the Jewish community whose support he had lost.

But in the early hours of 29 October, Milne was still seeking clarity. At 1.07 a.m. he texted Rayner again. 'Nothing came through from Ben, by the way.' Nearly seven hours later, at 8.01 a.m., the reply came: 'I'm on it now.' By then it was too late.

*

The EHRC ruled that the Labour Party 'had been responsible for unlawful acts of harassment and discrimination'. Under Corbyn's leadership, Labour had done too little to deal with 'harassment, discrimination and political interference' against its Jewish members. That, the commission ruled, was difficult if not impossible to reconcile with its 'stated commitment to a zero-tolerance approach to anti-semitism'. Over 129 pages the report unflinchingly described 'a lack of leadership'. Dozens of individual failures were identified: the party leadership interceding in the complaints process, or delaying the resolution of disciplinary cases. It cited the case of Ken Livingstone, the obstreperous old mayor of London who had called Adolf Hitler a Zionist, whose case languished before the party's disciplinary panel for seven months before it was heard. It had taken nearly a year – and the reporting in the *Sunday Times* that McSweeney had helped orchestrate – before a complaint against Pam Bromley, a councillor who had taken to Facebook to rail against the Rothschilds and dismiss allegations of antisemitism as the work of a 'fifth column' inside the Labour Party, was finally addressed, and another year before she was expelled. The pattern recurred, no matter how hard Corbyn's advisers insisted they had worked to break it. Jeremy himself was mentioned only in remarks made by others. The EHRC had no need to make the implicit – that these people were admirers of Corbyn, and that Labour had broken the law under his leadership – explicit. Nor did Starmer. To personalise and factionalise the report would overshadow a day for grieving, listening, and apologising. On the morning of 29 October he arrived at Labour's HQ on Victoria Street early, just after dawn, to give the speech that Chris Ward had written. The slogan on his lectern promised 'A NEW LEADERSHIP'. Now was not the time for an unedifying war of words with the old.

Two miles away at Africa House, the Holborn headquarters of the law firm Mishcon de Reya, the Jewish Labour Movement disagreed. As a complainant, it had the right to examine its findings an hour before their publication at 10 a.m. – a deliberately narrow window opened under duress by the EHRC, who were wary of leaks. Peter Mason and Adam Langleben, the JLM's leaders, had assembled in their 'war room' the leading lights of the Jewish centre left. Their host, the lawyer James Libson, had been immortalised in Hollywood as the defender of the libel claim brought by David Irving, the historian and Holocaust denier, and now assumed a new prominence in the public eye as the author of the JLM's case against its own party. Alongside him was Ruth Smeeth, the Labour MP who had been submerged beneath Boris Johnson's landslide. Under Corbyn she had been given a new, unwanted honorific – 'The Jewish MP' – as if her faith and politics were indivisible. At times she had concluded they were. Also present were Karen Pollock, of the Holocaust Educational Trust, and Ella Rose, a JLM official who had been filmed insulting a Corbynite activist by an undercover Al Jazeera crew.

For four years this unhappy few had worked to expose Jeremy Corbyn's Labour Party for what they believed it to be: antisemitic. Theirs had been a lonely struggle. For all their public defiance, they had wavered. They questioned themselves, their cause, in the face of the denials. Legal precedent seemed to stand against them. Victory – a ruling that Labour had indeed broken equalities law – was no inevitability. The JLM's other star lawyer, Anthony Julius – best known for his representation of Diana, Princess of Wales, during her divorce – had tried and failed before. His client Ronnie Fraser, the academic son of two Jewish refugees who fled the Holocaust, had taken his union to court after it voted to boycott Israel. He claimed, just as the JLM did, that it amounted to unlawful harassment of Jewish members. The law disagreed: a tribunal ruled that Fraser had made 'an impermissible attempt to achieve a political end by litigious means'. Would the EHRC make the same judgement? The complainants were motivated by politics as much as faith and morality. They wished to see Corbyn disgraced. In his lowest moments, Langleben – as combative a critic as any Corbyn had faced – asked himself whether he could ever succeed. 'Are we going mad? Can we actually stack it up? Can we go beyond the legal burden of proof?' The commission's answer was an emphatic yes. Libson examined the report alone, and relayed its conclusions. Each line was met with 'jubilation' and 'vindication', sources in the room recall now. As Starmer prepared to speak, a contented McSweeney took a moment to address Langleben in private. Over the phone McSweeney said: 'Now you know.'

They indeed knew they had been right about Corbyn's Labour – at least in the eyes of the law. What they did not know, however, was what Starmer's Labour intended to say at 10 a.m. Langleben and Mason took the view of Hillel, the Jewish sage of ancient Babylon: 'If not now, when?' If Starmer was not willing to rebuke Corbyn now, after the EHRC had ruled that his Labour Party had failed the Jewish community, when would he? Still the new leader stood firm: no blame, no names, just contrition. This would not be Corbyn's day.

Corbyn begged to differ. At 10.03 a.m. he published the statement that had taken so many torturous hours to write. It included both his expression of regret and his assertion that the scale of antisemitism within Labour had been 'dramatically overstated for political reasons'. That much was a victory for Milne and Murphy, who had travelled to Corbyn's Finsbury Park home to supervise his response. Upon their arrival, Laura had staged an eleventh-hour rearguard: Jeremy needed to change his statement. She had drawn inspiration from Evo Morales, the socialist president of Bolivia, who had been deposed in a coup the previous year. In the days before the EHRC's verdict she had tweeted a picture of the couple with Morales, who had told them that in the 1970s, 'coups were through the army and now they are through the law and reforms'. She added: 'I will never forget your words!' Indeed she did not. Jeremy, too, was the victim of a coup in which legal technicalities were deployed in place of machine guns. He had done nothing wrong. He had nothing to apologise for. She urged her husband's advisers to change his statement. 'No Seumas, you must do this!' Of Murphy, she complained: 'She's going to make Jeremy say certain things.' Again came the familiar warning: 'Keir will suspend him! Keir will suspend him!'

With such uncompromising counsel at home, Milne and Murphy thought the publication of *anything* that acknowledged that Corbyn had made mistakes was a small triumph. Soon it would bring his ruin. Team Starmer, preparing the leader for his press conference on the second floor of Labour HQ, took a less generous view. Having read Corbyn's words only, Ben Nunn resolved to tell Starmer only of its broad outline. There was no time to perform emergency surgery on a speech so delicately constructed.

Chris Ward called the leader. 'Corbyn's put this out,' he said. 'What do you want to do?'

Unmoved and resolute, Starmer said: 'The speech is right. It's what I believe. I'm not changing it because of what he said. That stops. If he said that, I'll handle that.'

The Irishman agreed. All knew that Starmer and Corbyn would now collide, publicly and violently, and that the press would demand an explanation. That would have to wait. If asked, Starmer would repeat his existing position: that denial or disputation was itself an integral problem of Labour's antisemitism problem. After he had spoken to a handful of journalists and a potted plant – the only audience permitted under Covid restrictions – that is what he did.

'I'll look carefully at what Jeremy Corbyn has said in full, but I've said a moment ago, and I'll say it again: those that deny this is a problem are part of the problem.'

'Oh my God,' thought Seumas Milne, watching on television. 'We have a problem.'

Starmer exited the stage and was met by Nunn, who told colleagues he needed to speak to the leader alone. The only available refuge was a multi-faith prayer room. Nunn pulled the door shut.

'Right,' he said. 'Jeremy is no longer going to be a member of the Labour Party later today. You need to gear yourself up for that.'

Starmer looked as though he had been passed a note by his junior in court. He gave Nunn a look that indicated he knew what needed to be done. Nothing remained to be said. By now it was just after 11.30 a.m. The two men went up to the eighth floor, to the office of David Evans. As general secretary it was he, not Starmer, who had ultimate authority over the disciplinary procedure that would soon be set in train. McSweeney joined them. So did Alex Barros-Curtis, head of Labour's governance and legal unit. Angela Rayner followed. Despite her links to the left, the deputy leader did not doubt that Corbyn was culpable. She told the room that he had been foolish. But was there a way out? Rayner suggested she establish whether he might delete his statement and apologise.

Starmer agreed, with one caveat. Ever the lawyer, he wanted legal advice before proceeding. Barros-Curtis, a former Magic Circle solicitor, knew the law was always open to interpretation. What mattered was what the client wanted. Politically, he said, there was only one option: Corbyn would have to be suspended or otherwise sanctioned. That, however, would wait until Rayner's spin doctor Jack McKenna – a millennial Lancastrian who had not yet recovered from two years working in Corbyn's office – had imparted a simple message to his old masters. 'He needs to walk that back, or he's going to get suspended.'

McKenna relayed a version of that ultimatum to James Schneider, to whom he had spoken the previous evening. Both had left the call believing they had reached an understanding. Schneider had sought to clarify Starmer's position: that his main priority was for Corbyn to accept the report and with it the existence of antisemitism within the Labour Party. That, Schneider believed, left him free to argue that the issue – and all now agreed there *was* an issue – had been exacerbated by factionalism. McKenna had sought to stress that Starmer meant business. If Corbyn did not make clear he accepted the EHRC's conclusions, then he would struggle to avoid the new leadership's wrath. On 28 October those positions were not irreconcilable. By 11.30 a.m. the following day, both realised that the earth had parted beneath them. Was there a way out? Schneider thought so, and assured his former colleague that Corbyn would soon clarify his position in an interview with Sky News. 'We're going to do a pool clip in fifteen minutes.'

It solved nothing. Corbyn would only make matters worse. He went to Brickworks, a Finsbury Park community centre. Waiting for him was Joe Pike, a Sky political correspondent. The interview commenced with Milne, Murphy, Schneider and Alvarez sitting behind Corbyn – squarely in Pike's line of sight. That a politician of such standing was accompanied by an entourage was hardly unusual. That they spent their short encounter sitting squarely behind their man, directly in Pike's line of site, was untypical. The reporter later texted his superiors to note the Corbynites had been 'trying to get me to wrap up'. Their instincts were right. Here was the worst possible version of Corbyn: tone impatient, brow furrowed, glasses skewed, red tie reluctantly fastened. As soon as the camera began to roll he began the defence that nobody had asked him to make. The EHRC's report did not 'acknowledge the work that I did' to improve Labour's complaints processes. Sixty seconds in, he lunged at the tripwire. 'The numbers have been exaggerated in my view.'

Word reached the office in which Starmer and his team had gathered. He insisted they find a full transcript of Corbyn's words before the interview was broadcast. Again the task fell to McKenna, who was promptly furnished with the audio by Schneider. He returned to the room and played the audio. Evans nodded along, processing each of the fateful words. There was, McSweeney said, 'no question' that Corbyn would now be suspended. He told Starmer: 'Corbyn's not withdrawing what he's saying. We have to suspend him. We have no choice.' Barros-Curtis agreed, but warned that suspension was as far as they could go. Corbyn could not be expelled from Labour altogether: his words did not merit it. If they tried, the courts would overrule them. Having consulted the party rulebook, however, it was clear that the statement and interview easily passed the threshold for disciplinary action: suspension pending a formal investigation. Starmer agreed with the verdict. Even if it was never said explicitly, all understood intuitively that Evans would now do the deed. Said one party official present: 'Everyone was clear that in order to protect the party, he had to be suspended.'

In Islington, the Corbynites reckoned with what was now inevitable. They were hurtling towards the very outcome they had strained every sinew to avoid.

At 12.37 p.m. Milne texted Rayner. Plaintively, he said of Starmer's speech: 'Wish we had had it . . . '

Moments later, a forlorn attempt to provide context: 'This is what JC has referred to in interviews; a March 2019 poll by Survation found that the general public thought on average that 34 per cent of Labour Party members had accusations of antisemitism and just 14 per cent thought the proportion was under 10 per cent. The real figure was less than 0.3 per cent. So, on average, people thought there was more than 300 times as much antisemitism among party members as there was.'

Rayner replied: 'This is seriously bad.'

Indeed it was. But by then it was too late. Rayner knew it. Milne knew it. So too did Simon Fletcher, who as the only adviser to have served both leaders was Starmerite unity made flesh. From his home in Gateshead, he called McSweeney to say: 'Jeremy's position and what Keir said are smashing up against each other, and it's going to be a very serious problem.'

It was some understatement. At 1.02 p.m., Evans emailed a letter to Corbyn's private address. The subject line of his message read: 'Important information regarding your membership.' Attached: a PDF notifying the former leader of the opposition of his 'administrative suspension from holding office or representing the Labour Party'. The offence: 'Your conduct on social media.' Corbyn, who had first joined Labour aged sixteen, shortly after Harold Wilson became prime minister, was told in straightforward terms: 'You cannot attend any Labour Party meeting, including meetings of any Branch or Constituency Labour Party, Labour Group, or the Parliamentary Labour Party; and you cannot represent the Labour Party at any level.' There followed a series of questions to which urgent answers were required. One read:

'The aims and values of the Labour Party include acting "in a spirit of solidarity, tolerance and respect". Do you believe that this statement is compatible with the aims and values of the Labour Party? If so, please explain why.' To Corbyn these impersonal administrative formalities were almost Kafkaesque. Still, help would be on hand as he processed this abrupt end to nearly six decades in the Labour Party. 'There are a number of organisations available who can offer support for your wellbeing.' Evans recommended Corbyn contact his GP, email Citizens Advice, or call the Samaritans. 'They offer a safe place for anyone to talk any time they like, in their own way – about whatever's getting to them.' He might turn to friendly colleagues, too: 'You should also feel able to seek support both through the whips' office and through the Leader of the Opposition's Office. Please feel free to contact Nick Brown, Opposition Chief Whip or Morgan McSweeney, Chief of Staff in LOTO [the Leader of the Opposition's office] if you would like to access this support.'

All that remained was to release the news to an expectant media. Nunn typed twenty-four words into WhatsApp. 'In the light of his comments made today, and his failure to retract them subsequently, the Labour Party has suspended Jeremy Corbyn pending investigation.' The hairs stood up on the nape of his neck. He pressed send.

7

'Let's all be friends'

The National Hemp Service, a little shop on the Stroud Green Road out of Islington North, sells relaxants infused with cannabidiol, extracted from marijuana leaves. Its proprietor was Tommy Corbyn, Jeremy's youngest son, and it was there that Milne and Murphy had retired to consider their options.

Relaxed they were not. The Corbynites were punch-drunk. They simultaneously declared war and sued for peace. Still unsure of Starmer's ultimate objective, their movement was divided against itself: had Jeremy been purged, or had his successor lashed out in a fit of pique? Each scenario had its adherents, yet proof remained elusive.

Nobody from the leader's office had called Corbyn to explain what had happened. He learned of his exile not from the personal email inbox he rarely examined but a cameraman from Sky News. Bewildered, devastated, he cycled through the stages of grief. Surely Starmer had not intended to do this? No leader of the Labour Party since the hated Ramsay MacDonald had been expelled by his successors. But Ramsay MacDonald had joined a coalition with the Conservatives. Jeremy Corbyn was an anti-racist.

Why had he been suspended? How they had laughed at Laura, ignored the melodramatic predictions of imminent doom: but Starmer had suspended him, just as she had predicted. There was no catharsis in her vindication. The old nightmare – Jeremy pursued by strangers through his own streets, accused of crimes he believed he was incapable of committing – began anew.

Milne and Murphy were told via texts from friends, forced to contemplate the end of Corbyn as they sat with his son. At the very moment of the suspension, at 1.03 p.m., Milne was still engaged in his futile back-and-forth with Angela Rayner.

'Obviously,' he wrote, still oblivious of the decision to which she was privy, 'we would have modified if we'd had what Keir was going to say in advance. He also told JC last night he would send, by the way.'

From Rayner: 'I spoke to JC as well. It's very bad. He doubled down on scale of the problem.'

Very bad – that said everything. The statement, the interview, the misunderstanding, the suspension – for the Corbynites there was nothing good to salvage from 29 October. And very quickly Len McCluskey was in a very bad mood. In his office at Unite, high above Holborn – and only a few hundred yards away from the temporary base of the Jewish Labour Movement – his mind turned to reprisals. Starmer had promised unity, as he had in return. The leader had reneged on their deal. Nobody, not least the leader of a Labour Party that needed Unite's money, reneged on a deal with Len McCluskey. He called Starmer to tell him so.

Starmer, too, was in a very bad mood. 'I'm beyond angry with Jeremy,' he told McCluskey. 'Jeremy put me in an impossible position. I had no choice.'

This was not the man McCluskey believed he knew – the very model of stolid, professional restraint. Starmer had snapped, lashed out thoughtlessly. Negotiation would solve everything, if he could be convinced to lay down his gun.

'Keir, before this gets out of hand, have you listened to the interview? Please listen to the interview, because it's not as though Jeremy is denying antisemitism. He's placing it in the context of the exaggeration of it, and how it's being used.'

That was unhelpful. Starmer had indeed listened to the interview. The only context that was relevant was that the leader of the Labour Party had said the opposite: that anyone who claimed antisemitism was exaggerated was part of the problem. Corbyn, he told McCluskey, had made a calculated attempt to undermine him.

McCluskey knew that fury would not be conducive to a deal. 'You need to have a wiser head. We need to step back, and we need to look at this,' he said. Their call ended without resolution but McCluskey told himself – and Starmer – that a deal would be done. He said as much later, when he called Starmer for a second time. Ominously, he did not pick up. For the benefit of the leader's voicemail he mounted another defence of Corbyn and his offending comments to Sky News. 'Jeremy hasn't done what you're accusing him of.'

McCluskey's intuition had not failed him. In the hours after their call, Starmer let it be known that his decision to suspend Corbyn had been no more and no less than a response to his comments. As had been the case with Rebecca Long-Bailey, there was no plot against him, nor the left. There need not be further escalation either. If he atoned, he might still be absolved. There remained the formality of the disciplinary process to which Corbyn, as a suspended member, was inescapably now subject. But, as the EHRC report itself revealed, those processes were political. If both sides wished to defuse the situation, they could be manipulated accordingly. A source familiar with those fraught discussions describes Starmer's thinking: 'You can't behave like this . . . I'm giving you a chance to just apologise and remove it.' There was indeed a deal to be done, and McCluskey would be the one to make it.

Or so McCluskey thought. His comrades on the Corbynite left – its praetorian guard in Parliament, union leaders, and the generals of the grass roots – were divided. It was a measure of their fury that they were soon convened via Zoom not for a strategy meeting, but what invitees excitedly described as a 'council of war'. Its members, so often derided as a cult by the Labour right, could not agree on anything. They disputed why they had lost the 2019 election, on the best candidate to carry their mantle subsequently, on whether to believe Starmer's homilies to their politics. Now they argued over whether to sue for peace or launch a retaliatory strike. Corbyn, taking refuge in the community centre where he had given his fateful interview to Sky News, cut the same miserable, withdrawn figure so recognisable from his final days as leader. Flanked by Murphy and Milne, he was a reluctant chair. Exercising executive power had never come easily, and so he struggled to make a decision on his own future. Plaintively he said he had 'no wish to place all our eggs in one basket'. It fell to his old friend Diane Abbott to speak for him. She denounced Starmer, whom she had never trusted even as their opposition to Brexit brought them together. Offering 'love and solidarity' to Corbyn, she cast him as the victim of a political assassination planned long in advance. 'I don't quite believe the decision was made on the spur of the moment,' she said. 'That's not how these

things work. It was politically pre-motivated.' Matt Wrack, the leader
of the Fire Brigades Union, agreed. 'Diane is probably right,' he said.
Corbyn's suspension was only the beginning: 'The people around Keir
are happy to see 100,000 to 200,000 leave.' To Richard Burgon, Corbyn
was a victim of 'lawfare' – just as Laura had predicted. His followers
had no choice but to punch back.

Dismayed, McCluskey dissented. These people did not know
Starmer as he did. As with any number of hard-nosed chief executives
and Tory ministers he had negotiated with, he assumed the Labour
leader was a man of good faith. More than that, actually. Nine days
earlier he had told the *Sunday Times*: 'I've always liked Keir . . . a very
decent man'. Their conversations that day had given him no reason
to alter his assessment. His blunt rebuttal: 'I am not of the view that
it was premeditated.' Reminding the call of his authority, he added:
'I speak for Unite.' Uncharacteristically, the trigger-happy Ian Lavery
joined the chorus for calm. As a former president of Arthur Scargill's
National Union of Mineworkers he was no stranger to self-destructive
protests against power, or kamikaze missions launched from the left
against Labour leaders. He proposed a middle way between insurrection and negotiation. Like the miners in 1984, the left were theoretically
the backbone of the nation. Without their hundreds of thousands of
members and millions of pounds of union money, the lights of the
Labour Party would soon go out. Starmer needed to know that he
could not survive without them, and that they were willing to walk
out. But an all-out strike was only advisable if there was no way of
securing Corbyn's readmission through peaceful means. 'Shouldn't we
try and do different things at once?'

Eventually, and as was often the case, it was John McDonnell who
won the argument. Like McCluskey, he knew Starmer well. He was
under no illusions as to his politics: this leader was not one of them.
Nor, however, was he unreasonable or factional. 'Before we start running around and overreacting,' he said, 'we need to know whether this
can be pulled back.' Corbyn's bottomless appetite for self-sabotage
should not be indulged. McDonnell recalled Stanislav Petrov, the
Soviet airman who had held his nerve when a malfunctioning nuclear
warning system falsely reported an incoming barrage of Nato missiles.
Then as now, return fire in ignorance guaranteed Armageddon. Before

it did *anything*, McDonnell ruled that the left first needed to establish the facts. McCluskey and Jon Trickett were deputed to negotiate.

Trickett had already spent much of the day in close contact with the men who had sacked him on the first day of Starmer's leadership. In the hours after Corbyn's suspension he had spoken with McSweeney in a futile attempt to seek resolution. He too suspected malign motive, and a broader plot to destabilise the left. At 2.51 p.m. he had texted the Irishman, accusing the leadership of launching a purge: 'Your staff are now trawling members' social media to find evidence for further suspensions. This is not what you said you would do.' McSweeney denied there was any such plan: insisting that Labour officials were targeting antisemites and not Corbynites.

By 5.17 p.m., formal negotiations had begun. 'I am authorised along with LM to try to see if we can find a way through this mess before we get to a complete meltdown,' Trickett texted. 'Any thoughts?'

'Shall we speak this evening?' McSweeney replied, seventy-three minutes later. 'Or have a zoom call tomorrow?'

'Good,' Trickett said. 'Of course. They are all good people and comrades . . . Obv Keir has to show leadership qualities but is he being painted into a corner? I hear he's doing a media round tomorrow – I am hoping that your extremely wise counsel will help him with some kind of formula.' He rued Labour's descent into internecine warfare at a moment of maximum difficulty for Boris Johnson's government: 'I am sure you are acutely aware of the consequences in a week when we had the Tories on the run on free school meals.'

By 11 p.m. the terms of engagement were set. 'I am told by Len M that you are going to set up a meeting at 3 p.m. tomorrow,' another text from Trickett read. 'He is speaking to Keir. We need to shut this down.'

★

At the appointed hour McCluskey strode into the boardroom of the leader of the opposition's office, with Trickett following behind. Across the table sat the Starmer delegation. To Starmer's right was McSweeney, an unknown quantity to both men. To his left was Angela Rayner, a familiar but not entirely reassuring presence. She opened proceedings with a request that their discussions remain confidential.

All were agreed: *We need to shut this down*. However hateful relations would one day become, on 30 October 2020 the past and present leaders of the Labour Party – and their advisers – just wanted the row to go away.

Starmer had said so on the *Today* programme that morning. 'There is no reason for a civil war, there is no reason to lean inwards,' he said. 'I want to unite the party. But I also made a very clear commitment to root out antisemitism. This is a matter of values for me.' So desperate were the Corbynites that they posed as supplicants, not revolutionaries. James Schneider – who would in time speak of Sir Keir with hair-raising vitriol – came directly to the leader with a long message whose deferential tone made its author queasy.

> Keir,
>
> I don't know your team well so I am writing to you directly in the hope of avoiding catastrophic factionalism and to find a way forward. I believe you desperately want to win to enact progressive social democratic reforms. I want that too. But this civil war could sink us all by plunging the party into perennial infighting when the whole party needs to be totally focussed on implementing the recommendations of the EHRC and how we deliver justice for millions in the face of this pandemic.
>
> I am more than willing to act as a negotiator in good faith to bring this about and help the movement in any way I can. Let me know what I can do.
>
> Best wishes,
> James Schneider

He did not mean it. Six months of Starmer's leadership had been more than enough to convince Schneider that he was *not* a progressive social democrat. To save its place within the Labour Party, however, the left had no choice but to prostrate itself before power.

Back in the leader's office, Starmer took the opposite view. It was the left's responsibility to lodge a convincing appeal, and a fair settlement. 'Over to you,' he told Trickett and McCluskey. The latter's mood had darkened overnight. Having exhausted his reserves of political capital in the hope of placating a furious left, he had begun to contemplate the alternative: that Corbyn's suspension was no accident.

He looked at McSweeney. Two weeks earlier, he had told the *Sunday Times* of his suspicions that McSweeney wished to kill Corbynism without the Corbynites ever realising. 'I thought, "My God, that's a very interesting observation." It's always been very positive with Keir. But then certain things happen which are slightly different from the kind of conversations I've had with him. So when somebody told me about that, I felt: I must keep an eye on that!'

Emollience gave way to anger. He withdrew from his pocket a piece of paper and thrust it in Starmer's direction.

'The NEC is going to meet tomorrow morning,' he said, 'and this is what it's going to say.' His paper dictated the terms for Corbyn's re-admission: the membership of the panel that would find him innocent, the statement it would make. 'This is your way out of this.' If Starmer did not take it, 'civil war' would follow: 'This whole thing's going to blow up.'

The machismo, the threats, the theatre, the factionalism: this was everything Keir Starmer hated in politics. He was the elected leader of the Labour Party. He would not be dictated to. He refused even to look at the paper, and flung it back across the table.

Appalled by the defiance, McCluskey demanded: 'Well, what's going to happen?'

Trickett intervened, seeking to remind both men that compromise would happen. 'Look,' he said, apologetically. 'We want to do a deal. We aren't going to say sorry, but we are going to issue a major clarification of what we were actually saying.'

Seven months earlier, Starmer had told the *New Statesman* of his admiration for Harold Wilson above all other Labour leaders. It was an artful dodge of the question whose most popular answers would cast him either as a sentimental leftie in the eyes of a sceptical commentariat (Clement Attlee) or a heartless sell-out in the eyes of wary party members (Tony Blair). But it also spoke to a deeper truth about the man and the politician. He would not slot neatly into someone else's taxonomy of the Labour movement. However simplistic his reading of history was, Starmer would unify, not divide along old sectarian lines. Of Wilson he most admired 'a mundane thing: the way in which he

actually managed to hold bits of the party together . . . he was spinning plates left, right and centre, but he actually steered through it
pretty well'.

Trickett reminded him of Wilson, whose enduring insight on party
management – quoted by the patron saint of Labour leftism, Tony
Benn – was that a bird needed two wings to fly. Starmer, Trickett said,
was suddenly 'flapping with one wing'. His attack on Corbyn had left
him in 'real danger' of shattering the very unity he had promised.

'We want to help, and you should have been talking to us, because,
you know . . .'

McCluskey interrupted. He corrected his comrade. The left *had*
been speaking to the leadership. He had, at least, for months: privately,
cordially, constructively. Why had Starmer, who had once sought his
benediction on appointments to the shadow cabinet, suddenly ended
that conversation?

'I think it's good to bring parliamentarians in,' he said.

Trickett resumed. McCluskey had said enough. Time for hard
truths. 'Look, Keir, I'm here on behalf of a lot of comrades on the left,
including trade unions, to know whether you're looking for a war. Or
are you looking for a way to reunite the party?'

Again the denial they had heard after the sacking of Rebecca Long-
Bailey. 'I definitely don't want a war with the left.'

Nor did Starmer accept that he had veered rightwards. Impatient
and incredulous, he said: 'I don't have any ideology at all. There's no
such thing as Starmerism and there never will be. I will make decisions
one after the other. But yes, I would welcome broad streams of advice
and information.' Corbyn had given him 'no choice'. But, he stressed,
he definitely did not want a war with the left.

'Hang on Keir,' Trickett said. 'Are you saying that if we could get a
statement agreed with you that you're happy with, and we could persuade Jeremy to issue that statement, that could resolve the matter?'

'Yes.'

Starmer agreed that McSweeney and Simon Fletcher – the honest
broker who had worked for Corbyn and Ken Livingstone – could help
formulate an agreed statement. A source in the room recalled: 'Keir
was quite explicit in that meeting that this could now all be sorted out.'
His preference was that his negotiators should meet with McCluskey

and Trickett the following day: the more protracted the negotiations, the greater the pain for the Jewish community.

'We can all come out and welcome his statement,' said Rayner, 'and that will set the climate.'

The next morning, Saturday 31 October, McSweeney called McCluskey. Starmer meant what he said. There was a way out. Corbyn could not be readmitted immediately: his suspension had set in train an internal investigation that could not now be avoided. 'He's going to go to a disciplinary process,' McSweeney said. 'He's probably going to get a warning or suspension. If he apologises, it will be less.'

McCluskey was at once encouraged and sceptical. Corbyn's clarification had already been drafted. But if he admitted wrongdoing, would that not be seized upon as grounds for his expulsion? 'No,' McSweeney said. 'It massively mitigates any action against him. But if he doubles down, if he goes and says more, that sanction will be worse.'

McCluskey was unconvinced. The Irishman tried again. 'Look: if he says that, if he apologises properly, he's going to have a much better chance. If you could get Jeremy to publish this statement today, Keir is on *Marr* tomorrow – and he will publicly welcome it.'

Trickett, meanwhile, made another appeal to Starmer. He texted the leader to say: 'We've now made contact with McSweeney . . . but I did mean what I said when I said you should be listening to the left.'

'I look forward to further conversation,' Starmer said.

In the hours that followed, all the Corbynites did was talk about Corbyn: to one another, to McSweeney and Fletcher, to Starmer. Within two days of Corbyn's suspension the statement that would secure his readmission to the Labour Party had been written. Later that afternoon, Fletcher shared it with Trickett:

The publication of the EHRC report should have been a moment for the Labour Party to come together in a determination to address the shortcomings of the past and work as one to root out antisemitism in our own ranks and wider society.

We must never tolerate antisemitism or belittle concerns about it. That was not my intention. I regret the pain this issue has caused the Jewish community and would wish to do nothing that would exacerbate or prolong it. To be clear, concerns about antisemitism are not 'exaggerated' or 'overstated'. The point I wished to make was that the vast majority of Labour Party members were and remain committed anti-racists deeply opposed to antisemitism.

I fully support Keir Starmer's decision to accept all the EHRC recommendations in full and, in accordance with my own lifelong convictions, will do what I can to help the Party move on, united against antisemitism which has been responsible for so many of history's greatest crimes against humanity.

'Thanks my mate,' said Trickett. 'That was the easy bit.'
'Yep,' wrote Fletcher. 'Jeez.'

★

Nobody made the ensuing weeks more difficult than Jeremy Corbyn. 'He more or less checked out,' despairs one of his intimates now. Starmer did not welcome his statement on *The Andrew Marr Show*, because it had not been issued. Corbyn had escaped. As his aides knew from their own difficult days in the leader of the opposition's office, he could not live in a world that had turned against him. When accused of antisemitism, he ran from the accusers: at first mentally, then physically. Emily Thornberry, his constituency neighbour, had urged Corbyn's staff to issue an apology, delete his offending statement from the day of the EHRC report, and move on. They agreed, but nobody could reach Jeremy. It was as if he had sunk into a fugue state. 'His face had gone solid,' a shadow cabinet minister said. 'He used to have this nervous tic, and if he did that, you just go: he's not listening anymore.' In the days after his suspension he disappeared. With Laura he left Islington for the Isle of Wight. Texts and calls were ignored. Once his friends had worked around his emotions. Now they were a firewall, trapping the left. No deal could be done without Corbyn's imprimatur. His reputation – and the existence of the left within the Labour Party – was at stake; and he was missing.

Corbyn could not hide for long. Under a dark grey sky on a wind-swept beach he was approached by a friendly stranger and asked for a selfie. The man transpired to be a nudist who had himself been suspended from Labour – for sharing a cartoon of Benjamin Netanyahu firing missiles marked 'defamation' at the helpless Jeremy. Corbyn felt that all too acutely. The bombardment went on and on and on. Len was calling. Karie was calling. John was calling. He ignored them all. Only Seumas Milne could reach him. On the eve of Starmer's television interview he had sent Corbyn a draft apology. Here was the script for his exoneration. Would he approve it? Corbyn said nothing. He did not say no. He did not say yes. Instead he changed the subject. An entire movement was chasing his shadow, wondering whether he even wanted to be found.

★

On the evening of 31 October, McSweeney had been traipsing the streets of Clapham with his four-year-old son. Lockdown had made trick-or-treating impossible: instead he doled out a sweet for each pumpkin they passed. His phone buzzed, flashing with the name Len McCluskey.

McCluskey, too, was struggling to navigate a new and unwelcoming world. 'I can't get hold of Jeremy,' he said, agitated. 'He's gone to the Isle of Wight.'

Matter-of-factly, McSweeney said: 'Okay, fine. Honestly, if you think you want him to apologise, the quicker he apologises, the quicker it gets accepted. In the end, this is about whether Jeremy can rebuild his relationship with the Jewish community after all this. Waiting to apologise is always a mistake.'

'I'll sort it out,' McCluskey said. 'Don't worry. I can deal with this.'

Could McSweeney believe him? Did McSweeney *want* to believe him?

Three days later, over dinner at Roger Liddle's, he apprised his friends of the political strategy that could – would? – make Starmer prime minister within five years. He told the room: his was not a ten-year project. Why would the Labour Party, still less the voters, permit them a stay of execution after losing another election? 'Everything we do must be subordinated to a one-term strategy.' Less than a year had passed since Labour's worst defeat since 1935 but the ambition no longer sounded like a delusion. The government's measures to contain the pandemic had unravelled and voters had tired of rallying around the Tory flag: the big two parties had drawn level in the opinion polls. There were two problems, however. The first was Starmer, not so much disliked by the public but unknown to them. Nearly half

of voters had no idea who he was. Those who did were as likely to dis-
approve of him as approve.

'Is he political enough?' asked one person present. McSweeney, who
was alone among the ageing Blairites in knowing Starmer well, did not
concede the point. During the leadership campaign his candidate had
likened himself to Bernie Sanders, the underdog of the American left.
Now, McSweeney said, he would follow the example of Joe Biden:
pursuing 'socially conservative voters reluctant to adopt transforma-
tive policy' and 'big-money donors'. Having built a big tent, Biden had
become more 'antagonistic' to the left. If he wished to endear himself to the voters that mattered, Starmer would soon have to do the
same. McSweeney called it Project Phoenix: his plan to rebuild the red
wall toppled by Johnson, and reunite Labour with the white working
class. 'In 2019,' he said, 'we lost twenty-four seats that Labour had had
for sixty years . . . and we lost twenty-eight seats in traditional wea-
thervane marginal seats. And ten more where the Brexit Party stood,
where we would have lost if they hadn't done so . . . Burnley, Hull,
Doncaster, Hartlepool.' For Starmer to win back those people, those
places, the left would have to lose. 'His rightward shift will cost him
votes to the left amongst the younger generation of voters.'

The other problem was Corbyn, and Corbynism. Starmer had spent
quite enough time compromising with the hard left. The time had
come for 'no compromise on the electorate', and no compromise on
everything McSweeney believed Corbyn personified: 'antisemitism',
'corruption', and 'Unite, whose officials milk Labour for money and
titles'. That vision of the future, starkly drawn, was clear enough. Jeremy's place in this post-apocalyptic landscape for the left was harder to
discern. 'We were always going to end up in this way with Corbyn on
antisemitism,' McSweeney said. 'His own world view is unshakeable.
It's not Milne's. It's his own. It was always going to be an exaggeration.'
In the immediate term, Corbyn would return to membership 'in a few
weeks' time, with a warning, but no longer to make his arguments'.
Then what?

The Irishman believed that denialism – antisemitism itself – was
'deeply baked into the party membership'. That, however, did not call
for the mass expulsions Angela Rayner had once dreamily described to
Trevor Chinn – losing 100,000 left-wingers to save the party from itself.
'Keir doesn't want to use the report as a basis of a factional attack, but

anyone not signing up will be taken out.' McSweeney's political prognosis was subtler than his Manichean rhetoric on the Corbynites may have implied. Over the preceding months the hard left had sought to draw any dividing line it could – war, refugees, austerity – anything that could convince MPs and members that Starmer was no true socialist. Yet this strategy was 'not possible with antisemitism', McSweeney concluded. If Corbyn's supporters wished to die on that hill, and discredit their movement as one long apology for his personal failings, so be it. In the event, few of them would. But there was a much broader swathe of the grass roots that saw Jeremy as something bigger: the 'key symbol' of their own ideals. If a vacancy ever arose on Labour's ruling NEC, McSweeney believed that Corbyn would 'top the poll'. If Starmer had fallen under a bus, there was every possibility that his predecessor would win that election too. Expelling him – declaring total war with the hard left – was for that reason a fool's errand. Corbyn's hundreds of thousands of followers would have every incentive to destabilise a leadership still struggling to find its footing: organise to avenge their fallen idol, seize back the party machinery, install their chosen candidates in parliamentary selections. They would weaponise the law, too. As Labour's head of legal, Alex Barros-Curtis had already warned McSweeney of a scenario in which the leadership went further than temporary suspension and sought to expel him permanently: 'Corbyn would win a case if he went to court.'

They could forget Project Phoenix, and Project Lazarus – McSweeney's blueprint for a Labour revival in Scotland; victimise Corbyn and there would be no project left at all. 'You'll turn him into a martyr,' McSweeney said. Starmer had two options. 'It's a choice between permanent parole on the basis of a final warning, or martyrdom.' The former would trap Corbyn 'in a vice', condemn him to 'suspended animation'. Unwilling to make the decisive breach with the only party he had ever known, the former leader would be cowed into compliance. All that remained was for him to accept the olive branch. 'If Corbyn doubles down . . . pending the investigation, it would weaken him. If he neither retracts nor repeats it, everyone's stuck.'

And for a few weeks, they were. Corbyn, distant and depressed, neither retracted nor repeated. His comrades grew anxious. Their conversations with the leader's office had been constructive, and their objectives shared. McSweeney did not want a civil war he might well

lose. The left wanted dignity. Starmer himself was still intensely frustrated by Corbyn's behaviour, but told Fletcher that he was in touch
with John McDonnell 'every day'. But with the accused refusing to
come to the dock, there was no guarantee of closure. That the EHRC
had appeared to rule that it was unlawful for the leadership of the
Labour Party to intervene in disciplinary cases added another layer
of complexity. But by Thursday 12 November – a fortnight on from
Corbyn's suspension – both sides were clear that Starmer's advisers
were not proposing to interfere in the process. They were proposing to
stage-manage it. That, at least, was the conclusion Milne and Trickett
drew from yet another Zoom call with Fletcher and McSweeney. The
Irishman had charted Corbyn's course back to Labour membership.
The following Tuesday or Wednesday, the NEC would convene a panel
to adjudicate on Corbyn's conduct. The desired outcome was his readmission. The question before the jury, said McSweeney, was: 'What
kind of sanction is appropriate in a case like this?'

Only Corbyn knew the answer, for nobody else knew what – if
anything – he intended to do or say. Would he withdraw his original
remarks and say sorry, say nothing, or clarify without apologising? 'If
there is no withdrawal,' McSweeney said, 'there will be an issue of
sanction. What we need is a constructive response.' Only then would
the nightmare end: Corbyn would be restored to membership either
instantly, with a reminder of Labour's values, or after a brief period
of continued suspension. Without the statement, everyone was stuck.
Starmer knew as much. The leader felt it would be 'helpful' if Corbyn
said something. As McSweeney explained: 'It helps with the politics
of the Labour Party and reconciliation and media interpretation.'
Without evidence of Corbyn's contrition, interviewers would make
mincemeat of the shadow cabinet. They would inevitably be asked if
they supported the NEC's verdict and the restoration of the Labour
whip to Corbyn. 'We need a statement from Jeremy, so the shadow
cabinet members know how to defend the reinstatement if the whip
is reinstated.'

There was no meaningful disagreement between the four men.
Trickett and Milne, however, had been reduced to parents pleading for
the headmaster to show leniency to their problem child: they could
not force the recalcitrant Corbyn to do anything. Ruefully Trickett
admitted the situation was a 'comedy of errors'. McSweeney preferred

to call it a vacuum. Something, preferably a statement from Corbyn, was needed to fill it. 'We can manage the front bench. We've talked to the Jewish community. We don't want antisemitism to be a factional issue, or about individuals . . . we *need* transparency on the statement.' Corbyn's motivations remained infuriatingly opaque. After the call, Fletcher again texted Trickett to warn that adding exculpatory 'context' to any statement would derail negotiations again – just as it had provoked Jeremy's suspension in the first place. It did not matter: Trickett still knew nothing of his intentions. 'Not heard anything yet,' he said. 'I won't agree to any additional words unless you sign off. It was right to hint that the best way to avoid sanctions is to go public.' Two days later, with only seventy-two hours remaining before Corbyn's hearing, Trickett confessed that things were moving backwards: 'In confidence: JC – very belligerent yesterday and today.'

His aides, despite themselves, were in dovish mood. On 15 November they finalised Corbyn's statement, still ignorant as to whether Corbyn would ever see it as such. It was written by Milne in consultation with Martin Howe, the lawyer whose services had been retained by Labour throughout the antisemitism crisis, and Howard Beckett, the dyspeptic Unite official who had helpfully taken to denouncing Starmer in public as a patsy of 'the oligarch class'. Their words had subtly evolved. Corbyn would make clear that he only intended to say that the 'vast majority of Labour Party members were and remain committed anti-racists', and that he supported Starmer's decision to accept the EHRC report in full.

Milne circulated the draft. His comrades were relieved. 'Seumas looks ok to me,' wrote McCluskey, with a thumbs-up emoji. 'Let's get this done and behind us.'

'Agree with Len. This is spot on,' said Trickett. 'The real task is how to persuade JC to do this.' The method: brute force and persistence.

The next day, 16 November, Milne and Murphy went to see Corbyn in Parliament. They found him in his office. He had returned to London after his holiday just as he had left: emotionally incapable of taking any decision whatsoever. Milne began a detailed explanation of the draft statement. Corbyn said nothing. To open his mouth was to invite yet another argument, another confrontation, more pain. His comrades were once again left to divine the significance of muttered asides and prolonged silence. The only thing that could be concluded with any confidence was that Corbyn was deeply uncomfortable. 'It's not that he was saying he wouldn't sign it,' one said. 'It's just that he was worried that it looked like backpedalling, selling out.' Not that he was prepared to say so explicitly. As another source recalls: 'He didn't really express it.' Milne and Murphy knew all too well that to paint Corbyn into a corner was to harden his resolve and sew his mouth shut. McCluskey, however, did not do passivity. He called Jeremy and demanded that the room hear his voice on loudspeaker. He 'pushed him and pushed him and pushed him'. His foghorn voice blew and blew, and still Corbyn did not blink.

Morning turned to afternoon, afternoon into evening. Milne, still trapped in the office, was alarmed, all too aware that Corbyn would not yield to pressure. Mindful of the cliché on insanity – doing the same thing over and over again and expecting different results – Milne resolved to do the opposite. Corbyn would only agree if he could be convinced that an apology was not a capitulation. Knowing him as they did, his friends grew fatalistic. 'He is extremely angry with all of us,' Trickett texted Fletcher to complain just before 4 p.m., 'and now Laura has turned up.' An hour later, McCluskey arrived for a private audience. 'Len has just gone to speak to JC privately,' continued Trickett's live commentary to Starmer's office. 'Punch up time.'

All of this had been expected. Even the communications strategy Trickett had written for those decisive days was laced with despair and derision for Corbyn's political myopia. He shared its text with Fletcher. 'I cannot see how he thinks this is a trap by LOTO – it was our side's suggestion ffs,' one line read. His refusal to engage risked destroying his movement: 'If JC doesn't stick to the framework as negotiated with LOTO then they may brief against him, his followers will continue to get expelled and his political leverage evaporate.' Petulant and child-like, he had turned against his friends: 'JC yet again thinks the very people who are fighting for him are the ones in the wrong – wtf does he think we get out of this??' McCluskey and Beckett would need to clarify that 'his political and legal guardians will not simply accept his self-centred behaviour'. The Socialist Campaign Group of Corbynite MPs were no use: 'The problem with SCG is they won't tell him, it's all vested interest there. And the people like Diane who could influence him, only tell him what he wants to hear.' Above all else, Corbyn was failing the very people to whom he remained a hero: 'This is one of the worst decisions that he has ever made as it compromises everyone who has tried to support and help him.'

Nothing helped. McDonnell and Diane Abbott tried. Both were suspicious of Milne and his claims of a monopoly on wisdom when it came to Jeremy's mind. They failed, too. McDonnell called, 'pressing him to do whatever necessary to apologise'. His pleas were pointless. Abbott, who felt she alone could impart difficult truths to Jeremy, was next. Corbyn could not bear to hear another variation on the same argument: that he was wrong, that he should give in, that he should apologise to his tormentors. Wordlessly, he passed the phone to Milne.

'I think we're coming in to land,' he told Abbott.

'Are you and Karie once again driving Jeremy off a cliff?'

'To be honest, Diane, I've really been here for a very long time to do the very opposite.'

After ten hours in his airless room, Corbyn finally agreed to do what had first been proposed nearly three weeks earlier. He would post the statement at 9 a.m.

*

17 November 2020 began just as planned. At 7.38 a.m., Fletcher texted Trickett to predict: 'This morning will be very interesting.' As a case study in political diplomacy, it certainly was. At 8.56 a.m., Fletcher made clear that the weight of Starmer's authority would be brought to bear on Labour MPs who wished to see Corbyn gone for good as soon as the statement was published. 'I have a lot of people awaiting my signal to start to put the political management into effect.'

McSweeney did not have time to waste. 9 a.m. came and went. A minute later, with no sign of the agreed words, he went to his Whats-App group with Trickett and Fletcher to ask whether the deal was off: 'Jon do you want us to pull the meeting?'

'We said 9.05, immediately after the 9 a.m. news.'

9.05 came. McSweeney asked again: 'Is it up?' Fletcher confirmed that it was.

'Good luck comrades,' Trickett said.

The Irishman was grateful for his efforts: 'Thank you very much Jon.'

Betraying his exasperation with Corbyn, Trickett signed off: 'It has been a pleasure to work with someone who knows how to take decisions.'

The day proceeded as agreed. The *Guardian* soon reported that Corbyn's case was likely to be resolved that evening. The names of the NEC members who would examine the evidence were published shortly afterwards. Conveniently, two were Corbynites: Yasmine Dar, a Momentum activist, and Ian Murray of the Fire Brigades Union. Another was diehard Corbynsceptic Gurinder Singh Josan, elected on a moderate slate coordinated by McSweeney. The fourth and final juror – the supposed swing voter – was Alice Perry, an Islington councillor whose longstanding personal relationship with Corbyn had engendered little sympathy in her for his predicament. In reality, she was prepared only to do what Team Starmer thought viable. And so it was inevitable that this panel of two friends, one enemy and a leadership loyalist would rule as both parties wanted them to. Corbyn had issued his statement in good time. He was clearly contrite. He would be readmitted with a slap on the wrist.

Was it a fix? McSweeney later told friends that he 'didn't know the panel' until the evening of 16 November, and had wished to end the era of 'stitch-ups' rather than exploiting them for his own ends. Simon Fletcher, by contrast, said to confidants that there had been lengthy discussions about its composition. A timeline of the process compiled by Martin Howe, the left's lawyer, notes that Trickett and McSweeney had discussed the 'timing and makeup' of the NEC panel. By accident or design, it had been perfectly calibrated to deliver the desired outcome and dispel any accusations of factionalism. Each member was instructed to discharge their duties independently – to make the decision that best reflected the party rulebook. Perry asked Alex Barros-Curtis what that really meant. Three weeks earlier, he had told Starmer that to suspend Corbyn was politically unavoidable, but expulsion was legally suicidal. He repeated that advice to Perry, warning of any attempt to expel Corbyn: 'It would be overturned, it would cost the party lots of money.'

He need not have bothered. Just after 6 p.m. the meeting concluded just as Corbyn had been told it would. He was issued with a formal warning, and readmitted to membership of the Labour Party with no further sanction. Chris Ward, McSweeney's deputy, congratulated colleagues on a job well done.

Immediately the left declared victory. It was Alex Nunns, Corbyn's speechwriter, who set the tone as Westminster sought to make sense of the verdict. He tweeted: 'Jeremy Corbyn's readmission is a huge climbdown from the leadership and a victory for the left. His statement released today didn't alter his original words – no grovelling. He clarified that he didn't mean concern about antisemitism was overstated, as opposed to the scale of it.' In an instant, after all the cries of zero tolerance from Starmer, the pendulum appeared to be swinging hard and fast towards a triumphant left. Momentum piled in, demanding rank-and-file members suspended for making the same mistake as Corbyn were readmitted with him. Despite the celebrations, the man himself had still had no formal confirmation of his readmission. The news had instead leaked from the panel itself, and the spin applied by the Corbynites soon riled Starmer.

Fletcher watched his old comrades revelling with some alarm. At 6.24 p.m. he wrote again to Trickett: 'Alex Nunns is briefing that the panel has readmitted him and it is a huge climbdown. His tweet about JC's statement is exactly the mentality that will lead to another round of infighting.' Then, at 7.05 p.m., 'There is too much cockiness around and it is fuelling a backlash.'

'Idiots,' said Trickett.

Labour MPs, who had gathered in Parliament to support their Jewish colleagues, were saying the same about the leader's office. Wes Streeting told Jenny Chapman, who as political secretary was forced to face the onslaught of outrage: 'He cannot come back. This is not good enough.' Margaret Hodge, the Jewish MP for Barking, called Jenny Chapman to express her incredulity. In 2018 she had called Corbyn an antisemite to his face: now he would sit alongside her. To readmit Corbyn as an ordinary member of the Labour Party was one thing – a legal inevitability. But if Starmer had restored him to the Labour whip, too, he had made a grave mistake. The leader had the right to give or take the whip to or from whomever he pleased: that was a matter of parliamentary privilege. Had Starmer invoked it to rescue Corbyn, who had only clarified, not even retracted, his original words on antisemitism? Hodge issued an ultimatum. There was room in the

Parliamentary Labour Party for Margaret Hodge or Jeremy Corbyn. Starmer could not have both.

Ruth Smeeth, the former MP whose enthusiasm for the leadership had – like Hodge's – become a bellwether for its credibility on antisemitism, said much the same. 'What on earth is going on?' she asked Chapman. 'Either you've done this knowingly – in which case, *explain* – or you've lost control of the party.' British Jewry, a community whose diversity of politics was inversely proportionate to its tiny size, rivalled the hard left for its tendency to split over small differences. But within minutes the Jewish Labour Movement, the Board of Deputies and the Jewish Leadership Council had all registered their dismay with Starmer publicly.

Let's all be friends. That was how McSweeney had described Starmer's politics: now Starmer confided in McSweeney that it was no longer possible. His reach for unity had exceeded his grasp. One side would have to be disappointed. One inevitability replaced another. Jeremy Corbyn had woken up on 17 November as an MP without a party, and he would wake up on 18 November as an MP without a party.

Necessity had forced Starmer and McSweeney to turn left in pursuit of peace. They had neglected to prepare their own people for compromise. Blairites had always assumed that unity was a byword for appeasement; many Jews within Labour had doubted Starmer's resolve. Both now made the same demand: withdraw the whip. Phil Rosenberg, a bearded PR man at the Board of Deputies, went pleading to Ellie Robinson, who did the impossible job of stakeholder management in the leader's office. Pacing around his tiny flat in West Hampstead, he said: 'I want to ask you a question. Technically speaking, as I understand it, there is a difference between membership and the whip. Now, it might be that Keir Starmer doesn't actually have the power to remove someone's membership. But he probably does have authority on the whip. *Please* consider not restoring the whip to him, even though he's got his membership back.'

'Okay,' said Robinson. 'Let's see what we can do.'

Jenny Chapman's phone was still ablaze, its list of incoming callers the stuff of Corbynite nightmares. Alan Milburn, the former health secretary and ageing prophet of Blairite fundamentalism, told her: 'Well, you've just got to fucking do something, haven't you?' Sally

Morgan, who had done Chapman's job for Blair in Downing Street, said: 'The whip *is* an option.' A third old Blairite, Charlie Falconer – who spoke as a lawyer as well as a senior member of Starmer's shadow cabinet – explained that removing the whip after restoring Corbyn's membership was perfectly legal. Starmer could invoke his parliamentary privilege if he so wished.

He did.

'What choice do you have?' Chapman told McSweeney. 'This is what we've got to do.'

The Corbynites, fleetingly intoxicated by power, crashed to earth. The hangover hit hard. From John McDonnell, the triumphalist tweeter Alex Nunns learned his declaration of victory had been taken as a hostile act. His post about the leadership's 'climbdown' had been 'unhelpful', McDonnell warned in a message relayed via a chain of trusted dissidents, like a samizdat pamphlet: first to the journalist Owen Jones, and then Joss MacDonald, another Corbyn speechwriter. Nunns must delete it. Sam Tarry, who of the few Corbynites who remained on the front bench was perhaps the most influential, made the same appeal to James Schneider. 'This is wrecking everything,' Tarry said. 'Keir is furious. You've got to get rid of it.'

Schneider assumed it was a joke. Keir Starmer was leader of the Labour Party. These had been his negotiations: this was his settlement. Surely it could withstand a single tweet. 'Are you serious?'

Tarry, a close friend of Angela Rayner, was in a position to know. 'Yes.'

'You're telling me that the leader of the Labour Party has taken a big decision based on him being annoyed *about a tweet*?'

It was more than a tweet. Starmer's very authority as leader was now at stake. At 7 a.m. on 18 November he arrived in Parliament, accompanied by Chapman and Ben Nunn. From the leader's office he called Nick Brown, his chief whip, with clear instructions: Corbyn was to be suspended from the Labour whip until such a time as he said otherwise.

If Starmer expected Brown to impart the message willingly, he was mistaken. These were not the methods of a chief whip – not as Brown understood them from his three decades of service to four Labour leaders. Under Tony Blair and Gordon Brown, his namesake and great patron, his business had been first sedition, and conciliation.

Under Corbyn, who had recalled him to the Whip's Office, it had been to maintain the unity of a parliamentary party whose behaviour he deemed needlessly hysterical. Jeremy, elected alongside Brown in 1983, was a harmless old peacenik. Karie Murphy was a friend. For those reasons Brown was an unwilling executioner. More fundamentally, he wished to avoid confrontation – not encourage it. He refused to remove the whip.

'This is wrong,' he told Starmer. 'I'll have nothing to do with it.' A friend privy to the discussion with the leader recalls Brown's belief that Starmer had wrongly chosen to humiliate Corbyn, and would 'pour oil on troubled waters' by doing so.

'No, it's not,' Starmer said. 'It's not what we're aiming for. We are trying to reestablish the credibility of the Labour Party and put right something very bad that we allowed to happen.'

Brown brought their conversation to an abrupt end. He would not negotiate over the phone. Meanwhile the Corbynites were still veiled in ignorance. Trickett, McCluskey and Milne had spent weeks offering assurances to Starmer and therapy to Corbyn. Would they now be wasted?

Trickett's day began as so many had in those weeks: with a desperate plea to Simon Fletcher. At 8.47 a.m. he wrote: 'Comrade, what is happening? We agreed reinstate with no further sanction except a reminder of values. Failing to restore the whip amounts to further sanction in my view. There is now a madness infecting the left. It's like what was the point? Any guidance off the record would be welcome.'

Fletcher, isolated from his own employer, could not tell him. 'I'm afraid I don't know what is happening Jon. It may be better for you to try Morgan. I've tried to do my best through all this to get a satisfactory resolution but as it stands this morning I don't know the position. I'm sorry about this.'

'Okay,' said Trickett. 'I fear what happens next.'

Next was another row between Starmer and Nick Brown, who came to the leader's office and named his price. Corbyn would inevitably sue the party if suspended again. As chief whip, Brown could be held liable. He would not proceed without a guarantee of legal indemnity.

Chapman was stunned by his insubordination. The chances of a lawsuit seemed infinitesimally small. 'What are you talking about?' she said.

Starmer, too, was furious. Friends of Brown describe his reaction as 'apoplectic'. He was 'screaming and shouting' so audibly that it could be heard through the thick walls of the leader's office. Another Labour official recalls Starmer kicking a bin in anger – an uncharacteristic lapse in discipline that does not feature in other accounts of that fractious morning. Allies of Brown are similarly dismissive of suggestions he demanded indemnity, as Starmer's team believed he had. He did, however, seek emergency legal advice from the Speaker of the House of Commons. Could the courts interfere in the sacred, privileged relationship between a leader and his whips? In principle, parliamentary counsel believed he was safe – though that principle had never been tested in court. Reluctantly, he did what was asked, calling Corbyn to impart the news that his successor had chosen not to restore the whip. At 11.02 a.m., Starmer finally spoke. He tweeted: 'Jeremy Corbyn's actions in response to the EHRC report undermined and set back our work in restoring trust and confidence in the Labour Party's ability to tackle antisemitism. In those circumstances, I have taken the decision not to restore the whip to Jeremy Corbyn. I will keep this situation under review.' Brown wrote to Corbyn to hand down the sentence formally: a suspension of three months.

Unity under Keir Starmer was now impossible. The Labour Party was again divided against itself. For doubtful Blairites on the front bench, it was a brave new dawn: 'Oh my god, this guy's the real deal. He's serious. I think this guy might just turn around the Labour Party.' For the Corbynites, an autocratic abuse of power. As Trickett wrote to Fletcher on the morning of 19 November: 'Jeremy suspended for three months "while investigations continue". What the fuck . . . ' Every illusion of Starmer shattered. To the Blairites he was no longer spineless, gutless, or hopeless. Observed from the left, he now took on the shape of every other Labour leader – the very categorisation he had always resented – an establishment turncoat. Wiser Corbynites had believed the initial suspension was a genuine, if misguided, attempt to restore trust with the Jewish community. Jeremy had erred, and Starmer himself had told them he had no designs on a civil war. Even pessimists like James Schneider, who believed Starmer wished to inflict 'moral death' upon the left after the EHRC report – Corbyn or no Corbyn – had not anticipated that he would seek their 'political death' within the Labour Party too.

In withdrawing the whip, Starmer resolved that ambiguity abruptly and conclusively. The facts had changed, and he had changed his mind with them. The left were not the partners he believed they could be. They could not be friends. Corbyn had disappeared. McCluskey had threatened him. Nunns had goaded him. Colleagues who had lived and breathed the toxic atmosphere of Labourism might have thought such behaviour inescapable. That was politics. But Starmer said no. To such a self-regarding professional it was all outrageous. From his earliest days in Parliament he had diagnosed in the Labour Party an abject lack of seriousness: the bitchiness, the bartering, the indivisibility of the private and political. The left were not alone in these failures but Corbyn convinced him to see them as McSweeney always had.

Bruised and betrayed, the left reckoned with the end of the beginning. The leader had told them that there was no such thing as Starmerism, and that there never would be. They disagreed. His politics were assuming an all too familiar form: rooted on the right, set against the left. Simon Fletcher concluded that in this hostile environment there was no more that he could do. He called Starmer and told him his continued employment was pointless. What was the point in the leader retaining the great organiser of sensible socialism if this is how socialists were to be treated? Fletcher had given old comrades his word that Corbyn's future would be resolved: Starmer had rendered it worthless, undermining his adviser and any future promise of unity either man would ever make. Still he pleaded with Fletcher to stay. There were 'many lessons to be learned' from the debacle, he said, and learn them he would. Unconvinced but unable to say no to the leader of the Labour Party, Fletcher did stay. It would not be for long. He well understood the grim subtext of all that had been said.

Len McCluskey never spoke to Keir Starmer again.

*

The Irishman was free at last. Friendship was no longer his leader's lodestar; no compromise with the electorate would replace no compromise with the left. His first opportunity came a week later, when the NEC came to elect its new chairman. First among the equals of the party's finely balanced ruling committee, the title came with moral authority and its holder cast the deciding votes. They had the power to bind Starmer's hands just as they had moved to hammer the left.

That was good news for Ian Murray, the big Yorkshireman from the Fire Brigades Union. He had sat on Corbyn's jury. Starmer had betrayed him. He had turned against his union, and his politics. Now he might drag him back. Everyone knew he would now chair the NEC. Buggins' turn: the deputy became the chairman, and Murray was deputy. In the party the unions built and paid for, that was how it had always worked.

Angela Rayner thought so. She too was a union woman. Even as the FBU and Unite and the Corbynites attacked the leader, she argued that it 'made sense' to elevate their opponent. It would 'keep the unions on board'. The alternative was to antagonise them into insurrection, to divert their financial firepower and political influence against Starmer. Unite had already cut its financial contributions to Labour by 10 per cent – or £150,000 – a warning shot. Why invite a barrage of machine-gun fire?

McSweeney was unmoved. He had questions of his own. Why should Starmer disadvantage himself for the sake of arcane tradition? Why should he defer to those who did not defer to him? Why should the left take charge of the committee that controlled everything, from parliamentary candidates to disciplinary cases? He was worn down by 'skirmishes every month'. Black Lives Matter, Long-Bailey, Corbyn. Margaret Beckett, the former cabinet minister, would chair the committee instead. He would not be friends with Ian Murray.

Nor would Starmer. McSweeney did not have to tell the leader to break with precedent, nor convince him to ignore his unifying instincts. He told him as much himself. 'Get a grip of it,' he said, unbidden, over the phone, on the eve of the meeting. 'Just grip it all.' He knew the left would oppose him. But that was now the price of power.

On 24 November, a week on from Corbyn's second suspension, Starmer would be vindicated. He told the NEC that Margaret Beckett would be their chair. Thirteen voices from the left denounced him, and walked out. That they were mounting their protest via Zoom rather blunted its rhetorical force. Unite's Howard Beckett struggled momentarily to log out. Colleagues with long memories were reminded of Eric Heffer, the argumentative left-winger who had marched out of an NEC meeting convened to expel the Militant tendency in 1986, straight into a broom cupboard.

Beckett became chair without a vote. One by one the Corbynites had disappeared from view.

*

But McSweeney wanted more. In early December he returned to Roger Liddle's dining table. He spoke with a new optimism. Corbyn had been humiliated, and 'civil war' – still less political Armageddon – had not come. The left were demoralised, not defiant. Starmer had once likened himself to the Good Samaritan. He could not pass by on the other side of the road if he saw a stranger lying stricken. His adviser's instinct was to exploit their vulnerability instead.

In time they would finish the job. Corbyn no longer had the option of purgatory: he was bound for oblivion. 'We cannot extinguish antisemitism as a problem in the party if Corbyn remains as an MP,' McSweeney said. Unite, the great immovable monolith of the hard left, would be next. To its members on factory floors: 'Unite is like an insurance company. You pay and get something when you need it, it doesn't matter who the chief executive is.' To the leadership of the Labour Party it was more like a protection racket. In the long term, McSweeney said, they would need to replace the chief executive with a more suitable candidate, prepared to work constructively with Starmer. As long as McCluskey was in post, however, their objective was to discredit him. 'Unite,' McSweeney said, 'must be turned into a pro-antisemitism organisation.'

Starmer had silenced his Blairite doubters, whose dinners had so often descended into counsels of despair. 'The PLP knows that Keir is the only show in town,' said Wes Streeting. 'Nobody ever thought of Ed Miliband like that.' If they were to be converted, they needed 'to feel loved and included and know what the plan is. They need to know what's guiding the thinking of Keir.' Starmer seldom narrated his motives. Yes, he had suspended Corbyn. Yes, he had given a speech – broadcast online, rather than before cheering activists at party conference – in which he defined himself against both the Tory right and Labour left. 'But nothing's happened since,' Streeting complained, 'we need to sort out our voices as well as our messages. We need our message carriers and enforcers.' Having vanquished Corbyn's movement, Starmer wanted for an army of his own.

The Irishman was optimistic. At last his leader had taken on the hard left. At last he had won. 'Keir's enlarging,' he said. 'He's a good performer, a good learner, and doesn't repeat mistakes.'

It was time to face the country. 'He's got to choose a direction. And equip himself with the people and ideas to get there.'

PART III: CHANGE

8

'Tell me and I'll go'

Jeremy Corbyn was gone, but the electoral inheritance he had left to Keir Starmer was not. In 2020 no British politician had been tested at the ballot box. Elections, like football matches, had been an early casualty of the pandemic. England's mayors and councillors had their terms extended for a year, as did the governments of Scotland and Wales. Lockdown made campaigning impossible. For Starmer, locked in the leader of the opposition's office, this was an ongoing torment. Ordinary people doing ordinary jobs, living on ordinary streets: they were his link to the world he had left for Westminster, the place that would never feel like home. For McSweeney it was a relief. There was too much to do.

Labour was bankrupt: morally, electorally, and financially – it had a huge deficit and Unite had cut its donations. In December 2019 it had lost *almost* everywhere. Had elections been held in May 2020, with Boris Johnson commanding 50 per cent in the polls, the losses would have been even worse. At that moment McSweeney's mission had barely begun. There was a war to wage, change to make. Much later he would claim he had always worked to a three-stage plan: reform the Labour Party, expose the failures of the Conservatives, and convince voters that Starmer had the answers. The first stage would be hard and ugly enough without the merciless judgement of voters, and the expense of an election campaign that could not possibly convince them that the Labour Party did not deserve it. Lockdown drove the leadership mad. But it gave them space.

It had not felt like much of a luxury, but in 2020 the only elections Starmer had to worry about – had employed other people to worry about – were those for Labour's NEC. He would soon fight thousands, in every corner of the country. The day-to-day business of leading a party that did not much like being led was so gruelling that Starmer and his aides seldom lifted their gaze to survey the horizon. When McSweeney did, he saw trouble. 'There's something stubborn about these voters,' he told his friends at Roger Liddle's in early December. 'They're going to be very hard to get back.' The voters of which he spoke had abandoned Labour for the Conservatives, Europe for Brexit. They were poorer, less educated, less comfortable with immigration, more exposed to the chill winds of globalisation.

These were the people McSweeney had always believed the Labour Party should be for, but they no longer believed the Labour Party was for them. That was the answer the general election had given a year earlier, and the opinion polls still said the same. Most of the electoral map was enemy territory, save for a few enclaves of urban liberalism. The numbers suggested Labour had further to fall. They also answered another question McSweeney posed of his friends, perhaps only rhetorically: 'Did they vote as a one-off to get Brexit done in 2019?' Whatever their motivations for voting Conservative then, Labour's old voters were not returning home. McSweeney went on: 'We're good at pulling Liberals and Greens, but not good at pulling Tories and ex-Labour working-class voters. 2019 voters are not yet coming back, and in some areas, we're going backwards . . . in Scotland, it's looking like we're going to be in third place.' Referencing the constituency that had returned Peter Mandelson three times, McSweeney predicted grimly that 'A lot of seats, like Hartlepool, we could lose if there was a by-election tomorrow.'

Among friends and in strategy meetings, McSweeney continued to speak of the need for a 'one-term strategy'. But if MPs or journalists had heard McSweeney speak of winning back Scotland or rebuilding the red wall, they would have laughed. Westminster assumed that Starmer's fate was to lose honourably, to fail better, and lay the groundwork for an election winner. Labour had been beaten so badly, and would continue to lose so badly, that newspapers would soon run headlines saying that Johnson would be in power for a decade. Starmer knew already that the left of the Labour Party was unconvinced of his abilities – they were not shy of saying so. Even outwardly loyal MPs and shadow cabinet ministers who served at his pleasure whispered to journalists that the art of politics might be beyond him, that he was a dullard and a dud. In the first months of 2021 they worked to disprove

McSweeney's predictions about Hartlepool and towns like it: sometimes methodically, more often messily.

By the time of the local elections on 6 May, they knew they had failed. Even Keir Starmer would ask the question so many in Westminster did: what was the point of Keir Starmer?

*

In 2019 there had been a simple answer: to discredit the Tory government's plans for Brexit, and secure a second referendum that overturned the result. It was a winning strategy for Commons votes and Labour leadership ballots. In a country that had accepted Boris Johnson's invitation to 'Get Brexit Done' it was a guarantee of defeat. Dominic Cummings dreamt of a Starmer victory in early 2020 for precisely that reason. On 10 January he had written to his friend Matt Zarb-Cousin, by then spin doctor for Rebecca Long-Bailey: 'Starmer wd be so easy for us, we'll see that dick coming a mile away, central casting London Remain beta-brain lawyer! Afraid I may have to tell the media that I'm terrified of RBL so they all write I'm secretly frightened of KS!'

Starmer knew he had been typecast and so his team sought new roles. On 30 January 2020, the eve of Britain's formal departure from the European Union, he rehashed the staple ingredients of his campaign speeches in a *Guardian* article headlined: 'Now Labour must end the Leave–Remain divide. Another future is possible.' The rules of the political game he had perfected as shadow Brexit secretary had changed. He wrote: 'Defining people by how they voted in June 2016 merely upholds a divide that we must overcome. There are no leavers or Remainers any more. In 2024 there will be no Leave or Remain constituencies.' Not quite: Remainers still existed, in their hundreds of thousands, in a big Remain constituency called the Labour membership. Before this audience Starmer kept playing his greatest hits, demanding that the free movement of people between the UK and EU continue after Brexit. The Ten Pledges made the same promise: to defend free movement and grant full voting rights to EU nationals.

That was what the Labour Party wanted to hear, but what Starmer said in pursuit of victory at the grass roots only hurt his chances in the country. It also blinded his followers to the inevitable. As soon as he became leader he braced himself to disappoint them. Johnson had only a year to strike a trade deal with Brussels. Whatever such a deal contained, no matter how comprehensively it failed to meet the standards he himself had set, Starmer would support it. His first slogan promised 'A New Leadership'. That, aides like Ben Nunn decreed early on, would mean voting for Johnson's deal. Nunn took advice from Peter Mandelson and Alastair Campbell on how Starmer could do so without shattering party unity. 'We were trying to find these cleansing moments,' says one of Starmer's friends in the shadow cabinet. 'There was never any question: we were going to vote for it. We were actively looking for the opportunity to clear the decks on Brexit.' Another close adviser to the leader explains: 'We actually thought voting for it would remove the original sin of a second referendum.' For Starmer himself, the conversion was more straightforward than his closest aides had expected. He had surprised them when, as they marked the moment of Britain's departure at 11 p.m. on 31 January with drinks in the bar of Bristol's Hilton hotel, he said: 'That's it. No more discussion about Brexit. It's done.'

By December 2020, just as McSweeney was warning that Leave voters were still wary of the Labour Party, Starmer was all but confirming that he would whip his MPs to make Boris Johnson's Brexit happen – the very last thing that would have been expected of him a year earlier. He told Johnson at Prime Minister's Questions: 'Labour will vote in the national interest, not in the party interest.' To the leadership, those were really one and the same. That month Marcus Roberts, the YouGov pollster whose data refined McSweeney's instinctive judgements into strategies, wrote a memo for the leadership that advised the best possible policy on Europe amounted to shutting up and moving on: 'Sir Keir's Labour Party can argue for a closer relationship with the European Union as long as it accepts that Brexit itself is the settled will of the British people for the foreseeable future and that people are exhausted by the idea of opening up the discussion again – even as the majority now think it was wrong.' More importantly, a leader that wished to keep hold of Hartlepool would have to let go of his old promises to Remainers. 'There can be no rapid return to the free movement of people,' Roberts wrote, 'as it makes no political sense for Labour to respond to both Brexit and the loss of its heartland seats with an argument for open borders.' At the same time, Labour's internal polling showed the advances it had made had come almost exclusively in metropolitan areas. 'We were making no difference in blue-collar places,' a senior adviser to the leader said.

The Johnson deal at last materialised on Christmas Eve. This left Parliament with only one week to ratify its terms. If it failed to do so, the alternative was the economic chaos of a no-deal exit – the only outcome that Labour had always been united in opposing. It had every appearance of an unenviable choice for Starmer, who would not countenance any decision that made no-deal more likely, but criticised the only available alternative as 'thin'. He now had only three days over Christmas to analyse its contents. Politically, however, the breakneck timing and high stakes provided the pretext his inner circle needed. MPs as much as voters needed to know that the party's culture had changed. One said: 'I think for Labour to have had legitimacy, then we had to vote for that deal. That was not an uncontroversial decision. But it wasn't just about those voters. It was about saying: "We're in the serious business of governing here." And in the serious business of governing, you take a flawed deal over a no-deal.'

The leadership was interested in symbolism, not substance. Entreaties from Neil Kinnock, Tony Blair and Gordon Brown to 'abstain and explain' were all ignored. By Christmas Eve, when Starmer responded to Johnson's announcement of a deal with the vow that Labour would 'accept it and vote for it' in Parliament, the refuseniks in the shadow cabinet – such as the former MEP and now shadow chancellor Anneliese Dodds – had given up. One said: 'The argument that won out was: "There's nothing we can do." We've been defeated, they've got their deal, there's no point fighting it. We've got to get power, we can't just keep picking at the scab.' None of them were among the thirty-seven Labour MPs who refused to vote for the deal: the largest rebellion of Starmer's leadership had the smallest impact, as for most the political logic was self-evident. As Rachel Reeves told colleagues: 'The politics are such that we cannot win an election if we don't get behind Leave.'

★

2021 would be one long test of that theory. Starmer's first year as leader of the Labour Party was an exercise in denial: of Corbyn, of Remain, of left-wing positions on the economy and national security.

He knew what he was *not*. What he *was* remained a work in progress, sketchy and indistinctly drawn.

'I'm in two minds about Keir,' Tony Blair told an old friend on 14 February. 'The plus side is he's intelligent, decent. He's not Ed Miliband, or Neil Kinnock. But he's not John Smith, either – I mean, he's like John Smith, but without his class. He's not a nutcase like GB. He's basically a London human rights lawyer who's not in touch with the people . . . he's perceived as an over-smoothed lawyer-like person. Too soft, not tough enough, inexperienced. Labour needs to find a new position as a combination of left: NHS investment, social integration, anti-poverty and unemployment; and right: crime, welfare rules, immigration, individual aspiration and reward. New Labour.'

New Labour? In the public's eyes – in Westminster's, too – it was anything but. As Chris Ward had written to LOTO colleagues in October, leadership's official policy remained the Ten Pledges, which limited their room for manoeuvre. 'I remember Ben Nunn doing some brand commissions and brand polling at the beginning of 2020,' said a Starmer confidant. 'Terrible. It was the age-old classic of: you come up with a policy, put it in the Conservatives' name, it polls ten points higher than it would have otherwise. You say it's from the Labour Party, it goes down ten. The brand was trash. We hadn't realised that.' That disadvantage – structural, inherited – was only exacerbated by the horrifying contingency of Covid. Over the second six months of 2020 the government's confused and chaotic reopening of the economy had helped Labour draw level in the opinion polls. So battered was Boris Johnson's reputation that Nicola Sturgeon, the nationalist first minister of Scotland, was briefly the most popular politician in England. In July, England's lockdown had been lifted; over August, localised restrictions were imposed on areas of high infection; in October the country was divided into three tiers, with freedoms varying from county to county; in November there was another four-week lockdown; in late December, Christmas was effectively cancelled in the south-east; and in January came the third and most draconian lockdown. Nearly 70,000 people died.

This never-ending assault on the ordinary lives of an exhausted public had hurt Johnson's popularity and undermined faith in his government. Starmer, however, remained pessimistic. Whatever the pandemic had taken from the Tories, it would soon give back. As early as September he was remarking to aides: 'As soon as there's a vaccine, they're going to get a bounce.' By November, the first was approved for use in Britain – ahead of the EU, Johnson never tired of declaring – by December, the first doses administered. For Johnson the end was in sight; for Starmer, a new world of electoral pain awaited. Polling did suggest that the Labour Party's vital signs were healthier than its own MPs and members were willing to admit. It was not that Starmer offended the public, as Corbyn had, nor that Labour was as comprehensively distrusted: by early 2021 it had narrowed the Tory lead on economic competence to only a few percentage points. Instead he was irrelevant and ignored. His first speech of the new year, on 11 January, compiled a litany of government failures on the pandemic but made no impact. Rafael Behr, the influential *Guardian* columnist, wrote that it 'mostly . . . sounded as if it had been composed on a spreadsheet'. The second, a month later, sought to rebut already persistent criticisms of Starmer's timidity with an incomprehensible new economic policy – 'British recovery bonds' – and barely troubled the front pages either. By then Nunn had taken to briefing the newspapers a mix of Starmer and McSweeney's electoral analysis: when the local elections came in early May, voters would take the opportunity to thank Johnson for the vaccine.

★

They knew that first weekend in May would be difficult. It was a chain-smoking librarian who made it a full-blown crisis.

Mike Hill was never supposed to become a Member of Parliament. He was thin and drawn, as grey and unprepossessing as his suits. He had spent a lifetime working quietly in council libraries, and for his trade union. In 2017 he became Labour's candidate in Hartlepool, and won. In 2019, when the Brexit Party cannibalised the vote of his Conservative rival, Hill won again, isolated on a small island of red in the new Tory heartland of north-east England.

Upon his election as an MP he felt out of his depth. In Hartlepool he visited a woman he helped as a union official, fell to his knees and begged her to work for him in London. He promised her a place to live. When she arrived in Westminster she learned her new home was Hill's bedsit in Pimlico. She also learned that Hill was in love with her. She said she was uninterested but still the married man climbed into her bed and sexually assaulted her. He also touched her as she worked in his parliamentary office. When she protested, he victimised and threatened to evict her. When she told the Labour Party, she was told to quit her job, not to complain. She ignored the advice. In 2019, Hill was briefly suspended, but soon he was allowed to stand for election again. He returned to Westminster the subject of three investigations: by the Metropolitan Police, Parliament's sexual harassment watchdog, and an employment tribunal. His victim would have to wait until 2021 for her day in court. Only then could she finally reveal the extent of her suffering – and how much of it the Labour Party had known. Parliament's Independent Complaints and Grievance Scheme would soon issue its detailed verdict on his conduct too. Early in 2021, Jenny Chapman – whose role as Starmer's political secretary obliged her to play disciplinarian and agony aunt – had received a call from Karl Turner, the Labour MP for Hull East. 'You need to know about this,' he said, furnishing Chapman with every harrowing detail of the woman's ordeal. The accusations were already an open secret among Labour's women in Westminster, several of whom had spoken to the victim. Turner told Hill to speak to Chapman too. As a former MP herself, old colleagues thought her a straight dealer.

Nor did Hill expect hostility. Chapman's old seat of Darlington was near Hartlepool. His Constituency Labour Party had nominated Starmer for the Labour leadership, as had he. They had been friends. What Hill told her would bring their professional relationship to an abrupt end. In time it would sever the ties between Labour and the seat synonymous with its former MP Peter Mandelson too.

'Mike, I've been told words to this effect,' she said, as she detailed the charge sheet. 'Have you come to talk to me because you want me to know that this is coming?'

'Yes,' he said. Hill told her of the looming judgement: that he had breached Parliament's sexual misconduct policy at home and at work, and that he had discriminated against the complainant after she had summoned the strength to report his behaviour. He insisted the report was unfair. It had taken his behaviour out of context. He complained of suffering imposter syndrome in an unwelcoming Westminster. He intended to appeal any ruling against him, and wanted the Labour Party's support as he did so.

'Oh my God,' thought Chapman. Hill had been her friend. Now she was political secretary to the Labour leader she valorised as 'Mr Rules' and 'Mr Integrity'. When she told Starmer the extent of Hill's misdemeanours, he reacted accordingly.

'I can't look at you while I tell you this,' Chapman said to Starmer, before recounting what she had learned.

'We can't have that,' he said. 'We just can't have that.' Hill was told to resign.

To McSweeney the case represented everything he hated about Labour politics: Hill's entire political career was a moral catastrophe, aided and abetted by the party's powerbrokers. Almost as soon as he had become an MP, he was sexually harassing his assistant. His suspension had been overturned so that he could stand again in 2019. For that decision McSweeney blamed Corbyn's advisers, but also Nick Brown. The chief whip was not a Corbynite. But nor was he the ruthless disciplinarian or enforcer of legend. Instead McSweeney and others in the leader's office saw Brown as leader of 'a trade union for MPs'. He was a powerful man seeking to protect other powerful men, like the Catholic bishops McSweeney had known as a boy, like Ted Knight in Lambeth. Under Brown's watch, McSweeney believed that disciplinary cases against MPs went nowhere. The two men had already clashed over Claudia Webbe, a hard-left MP who had been charged with harassment in September 2020. She was accused of a string of silent phone calls and threatening to reveal naked pictures of her partner's lover. Nonetheless Brown told McSweeney that she should keep the Labour whip unless and until she was found guilty. He had phoned her, and she had told him it was untrue. Surely the Labour Party should stand by her?

The leader's office thought not. And they thought the same of Hill. 'The truth is,' said one leading adviser to Starmer, 'he shouldn't have been able to stand in 2019 . . . he didn't meet the bar to be a Labour candidate.' Said another: 'I profoundly disagree with anyone who thought that we should have let Mike Hill carry on being an MP.' Only Nick Brown did. He believed the job of a chief whip was to avoid unnecessary confrontation with the electorate. He knew that in Hartlepool the confrontation would end only one way: in defeat for the Labour Party. There had not been a parliamentary by-election since August 2019. Losing councillors to the Conservative Party in May would be painful, but in Westminster politicians could tell themselves that there was still time to avoid oblivion. Losing a parliamentary seat that had been held by Labour since 1964 would generate fear and panic. Having sought salvation in Starmer, they would be forced to reckon with the inevitability of their own political deaths.

Hill eventually resigned on 16 March. Breaking the news, Henry Zeffman of *The Times* echoed Brown's assessment of the stakes: 'Mike Hill, Labour MP for Hartlepool, is quitting the Commons. Prepare for a dynamite by-election deep in "Red Wall" territory.' Writing in the same newspaper the next day, Peter Mandelson – who had heard McSweeney's private prediction that the seat would be lost – warned: 'Keir Starmer will be hoping that normal service can be restored in Hartlepool but it will be a tough fight. The Tories feel they have the wind in their sails and the town will drop into their lap.'

Team Starmer now prepared for a controlled explosion. Almost immediately they moved the writ for Hartlepudlians to elect a new MP on the same day as the local elections, a decision all involved would later regret. Labour's candidate would be chosen from an unusual shortlist: it had one name. Laura Pidcock, the great hope of the hard left who had been Corbyn's heir-designate before she lost her seat in 2019, was briefly mooted. But Chapman had only one man in mind: her friend Paul Williams, a GP who had unexpectedly won the neighbouring seat of Stockton South in 2017, only to lose it again two years later. To put only one hopeful before members was unheard of. It was a stitch-up. In his Ten Pledges, Starmer had promised that the 'undemocratic' imposition of parliamentary candidates by the leadership would end, and in Hartlepool that promise was broken in order to avert the disaster of a Corbynite candidate running in the red wall. That it was broken so brazenly discomforted some in the leader's office, who took the opposite view of questions of discipline and process to Chapman and McSweeney. 'There was a cavalier approach to these matters that started to develop,' said one disgruntled LOTO aide. Some in the leader's office had begun to diagnose in Starmer's inner team a preference for gung-ho decision-making. 'I think that was completely exemplified by the decision to have a one-person shortlist in Hartlepool,' one said.

Even the leader's allies on the NEC agreed, with a handful – including McSweeney's friend Alice Perry – refusing to endorse the selection. Williams, a Remainer sent to Brexit-backing Hartlepool to fight a losing battle, spent much of the campaign apologising for historic tweets in which he had mused on the identity of his favourite 'Tory milf'.

★

They knew they would lose. 'Getting Mike out was totally the right thing, given what he had done,' says one of Starmer's inner circle now. 'But I think what we should have said is that we'd lose Hartlepool as a result of doing the right thing.' Another agrees: 'It was the right thing to hold a by-election. But we should have been really clear from the start. We're going to lose this. And we're going to lose badly.'

Yet Starmer was told that he might win.

Early on in the campaign, Chris Ward had asked Labour's field team: 'Do we have any chance of winning this?'

'We have a chance,' said an official. 'But not a good one.' Starmer heard much the same. 'You have a chance here,' he was told.

As well as predicting a defeat in Hartlepool, McSweeney had told his friends at Roger Liddle's dinner table that the May elections would 'test all our systems as if running a general election campaign'. To that Angela Rayner said: what systems? She had three titles: deputy leader of the Labour Party, Labour Party chair, and national campaign coordinator. To outsiders the last might have implied at least some oversight of the first campaigns Labour had run since 2019. In reality it was a sinecure. She coordinated nothing. She had become used to Starmer and McSweeney inviting her to work with them, and nothing materialising. But one of her advisers recalls: 'She didn't have any authority. Jenny Chapman was running the campaign, Simon Fletcher – the head of campaigns – was ignored by the comms team, and we didn't even know what the grid was.'* Chapman, one of the few northern women in the Labour Party who had not struck up a friendship with Rayner, had taken control of the by now totemic contest on the Tees. The deputy leader felt frozen out. A Starmer aide agrees that in no meaningful sense was Rayner controlling the campaign. 'No, not really. The leadership is very suspicious of her.'

Just as her chief of staff Nick Parrott had warned before her election, she had become Labour's version of the Queen. There were

---

* The 'grid' is the coordinated diary of all announcements, appearances and events.

warm and cordial weekly audiences with Starmer, but meaningful power was exercised by his team. 'She would have these meetings with Keir where they would agree on a way of working . . . Keir would discuss with her, consult on things with her, obviously value her input, role, influence, and then a couple of days later, something would happen, or something wouldn't happen, that wouldn't match up to that.' To her dismay, Rayner found her advisers were initially excluded from campaign meetings. When they were finally invited in, they discovered she had been omitted from the grid entirely. 'I saw a grid and it didn't have Angela on it,' said one. 'I thought: this is gonna be a problem . . . not that she needs to be front and centre, but what are we going to do with her for six weeks?' As far as Rayner's team was concerned, that Labour's most recognisable northern woman did not feature in its charm offensive of northern voters was an ominous sign. Through no fault of his own, Starmer had been dealt a terrible hand. 'It was a fucking shit show in the fuck factory,' said a senior Labour official. 'In the context of Covid: can you campaign? You can't really campaign. And the national political headwinds were nationalistic: Captain Tom,[*] Boris.'

McSweeney despaired. By the end of March both he and Chapman were regularly subjected to hostile briefings in the newspapers. Speaking anonymously, shadow cabinet ministers would bemoan his caution, the apparent lack of vision. They did not know that he agreed with them. He too was horrified by the campaign grid. The notional focus of its first week was crime, but instead Labour was sucked into three days of commentary on the Sewell Report – a Johnson-commissioned inquiry that had concluded that Britain was not an institutionally racist country. Another senior Starmer adviser sums up the problem: 'Sewell said: "Look, there's problems with racism in this country, but Britain isn't institutionally racist." And then we spent three days talking about how institutionally racist Britain was.' Once again McSweeney felt as if his trenchant criticism of Labour's most persistent habits had, if anything, been too mild. Given the opportunity, his party too often spoke only to itself and for itself. He would eventually coin a self-denying

---

[*] Captain Sir Thomas Moore, a former army officer, had raised tens of millions for charity in the weeks leading up to his hundredth birthday in April 2020. He died in February 2021, three months before the May elections.

ordinance called the Tinkerbell Rule: 'Every time we are talking about things that are on the Tory grid, a Labour councillor dies.' He was embarrassed that a prime minister as disorganised and self-destructive as Johnson could derail the opposition's communications strategy. Boris laid traps, baiting liberals into outrage, and Labour MPs leapt into them. Even more concerning was the party's lack of data. In his past life at Labour Together he had no shortage of money to spend on polling: indeed, he had spent more than both Labour and the Conservatives combined in a little over three years. Now he had nothing. On one call with Labour's field operatives, Starmer asked: 'How is it in the West Midlands?' They replied: 'It feels good.' Had they spoken frankly with Rayner during those weeks, Starmer's advisers may have empathised with her. They too felt they had no control over the Labour Party's campaign operation. 'There was a disconnect,' says one of Starmer's advisers, 'between the expectation management that we were doing and the campaign we were running. We just had no data. Nobody knew what was going on.'

What little detailed data that did exist told a different story. It did not come from Labour HQ. On 6 April the Communication Workers Union, led by the left-winger Dave Ward, handed the first constituency poll of Hartlepool to *The Times*. It projected that the Conservatives would take the seat and win by seven percentage points. The Corbynites had emerged from the hard winter of Jeremy's suspension and once again asserted themselves. Ward derided Starmer as 'far too timid'. In a merciless piece accompanying the poll he wrote: 'The country has been left shrugging its shoulders asking, "Who are you?"' Ben Nunn, who had the impossible job of spinning the looming disaster into something the press might write up as a triumph, privately believed there was an easy answer to Ward's question. Starmer was not an incumbent. With the worst of the pandemic at last behind them, voters were likely to thank those in power – whichever party they represented. He privately told Beth Rigby, the political editor of Sky News: 'I will literally hand you over my dog, my cat, and my house if we win in Hartlepool.' As they staggered towards defeat, Starmer's advisers wondered why they had bothered going through the motions of a by-election campaign at all.

Yet the leader himself was up for the fight. Lockdown's end may have posed a new political challenge to Labour but for Starmer it was a great liberation. McSweeney had noted his leader's struggle to adapt to life in Westminster's gilded cage. As soon as he could escape captivity, he did. Having visited Hartlepool three times, there was no question that this was *his* by-election. In the company of trusted friends he confessed his doubts. With polling day on the horizon he took tea in his office with Carolyn Harris, his parliamentary private secretary and cheerleader. He wondered whether he would ever be good enough. 'Whatever happens, this will be okay,' Harris said. Cackling dramatically, she added: 'I've got a feeling in my water! I'm a witch. You know that!' From Teesside, the shadow cabinet minister Jim McMahon told Starmer the polls were neck and neck. Pessimists at the top of the party thought that assessment – and McMahon himself – was ridiculous, delusional. They saw the campaign as a bad imitation of *The West Wing* on England's north-east coast. One official said of McMahon: 'He was the worst political leader I've ever seen. He was absolutely atrocious, but he thought he was Bruno Gianelli.'

6 May 2021 remains the most fateful day of Keir Starmer's leadership of the Labour Party. On that, all who lived it with him now agree. That morning there was no consensus. What little Starmer said publicly on the eve of the elections reflected the confusing cacophony of voices he was hearing in private. 'When things go right, the leader takes the plaudits; when they don't go right, the leader carries the can and takes responsibility,' he said. Which was it to be? The leader had no idea. Only a day earlier, leaked canvassing returns had suggested that fewer than half of the voters who had backed Labour in 2019 would do so again. Yet Labour HQ told Starmer he would win by at least 5,000 votes. That had sounded implausible to staff in the leader's office even before they went to Hartlepool on polling day. It was a crash course in the new political reality. Yasmeen Sebbana, Starmer's private secretary, knocked on the doors of lifelong Labour voters and was told: 'I'm never voting Labour again.' Another told Ben Nunn: 'Your guy seems fine, but Boris is paying 80 per cent of my wages at the moment, and he's just given me a vaccine. I'm going to vote for them.'

Starmer, stuck in London, remained oblivious. As his aides heard no after no from the people of Hartlepool, he demanded they tell him yes. Chris Ward was gathering his belongings in a hotel, preparing to return to Westminster, when the leader called. 'How is it on the doors?'

'We've obviously lost,' Ward said. 'We've lost by a long way . . . '

Starmer interrupted. 'That's not what I'm being told. Go back out there. Go and find more voters. There are more voters there. I'm being told there are.'

'You have lost this fight,' Ward said. 'This is not close. Morgan will phone you in a minute and talk you through it.'

Starmer asked the same of McSweeney. 'How's it going?'

'We're definitely going to lose.'

'How do you know?'

'Everyone who's not down as Labour – there's only 6,500 who are – is anti us,' McSweeney told him. Party officials had told Starmer: 'The doorstep seems really positive.' They were wrong.

When they spoke for a second time, McSweeney told Starmer: 'We're going to get walloped.'

Still unwilling to believe it, the leader texted Simon Fletcher instead. What was *his* take on Hartlepool? Fletcher warned that turnout was higher in Tory wards than in old Labour strongholds. Yet even after polls closed, Starmer was told that Labour had won Hartlepool by 1,000 votes. Surrounded by reporters in the sports hall of a municipal leisure centre, Chapman quickly realised they were wrong.

Just after midnight, Starmer texted Simon Fletcher and at last reckoned with reality. 'I'm assuming we've lost Hartlepool,' he wrote. 'I'm going to go there tomorrow to make clear that I care. We're not walking away. And I'll take full responsibility for the results and not cast around for excuses.'

At 4 a.m. the verdict was announced. Labour had lost Hartlepool by 6,940 votes.

★

His team had arrived at that assumption much earlier. At 3 p.m. on polling day, Ward and Nunn had left Hartlepool at McSweeney's suggestion to return to London. There were statements to write, politicians to brief – a storm to weather. Unbeknown to Starmer, the plan for defeat no longer included a return visit. The previous evening Chapman described that plan as 'insane'. 'The party members won't speak to you, the staff won't want to speak to you, everyone will be knackered and upset . . . the Tories will have their victory lap, and you'll be there. No one will want to know you.' She was right. On the morning of Friday 7 May, Johnson flew to Hartlepool and landed a hero. He went to the marina that had been built with money from New Labour and the European Union, stood before a thirty-foot inflatable effigy of himself, and claimed the entire country thought like Hartlepool. 'If there is a lesson out of this whole election campaign across the whole of the UK,' he said, 'it is that the public want us to get on with focusing on their needs and their priorities, coming through the pandemic and making sure we build back better.'

Starmer was miles away, in mind and in body. Like Johnson, he had stayed up to hear the verdict. Deflated, he spoke briefly to Ward, and approved the statement that was issued to the press two hours later: 'We've said all along the north-east and the Midlands would be difficult. We also said the places declaring Thursday would be particularly difficult. But the message from voters is clear and we have heard it. Labour has not yet changed nearly enough for voters to place their trust in us. We understand that. We are listening. And we will now redouble our efforts.' In truth, they knew that they had done too little to prepare Westminster for a rout of such a scale that it led *The Times* to declare on its front page: 'Johnson eyes decade in power.' In the *Guardian*: 'Labour in turmoil after Tories inflict huge defeats.' Nothing they said would disrupt that narrative, which by then had a lethal momentum. Starmer's aides retreated to the safety of rhetoric. 'People don't want to hear excuses. Keir has said he will take responsibility for these results – and he will take responsibility for fixing it and changing the Labour Party for the better.'

But what did change mean? On the *Today* programme, opening bids came from Peter Mandelson and John McDonnell. Mandelson for once dispensed with his waspish stage persona. He did not blame Starmer, acknowledging Labour had suffered from 'long Covid' and 'long Corbyn'. But his patience was wearing thin: 'What I would say is this, and remind the party we have not won a general election in sixteen years. We have lost the last four, with 2019 a catastrophe. The last eleven general elections read: lose, lose, lose, lose, Blair, Blair, Blair, lose, lose, lose, lose. We need for once in this party to learn the lessons of those victories as well as those defeats, and I hope very much that Keir and his colleagues in the shadow cabinet say this means that we have got to change direction and that they actually mean it.' He angrily spat out every word. McDonnell, who instead adopted the tone of an oncologist giving a terminal diagnosis, accused Starmer of sending candidates 'almost naked' and 'almost policy-less' into the electoral fray. When he added that his leader should be 'given his chance' to 'demonstrate to people the sort of society you want to create', it sounded less like a peace offering than a threat.

Turn right, turn left: that morning neither vision appealed to Starmer. If the Labour Party needed to change anything, it was him. By the time he returned to the leader's office he had resolved to leave it for good. He wanted to resign. With Chapman and McSweeney still in Hartlepool, he was met by the small team he had employed in the months after his election as an MP: Ward, Nunn, Sebbana, and Stuart Ingham, his policy adviser. They had witnessed the very beginning of his journey to the Labour leadership, and now they would witness its end. The most important adviser of all had failed to dissuade him. Friends privy to their anguished conversation that morning say Victoria, his wife, had disagreed with his conclusion, but resolved to support him nonetheless. All that remained was to inform his staff. Ward was already waiting in Starmer's room.

'I think I have to go,' he said.

'What the hell are you talking about? Obviously you're not going.'

Starmer explained his reasoning. He had no wish to lead the Labour Party to another crushing defeat. Other leaders had been forced to carry the burden to the end by colleagues that knew they would lose but had never had the guts to say so.

'Do you think I can win?' asked Starmer. 'If you don't, tell me now, and I'll go.'

Ward protested. Starmer would not listen. For ten minutes he went on, damning himself.

'We're going backwards. We're losing seats that Corbyn won. I don't want to be one of those people who puts himself before the party and ends up having to be propped up when he's holding the party back. *I* was on the ballot, *my* party, *I've* been doing this a year, *I* said we'd changed, and we're going backwards.'

Nunn arrived and joined Ward in trying to dissuade him. 'Let me think about it,' Starmer said. 'I'm going to talk to Vic.'

He left the room for ten minutes and then returned. 'I still think I have to go.'

Ward remained adamant that Starmer should not quit. Nobody who had opened their door to Labour canvassers in Hartlepool had told them that they were voting Conservative because of Keir Starmer. They were voting for Boris Johnson, for Brexit, for the vaccine. They liked Ben Houchen, the Conservative mayor of the Tees Valley, who won that day with an almost North Korean vote share of 72 per cent. Some doubted Labour was ready for government. It was not personal.

'Don't do anything until Morgan gets back,' Ward said. 'We've got to talk to Morgan. We've got to talk to Jenny. They're on a train back from Hartlepool. This nonsense has to stop until they come back.'

Hours passed. Just after lunch McSweeney was met by colleagues who were by then hysterical. At midday the former cabinet minister Andrew Adonis, the Blairite's Blairite, had called for Starmer's resignation in *The Times*. Keir, he wrote, was 'a nice man and a good human rights lawyer, but without political skills or antennae at the highest level . . . the question now is what Keir transitions to and when; and whether Labour needs to lose another general election, to Boris or Rishi Sunak, before choosing a leader who can win.' Not only was it merciless, but Starmer agreed.

Ward grabbed McSweeney by the shoulders and dragged him into another room. They spoke alone with Ben Nunn.

'McSweeney. We've got a problem.'

'What?'

'Keir's going to resign.'

'This is awful,' Nunn said.

McSweeney struggled to take them seriously. He had known Hartlepool was a lost cause. As far as he was concerned, all Starmer now needed to say was that he would change the Labour Party. 'What the fuck are you talking about? We've got a plan. Let's just implement it. *Let's go and just do this.* What's the problem? We've got a script. Why is he still here?'

He too found the leader sitting alone, dour and disconsolate. 'Nobody was not voting for us because of you,' McSweeney said.

Starmer had not budged. 'I think I have to go.'

The Irishman was baffled. One day, years earlier, he had been plotting at his office in China Works when Labour Together's tame academic Jonathan Rutherford had appeared from behind the door, quoting Gramsci. 'The old is dying,' Rutherford said, 'and the new is struggling to be born.' Starmer was trapped in the same interregnum.

Once they had spoken of damning Corbyn to political purgatory: now his successor struggled with the same enfeebling fate. McSweeney's view was that crisis was their opportunity. Advocates for unity like Nick Brown, who had fought against a by-election and was still taking secret trips to the Wimbledon headquarters of the Communication Workers Union to discuss a deal to readmit Corbyn, could finally be silenced. Towns like Hartlepool had emphatically rejected the left. If they wanted unity, it was unity of purpose – behind a strong leader. For McSweeney, that meant change. Starmer needed to say so.

Plans for this moment of truth had been in train for months. In the weeks before the by-election the leader had finally acceded to requests to discuss strategy with his shadow cabinet. With Rachel Reeves, Lisa Nandy and Jonathan Ashworth – the shadow health secretary who had once tried and failed to convince him to stand for Gordon Brown's Labour Party fifteen years earlier – he met to discuss what change might look like. But their discussions leaked. Most blamed Nandy, the perennial suspect. Soon they stopped. McSweeney knew too that the press were right: Labour had yet to offer a clear alternative. With the help of Peter Mandelson, he had written a paper, *Labour for the Country*, that argued for all-out war on the Corbynites. It was to be implemented after the local elections. As the Hartlepool reckoning approached he was seized by an almost millenarian zeal for destruction. He needed proof that nothing was working. Privately, he almost longed for defeat. Only then would the wisdom of his strategy seem self-evident to Starmer. He had been careful to ensure that the first two shadow cabinet ministers dispatched to speak to the media in the morning after the by-election were Steve Reed, his old boss from Lambeth, and Nick Thomas-Symonds, the loyal shadow home secretary. Those two friends would call a spade a spade, not repeat lines about mixed results.

McSweeney did not want to say, as others had, that Hartlepool could never have been won. He had no time for the other strategies that were suggested before the defeat. As a colleague said: 'The alternative was to pivot back to our base, and say: "Look, actually, there is an argument for social democracy." Keir could have doubled down on a lot of the stuff we were saying about inequality, that it was the thing Blair missed out.' Starmer had been obsessed with the Marmot Report, a 2010 review of health inequalities, and had invited its author, Professor

Sir Michael Marmot, to address an early meeting of the shadow cab-inet. 'This is what we base the manifesto around,' he told them. 'This is it. We've got to do this stuff.'

McSweeney feared nothing more: that Labour would look for excuses, retreat into its ideological comfort zone, and talk even more loudly about inequality and unfairness; that it would wait for victory to be declared in the West of England mayoralty, conclude it could improve the wording on its leaflets, and settle for incrementalism. These were the 'forces of conservatism' that would strangle the life out of his project. He had to defeat them. Starmer had to resist them. But neither man could do so without the other. 'Morgan was brilliant afterwards,' an aide in the room during those uncertain hours said. 'He spoke in terms of: this result is why we've got to sort this out. It was the kick up the arse the party needed. He had been talking about what we needed to do to reset for some time. The elections gave him a mandate to really start.' Another recalled: 'There were so many ways we could have explained it: "This was never going to be a winnable by-election and it's not a true test of how far we've changed the party." That's how we could have done it. Morgan takes the other approach. He says: "We need to be smashed to rebuild, and we need a Hartlepool moment to rebuild the party." '

After an hour or so, with his team returned from Teesside and fully assembled, Starmer emerged from his stupor. Some staff who spoke to him that morning now suspect he had never resolved to resign, but lashed out in frustration. Once his despair subsided he turned again to face the future. He took heed of Denis Healey's first law of holes: that politicians who found themselves in them should stop digging.

'You've got to do a press clip,' Nunn said, 'and we need to agree what we're going to say.'

From McSweeney came one phrase, over and over again: 'Change the party. Got to change the party. Haven't changed enough. Change the party.'

The BBC arrived to record Starmer's first public statement later that afternoon. In the intervening hours Len McCluskey had joined the Blairites in filling the vacuum with *ad hominem* criticism of a leader with neither principles nor a plan. Staff for Sadiq Khan, the mayor of London, called to warn Ward that, if he did lose City Hall to his Con-servative rival, they planned to tell the media that the leader had been a drag on the ticket. It was open season. When their quarry finally broke his silence, he stood alone before two shelves of Hansard and a large succulent as if held hostage in the leader of the opposition's office. Johnson, by contrast, was filmed swaggering through Hartlepool like a conquering hero: all smiles, mobbed by adoring voters. Starmer's face was red and puffy, his voice raised. He looked and sounded devastated, but was clear he would not quit. As if he had short-circuited, he declared: 'Changing the things that need changing, and that is the change that I will bring about.'

Nobody was impressed. As he faced the BBC, Starmer's team addressed a more difficult audience: Labour staff. Jack Bond, the party's head of social media, spoke for party and nation when he said: 'That clip was rubbish.' Who disagreed? Not McSweeney. Not the rest of the leader's praetorian guard. They remain scarred by the memory of that afternoon in May 2021. Every testimony ends with 'really bad', 'terrible', 'awful'. Somehow, they fell even further over the weekend.

Next on their agenda was a long-planned reshuffle of the shadow cabinet. Ward wondered whether the weakened Starmer still possessed the authority to hire and fire. 'Should we really be going ahead with this now?'

'If we stand still, we're dead,' said McSweeney. 'Got to keep going.'

Starmer was no longer in the unity business. His new shadow cabinet would prove it. If his advisers had managed to convince him, there would have been a new shadow chancellor long before Hartlepool. Chris Ward had drawn up a new front bench that January. Ben Nunn wanted Rachel Reeves to respond to the budget in March. Starmer wanted them to go away. Whenever the prospect of a reshuffle was raised, however tentatively, he said: 'I haven't got time for your fantasy politics.' On one occasion: 'I've got no time for your fantasy politics. Put your list away. We'll talk about that another day. I'm not doing that today.' On another: 'It's all fantasy politics, moving people around a chessboard . . . you guys can talk about that, I don't want to get into that. I believe in these people, I put them there, I don't want to be one of these people who just discards them.' It was too soon. He wanted his team to have the time and the chance to prove themselves.

Eventually, he agreed: 'I've got to do it after Hartlepool.' He finally looked at the list he had so studiously ignored. Fantasy politics suddenly felt very real. Was he too weak? 'Staying put would not have been tenable,' said a Starmer adviser. 'The lobby would have all been: "*Seriously*? You're going to keep your shadow chancellor? You're not changing anything? This guy's so weak, he doesn't even know how weak he is."'

Much worse was said over the ensuing days. On the morning of Saturday 8 May, Team Starmer – McSweeney, Ward, Nunn, Chapman and Claire Ainsley, Labour's director of policy – reconvened on the eighth floor of Labour HQ. Starmer arrived a changed man. 'Let's not talk about yesterday,' he said. He was chipper, focused anew on the mantra McSweeney had scrawled in his slapdash hand on a white-board: 'CHANGE LABOUR. CHANGE BRITAIN.'

Beneath it was a media grid for the following week. Day one: reshuffle. Day two: a major policy announcement. Day three: Deborah Mattinson, the former pollster to Gordon Brown and author of two well-received books on the voters lost in 2010 and 2019, would be announced as Labour's new strategy director. And so on. For two hours Starmer pored over the plans, optimistic and energised.

This new-found positivity didn't last. Day one – the reshuffle – would last nearly forty-eight hours, make all the plans for the rest of May redundant, and permanently disfigure the leadership of the Labour Party.

9

The Reshuffle

It was all about Angela Rayner.

If Morgan McSweeney had believed the Labour Party could change with its deputy leader holding the keys to party headquarters then it is unlikely that the events of 8 and 9 May 2021 would merit their own history, still less one that remains bitterly contested by the politicians who lived it. But McSweeney thought the opposite. By that afternoon everybody else in Starmer's team agreed Rayner needed to move. Having been elected to the deputy leadership, that title would remain hers unless and until she resigned. That, however, was a bauble. It gave her a seat on Labour's NEC, but little else. Party chair, national campaign coordinator – her other titles were what really mattered. Candidate selection, policy processes, party conference – all were in Rayner's gift. There were two seats of meaningful power in Keir Starmer's Labour Party, and only one of them belonged to Keir Starmer. He and McSweeney could not have that. They had sacked Jennie Formby. They had sacked Michael Sharpe, the general secretary of the Scottish Labour Party, and then Richard Leonard, its leader. They sacked Jeremy Corbyn. All were necessary preconditions for the kind of change McSweeney wished to see. They could not sack Angela Rayner.

But they had to move her. Then, others in the leader's office said, Starmer might make better use of her formidable talents. Ben Nunn would say to colleagues in the leader's office: 'She's a great communicator, but I can't get her on TV because she's in NEC meetings.' In April 2020, the relative anonymity and inexperience of the shadow cabinet had been an asset. It had not upset the delicate balance of Labour's internal politics. It had even delighted Len McCluskey. Now it was nothing but a hindrance. 'I need five media performers,' Nunn said, 'and I've got none.'

The plan was that Rayner would shadow a major government department. Anneliese Dodds would be out as shadow chancellor, replaced by Rachel Reeves. Ed Miliband would lose the business brief, too. As a senior Starmer aide explained: 'He won't meet with businesses. Every business thinks he wants to renationalise them. Keir's having to do the heavy lifting on business.' After the Corbyn debacle, the Claudia Webbe debacle and the Mike Hill debacle, Nick Brown *had* to go. That aide again: 'I would describe him as being at best agnostic, periodically openly unhelpful.' Blairite media darlings like Wes Streeting and Peter Kyle were destined for promotion. *Telling* voters that they had changed would not be enough. *Showing*, with a new team of spokespeople and shadow cabinet ministers prepared to think what had been unthinkable under a unity banner – that might be.

But it was still all about Angela. As an elected deputy, it was in her gift to dictate terms. Only once she had agreed to move to a new shadow cabinet brief could others be moved in turn. Yet the Starmer court discussed her future for only ten minutes. Would she accept shadow health secretary? Would shadow culture be taken as an insult? Would she accept any offer *at all*? These were questions nobody but Rayner could answer. Starmer would ask her what she wanted instead. His advisers planned for their conversation to begin like this: 'Look, I want to do a reshuffle today. I want you in a front-facing department. You can have your pick. I want to put a new shadow chancellor in. I want to change the chief whip, but I want to do this with you and I want to talk about how it's going. That's how I want to do it.'

Rayner did not yet know what *it* was. Her staff had been assured by the leader's office that there would be no overreaction to the results. Nor had she panicked as Hartlepool declared. It was merely the coda to the electoral story that had played out elsewhere in the north of England two years earlier. 'The results as a whole were actually not nearly as terrible as they were made out to be,' said an adviser to the deputy leader. 'It just happened that the red wall had declared earlier on.' Indeed, so confident was Rayner that her role would remain unchanged that she travelled down to London with her spin doctor Jack McKenna to prepare for a series of media interviews where she expected to play defence counsel for Starmer.

Over the course of the journey her mood darkened. The *Sunday Times* had been in touch with McKenna. A party official had told the paper she had demanded the party pay for her first-class train tickets. The cause of her request was her fear of travelling alone and anxiety in large crowds. Death threats had done that. The effect was to portray her as a preening diva, a self-styled working-class hero enjoying the taxpayer-subsidised trappings of power – like Nye Bevan drinking Bollinger or John Prescott playing croquet at Dorneywood, the deputy PM's country home. Yet all Rayner really wanted was to feel safe. The abduction, rape and murder of the thirty-three-year-old marketing executive Sarah Everard from a south London street seven weeks previously had terrified and destabilised her as much as the near-constant abuse she herself received. 'She was fucking scared for her life,' another adviser to the deputy leader said. 'She's a very anxious person.'

By the time she arrived at Southside, Labour's Victoria Street HQ, her team feared the worst. They had watched David Evans, ordinarily able to access all, walk to the door of the room where the reshuffle was in the works – only to be barred from entry. Whatever was coming, they inferred, must be big. And Rayner assumed that big meant bad. Just before 3 p.m. McKenna received another text from the *Sunday Times*, informing him that the deputy leader had lost her job as chair of the Labour Party. Moments later, Starmer asked to see her.

At quarter past three he returned to his own team. 'It was really bad,' he said.

'How bad?' asked Chris Ward.

'She swore at me and walked out. I told her exactly what we talked about and she thought we were blaming her for Hartlepool.'

'So what happens now?'

'I said to her, "I'm still going to be sitting here if you want to come back and discuss it. We'll talk about the reshuffle together and discuss it like grown-ups." And I'm waiting for her to come back.'

Rayner had said something unexpected: no. She opened by telling Starmer: 'I'm going to tell you what you're about to say,' predicting he was going to strip her of her brief in an attempt to blame her for the defeat. When Starmer tried to deny it, she read Starmer a text from the *Sunday Times* forewarning her demise. He was shocked, not least by the accuracy of what had been briefed to the papers. No attempt had been made to prepare the ground for a move that would inevitably be interpreted by the media as a judgement on the success of an election campaign which, by her own admission, she had very little to do with.

She knew her partnership with Starmer was not working as planned, but did not know *she* was considered the problem. He tried and failed to disabuse her of the view that she was being made a scapegoat. 'I'm going to consider the whole shape of the shadow cabinet,' he said.

Rayner was unconvinced. 'What job do you think I want then?' she said. As the texts in her possession had predicted, he raised the prospect of health secretary. It seemed to her that Starmer was now trying to blame the occupant of that role, Jon Ashworth, as well. Rayner wanted no part in it. She swore and left for the pub. Jack McKenna followed, but not before confronting a bewildered David Evans, who was oblivious to the chaos unfolding in the building he notionally ran.

'What's going on?' asked Evans.

'I'll fucking tell you what's going on,' said McKenna, who told the general secretary his boss had been sacked as party chair.

News that Rayner had been sacked as party chair – only one half of the leader's plans for his deputy – spread across social media like Covid. Nunn's phone buzzed incessantly. He had promised to be home for dinner – it was his wife's birthday. It would be 2 a.m. before he could leave. Whether he would do so as director of communications to the leader of the Labour Party was also in question. In the Duke of York, a pub a short walk from Labour HQ, Rayner too was inundated by calls. Journalists were calling, asking of her intentions; MPs and trade unionists were calling, telling her that those intentions ought to be a leadership challenge. As *The Times* reported two days later, she had made that very threat to Starmer's face.

★

While the deputy was in the pub, the leader was in shock. His advisers told him to carry on regardless. One recalls: 'My argument was: fuck her. She's stormed out. We'll go ahead and do it, and she can have what's left.' Starmer disagreed. 'Keir didn't want to do that, probably rightly. We agreed that we couldn't proceed with the reshuffle until Angela had agreed to something.' They were in for a long evening, fuelled by industrial quantities of McDonald's fetched – in a moment of bathetic physical comedy – by the diminutive McSweeney. Before long, at 5 p.m., Starmer left. 'If she wants to talk to me, that's great. If not, I'm not going to sit around here waiting all night for her. I'm going to go home to my family.' Disbelief curdled into cold fury. Said an adviser to the leader: 'He just thought Angela was being unreasonable. He didn't want to concede to that, so he digs in much more at this point.'

That was not a luxury available to his staff. They spent the following hours fielding angry calls from Andy Burnham, the mayor of Greater Manchester, who saw himself as the patron of northerners in the shadow cabinet. Nobody could find Rayner, whose phone was switched off at the instruction of her chief of staff, Nick Parrott. He had himself only learned of her whereabouts from a tweet from the *Guardian*'s political editor, Pippa Crerar, who had spoken to McKenna: 'I can confirm she *is* down the pub.' Nor did they know where she planned to go. One of Rayner's closest confidants now says categorically that she was ready to launch a coup: 'We could have taken him out there and then, without a shadow of a doubt. All of the unions were on board. We had Unite. We had the money. Momentum were lined up. We were done. We had a rally of 5,000 people ready to go.' In those fevered hours Rayner's inner circle were confident that the GMB and CWU would have endorsed her platform of high tax, high spending 'Scandinavian social democracy' infused with the cultural conservatism of Blue Labour with tough lines on crime and immigration. Trusted intermediaries spoke to Len McCluskey, whose own intimates confirm that he was prepared to fund a putsch: 'Len was completely alienated from Keir by then, and felt he'd been dishonest over the matter of Jeremy getting the whip back. He was fed up.' So too Starmer's stalwart friends in Unison, the largest union of all. 'There was a sense in the party: "Fuck me, they're trying to take her out and pin blame on her that's not hers."'

One leading adviser to Starmer rang Rayner in tears, begging her not to run. They begged because they were scared. 'If there'd been a concerted challenge from the left,' said another aide involved in crisis talks that night, 'Morgan was worried that Keir wouldn't fight it. He didn't think he was making headway. He wasn't enjoying it. We were worried he wouldn't fight it. And if we did, we worried that it would take so much out of him that it would kill him.' Midnight approached, but resolution did not. Helpless and besieged, Starmer's aides reckoned with the realisation that they had indeed changed the Labour Party. It was now united in contempt for its leader. At 11.43 p.m.,

Burnham – whose own designs on Starmer's job were no secret, and now looked increasingly plausible – delivered what felt like the final humiliation. He publicly declared: 'I can't support this.'

*

What would Angela Rayner support? When Starmer's team reconvened in Parliament at 8 a.m. the following morning, they found the premise of that question was built on an absurdity. There was no such person as 'Angela Rayner', singular. There was *the* Angela Rayner, the woman who felt she had been taken for a fool. She wanted dignity and respect. There was Nick Parrott's Angela Rayner, a cipher for the canny organiser's own influence within the parliamentary party and his friends at the top of the unions. He wanted to cling on to the jobs McSweeney was desperate to wrest from his control. And there was the hard left's Angela Rayner. They wanted a battering ram to smash open the doors of the party that had been locked behind Jeremy Corbyn. Hour by hour the terms of the negotiations changed peremptorily. Could a deal be done if Rayner was given responsibility for policy on employment rights, and another shadow cabinet role? No: it was party chair or nothing. Then came the threat of a leadership challenge.

From the outside it appeared as if the problem was paralysis. Wes Streeting, the great white hope of continuity Blairism, was being interviewed when his phone rang.

'Oh, have you been offered the job?' asked a journalist of rumours he was set to be appointed party chair.

'My phone is ringing now,' Streeting joked, 'but I don't think it's Keir Starmer.'

In reality the ground on which Starmer stood was shifting too violently for any decision to be taken. Exhausting rounds of shuttle diplomacy ensued as McSweeney and Parrott hammered out the terms of an armistice. That paparazzi were documenting LOTO's despair in real time did little to lift the oppressive air of hopelessness and paranoia. As he awaited white smoke, Starmer was snapped on the balcony of his office, staring into the Thames as if contemplating the end. The leader had only one demand: that there could be no return to the status quo ante. That, he thought, would be an even greater indignity than any meted out to Rayner the previous day. Nor, in her heart, did Rayner wish to humiliate Starmer. After one conversation with her that afternoon, McSweeney told colleagues: 'I've spoken to Angela. She doesn't want this at all. She wants to put this back in its box.' Parrott, her plenipotentiary to these hastily convened peace talks, had revealed the same preference. The back benches were no place for a deputy leader. He knew enough of Labour's history to recall the sad story of George Brown: the deputy to Harold Wilson, a union organiser of working-class stock, just like Rayner, whose cabinet career had collapsed in 1968 under the weight of alcoholism, economic policy disputes and petty resentments. Brown had retained the paper dignity of the deputy's title but nothing of power. Even in anger, Rayner could understand that was a warning from history and not an example to follow. De-escalation was the order of the day. Yet that did not stop a salivating media from interpreting the eventual settlement as a resounding defeat for Starmer: a job title of shadow first secretary of state, shadow Chancellor of the Duchy of Lancaster, and shadow secretary of state for the future of work. 'They backed down,' said a friend of Rayner later, 'because they realised if they wanted to go toe to toe, we'd have landed a nuclear missile on their faces.'

In that moment the mocking laughter was deafening. Yet inside the leader's office they believed that they might now make their true voice heard. With Rayner placated, their most consequential moves could at last be made. In time both would prove that the left had won a pyrrhic victory. Rachel Reeves was appointed shadow chancellor, replacing Anneliese Dodds. The woman that everyone from the *Guardian* columnist Owen Jones to Nick Brown considered frighteningly right wing was installed at the very heart of the leadership. Shabana Mahmood – an old ally of the Irishman from Labour Together – assumed the power McSweeney had coveted for as long as it belonged to Rayner, and became national campaign coordinator. Brown was sacked. Streeting was given the invented role of shadow secretary of state *for* child poverty, a title both leader and appointee knew to be absurd. Yet by 10 p.m. Starmer was crankily uninterested in keeping up appearances. On being told to call another shadow cabinet minister to impart news of their sacking, he told aides: 'It's ten o'clock. I'm not doing it. They can stay.' Victims of the cull likened him to a partner in a City law firm sacking his paralegals. 'He just kept looking at his lines and saying: we need to change, we need to show we've changed, if it hasn't worked out, I'm going to have to let you go.' To a new appointee he wearily said: 'As you can see, it's not been a great day.' His aides begged to differ, even if they did not dare say so.

'We're still alive,' McSweeney said. 'We're still moving forward.'

★

On the morning of Monday 10 May, the new shadow cabinet savaged Starmer. 'Angela was criticising Keir, various people stood up and criticised the reshuffle,' one attendee said. 'It was fucking dreadful. It was just bad. *But we were alive.*' Another recalls: 'You had Andy McDonald asking about the status of Keir's Ten Pledges, and if he was still committed to them, Rosena Allin-Khan standing up and saying the Tories had literally killed people during the pandemic, and I was side-messaging people saying: "What the fuck is this circus?" I just couldn't believe it. It was like *The Vicar of Dibley*, with even more deranged characters.'

But the course was set. Simon Fletcher, who had reluctantly stayed in post in the leader's office after the suspension of Jeremy Corbyn, soon left. As he parted with Starmer for the final time, the leader proposed they meet when he next visited Westminster. The niceties were no disguise for the new reality. Fletcher was deserting the party because the Starmer project had deserted the left.

Tony Blair agrees. 'He just decided: "OK, I'm going to lose if we don't change. Therefore, we're going to change."' Soon the two men began to talk. 'I think he realised pretty early on – and Hartlepool confirmed that for him – that the Labour Party was just in a fundamentally bad position, needed to be shifted, and then he started to do it. It's possible that his journey isn't like Neil Kinnock, where you start on the left and then you move to the centre. I don't think he really started anywhere except vaguely progressive. And then, very unusually, only when he was leader did he really start to think about politics in a different way.'

10

Deconstruction

Starmer thought that Hartlepool would be rock bottom. His team knew otherwise. Even before the result, Jenny Chapman, his political secretary, had wearily confided in Chris Ward over fish and chips: 'It gets worse.' She told him: 'Tracy Brabin is going to win in West Yorkshire. We're going to have a by-election in Batley and Spen.'

As the most difficult seventy-two hours of his professional life came to a close on Sunday 9 May, Starmer told himself it might have been the darkness before dawn. Dawn refused to break. Still just about alive, his team staggered on to another fight they could not afford to lose.

The essence of the consensus that took hold of the Labour Party beyond the leader's office in the hours after Hartlepool was that Starmer had chosen a disaster movie over a feelgood story in which the underdog won – that in sacking Angela Rayner he drew attention away from promising results elsewhere. Labour had won the new mayoralty of the West of England. Andy Burnham had won every single ward in Greater Manchester. And Tracy Brabin, the MP and former *Coronation Street* actor, had comfortably won another new mayoralty in West Yorkshire. Jeremy Corbyn had lost four of the county's parliamentary seats to the Conservatives in 2019 but two years on his successor had swept the board. That was the story Starmer might have told to voters, had Morgan McSweeney wanted him to.

But even before the rout in Hartlepool his advisers knew they could not be sure of a happy ending. When Brabin had put herself forward for the mayoralty nobody had seemed to notice that her victory would almost certainly mean defeat – nobody seemed to have checked that she would be legally required to resign from the Commons, as the mayor of West Yorkshire would also become the county's police and crime commissioner; and nobody was confident that any Labour candidate would win a by-election in Batley and Spen. Brabin's was another seat haunted by its own past, full of fading mill towns that once spun woollen cloth – Batley, Heckmondwike, Cleckheaton – and posh villages where the rich men and women of Bradford and Leeds whiled away their retirements. Red wall and true blue. 'Tracy should never have been allowed to stand,' a leading adviser later said. They braced themselves for another punishment beating from voters who either disliked or distrusted Keir Starmer. The only hint of their anxiety was a brief story on page ten of *The Times*, published on the morning voters in West Yorkshire went to the polls: 'Mayoral victory could set in train another Labour defeat.'

Defeat in Hartlepool had brought with it the threat of a challenge to Starmer's leadership. Defeat in Batley would make it a reality. The seat's recent past cast a darker shadow than its industrial past. In 2016, in the week before the Brexit referendum, its Labour MP Jo Cox had been shot and stabbed to death by a far-right loner who later gave his name in court as 'Death to traitors, freedom for Britain'. To hold its second by-election in five years quickly – as the Labour leadership wished to do – meant the campaign would coincide with the anniversary of Cox's death. Confined to his car by torrential rain in Hartlepool, McSweeney called her family as a courtesy.

'This by-election, it's going to come up, because Tracy looks like she's going to win. If we do it quickly, it'll coincide with the anniversary of Jo . . . look, we could lose the seat.' McSweeney asked if the family had a preferred candidate. To his surprise, Kim Leadbeater, Cox's younger sister, suggested herself. He warned that the campaign was likely to be ugly – a crude inversion of the line from Cox's maiden speech to the Commons that had taken on its own life after her death: 'We have more in common than that which divides us.'

Leadbeater was undaunted, but McSweeney was right. She had been the Labour candidate for only five days when George Galloway's circus rolled into town, as it always did when a by-election was called in a place of tension like Batley – where 20 per cent of voters were Muslim and a local schoolteacher had been forced into hiding after showing his class a cartoon of the Prophet Muhammad. To his supporters the Scotsman in the fedora was a maverick and champion of the Palestinian people; to his detractors – many of them the Labour MPs on whose benches he had once sat – he was a race-baiter and demagogue. But as Tony Blair had learned in Bethnal Green, and Ed Miliband had learned in Bradford, he knew how to win elections. In Gaza, Hamas and Israel were exchanging rocket fire. In discussions with Labour's Indian activists the previous year, Starmer had described independence for Kashmir as a 'bilateral issue', seemingly dismissing the region's right to self-determination. Both had left British Muslims angry. In Galloway, they had an outlet for that anger. He did not need to win. 'Even if he only wins 2,000 votes,' a local Labour figure fretted at the time, 'they're coming straight off our pile.' One charismatic populist, Boris Johnson, had badly wounded the stolid and managerial Starmer. Another might now deliver the *coup de grâce*. One of Starmer's closest aides recalls: 'We had a problem with Leave-voting white men in Hartlepool. That was our working-class industrial vote. We're not winning in Scotland either. If we're suddenly losing Batley because we've now got a problem with Muslim voters as well . . . where is our voter coalition coming from?'

Polling day, 1 July, had become Starmer's next date with destiny. They had less than two months to save him.

★

Batley would be more than a by-election. It was bigger than Hartlepool. Immediately his advisers knew that he would not survive another defeat so quickly. They feared another challenge from Rayner, whose own aides had not been placated by her elevation to every lavish title short of a peerage. They were also wary of Tony Blair. Over a year of lockdowns his grey hair had grown long. His ambition went untamed too. Brooding deep in the English countryside at a stately home once owned by the actor John Gielgud, he dreamt of a return to the political stage. In the days after Hartlepool he had written a long essay for the *New Statesman*. Its headline read: 'Without total change Labour will die.' It argued that only 'total deconstruction and reconstruction' would save a party he no longer recognised. It asked whether Starmer was 'the right leader', criticised his lack of a 'compelling economic message', and damned him as a prisoner of 'the "woke" left'. Perhaps, Blair wondered, British progressivism would only be saved by bold and like-minded radicals in Labour and the Liberal Democrats.

He said so for two reasons. Like his disciples, he felt ignored by
Starmer. The leader's office treated Labour's last election winner like a
disgraced and demented relative. Until then the two men had seldom
spoken. During his leadership campaign Starmer had refused to meet
with him. Any suggestion that he had sought advice or benediction
from Blair would have destroyed his candidacy. For his part, Blair was
nonplussed. What he had written about the future of the Labour Party
was alarming enough if read literally. McSweeney understood what
lay between its lines. The Irishman knew that Blair's standing army
of advisers was courting the same donors he had once warned against
funding any new party of the left. He was not offering advice to the
Labour Party, but reading its last rites.

Blair was wrong. He would not return to elected office. There
would be no new party. Labour *would* be deconstructed and reconstructed, but by Starmer. But first he needed to survive. Starmer had
only six weeks to disprove the judgement the public and his party had
made at Hartlepool.

Much of that work would be done by two politicians he barely
knew. When McSweeney and the MPs who made up Labour Together
had defined their project in 2018, they had said of their party: 'It
brought together Protestants, Jews, Catholics, socialists, Irish and English, middle class and working class. It united estranged interests. It
defended the poor. It overcame racial prejudice.' No two members of
the Parliamentary Labour Party knew what those sentences meant like
Shabana Mahmood and Conor McGinn.

Mahmood was a barrister from Birmingham. She knew McSweeney
from Labour Together, on whose board she had sat since the beginning. She knew his world view, too. In 2010 she was elected to represent
the people of the Ladywood streets she had grown up in – where her
father, a Pakistani immigrant, had run a corner shop. Many, like her,
were observant Muslims. They endured appalling racism in the only
home they had ever known. As a girl Shabana knew where not to
walk in Birmingham: the places where she was called a Paki. Bigots
ransacked the family shop. This unasked-for education in the uglier
ways of English life might have made her an unlikely match for Labour
Together – whose roots, after all, lay in the Blue Labour movement
which had defined itself against migration and cultural change. Yet in
Ladywood she had seen what McSweeney had seen in Dagenham. Her

Muslim voters were poor and conservative too, just as rooted in the places they had come to call home, and just as dismayed by what the Labour Party had become when it embraced globalisation and break-neck social change. She learned her politics from the former deputy leader and mafia don of Labour in the West Midlands Tom Watson, a man to whom her family had become so close that had he too been Asian, she joked that she would have called him 'Uncle'.

In 2016, in the days after the Brexit vote, most of her friends had resigned in protest from Jeremy Corbyn's shadow cabinet. Yet she never left the NEC, where she waged a lonely war of attrition against the hard left. Privately she called the Corbynites 'bastards'. On the NEC she opposed everything they did, not least their attempts to allow the party membership to deselect MPs opposed to Corbyn. To Mahmood, resistance was God's work. Accusations of antisemitism against the Labour Party enraged her. She saw Britain's Jews as she saw her own people: a community besieged by racists and liberals suspicious of their traditional religious practices. It was also thankless work. In 2017, Starmer had asked her to return to the front bench as a junior shadow minister in his team. She declined the promotion. It would have required her to leave the NEC. He did not understand why. Mahmood knew the raw and bloody power politics of Labour's internal democracy were more important than parliamentary titles, even if her place on the barricades denied her the profile she had once enjoyed.

When Starmer ran for leader she declined to endorse him, or anyone, lest she leave the moral high ground from which she lectured the leftists who sat alongside her. But once he became leader, and that battle was won, she thought she might be rewarded for her service with a post in the shadow cabinet. She was not. McSweeney told her she was to stay on the NEC, to finish the dirty work her new boss had never done: appoint a new general secretary, purge the hard left. Vacancies came and went. When Rebecca Long-Bailey was sacked Mahmood wanted to become shadow education secretary. Given her religious conservatism, she was told the post was 'too hot to handle'. Irritated and impatient, she asked Conservative ministers whether she might become a government trade envoy instead.

During the weekend after Hartlepool, though, several calls were made to her. At first they went unanswered. Mahmood was driving through Birmingham with her father, delivering food parcels; her phone had been left in the home she shared with her twin sister. It rang and rang. Eventually her sister snapped.

'Tell her to come and answer her fucking phone,' she called the car to say. 'It's driving me insane. Morgan fucking whatever his name is wants to talk to you.'

Mahmood went home. She called back. McSweeney handed the phone to Starmer. 'Shabana,' he said. 'I really want you to be here.'

Here meant two things. The shadow cabinet – at last – as national campaign coordinator. More pressingly, it meant Batley. Everyone party to that brief conversation knew that it might have been the first and last campaign Mahmood would coordinate for Starmer. There was no detailed discussion of her brief, the limits of her authority, or their shared objectives. She understood it all intuitively, even as it went unsaid. With Starmer, it always did. 'He gives people a job,' said another shadow cabinet minister appointed that May, 'and then he disappears.' Mahmood's job was to save him.

At her side was a second Irishman. When Mahmood called the Corbynites 'bastards', the man who became her deputy thought she flattered them. Conor McGinn came from South Armagh. He grew up in Camlough, a garrison town. The soundtrack to his childhood had been rebel songs and the ceaseless thud of British army helicopters. His father, Pat, was a Sinn Féin councillor when that party's name was always followed by the letters IRA. He never imagined that his son would swear allegiance to a British queen as the MP for St Helens North, the rugby league town in Lancashire once known for its coal and glass. But like McSweeney, McGinn had come to London as a teenager, lived with his aunt, dropped out of university, and joined the Labour Party. He pulled pints for other Irishmen. He drank them too. When he was not scheming, he was reading. McGinn studied power and acquired it, quietly, in the pubs where Labour's London Irish did their politics, on the NEC, and as an adviser to shadow cabinet ministers. His heroes were the Chicago mayor Richard J. Daley, the last of America's Democratic boss politicians, and wily social democrats who had dragged their parties to power against the odds, like François Mitterrand, the president who remade the French left in his own image.

By 2021 McGinn was still a young man – at thirty-six, younger than Starmer, McSweeney and Mahmood – but an old-fashioned politician. To look at him in his thick glasses, and listen to him, was to experience not the Troubles of his native Northern Ireland but Labour in the 1980s. Even as he sang the old songs he had adopted another country's tradition. His politics were those of Labour's old right: conservative, unsentimental, muscular in their assertion of state power, and implacably hostile to the activist left on the streets, in Parliament, and at the top of the trade unions. This was as unlikely a journey as that Mahmood had made from the flat above a Birmingham newsagent to Oxford and the bar. After all, Jeremy Corbyn thought himself a steadfast friend of Irish Republicans, especially those who lived, like McGinn, in Islington North. But this Irishman loathed him. From the moment Corbyn became Labour leader McGinn had worked to destroy him, even when employed as one of his whips. One afternoon in 2016, Seumas Milne had walked alone along a quiet parliamentary corridor. From its opposite end approached McGinn. They passed one another in silence. As Milne strode on he heard a single word.

'Cunt.'

That said everything. It was McGinn, plotting sedition from the Whip's Office, who had orchestrated the hourly resignations of the shadow cabinet that year. When that failed to dislodge Corbyn, he busied himself legalising same-sex marriage in Northern Ireland. Yet he remained restless. Later, as Starmer's shadow security minister, he sat opposite the heads of MI5 and MI6. Like them, he operated in the shadows. He had learned his guiding mantra from John Spellar: 'If you don't have to write it down, say it in a phone call. If you don't have to say it in a phone call, say it in person. If you don't have to say it, nod.' The leader's office knew the influence he wielded. 'People listen to you,' said Jenny Chapman. 'I don't know why, but they do.'

Hartlepool and its messy aftermath gave McGinn his opportunity. MPs were dismayed by what Starmer's leadership had become, and not just because the local elections suggested that more of them may yet lose their jobs. They thought his aides were haughty and aloof. To outsiders the leader's operation looked like it was all tactics and no strategy. There was no great love for the leader either. As early as February, the *New Statesman*'s well-connected political editor Stephen Bush had reported of growing resentment among the PLP and declared: 'A consensus is forming among the commentariat that Keir Starmer is not up to the job.' Now, however, the vultures circled, and the MPs who had waited so long for the end of Corbynism had no option but to rescue him. Lucy Powell, the canny Mancunian recalled to the shadow cabinet that month, told McGinn to offer his services to Mahmood. So he did. These two outsiders thrust implausibly into the British establishment would together save a leader who seldom spoke to them.

What followed was the archetypal story of Labour politics under Starmer, because it did not involve the leader at all. Mahmood and McGinn would deal in discipline. Unusually for two Irishmen in the Labour Party, McSweeney did not know the younger man. McGinn began their first conversation with a question: did McSweeney prefer the small ball of hurling, or the big ball of Gaelic football? On that alone they begged to differ. In the ensuing years their conversation never stopped. In a memo McGinn sketched out how he and Mahmood would run the Labour Party – as 'an army, not a hippy commune for freethinkers'. They instituted an 8.30 a.m. call for political advisers, so that Labour would know what it had to say about the politics of any given day. It was hardly a radical innovation but over a year of lockdown and the cessation of factional hostilities, Labour's political muscles had atrophied. At one early meeting McGinn asked Ben Nunn to brief his colleagues on the morning's newspapers.

'What do those six stories have in common?' asked McGinn. No aide could say.

'There's not a single Labour quote in any of them.'

Disappointment was expressed bluntly. Mahmood and McGinn said what they thought. What they thought was often unprintable. 'They'd just be really sweary,' recalls one senior aide to Starmer. Said a shadow cabinet minister: 'There was a lot of: "Shabana is a bitch."' Staff did not like being shouted at, and complained. Mahmood had concerns of her own. While McGinn cracked the whip in Westminster, she had bedded down in Batley. Leadbeater had been selected on Sunday 23 May. The following weekend was to be her proper introduction to voters. By convention, by-election weekends are blazes of campaign activity. Canvassers from across the country invade the given constituency, marshalled by Labour staff. But despite the existential stakes, Batley was a ghost town. To Mahmood's fury, its Labour councillors were campaigning lackadaisically. She told their leader, Shabir Pandor: 'I'd deselect the lot.' The salaried employees at her disposal were hardly more dynamic. On one Sunday afternoon early in the campaign – a week after Leadbeater's selection – Mahmood was on the phone to McSweeney when she was interrupted by a staffer.

'I'm really sorry,' they said. 'Are you going to be any longer? I need to lock up.' Mahmood checked the time. Perhaps it was later than she realised. No – it was 3 p.m.

'What do you mean you're locking up?'

'They've gone to the pub.' As a sympathetic shadow cabinet minister subsequently recalled, Mahmood 'lost her shit' – and remained furious with her own colleagues for the duration of the campaign.

Others were *too* engaged, and unhelpfully invested, in the battle that by rights was Mahmood's to lead. Broad-shouldered and hard-nosed, Wajid Khan – Lord Khan of Burnley – saw himself as Angela Rayner's representative on earth. Or at least in West Yorkshire. Across Batley and Spen he was everywhere – a living, wheeling and dealing reminder that the deputy leader had not been cowed by the reshuffle. Even as he assured McSweeney that he could deliver the constituency's restive Muslim voters for Labour, Mahmood saw his mere presence as a threat. 'Angela had an agent in the field who was reporting back to her minute by minute, hour by hour,' a source intimately involved in the Batley campaign said. To Starmer's new praetorian guard, it appeared that Rayner was preparing for his defeat and her final victory. She thought those rumours laughable, having actually used her local influence – and Khan's – to install Leadbeater as a candidate. Similarly unhelpful, if not malicious, was the suggestion her chief aide, Nick Parrott, had sought to have his partner stand in the seat. Yet in those days, perception, or paranoia, became reality. News of her supposed ambitions had even reached Roger Liddle's dining table, where, in the aftermath of Hartlepool, McSweeney and his friends speculated that the strutting left-winger Sam Tarry – a shadow minister and later her partner – was laying the ground for a leadership challenge.

On that particular point their intelligence was accurate, whether or not Rayner had given her blessing. Who could have blamed him? Week after week Mahmood told shadow cabinet meetings that Batley would indeed be lost. 'This is probably not a winner,' she said.

It helped that she happened to be telling the truth: Batley was bad. While less convinced of her own infallibility than the headstrong Khan, Mahmood thought she understood Labour's Muslim voters. They were *her* voters – *she* was such a voter. And she did recognise the communal politics that would determine Labour's fate. Mahmood confessed to being taken aback by the enduring power of West York-shire's Biradri clans and the influence of their patriarchs. She phoned her father: 'I can't believe it. I remember this from when we were kids. Batley people are weird.' To Kim Leadbeater, who was equally unfamiliar with the ethno-religious intricacies of her new electorate, she said: 'I'm sorry, Kim, but this is like Birmingham twenty-five years ago.' Such tensions would have been difficult enough for an unpopular Labour Party to navigate without the added complication of an Israeli attack on Ramadan worshippers at Jerusalem's Al-Aqsa Mosque at the outset of the campaign – and the background hum of criticism of Starmer's position on Kashmir. With Galloway reprising the old tunes that had found such a receptive audience at Bradford nine years earlier, they now struggled to make themselves heard.

Locked into a fight for her leader's political life, Mahmood fought dirty. Nobody who campaigned alongside her in Batley pretends that those weeks were anything but a prolonged exercise in low cunning and heavy cynicism. Leadbeater was given tacit licence to stray as far from the party line on Palestine as she felt necessary. Mark Simpson, Starmer's foreign policy adviser, was hauled into the war room when LOTO was struck by the realisation that 'not being pro-Palestinian enough, or Keir not saying anything about Palestine, meant we'd lose'. One of Leadbeater's leaflets promised a 'strong national voice on Palestine in Parliament' and 'a strong national voice on Kashmir'. It did not condemn Israel explicitly – as Galloway did constantly, his denunciations laced with innuendo about Starmer's advocacy against antisemitism – but condemned the behaviour of its troops in Jerusalem and demanded the recognition of the Palestinian state. The scream-ing subtext was not lost on Jewish community leaders. They promptly complained to Lisa Nandy, the shadow foreign secretary – who vented her spleen to Mahmood in turn. Undeterred, Mahmood authorised another leaflet for distribution to Muslim voters in the final days of the campaign. This, one of the most incendiary things committed to print under Starmer's leadership, dispensed with the subtext entirely. It pictured Boris Johnson embracing Narendra Modi, India's Hindu strongman prime minister, and warned: 'Don't risk a Tory MP who is not on your side.' It was shameless sectarianism. Everyone involved now admits that it was a desperate measure at a desperate time.

For a party unacquainted with winning – still less winning at all costs – Mahmood's tactics were nauseating. Right on cue came condemnation from Nav Mishra, a Corbynite MP who sat in Rayner's kitchen cabinet. Accusing the leadership of embracing a 'hierarchy of racism', he fumed: 'We beat our opponents based on policies, not dog-whistle racism.' At the shadow cabinet's final meeting before polling day Mahmood was assailed on all sides by furious critics, led by Rayner and Nandy. Having tried and failed to have the flyer pulped, Nandy claimed Mahmood had breached the collective responsibility to which frontbenchers were bound: 'How dare you change foreign policy in this leaflet.' Mahmood told them their objections were absurd. Collective responsibility was always suspended during by-elections, precisely because of little local difficulties such as those in Batley: 'You will not, and will never have, a say on a by-election leaflet. I'm in this job, and the one thing you don't want is to have a say on a by-election leaflet . . . you will hate me within two minutes because there'll be so much coming to you for sign off.' As the row over who wielded ultimate authority in his Labour Party raged on, Starmer sat silently. Little more than forty-eight hours remained of the campaign that would make or break his leadership, yet in his darkest hour he seemed to have disengaged completely.

Were there any limits to what the leader was prepared to permit others to do in his name, so long as he won? He pursued power vicariously, through shadow cabinet ministers and advisers. In the weeks after Hartlepool his leadership had been put out to tender, and he appeared untroubled by the less scrupulous practices of his chosen contractors. They – not the leader – set the parameters of decency. For McSweeney and Mahmood only one tactic was beyond the pale. Before his sacking as chief whip, Nick Brown had wasted several afternoons at the Wimbledon headquarters of the Communication Workers Union, negotiating the terms of Jeremy Corbyn's reinstatement as a Labour MP with its general secretary, Dave Ward, who had inherited McCluskey's role as the left's chief negotiator. On the eve of the local elections Brown told the leader's office that a deal had been done. McSweeney was horrified.

'Please can we wait until after the local elections?' he said.

The prevailing mood was Brown's. None of Westminster's hoary old clichés had as much purchase in the Labour Party as the maxim that divided parties cannot win elections, and by that seductive logic the reconciliation of Starmer and his predecessor could only have been a good thing. That plan was scotched when Liam Byrne, swimming against the tide in the race for the West Midlands mayoralty, said Corbyn could only lose him votes. Brown was gone by Batley but as the campaign stuttered his plan was revived again. 'The argument was that we were losing support among Muslim voters because Corbyn was so popular, and that we would otherwise lose,' one official present for discussions said. 'We were going to bring him in before Batley and Spen.' McSweeney felt he had lost the room, and the argument he had lost his youth winning. Only Rachel Reeves refused to accede. She dragged colleagues to her view. If Starmer was to lose, it would be on his own terms.

*

'If you lose this, are you going to fight, or are you going to resign?' Chris Ward had asked many difficult questions of Keir Starmer, but none as difficult as that. 'Are you up for this? If we lose, this is going to be bad.'

1 July might have been the last day they met in a leader's office that belonged to them. Two futures were now possible. Labour's internal data – much improved in the seven weeks since Hartlepool – suggested only 500 votes would stand between the two. Whether they would fall to Starmer's advantage was too tight a call to make. Win and he would remain the leader of the opposition, at least for a little while longer. His team might at last exhale and take stock.

Lose and open season would commence. 'We were planning our last stand,' said one. That much had been clear to those manning the front in Batley. 'I think the campaign was always conscious of operating on two levels: one was the grim street-by-street fight with George Galloway, and the second always in our minds was the national significance of winning or losing,' another senior adviser to Starmer said. That significance was clear from the front page of that morning's *Times*: 'Rayner supporters prepare leadership challenge to Starmer.' It was read by Starmer and his team with weary resignation that turned into fury. 'I can't think of a single time a sitting deputy leader is preparing to openly challenge a leader and has a campaign ready to go on the night of a by-election . . . that was what our deputy leader was doing,' another member of the leader's inner circle says bitterly. They suspected that she would invoke her own mandate to justify a hand-brake turn back to the left and a return of the whip to Corbyn.

Rayner was not alone. Lurking stage left was Andy Burnham, whose own naked ambitions unsettled LOTO too. The day after Hartlepool he had said: 'If the party were ever to feel it needed me, I'm here and they should get in touch.' How he would make the long leap back from Manchester to Westminster just weeks after his re-election as mayor was a matter of some debate. Rumours persisted that he had agreed to swap jobs with Lucy Powell and claim her safe seat of Manchester Central. Further left, Dawn Butler's denials that she would mount a Corbynite challenge to Starmer in the week before polling day had convinced nobody. Ian Lavery was forever threatening to go over the top. The identity parade was endless and not a little ridiculous. Yet as much as Starmer's intimates distrusted Rayner, they worried less about the challenger than the fact of a challenge alone.

As one recalls of those events: 'The Angela campaign is real, and it's there. But the bigger problem is that we're going to have to go back to the membership [for another leadership election] – having lost two by-elections, being fifteen or more points behind in the polls, and with three years to go until an election. We don't know how that's going to play out. Even Morgan didn't know how the membership would vote at that point. Nobody knew. It was totally fluid. So whether it was Angela or not, there would have been a challenge . . . and if other candidates had declared, it would have been very messy.' Mutiny by other shadow cabinet ministers and back-bench grandees could not be ruled out either. John Healey, Ed Miliband, Yvette Cooper: if Labour was losing Batley, then they were losing too.

Reckoning with the possibility of catastrophe tested LOTO's sanity as much as their resolve. Days before the by-election, a shadow cabinet adviser had crossed paths with McSweeney.

'How's it going?'

'Great. I'm just on my way to sit outside the office with a sword and shield in case we lose and John McDonnell comes and launches an assault.'

Ward had written two scripts, one for each outcome. Three days earlier, on Monday 28 June, McSweeney had told colleagues how the lines to be delivered in the event of a loss ought to read: 'Stick to the strategy. Change, change, change.' Together with McGinn and Ward he had prepared a ninety-six-hour grid of announcements in the expectation of 'people suddenly doing something stupid', with its final entry Starmer's arrival back to his home in Kentish Town – still leader of the Labour Party. Starmer hated mess. He thought most politicians were stupid. It was all inimical to his sense of self – not just as a politician, but as a man. But he did not blink. He had stared into the abyss only weeks earlier and turned back. His flirtation with political oblivion was over. He wanted to be leader of the Labour Party for as long as it would let him lead it.

He endured a long night before he knew that was possible. Mahmood held the fort in Batley while McGinn ran the show at Labour HQ, arriving well refreshed after a long day in a hospitality tent at Wimbledon. Starmer, as ever, had placed himself at a degree's remove from the business of his own future. He retreated to the safety of Kentish Town. For once, home and family offered no respite from politics. At 4 a.m. he called the pollster Deborah Mattinson, who was soon to join his office. 'I've worn a hole in my carpet pacing up and down.' At Southside his staff readied themselves for four days of frenetic activity. They would not sue for peace with the left. Starmer and Reeves would go unbowed into the television studios, address the PLP – Starmer would even do what he hated more than anything, and spend Monday evening drinking with the PLP. The message to country and party: 'We haven't changed enough. We're not ready.' To the challengers using defeat at the hands of 'Gorgeous' George Galloway as a pretext for rebellion, condemnation. 'Galloway ran a homophobic, divisive and hateful campaign,' explains a party strategist. 'I thought we'd use it to enhance our strategy.' Said another of the script's authors: 'We would have said that Kim would have won if it hadn't been for George Galloway – the plan would have been to park it on him and his behaviour.' The invitation to Rayner, or whoever else, was to side with the populist over the Labour Party. For his part, McSweeney was particularly dismayed by the friendly fire directed at Mahmood and her campaign. He moaned to friends that her only crime was to have attempted to win by uniting the white voters of the red wall with their Muslim neighbours.

None of it mattered. George Galloway won 8,264 votes. Ryan Stephenson, the Conservative candidate whose name has since passed into obscurity, won 12,973. At 5.41 a.m., Kim Leadbeater learned she had won 323 more and assumed the office her elder sister had never intended to vacate. The margin was tiny; the result enormous. On a conference call, McGinn sang Barbra Streisand: 'Happy days are here again.' Rayner was listening.

That afternoon Starmer went to Batley and stood before a small crowd of activists holding placards that declared it was time for a winner. He celebrated as if he had become prime minister with a landslide. His smiling face appeared only briefly on the bulletins, between anticipatory coverage of England's quarter-final in the European Championships. That context was camouflage for what was to come. He quoted Blair.

'Labour is back!' he shouted. 'Labour is coming home.'

What did that mean? Really the last remaining links between Starmer's politics and his home – the private world of friends and old colleagues he so jealously guarded – would soon be severed without ceremony. His project was at once unmoored from its own past and cast back into a history that belonged to other people. New Labour was coming home.

11

Reconstruction

Morgan McSweeney called them 'The Librarians'. Too many colleagues seemed drawn to the quiet life: prepared to bank the win, then revert to the unity approach and the defeat it portended. He spoke contemptuously of its members. Librarian Labour were the people who had been 'terrified of the Corbyn machine': 'First they went along with it, and then they realised now he's gone, and all they want is quiet.' Said one person: 'Morgan had concluded that too many people around Keir simply had the party as their reference point: comfort, keep everyone together, as opposed to Labour having to change to win.' McSweeney himself put it more caustically. He told friends: 'Labour was so good at losing, we had options for how we could lose. You could follow Neil Kinnock, so you change the party but you hand over to Tony Blair. Or you could do a ten-year strategy. Or you could get all these other losers together and see how that works.' In this respect, Kinnock was just as dangerous as Corbyn. In their different ways, neither man accepted that their task was winning power in a single term.

In the days after Batley, one of Starmer's younger aides, never away from his side in Westminster, reported that the leader was 'mightily relieved' to have been given a stay of execution. He had a 'spring in his step'. Morgan McSweeney did not. The by-election may have been a victory for Starmer, but the pendulum was still swinging away from Labour: the party's share of the vote had fallen substantially. Its majority, of 323 votes, flattered to deceive. The Irishman was determined that the party should not over-interpret – or misinterpret – the results. They still pointed to a general election defeat. If he had one aim for Labour, it was to cure it of its culture. As he surveyed the leader's office and shadow cabinet, he detected a party comfortable with the prospect of losing.

At times, McSweeney wondered if even Starmer was a Librarian.
To a tiny circle of friends he confided his fears that his principal might
be too timid. The leader was prepared to work with people who either
did not understand the urgency of the change required, or appeared
inclined to sabotage it. He told one friend in the summer of 2020:
'Keir's very bright and picks things up very fast. He's not completely
unpolitical. He has some sense of skulduggery. But not like these
people. Angela is political all the time, she manipulates people . . . all
of her people come from Unite. Keir doesn't realise these are people
he cannot do business with.' To another, he was openly fatalistic, questioning his lack of politics: 'Keir acts like an HR manager, not a leader.
What's the point of circling the wagons if you can't last?'

In this one respect, McSweeney was wrong. Starmer was far more
spooked by his party's predicament, and his public opinion, than he
let on. He knew voters were not listening. Those who remained were
unconvinced. Focus groups damned him. Was Starmer not a posh
London lawyer – an aristocrat who had inherited his title? Was he not
a lefty lawyer who had served under Corbyn? Did he stand for anything at all? After watching an online focus group from the comfort of
his home, he confided in a friend: 'I thought at the beginning of this
I'd have a glass of wine, but I seem to have drunk a bottle.' He knew
self-medication was only a temporary reprieve. His resolve had been
hardened by wizened friends. Over the summer, Charlie Falconer and
Ed Miliband were even moved to visit his home. Starmer was unlike
any other Labour leader they had ever known. To Falconer, his old
flatmate Blair had stood for the modernisation of Britain. Miliband
knew Brown's lodestar was the eradication of poverty, as far as prudence with the public finances permitted him to do so. Summarising
Starmer in a similar sentence this way felt impossible. As one person
present for the discussion recalled, the basic questions the leader had
not yet answered, even in private, were: 'Are you left? Are you right?
Are you middle? Why should we be in power? What are we for at the
moment? We're not really for anything.' Impatient, Falconer advised
Starmer to adopt a pet cause: social care, childcare, or crime. Miliband
urged him to seize the green agenda. Both feared Starmer had yet to
grasp what George H. W. Bush so memorably called 'the vision thing'.
Their concerns were representative of countless discussions in that
month, as the party's politicians struggled to reconcile themselves to

the realisation that they worked for a leader who did not much like politics. 'There's not a culture of political discussion with Keir,' the aide said. 'He doesn't do group discussion . . . he doesn't let people know if they are performing, or disappointing him. He's completely unreadable.' Starmer appeared to have retreated to the comfort of bureaucratic routine. 'Keir doesn't work like a leader,' they went on. 'Morgan does try to draw out the politics and debate it, but there's a massive problem with Keir's time and diary . . . Monday to Wednesday, he has eight-hour meetings every day, and then he's on the road [until] Friday. There's no time to talk politics unless there's an emergency; even then, it's very fragmented.' Most damningly: 'Keir doesn't engage in the political process. He got this far by not expressing any political opinions. You don't get to be Labour leader without being political. He's good with people, but he doesn't debate big ideas. He's curious about ideas, but doesn't engage with political discussion about them.'

In fact, Starmer had grasped the urgency of the situation far more than he let on. Privately, he concluded permanent change was the only option: not just of his shadow cabinet, but his tight-knit circle of advisers. Until then, Starmer's Labour had always been the political equivalent of a family firm. What few friends the boss had made in Westminster worked for him. Together they had built the leader of the opposition from nothing. Over the space of a few short weeks every one of them would leave: some voluntarily, others at gunpoint – mates dispatched with the same ruthlessness he had shown Corbyn. For a time, even McSweeney's fate was uncertain.

*

One by one they went. First Ben Nunn, the only spinner Starmer had ever known, announced his resignation on 18 June. After fourteen months he felt it was his only choice. He had wanted to think strategically about McSweeney's favourite word – *change*. Yet events had seldom given him the time or space. His press office was small and staffed by Corbynites. What little thinking he did find the time to do was leaked. When he told Labour staff that the party intended to make more use of the British flag in its communications, they told the

Guardian it was tantamount to racism. That he had spent the weekend of his wife's birthday fielding inquiries about Angela Rayner was the final indignity. He had watched every stage of Starmer's political career, from meetings of the Constituency Labour Party of Holborn and St Pancras, through Brexit, Corbyn and Hartlepool, but no more. Next was Jenny Chapman, who, like Nunn, belonged to what Labour MPs dismissively called the 'Camden Clique' in the leader's office. On one level that insult was literal. Starmer lived within its precincts in Kentish Town. His leadership bid had been planned at Chapman's home on Arlington Road or in nearby pubs. But the epithet had an edge. 'Camden' denoted detachment from the world which many of her parliamentary colleagues claimed to inhabit. Chapman was from Darlington and until 12 December 2019 had been its MP too, but as polit-ical secretary she became a lightning rod for their anger. MPs blamed her for the calamity of the Hartlepool campaign. Rayner loathed her. By June the briefing against her had become unbearable. On the night of the reshuffle her husband had appeared unannounced and emotional at Labour HQ after a libellous allegation about her personal life was published online, a scene pained spectators likened to the denouement of an *EastEnders* episode. The devastated couple were forced to sue, and were paid damages. Enough was enough. Chapman became a shadow minister instead. Carolyn Harris was the other woman responsible for the leadership's liaison with MPs. Like Chapman, she had encouraged Starmer to stand for the leadership, long before he had been prepared to admit that he nurtured that ambition. She was sacked without cere-mony as his parliamentary private secretary. That should have hurt, but Starmer proceeded without sentiment. He had no firmer friend than Harris, who defended his honour as if she were his mother. Yet in the days of hate that followed Hartlepool she had erred. Outraged by Rayner's disrespect for his authority, she gossiped to her fellow Welsh MPs, suggesting that Rayner was engaged in an adulterous affair with another shadow cabinet minister. Chris Bryant, the former vicar who sermonised to colleagues from his back-bench pulpit, warned her against spreading untruths. He told the wrongly accused of her rumour-mongering. The shadow cabinet minister complained. With Starmer's blessing, Harris was gone. That she had responded to media inquiries by blocking lobby reporters on WhatsApp was a tragicomic testament to the siege mentality that now gripped LOTO. The old gang was parting ways with alarming speed.

★

Still, he would always have the Irishman. At least, that had been the plan. Yet over the preceding weeks, one suggestion recurred as Starmer took soundings and unsolicited advice, as recorded in a contemporaneous note of plans for a new regime: 'Keir being told he needs administrator, executive, civil servant-type chief of staff.' If one had asked a friend of Morgan McSweeney to describe him in a single word they might have picked from any one of hundreds of admiring adjectives. 'Organised' was never one of them. McSweeney himself knew it. He had little interest, still less enough time, to manage Starmer's private office. 'Keir thought he needed someone to make the LOTO trains run on time,' said a friend of McSweeney. 'Morgan did not see it as his role.' He fought constantly, on too many fronts. What mattered, if the Corbynites were to be consigned to history, was headquarters and its bureaucracy – not that musty warren of rooms in Norman Shaw North or even the Commons chamber. 'Keir doesn't understand Parliament,' a shadow cabinet minister said. 'Nor does Morgan. They've got all the same blind spots.' McSweeney spoke of crucial votes as 'whatever that thing is that's happening in Parliament tomorrow'. David Evans, his chosen general secretary, had told the shadow cabinet: 'I just need you out of that place, out there campaigning.' Labour's machine mattered to McSweeney above all. The speed with which he had sought to wrench the controls of the Batley campaign from Rayner's hands was proof of that point. 'We were trying to get control of the party,' said one of McSweeney's allies in LOTO of the reshuffle. 'Who's the best person to be in control of the party? Morgan. He couldn't do that as chief of staff, and one of the things Keir concluded was that because Morgan was spending 90 per cent of his time as acting general secretary, he wasn't really acting as chief of staff as well.' It was a conclusion on which both men would agree, and in time profit handsomely. It was also a discussion that was best had privately. Instead it was leaked to the *Sunday Times*.

On 19 June, little more than a fortnight before the Batley by-election, its front page said: 'Sir Keir Starmer has removed his chief of staff as part of a reorganisation of his senior team ahead of a second potential by-election defeat in Labour heartlands.' 'It's safe to say it didn't go down very well. It went down particularly badly given that we'd just spent weeks fighting for the life of the project, and Keir's leadership,' said one of the leader's advisers. And what was their project without McSweeney? Chris Ward, Starmer's first and longest-standing staffer, posed the question to Starmer directly. Ordinarily placid – and unfailingly deferential to his boss – Ward shouted his objections at Starmer, the first and only occasion on which he would ever raise his voice to his leader and friend. These rancorous scenes would have surprised the PLP. The inner circle no longer felt like a clique. Focused dispassionately on survival, he had abandoned them. Said one member of Starmer's senior management team: 'He was talking to people he shouldn't have done – he asked a lot of grandees their view on what he should do with his office.' Another adds: 'It was extraordinary, really, and obviously very destabilising. Lots of us had been brought in by Morgan. There was loyalty to Keir, but a lot of us were very loyal to Morgan . . . he certainly deserved better than being named in that particular way.'

Starmer did not appreciate being challenged. But to those around him it was born of necessity. His failure to communicate had left those around him to assume the worst. In the event, there was reason to his new-found ruthlessness. Although Starmer rarely narrativised his own actions in real time, he had developed a clear-eyed view of what needed to be done. McSweeney was safe. The leak forced him to reveal what that meant in practice. 'He always wanted him around – just not in that role,' a colleague recalled. Starmer knew exactly what he wanted – *needed*. The Irishman was not an administrator, nor a civil servant. He was a campaigner. Everything in his life was subordinate to winning votes. No anecdote from McSweeney's past amused Starmer like the first act of the courtship that became his marriage. One of the councillors who delivered McSweeney victory in Lambeth in 2006 was Imogen Walker. Before long that name was indivisible from his. Not then. 'You just keep calling me Stockwell Five,' she complained. 'You don't know my actual name.' Even the love of McSweeney's life was a number on a spreadsheet. Weeks passed before his new role was formalised but the offer was of total control over campaigning. Labour's political strategy would be his to write.

★

To repopulate his office, Starmer summoned the political undead. Starmer had defined himself against New Labour as much as the hard left. In 2021, New Labour consumed him. His original cast of advisers had been too young to know Blair and Brown as anything other than important men on television screens. The few who did, like McSweeney and Chapman among them, had lurked on the margins of the movement: at local councils, in constituency offices and trade unions. They knew nothing of winning general elections and working in government: Blairites and Brownites did. They were people he did not know, but now had no option but to trust. The suspicion was mutual and the risks considerable – but for the ageing men and women of the party's last government the opportunity was too good to miss. The first to be summoned was Deborah Mattinson. She was New Labour before New Labour existed – before several of Starmer's aides had even been born. With other young advertising executives in the 1980s she had introduced an old-fashioned Labour Party to market research and branding exercises its flea-bitten union men regarded with suspicion. With Philip Gould, the adman who invented Blairism, she helped poll the party into winning shape in the 1990s. In the first decade of the new millennium she was Brown's pollster: measuring his success as chancellor and then his failures as prime minister. Mattinson knew what Labour leaders needed to do in order to win. Arguably more important was her deep understanding why they had lost – who they had lost. Her focus groups in south-eastern seats had informed *Southern Discomfort*, the influential study of Neil Kinnock's loss of the aspirational working class in 1992. In two books of her own – *Talking to a Brick Wall*, published after Brown's defeat in 2010, and *Beyond the Red Wall*, a brutally objective analysis of the loss of Labour's old heartlands – she had laid bare the electorate's collapsing faith in the party she had taught to win. Labour no longer respected the kind of voter that had abandoned Kinnock in 1992, Brown in 2010, Miliband in 2015, or Corbyn in 2019. It needed not only to engage with them but venerate them. She developed her own coinage to describe them, one she conceded was cringeworthy, if helpfully unambiguous: 'Hero Voters'.

The question for her was whether Starmer could reach them. She could not make that judgement yet, but was reassured by his willingness to face the music. The pair knew one another vaguely – he was a five-a-side teammate of a close family friend – and the previous summer they had spoken privately, discussing her research on the red wall in the garden of a Crouch End pub. He watched her focus groups and flinched. Occasionally she dispensed her candid advice in public. 'Sir Keir's focus-group animal is an eagle,' Mattinson had written in December. 'At first sight this looks encouraging – much more flattering than a sheep, surely? But, on closer examination, the choice reveals a problem, for Sir Keir's eagle is circling above the fray, calculating but distant. The need for Labour to set out its stall grows increasingly urgent.' Starmer listened carefully. So did Rachel Reeves, whose own belief that Labour had no option but to vote through Johnson's Brexit deal had been clarified by a long paper from Mattinson. It was Reeves, not Starmer, who ultimately asked her to join LOTO in February. 'Keir has decided he wants to hire a director of strategy,' Reeves called to say. 'Would you be interested?' At first she demurred. After another conversation with Starmer she relented. Mattinson's appointment, long in the making, was announced the weekend after the Hartlepool election – a vain attempt by the outgoing Ben Nunn to magic up a good-news story. Her first day was 5 July, the Monday after Batley. Who, if not McSweeney, was to be Starmer's chief of staff? That question weighed more heavily on the leader than any other, and its answer would bring more profound disruption. Before he could go forwards, the leader was once again impelled to look backwards. Sam White personified New Labour. Like Mattinson he had felt the traumatising jolt of its fall to earth in 2010. Through the Brown years he had been at the right hand of Alistair Darling, the chancellor who dared to say no when the prime minister demanded an alternative to austerity during the financial crisis. As so many of that project's sons and daughters had done, he disappeared from Whitehall into the corporate world. With his bald head and neat, tieless shirts, he looked and sounded like a public affairs executive – for that was what he had become. White's sentences were salted liberally with the euphemisms of management speak, nothing like the honeyed prose for which his father, Michael, had become

famous as political editor of the *Guardian*. He had met the young
McSweeney during the 2005 election and it was the Irishman who
asked him to advise informally on Starmer's response to the pandemic.
With the virus in retreat he had returned to his comfortable life in
the insurance industry but lingered, silently, on the WhatsApp groups
that coordinated the day-to-day work of the leader's office. That July,
Starmer invited him to speak again.

He mulled the offer, seeking Mattinson's counsel. 'Obviously, Deborah, you think this is turnroundable.'

'Yeah, I do.'

'I do, too.'

White spoke to Jonathan Powell, too – the former diplomat whose
cut-glass vowels had informed every decision of consequence made by
Tony Blair. White hoped to be chief of staff to a Labour prime minister, too.

He took the job and in so doing created another vacancy. White
was too much for Chris Ward. Six years of his life had been sacrificed
on the altar of Starmer's ambition. The leadership was *their* project.
Starmer had never known politics without Ward, who had schooled
him in Parliament's arcane customs. He had written the pledges on
which the leader was elected and knew the mind that was now scrambled by advice from people who had never believed in Starmer as he
had. Already smarting from McSweeney's humiliation of him in the
press, Ward was livid to learn of White's arrival in a private conversation with Starmer on Saturday 24 July. Starmer never took decisions of
consequence without consulting him. They never did faits accomplis.
Now the team that had made Starmer leader of the Labour Party had
been thrown to the wolves of New Labour. By the following Wednesday, Ward had left. His once constant conversation with the leader
would not resume for the best part of a year. Nunn, Starmer's other
steadfast friend, was replaced by another Blairite stranger. Westminster knew Matthew Doyle as his master's voice: he had been Tony's
final spokesman in Downing Street and followed him to the capitals of
the autocratic states that sought his expensive advice, defending those
murky deals to journalists who asked whether this was how a former
prime minister really ought to be earning his living. His head of dense
curls had greyed, but he still played the straight bat that older lobby
journalists remembered. From their misspent summer on Liz Kendall's

kamikaze leadership campaign McSweeney knew that Doyle could spin the impossible. Doyle was known to McGinn, too: even at the zenith of Corbynism they had together ensured that the Labour Party Irish Society had remained the last redoubt of resistance to the hard left. He was not their first choice to become the director of communications charged with talking Labour back into relevance. Others tried to lure another old stager with an Irish name, Paddy Hennessy – spin doctor to Ed Miliband and then Sadiq Khan – out of retirement. But Hennessy said no, and Doyle was next on the list. He was busy in Batley, working for Kim Leadbeater, when McSweeney called.

'If Keir was to call you, would you say yes?'

Doyle ruminated for a little while and phoned back. 'Yes, I would say yes.'

Starmer followed. 'A lot of people I respect say that I should hire you.' He did. Doyle arrived in LOTO on the same day as Mattinson. They took up their roles alongside Stephanie Driver, another experienced operator who joined in March as Starmer's personal communications chief. So straitened were the party's finances that her salary was cobbled together from the leftovers of its budget for leaflets.

*

The complexion of his new operation revealed more about Starmer's state of mind, about his precarious sense of self as a politician – about the priorities that cut so sharply across the human relationships he supposedly cherished above all else – than almost anything he said publicly in the first year of his leadership. His political mind was a closed book even to those who believed they had written its contents. Decisions were taken deliberatively, his thinking opaque. Only once he had come to a conclusion, inevitably a long and private process, did he reveal it to his intimates. And in 2021 he concluded that to survive he must hand the reins of his political project to people he did not know, on the recommendation of people he knew to have doubted him. That much was obvious to Angela Rayner. To friends she fumed that Starmer was incapable of running a bath, let alone the opposition. Who really controlled the Labour Party? She said she did not know. All she could say was that it could not be Keir Starmer.

The ambiguity on which his leadership was built had at first been constructive. In 2020 he had rejected the binaries of left and right, of Blairite and Corbynite, that made so many of Labour's factions mutually exclusive. By the following summer Starmer had left that all behind. He would never see himself as an 'ite' or think in terms of 'isms', but recognised more definition was needed.

It fell to McSweeney to spell out what that definition looked like. Unbeknown to Starmer, he had been working to ensure that their project *would* last. Summer would soon give way to September and with it their first party conference. For once the eyes of the country would turn, if only fleetingly, to the Labour Party – to its leader, its trade unions, its members and its left wing. They would learn the answer to Rayner's anguished question: who really ran the Labour Party?

Secretly, just as before, the Irishman had a plan to settle it.

12

'Pin it to the wall!'

What constrained McSweeney was the membership of the Labour Party. These 500,000 or so people had their uses to him, of course. Most of them had voted for Keir Starmer to be leader. But the electorate McSweeney now wished to convince of his employer's merits was one hundred times larger. It shared neither the politics nor the priorities of the minority of the country that paid its subscription fees to party headquarters, nor the minority within that minority who showed up to constituency meetings and voted for conference delegates, parliamentary candidates and members of the NEC. For a strategist who wished to uncouple the party from its activists and drag its agenda towards the sensibilities of the voter for whom even Ed Miliband seemed dangerously left wing, their influence was a running sore. What if someone just took it away?

Such a question could not be asked openly, which was why, on 17 March 2021, McSweeney set up a secret WhatsApp group to which a handful of comrades were invited. He called it 'Project Ex' – an apparent homage to the low-budget American film in which three teenagers live out their wildest dreams as the hosts of a house party thrown in their parents' ignorance. It was party members who had given Starmer the majority on the NEC that he needed to push through the reforms McSweeney thought necessary. Four and a half years of Jeremy Corbyn – a man to whom their democratic rights meant everything – had increased their power only marginally. Radical proposals to allow them to deselect parliamentary candidates at will had never come to pass. What little change that had occurred was modest. 33 per cent of local members were required to trigger a reselection contest if they no longer liked their incumbent Labour MP where once a majority had been needed to oust them. Only two Corbynsceptics had fallen foul of this new system and both survived. The predicted bloodbath never came. Candidates for the leadership and deputy leadership now required nominations from 10 per cent of the Parliamentary Labour Party, down from 15 per cent, after which point a majority of members was the aim. That too might have made life easier for the hard left, but it was Starmer who had won.

These new technicalities of the Labour rulebook seemed to suit everyone. McSweeney's friends, led by Nathan Yeowell, had out-organised the Corbynites twice over: when MPs faced their trigger ballots for reselection, and then in the leadership contest. But the resurgent right still thought the left was debilitating, sucking the life from the Labour Party. He thought his parliamentarians worried about the wrong electorate. Some spent their five-year terms fretting over the Damoclean threat of deselection. What happened on a 'wet Thursday afternoon' at some constituency branch meeting or other came to matter more than the thoughts of the tens of thousands of locals who lived their lives unaware that those meetings ever occurred. Others, namely the shadow cabinet ministers and ambitious MPs who coveted selection as mayoral candidates – or, indeed, Starmer's job – sought only to please the members that might make them so. When Starmer himself was seeking to please the same people, he had vowed to do the opposite of what McSweeney really wanted. 'The selections for Labour candidates need to be more democratic,' he said. 'We should establish an assembly of members and trade unionists to look at how we can develop policy in a more democratic way.'

McSweeney came to believe that the empowerment of party members was Labour's original sin. Nobody, not even Blair, had bothered to contest with much vigour the argument first made by Tony Benn: 'Parliamentarianism is the disease that has infected the Labour Party . . . the idea that when you have elected MPs they join a little club of people who know better than everyone else.' New Labour had merely slowed the stream of this logic. If Starmer was to exercise total control as leader, he would have to reverse it. The Irishman and his co-conspirators thought a party democracy that obliged elected representatives to put members before voters was the real elitism. Too many of the changes Starmer had wanted to make were vetoed in the

name of membership unity. McSweeney believed unity was a euphem-
ism for political cowardice.

Consider the case of Richard Leonard. The leader of the Scottish
Labour Party was doomed from the start. To McSweeney, his socialist
political project was a period piece: heavy on nostalgia for a lost world
of Red Clydeside, trade unions and heavy industry. These were not
Starmer's politics, nor those of the Scottish public. In 2019, Labour
had come fifth in the only national election Leonard had ever fought.
McSweeney had wanted to sack him the moment he arrived in the
leader's office. Starmer, fearful of a backlash, initially suggested that
he be put on a performance improvement plan – as if he were a sales
rep who had failed to meet his targets. It took months to force Leonard
out, which finally happened in December 2020 when Starmer enlisted
his union, the GMB, to tell Leonard his time was up.

Consider the case of mandatory vaccines for workers in care homes,
which voters supported and the leadership of the Labour Party had
wanted to support when it was proposed in early 2021. Yet when its
Covid committee came to meet, it concluded that it could not split
with Unison, the trade union that opposed the policy for fear it would
put its low-paid members in the care sector out of work. 'No matter
what the issue was,' an adviser present at the meeting recalls, 'the
thinking would be: voters think x, members want y. But voters want a
united party, so let's do y.'

Consider the case of Joe Anderson, Liverpool's all-powerful mayor,
who had been arrested on suspicion of bribery and corruption. Labour
established an inquiry into how the politics of its safest city had gone
so badly awry. McSweeney wanted Jacqui Smith, home secretary under
Gordon Brown, to chair it. Left-wingers on the NEC thought the mere
fact of her service to New Labour disqualified her. Rather than defy
the left, Margaret Beckett, the grande dame of the moderates, joined
them in vetoing Smith's appointment. McSweeney was angry and dismayed. Not even when criminality was alleged could the leader impose
his will.

After Liverpool, he resolved to 'pick the Labour Party up and smash
its head open'. He told Starmer: 'If you want me to get a grip of
things, I can't – because everything and everyone is wired completely
on focusing on the party. We have to make a big change . . . I can't fix

this problem without a fundamental shift. We need to be for the country, not the party.' The time had come to clarify where power truly lay.

★

Project Ex was untypical of the WhatsApp groups on which
Westminster does much of its business. Its membership was small:
McSweeney and just three others. Nor did its contents ever leak. The
names alone would have revealed the radicalism of their plans to take
back control of the Labour Party.

Any scheme to marginalise the left naturally involved Luke Akehurst. For a man of such a bookish manner and negligible public
profile – he had never held a public office beyond Hackney Council –
Akehurst provoked extreme emotion in the Corbynites. It felt as if he
had always been on the NEC, needling them at every turn. His politics
were those of the old right. As leader of Labour First, the tiny band of
brothers that kept this unfashionable and traditionalist faction alive, he
believed in everything the hard left did not: foreign military intervention, extreme fiscal discipline, the Jewish state – for which he advocated
tirelessly in his day job as the director of an organisation called We
Believe in Israel. But for Akehurst crushing the Corbynites was an
enjoyable end in itself. They called him Luke the Nuke and mocked his
ginger hair and ruddy complexion, the latter brought on by the neuro-
logical disorder that forced him to walk with a stick. In boyhood he had
been one of them. Akehurst's father recited Benn's *Guardian* columns
from memory and the son revered him too. As a ten-year-old he won
a school election on a promise to install Benn in his cabinet. But after
Labour lost in 1983 he devoted his life to stopping the left from coming
close to the leadership again.

In 2020, Akehurst had helped deliver Starmer his slender majority
on the NEC. With Nathan Yeowell of Progress, he had built Labour to
Win – an organising machine that sought to drive out the Corbynites
from every obscure committee of the party, vote by vote. In days of
old this collaboration may have felt implausible. Labour First had been
Gordon's people. They were suspicious, too, of the cosmopolitan slick-
ness of the Tony project – as well as its disdain for trade unions, which
Labour First liked provided the hard left was nowhere near the offices
of their general secretaries. Akehurst in particular resented how the

long history of Labour's moderate tradition had been flattened and truncated by the Blairites, who sometimes spoke as if it all began with Tony's election as leader in 1994. When he met new party members he confronted them with an hour-long slideshow that taught them of Hugh Gaitskell's opposition to unilateral nuclear disarmament and Neil Kinnock's war on the Militant tendency. But under Starmer, necessity brought old right and new right together, as illustrated much later in a joke told by Peter Mandelson: 'Contrary to what people believe, I've always thought it was really important that the Labour Party should have two wings. Those two wings being Labour First and Progress.'

McSweeney turned to Akehurst because he knew the Labour rulebook – the subtlety of the changes to it the Corbynites had wrought, and how they might be altered to freeze them out. It was never Akehurst's aim to eliminate them entirely. A friend describes his politics thus: 'The hard left should be part of the party, we don't want them all out. Their views are welcome. But don't mistake that for giving people whose views are pretty abhorrent to the vast majority of the British public the levers of power, because it all ends in tears.'

Roy Kennedy – Baron Kennedy of Southwark – was a scholar of the party constitution too. Born to Irish parents in a poor home in Lambeth, he had made an unlikely lord but a natural opponent of the activist left. For two decades he had fought and sabotaged them at Labour HQ. In his days as an apparatchik he had been custodian of its ever-changing rules and knew how the subtlest shifts in its wording could be weaponised.

Charged with ensuring their discussions became reality was Matt Pound, who had once been Akehurst's only employee at Labour First. Much younger than his three comrades, he had been recruited by his friend McSweeney – first to grind out constituency nominations for Starmer's leadership campaign, and then to work as his mechanic on a stuttering party machine. All, to one degree or another, had been schooled in the brutality of grass-roots organising by John Spellar, the ageing warhorse of the old right who made a point of reading the communist *Morning Star* each morning: to learn of his enemies' activities, and to celebrate if a hard-left organiser of his acquaintance was on its obituaries page. Margaret McDonagh, Blair's chief bureaucrat, willed them on from afar.

In the first months of 2021 the four men had been trapped – not only by lockdown, but the limitations the rulebook imposed on their ambitions. But McSweeney's mind had wandered and even before they convened virtually that March they had set their sights on reforms even they knew to be unrealistic. They were first committed to writing in the first message to Project Ex, which came – predictably – from Akehurst. There was no mistaking what they wanted: to formalise and codify the new powerlessness of the Corbynites. They would abolish the leadership rules introduced by Ed Miliband and exploited so deftly by Jeremy Corbyn. No longer would members of the public be able to pay a small fee for the right to elect Starmer's successor. Nor would members of the party's votes weigh the same as those of an MP. Instead, the electoral college – the tripartite structure that split the selectorate between the MPs, members and unions – would return. Those two changes alone would render the election of an out and proud leftist as good as impossible. A third aimed to ensure they had little chance of ever reaching the ballot by raising the threshold of nominations required from Labour MPs from 10 to 20 per cent.

When the work of Project Ex was finally revealed, on the eve of Labour conference in September, disgruntled shadow cabinet ministers suspected its true purpose was to rig the succession. Allies of Angela Rayner in particular believed McSweeney and the old friends from south London who worked with him – namely Matt Pound and Matthew Doyle – were in reality working not for Starmer, but to create the conditions in which Wes Streeting could be elected leader on a manifesto of unabashed Blairism. One member of the Project Ex WhatsApp group insists they were preoccupied only by the present: 'They said we were doing it to line up Keir's replacement. This was never true. The leadership election rule was about changing the reference points and the motives for shadow cabinet members . . . the shadow cabinet would get regular presentations on how to win an election, and were told that we had to get people who voted Tory in the last election to vote for us now. We had to get people who voted Leave. They'd say: that's great. And then they'd go out and do the opposite, because they were thinking about party members.'

The irony was that McSweeney now had little choice but to think of party members. Changes to the rules of the Labour Party could only be approved by conference, whose voting delegates were elected by constituency parties and the unions. The leadership did not control either bloc – not yet. Akehurst set to work. Ignored though they were by the Westminster media, votes for the conference delegates of local parties – elected on the wet Thursday evenings McSweeney so hated – were as formative and consequential to Labour leaders as the Iowa caucuses were to the presidential wannabes of the United States. Before the four men was a chessboard of 650 squares. To win any one required them to out-organise and out-vote the Corbynites. It demanded sympathetic volunteers book a week off work to cast votes for which they were unlikely to be thanked. It needed deep knowledge of who exactly Labour's 500,000 members were as individuals. 'This was all coming down to one or two people turning up, or not turning up, in a draughty church hall in West Dorset in February.' Armed with a 7,000-strong spreadsheet of names, numbers and email addresses harvested through years in the trenches of factionalism, Akehurst called and called and called.

★

The work of Project Ex was clandestine and risky. But before long the circle of trust expanded, if only by three. The first was Phil Gaskin, the party's regional director in the south-west. Then came Hollie Ridley and Teddy Ryan, a young married couple who together ran the Labour Party in the east of England. They were so schooled in subterfuge that they had named their daughter after Violette Szabo, a British spy executed by the Nazis. To the Corbynites they were the mob bosses of a fiefdom so impregnable to the left that they referred to it as District 13, a resentful reference to a film about a crime-ridden Paris *banlieue* of the same name, deemed so dangerous by the powerful that it was isolated behind barbed wire. Ridley, like McSweeney, came of age in Dagenham – discovering the Labour Party as the BNP reared its ugly head. Ryan was a third-generation dustman from Lambeth who came to Labour through the Blairite madrasa of its student wing. Somehow, despite their politics they had survived Corbynism. Yet even after Starmer's election they were anxious that the civil war had been stilled by a ceasefire, and not by lasting victory.

As early as November 2020 the couple were embarked on a similar mission as the men from Project Ex – though neither side knew it at the time. If Starmer entered the conference hall without a slate of delegates on whom he could rely, he would be humiliated by the left at the precise moment the national media had turned its gaze to Labour. Everything he had said about change – and every move he had made to effect it – would be rendered worthless by the spectacle of victorious Corbynites winning vote after vote. Ridley and Ryan did the same grinding work as Akehurst: moving methodically from constituency to constituency in Essex, East Anglia and further afield. They encouraged reliable delegates to stand up and be counted.

Some notional strongholds of the left were neither meeting nor holding elections at all. In violation of the rules, their delegates were instead appointed. One by one these political shell companies were asked to furnish the party with minutes of meetings that had never happened. None could comply, losing their delegates and opening the door to friends of the leadership.

As a courtesy, Ryan told McSweeney of their work. 'This isn't a request for permission,' he said, 'because I would not put you in a position where you have to give permission. But I am letting you know so that you have the opportunity to stop me should you so wish.'

'Absolutely not,' said McSweeney. 'We need to be fucking doing it.' He well understood Lyndon B. Johnson's first rule of politics: be able to count. But he knew too that counting was pointless if the sums in question added up to defeat. Ridley and Ryan joined Project Ex. In May, as the instability that followed Hartlepool gave a beleaguered left new energy, Labour's newly appointed general secretary David Evans gave their work his official imprimatur. 'We have to do this,' he told a meeting of Labour's regional directors. Soon the entire bureaucracy of the Labour Party was directed to construct an electorate whose significance its leader would not know for four more months. The name of every delegate was entered into a spreadsheet, their obedience to the project ranked.

The margin would be painfully tight.

*

Activists alone were not enough. Without a majority of delegates appointed by the trade unions, who had the other half of votes of the conference floor, the plan was doomed. They, however, were busy with their own internal elections, and their own precarious politics.

Unison, the largest affiliate of all, was led by Christina McAnea. Her Glaswegian burr disguised the depths of her links to McSweeney, alongside whom she had tried and failed to prevent the hard left from taking control of the Labour Party in Streatham, where her husband was a councillor, in 2019. She was instinctively sympathetic to Starmer, not least because she lived his predicament. Elections to her own executive committee loomed, as did the hard left. She would suffer the consequences directly if she backed reforms designed to kill the Corbynites.

At Unite, the most generous in its donations, Len McCluskey had finally retired. But regardless of who succeeded him, Unite's delegates were already elected – and were unlikely to offer their services to the destruction of the Labour left.

That left the GMB. That March, just as Project Ex had begun its covert mission, GMB members had elected Gary Smith as their general secretary. The garrulous Scotsman had, like McSweeney, made it his mission to reconnect the GMB's leadership with its lost purpose: to serve its workers. Most of them worked in industries to which the activist left were hostile: armaments, oil and gas. The enmity was mutual. Smith had a special contempt for the 'hard-core tankies and social misfits' he believed to have hijacked the union movement to fulfil their own ideological fantasies. Though he lived among such people in Brighton, he revelled in insulting them. Both men relished symbolic confrontation. Smith had noted approvingly the picture of the Irish revolutionary James Connolly that hung above McSweeney's mantelpiece. He was less taken with Starmer. The leader had upset Smith with an ill-judged speech to his first union congress as general secretary, in which he adopted a performatively blokey register and said hopefully: 'Gary and I are going to go for a pint.' The damage was compounded in the weeks before conference when Smith visited Westminster to catch up with Judith Cummins, the Bradford East MP he knew from university. Starmer strode past the pair as they ate a pizza, ignoring entreaties to pause for a conversation. Shadow cabinet ministers sought to reassure Cummins that Starmer had intended no slight and was well aware of the importance of the GMB's support. 'Well,' she said, 'it would help if he was nice to people.'

Nice or not, the odds were stacked against the leader's office, which told unions of the broad thrust of proposals to limit the membership's influence over the summer. At first they were sounded out, a little disingenuously, with reports of MPs' ongoing anxiety over deselections. When the plan was set out in full, the overwhelming reaction was one of scepticism and hesitation. Unison could not commit. Smith did not want to strike out alone. Usdaw, the shopworkers' union whose support for Starmer was never normally in doubt, thought it all too radical. The secrecy unsettled them. Michael Wheeler, its political officer, told Matt Pound: 'It's all too late . . . this isn't right. You can't just bank on the support of an individual union.' Undaunted, McSweeney pressed on. As August turned into September his plans had left the digital realm and entered the material world of the leader's office. Sam White, his new chief of staff, was briefed by McSweeney as they climbed Arthur's Seat on a trip to Edinburgh, and agreed immediately with the logic of reforming the party's rulebook to liberate MPs from placating their most vocal activists.

Only then was Starmer informed of the specifics. He had known in vague terms what McSweeney hoped to do. In April, just before Hartlepool, he had been the grateful recipient of McSweeney's memo on *Labour for the Country*, which ended with the mention of 'a conference that illustrates the struggle to change the party'. But he knew nothing of the elaborate plans to effect that change, until September. That, however, was McSweeney's modus operandi. He knew that Starmer would agree to almost everything if he could be convinced it represented the shortest possible route to Downing Street. The leader's prolonged ignorance was also explained by the fact that constituency delegates had not been confirmed until June. McSweeney and Pound saw little point in seeking Starmer's approval before they knew which delegates would be willing to vote with him. In his diary, a friend of the Irishman wrote: 'Party conference – keep our mouths shut until the delegates are locked up.'

Despite Starmer's hardened resolve, however, he had not suddenly developed the close interest in internal Labour politics that had always eluded him. That much was all too clear to a baffled shadow cabinet. Said one of its members: 'Gordon, Tony, Jeremy, Ed, they basically just wanted to talk politics the whole time. The moment something happened, they'd be making excuses to get away and talk politics with their pals. Whereas Keir doesn't want to be sitting around the table talking. He's much more bored with the detail of politics than any previous leader of the Labour Party I've ever seen.' Tellingly, a select subset of shadow ministers had known of the reforms before their leader – with the rest told at an awayday at the headquarters of the Local Government Association in early September. The chosen few thought this curious imbalance of knowledge immaterial. 'If he was aware,' another member of the shadow cabinet adds, 'it was only in the broadest of senses. All I really cared about was that there was de facto permission, I didn't even care if there was explicit permission. As long as we had that, it almost didn't matter.'

Yet explicit permission would at some stage have to be given. McSweeney and White made the pitch for it together towards the end of August. 'You can fight on the back foot or you can fight on the front foot,' White, who had sold himself to Starmer as a purveyor of hard truths, told the leader. 'But we're going to have to fight.' Characteristically, Starmer at first gave little away. It was unclear whether he agreed with the conclusion most of his team had then reached, which was that changing the rules offered him a similar opportunity to that seized by Tony Blair when he abandoned Clause IV of the Labour constitution. As one of his senior advisers explained: 'Voters were only going to come back to us if they heard from us: "Yeah, look, I'm sorry, we kind of fucked up, and we presented a party and a candidate for prime minister that wasn't fit for your vote at the last election. We heard you loud and clear, we've changed, and so therefore can you please vote Labour?"' McSweeney laboured the point. 'I completely agree,' White went on. 'This is a high-risk strategy, but I think you've got no other.' He too was confident in Starmer's appetite for change, however perilous its pursuit. At an earlier meeting in the depths of August at which they discussed White's appointment, the leader had said: 'You're here to shake things up. You're not here to keep things the same. We're not on a trajectory to win today. We need to get on to a trajectory to win.'

★

'People thought we had lost our minds, because obviously we weren't going to tell people that we were going to do this. We're planning an

ambush. You don't tell people you're planning an ambush.' So goes
the official explanation, offered by one of the men who had known of
the reforms from the beginning, of why Starmer only told the unions
and his deputy of his plan to rewrite the rules of the Labour Party a
week before it went to Brighton for the conference that would make
or break him. The full story is rather more complicated.

In an ideal world, Starmer would have broken cover much earlier
than Monday 20 September. But in the first weeks of that month came
two sharp reminders that they inhabited an imperfect world. Just as
McSweeney and Christina McAnea had feared, the hard left won control of Unison's national executive. Enthusiastic support was now out
of the question. Abstention was the best she could do. McAnea's disap-
pearance left Gary Smith, of GMB, and Paddy Lillis, of Usdaw, out on
their own. Neither man wished to be there.

Still, they planned to take a final decision on whether to press on.
That Saturday, however, Starmer learned of the death of Jonny Cooper,
an old friend from his Doughty Street chambers. When he delivered
Cooper's eulogy, Starmer described the loss as 'unbearable'. Suddenly,
the work of the leader's office seemed irrelevant. Distraught, he could
barely focus when his team met on Zoom to consider its verdict on
the reforms. When he did speak, he radiated uncertainty, and worried
the unions might abandon him en masse. 'Well, I'm not sure,' he said.
'What happens if we get none of them?' McSweeney pushed for an
answer. TULO, the talking shop at which leaders of Labour's affiliated
unions had their chance to air their grievances to Starmer's face, had
been called for a meeting on Tuesday the 21st – and its agenda had yet
to be written. For once that meeting was taken seriously by LOTO,
who had promised Usdaw that they would make a serious attempt to
convince the doubters. 'Look,' McSweeney said, 'we have to make a
decision tonight.' The green light flashed. 'Let's go for it,' said Starmer.

'Keir could have been a wimp, and said: "No, not interested in a
confrontation at this conference,"' a member of the Project Ex group
recalls admiringly. Yet confrontation was the course he had chosen,
even as he grappled with the pain of loss. The following morning
McSweeney invited the regional directors who had not enjoyed the
same privileged access as Ridley and Ryan into his confidence. He
was visibly and audibly excited as he addressed them virtually, from

the new home in Lanarkshire he had bought the previous year, and so were they. Months of secrecy had ended. By 4.56 p.m. news of the plan was disseminated publicly by the journalist Aaron Bastani, whose Novara Media website spoke for the very politicians the reforms intended to enfeeble. 'HERE WE GO?' he tweeted. 'Whispers of Labour going back to electoral college in selecting next leader with it being 1/3rd PLP, 1/3rd trade unions & 1/3rd CLPs. Could be going to NEC Friday . . . Corbynite legacy may be little more than reversal of Miliband reforms. Unison & GMB may decide it.' He had called the stakes – and the risks – with uncanny perception. At 6.27 p.m., Sienna Rodgers, the editor of LabourList, added drily: 'The next TULO meeting will be interesting.'

Indeed it was. McSweeney likened TULO to the UN Security Council. Meetings were too long, too tense, and almost always ended with a superpower wielding a veto. The next morning all thirteen union leaders said no to the reforms. They demanded a halt and claimed they could not agree to such consequential rule changes tabled at the eleventh hour. In truth most were happy to see it postponed indefinitely. 'It's too late,' they said, one after the other, as Starmer and his aides sat listening to the call in the boardroom of the leader's office. 'Okay,' he said, a little awkwardly. 'We'll take this away and reconvene.' The leader's tone was so audibly uncomfortable that when Gary Smith took stock with Christina McAnea, she collapsed into fits of laughter. Starmer found the experience less amusing. He held out the prospect of a negotiated compromise. For months the intricacies of the plan were so jealously guarded that even Starmer himself had been unaware of them: now his every utterance was published in real time by journalists. Any concession would now be reported as a humiliating submission to the strength of the left. That alone convinced Matt Pound that they had no choice but to hold their nerve. As the meeting adjourned he grabbed McSweeney and Matthew Doyle. 'This is bullshit,' he told them. 'Of course they're going to say no. Obviously their starting position is no. We've just got to keep pushing. We're boxed in now. If there's any climbdown, it looks like we've caved ten days ahead of conference.'

Pound was right. The left began its rearguard. Just after 5 p.m., Momentum emailed its supporters with a fundraising appeal from

Zarah Sultana, the Corbynite MP: 'The leadership is trying to introduce an electoral college to elect the Labour leader. This would massively increase the power of MPs at the expense of ordinary members. This would be a shameful attack on democracy.' At 9.43 p.m., Sharon Graham, Len McCluskey's successor as general secretary of Unite, spoke in neither sorrow nor rage, but condescension. 'I wasn't even angry,' she said. 'I was bemused . . . they've lost touch with reality. Who thinks this is a good idea? It's just strange.' She declared Labour so irrelevant to the industrial struggle that she declined to come to Brighton altogether. Yet in urging Starmer to postpone the changes for another year, Graham convinced the leader's office to do the opposite. 'It was done,' one said. 'We had to go ahead, and we were going all the way.'

Over the following days McSweeney barely slept. He rose at 5 a.m. each morning to call Pound for an update on the arithmetic of conference votes. At 7 a.m. he would call Smith, Doyle and anyone else who might help him. Friends began to disappear. Colleagues challenged him. Deborah Mattinson, who had not been consulted, objected outright. Starmer's year had been defined by jeopardy and he had only just survived. Why invite more uncertainty? Luke Sullivan, the new political secretary whose old habits from the chief whip's office died hard, sought to do a deal with Unite. Unions sued for peace. Some promised to back the leadership's plans to make it harder to deselect MPs if the rest of the reforms were dropped. Others proposed a special conference be held in the spring.

Neither offer was accepted. LOTO listened to only one outsider. White, whose own conviction that conflict was a precondition of change never wavered in that trying week, called Tony Blair. 'The mess is the way,' Blair said. To White he sounded like a Stoic philosopher. 'The mess is the way.'

★

What a mess it was. By Friday, Labour's dysfunctional family had decamped to Brighton for its first conference since 2019. Nowhere else did left, right and unions meet as equals: voting against one another, drinking alongside one another in the same hotels and pubs. Nowhere else did the national media pay such close attention to all the Labour

Party did. Starmer had arrived unproven and had only one opportunity to defy the narrative that still prevailed after Hartlepool: that he was weak, indecisive, a prisoner of the untamed left. Arriving in Brighton as the rest of the country ran out of petrol, a crisis Tory ministers struggled to resolve, the government lay vulnerable. But his authority teetered on a deal whose imminent failure risked conveying the very opposite of authority. TULO met again that afternoon, as did the NEC. McSweeney barely recognised himself. Inscrutability had been the defining feature of his work for Starmer. The left had always failed to read him. Now the Irishman was utterly transparent. As he waited to meet the unions he physically shook. Having come to Sussex to kill off the left, he instead reckoned with his own political mortality. Before leaving home he had told his wife: 'If we lose, I'm fucked. I've got to go.' His mind wrote his own obituary. People would say that Morgan McSweeney did not know how to count. That hurt most of all. The job was neither here nor there. To be campaign director of the Labour Party meant nothing if the left was to control him forever.

The unions were all sound and fury. Starmer stressed that he was seeking consensus. One by one, this time looking the leader in the eye, the general secretaries 'bollocked' him for his failure to consult them. Smith, in what transpired to be a fit of performative anger, took the opportunity to deride the leader for his failure to endorse the £15-an-hour minimum wage supported by the GMB and asked repeatedly if he was embarrassed by its green energy policy. That every criticism was leaked to the leadership's most outspoken critics only compounded the indignity. 'I'm told Keir Starmer's meeting with trade union leaders was a "shit show",' declared the *Guardian*'s Owen Jones. Starmer's humiliation was so comprehensive that his team could not bring themselves to table the rule changes at that evening's meeting of the NEC, whose moderate members openly questioned the leadership's wisdom too. 'Why do we want confrontation?' one asked Akehurst.

Events made a beggar of the Labour leader. That evening he went from union to union, like a travelling salesman fallen on hard times. First he met Paddy Lillis, who arrived in Starmer's suite in the Brighton Hilton with a lifeline. 'If you can get at least one other general secretary with me, I'll be with you,' he said. McAnea was immovable. The most she could do was abstain. Where was Gary Smith? They asked that question literally. 'Track him through every fucking reception he's going to,' McSweeney told Drew Smith, a GMB official. 'Don't leave him out of sight. He's got to meet Keir tonight.' It was midnight before he did. The long wait was no power play. For all his swagger, Labour politics mattered less to him than his own union. The GMB's offices had been flooded before Smith's arrival, destroying many of its records. His most valued member of staff was seven months pregnant. Other trade unionists thrived on the leverage they had over the leadership of the Labour Party: Smith could barely summon the energy to care. However irritated he had been by Starmer's slights, he did not dislike him. They had been for that pint. Indeed, to his surprise, they had been for three. 'What does Keir want?' Smith asked his staff that night. He was prepared to negotiate.

Smith did dislike the Corbynite left. That was decisive. He loathed Unite, whose members had scabbed on strikes called by the GMB's refuse collectors and gas workers. 'Fuck them,' he told fellow union leaders, in a voice that sounded like crunching gravel. 'We're not getting pushed about by McCluskey's mob anymore.' He would do his so-called comrades no favours. Jon Lansman, the godfather of Momentum, called Smith's adviser Rhea Wolfson in a vain attempt to barter. If the GMB opposed Starmer, he would ensure his activists voted for its motion on energy policy. This she rejected out of hand: 'You don't have any currency.' Besides, for all his pantomime opposition, Smith had no issue with an electoral college which, after all, would endow the unions with a third of the vote in leadership elections. 'Why would we surrender union power?'

He asked if Starmer knew how to count. 'How many votes have you got, if you've got the GMB?'

'50.3 per cent.'

'Are you fucking sure?'

'We've got 50.3 and 49.7.'

'Okay. Don't do this again.'

An hour later Smith called McSweeney. He could count on the GMB. Ecstatic, the Irishman went to Starmer's room. Uncharacteristically, he met him with a long embrace. Together they had survived again.

Unison's intentions remained unclear. That night McSweeney had fallen into conversation with Rob Hill, McAnea's husband. They spoke of old times in south London. 'The Trots are still in control of

Streatham,' moaned Hill. McSweeney did not say what he wanted to say: that McAnea could marginalise the hard left if she shifted her position. But that seemed unlikely, so much so that he had given up on them.

Overnight, McSweeney and Pound tempered their ambitions. They would no longer seek to reintroduce the electoral college, enhance the power of MPs to pick their leader, and abolish the Miliband system of one-member, one-vote. The increased threshold for leadership nominations, from 10 per cent to 25 per cent of Labour MPs, now stood alone on the agenda. The principle of one-member, one-vote would remain unchanged. But what appeared to be a gesture of goodwill was in fact a deliberate attempt to heighten pressure on the unions. Mark Ferguson of Unison had been happy to talk about thresholds. They had no wish for another Jeremy Corbyn to reach another ballot. Others complained that they would now have less power over the process than under the electoral college they had opposed. Expecting another concession, they proposed a threshold of 15 per cent. Then 17.5 per cent. Tough luck, said LOTO.

Angela Rayner made a final play for compromise. When the NEC met on Saturday morning to decide the package that would be put to the conference floor, she arrived with an amendment of her own. Yes, nominees for the leadership would require 25 per cent of MPs to back them. But if no woman met the threshold, then they would be included regardless. This gesture towards gender equality was inevitably interpreted as an attempt to ensure Rayner herself would fight the next leadership election. Her team saw it quite differently: by tabling the caveat, they say now, she was seeking to pacify both parliamentary colleagues on the left and unions who feared the coronation of the Labour right's great hope, Wes Streeting. If gender equality was the only way of avoiding a shortlist of one, they were happy to advocate it. In the event, the leadership contacted Rayner's team over WhatsApp as the meeting took place, prompting a series of 'under the table' discussions that led them to think again on their threshold. At the eleventh hour, the meeting considered a proposal to reduce the threshold to 20 per cent. Tacked on to it was a proposed working group, to be chaired by Rayner, which would review the party's rules more broadly. That McSweeney had no intention of it ever meeting was necessarily not disclosed in the moment. When it came to the vote, the new motion passed. Triumphant, Shabana Mahmood told the BBC: 'The changes that have passed the NEC this morning . . . show we are a serious political party under Keir's leadership.' Only the delegates remained to be convinced.

Those supportive of Starmer received their instructions from Ake-hurst at the Sussex County Arts Club. Ryan and Ridley pored over spreadsheets that described every delegate in minute detail. What were their politics? Would they need their children looked after if they were to attend votes? Delegates who did not need convincing were secretly assigned to those who did. Said one official: 'Wavering or undecided delegates were buddied up with the staunchest believers of the project, whose job was to stick to them throughout the duration of conference and become their best friends.' People like 'little old Ellie from Braintree CLP' – a charming and gently persuasive pensioner with 'sound politics' – were reborn as evangelists for the leadership. McSweeney obsessed over every vote. The day before conference, he had texted Ridley and Ryan at 5.51 a.m. to ask: 'Are any delegates not going to make it to conference?'

David Evans was their guinea pig. After a jittery speech in which he asked delegates to think of why they had joined the Labour Party – a rhetorical question that was nonetheless met by cries of 'JEREMY CORBYN!' – the general secretary called a vote on his own future. He won by 59 per cent to 41 per cent. The leader's office exhaled. McSweeney asked Ryan whether the reforms might pass too.

'After David,' Ryan said, 'we're fairly confident that our numbers are accurate.'

'Keir has said this has got to be done. We've got to go for it.'

That evening Margaret McDonagh reminded Blairism's past and future of the price of failure. Ridley, Ryan, Pound, McSweeney and Kennedy met in the Hilton. Confined to her home by terminal cancer, she told them that the future of the Labour Party rested on the reforms. McSweeney went to bed knowing that it might still be lost. He knew, too, that they would not give up. Having consulted Nick Thomas-Symonds, the shadow cabinet's resident historian, he had ensured a second speech was prepared for Starmer. Like Hugh Gaitskell, Starmer would respond to defeat by vowing to 'fight, fight and fight again' to save Labour from the left. On the promenade, Pound was still cursing Unison. He crossed paths with Wendy Nichols, the union's elder stateswoman. He complained that her comrades were doing nothing to help. They refused to stand up for Starmer because they feared the hard left. What kind of logic was that? His humiliation would only encourage them to organise. Nichols vowed to help, and exerted pressure on McAnea and her delegates.

Sunday had the appearance of another difficult day. As was customary, Starmer ran the gauntlet of television cameras that morning. His interview with Andrew Marr on the BBC was largely given over to questions of his deputy's decorum. As the leader's office had marinated in its own anxiety, Rayner had spent the previous evening addressing activists in her own inimitable style. 'I'm sick of shouting from the sidelines,' she told a reception full of friends from her native northwest. 'I bet yous lot are too.' She turned her fire on Boris Johnson. 'We cannot get any worse than a bunch of *scum*. Homophobic, racist, misogynistic, absolute pile of banana republic . . . Etonian . . . *piece of scum* – and I held back a little – that I have ever seen in my life!' More disruption followed. At 5.20 p.m., Andy McDonald quit as shadow secretary of state for employment rights in protest at Starmer's failure to endorse a £15 minimum wage. The leader was so rattled by this show of sedition that he demanded the television be turned off. 'I don't want to look at that.'

It was nonetheless the best day of McSweeney's working life. That morning his phone had buzzed with a text from Liz Snape, Unison's assistant general secretary. They would vote for the reforms.

Later he asked Rob Hill what had changed McAnea's mind. With the GMB's backing, Starmer already seemed set for a narrow victory. 'Why did she do it, Rob? We had won. She doesn't need to do this.'

'She couldn't sleep. She knew it was the right thing to do. She wanted to back you.'

To outsiders his elation might have been incomprehensible. All he had done was edit a few lines of Labour's rulebook. That, however, meant everything to McSweeney. He had severed the link between Ted Knight and Jeremy Corbyn and power within his party. The war was over. Unite no longer held the union movement and the Labour Party in its vice. Morgan McSweeney knew how to count.

*

The reforms went to the conference floor under a title that understated the emotional toll they had demanded from their authors: 'Getting Labour Election Ready'. Dave Ward, the Corbynite leader of the CWU, spoke first. He railed against the leader's office as Starmer sat silently on the same stage. 'We have not been consulted . . . we feel we have been bounced, and even at this late stage I think Keir should reflect on this.'

'Welcome to the red wedding!' shouted McSweeney, who struggled to contain himself. He left the room to await the result. Once he had, another delegate complained that the new rules were so restrictive as to constrain the choice before members to an undemocratic degree. Margaret Beckett, Ed Balls, Andy Burnham, Diane Abbott: not one of these 'Labour giants' could have run for leader under this regime. 'In 2020,' he said, 'we would have been faced with Keir Starmer or Keir Starmer.'

It was a fair point. To McSweeney, it was *the* point. Unknowingly, the delegate had described LOTO's new definition of unity. Twice now the Irishman had planned in secret to shift the ground of Labour politics in directions only he knew. For as long as he could he had told nobody, not even Starmer, of his true intentions. Now the party would inhabit a reality that bore no resemblance to the party Starmer had promised to build in 2020.

Until that Sunday evening, at least. Once the ballots had been cast McSweeney ran to Alex Barros-Curtis, the party's legal director. Printers whirred. Barros-Curtis presented the numbers to McSweeney: 53.67 per cent of delegates had voted with the leadership. At 6.34 p.m. on Sunday 26 September, Project Ex concluded its work. McSweeney believed that Starmer might now face the country. The Conservative Party would soon ensure the voters were willing to pay attention to him. His new priorities were distilled into a put-down of leftist hecklers, texted by McGinn to White: 'Shouting slogans, or changing lives, conference?'

'We need to control this narrative,' McSweeney said, at last acknowledging the need to tell the world of what he had done in secret. The last-minute compromise on the electoral college meant journalists would leave Brighton believing that the leadership had been forced to concede by a resurgent left – that the story was still one of weakness and division. Yet McSweeney had everything he wanted.

'Pin the results on the wall. And then they're public. That's it. They're published. We don't need to do anything else.'

Barros-Curtis dithered with the papers. Ridley arrived with a stapler and tape. Matthew Doyle went to tell the press.

By now the Irishman was laughing manically. 'Pin it to the wall! *Pin the fucking result on the wall!*'

13

Partygate

First, Dominic Cummings offered to help make Jeremy Corbyn prime minister. Then, he succeeded in making Sir Keir Starmer prime minister. The ends were at odds with everything the strategist who had transformed Conservative politics appeared to believe. The means were never revealed.

On 7 January 2019, Matt Zarb-Cousin, an Essex Boy recovering from a draining year as Corbyn's spokesman, was scrolling through Twitter. Though no longer employed by the Labour Party, he continued to make his profane and lively case for socialism online. Messages from admirers – and detractors – came readily. Another landed. The sender said they admired Zarb-Cousin's work. Then they claimed to be Cummings, the man who had made Brexit happen. They asked to meet him.

Zarb-Cousin turned to his wife. 'This is a stitch-up,' he said. 'I might get whacked.' Just what, after all, could Dominic Cummings want from a Corbynite? His Vote Leave campaign had divided Labour against itself. His politics – that bracing brand of anarchic, right-wing populism – were everything that Jeremy defined himself against. David Cameron, tormented by Cummings as prime minister, had called him 'a career psychopath'. He looked like one, too: wild-eyed and dishevelled. His business was destroying the left, not helping its leaders. So what did Cummings want from this Corbynite? And what could a Corbynite possibly want from Cummings?

But the two men did meet, for dinner at Dishoom, an Indian restaurant in Shoreditch, four miles but a world away from Westminster. They were joined by James Schneider, who still worked in the office that Zarb-Cousin had left. Cummings wanted his life's work to be saved by Corbyn from the grinding jaws of parliamentary process. Conservative MPs refused to back their government's Brexit deal. So too did Starmer, who as shadow Brexit secretary had been as obstructive as any Tory Eurosceptic. Progressives rallied around the banner of the People's Vote campaign. All that Vote Leave had fought for seemed lost. Only Corbyn could save them now.

Cummings explained how. If Labour whipped its MPs to vote for Theresa May's withdrawal agreement, it would pass the Commons. The Tories would split and May would resign. No longer hamstrung by his own party's divisions on Europe, Corbyn – promising to fund the NHS and public services – might win the general election that would surely follow.

At this moment of deadlock and uncertainty it no longer mattered that Cummings thought Corbyn's socialism was deranged. Through his Labour Party ran the most straightforward escape from Brussels. In power, the radical left might do what Cummings most wanted, dismantle the Civil Service establishment, and take a sledgehammer to the old ways of Whitehall. Cummings was willing to help them do it. Schneider listened with interest. Corbyn's inner circle was as hostile to a second referendum – and to Starmer, its chief advocate within the Labour Party – as Cummings. Schneider referred the proposal to his superiors. He recalls now: 'I wanted Brexit to pass, the Tories to split, us to run a left-populist insurgent campaign, have a proper operation to do that, and therefore win.' The plan proceeded. Cummings drew Corbyn's roadmap to power in a text to Zarb-Cousin. 'Thanks for dinner comrade! You get Brexit through, [People's Vote] fucked . . . high chance of Govt collapse and election pre-August but Tory civil war guaranteed for years in any scenario . . .'

From focus groups in Labour's battleground seats in the West Midlands, Cummings had learned that Corbyn could not afford to decline his offer. With uncanny prescience, he wrote: 'My view has been strengthened that 2REF = crackup for both parties, it will be a messy race to see which party collapses fastest under the pressure. Jeremy on the same side as Blair and Chuka [Umunna] when a tidal wave of hate is unleashed outside the M25 wd be disaster for him in marginal seats but ditto for Tories. Long-term strategic danger for LAB is the crackup gives Tories a big strategic advantage with working classes for years to come, after they re-form as a clearly Brexit party . . . and they brand Labour as "against working-class people on Brexit and immigration, and Labour doesn't respect democracy".'

Cummings was right. The Corbynites knew he was right. Over the ensuing months he kept sending his messages, promising electoral riches and warning of disaster if the left did not claim them. As May announced her resignation, he crowed: 'The destruction of the Tories proceeds apace, comrade. Boris is their last gasp at ignoring reality. When that fails . . . kaboom.' What he did not know – what nobody knew, not least Corbyn – was that Starmer was already preparing himself. The shadow Brexit secretary began every week at Jenny Chapman's kitchen table. There he and his Arlington Group were plotting the opposite course for power. Starmer knew that to support a second referendum was to win the affection of the members who would be asked to choose the next leader of the Labour Party. John McDonnell knew that without a People's Vote the Remain voters of the middle classes would vote for anyone other than the Labour Party. Together they were unbeatable, even by their leader.

Corbyn endorsed a second referendum. Cummings went to work for Johnson. He did for Boris what he might have done for Jeremy. The Tories were remade as a party of Brexit. Johnson read the lines that had been written for Corbyn – get Brexit done, Labour don't respect democracy – and annihilated him. Starmer, derided by Cummings in another text to Matt Zarb-Cousin as the 'central casting London Remain beta-brain lawyer', posed no threat to Johnson. But power always reveals, and as the pandemic placed unprecedented strain on the state it revealed to Cummings that Johnson was all he had feared: lazy, disorganised, too hungry for the media's approval. By November 2020, not even a year after the election that had gone exactly to plan, Cummings walked out of Downing Street with a cardboard box and an appetite for vengeance. He knew every secret. He knew *the* secret. Johnson and his government had told the British people to stay at home. They criminalised birthdays, weddings, funerals – even Christmas dinner. Parents died alone as their children followed the law. In Downing Street, they broke it. They partied and they drank while ordinary people were prosecuted for doing the same. Cummings knew.

★

McSweeney knew too. He knew that to be inside Downing Street that winter was to enjoy a kind of privilege that Starmer never could. Isolation disempowered the Labour leadership. Conversation, particularly the kind the Irishman liked – long, discursive, inconspicuous – became harder to achieve through a screen. He went for winding walks instead, for miles across London. He walked with Steve Reed, his mentor from Lambeth, or with Marcus Roberts, the pollster whose data had made Starmer leader.

They talked about how difficult it was to do politics in a party forced to litigate its furious disagreements online, and looked enviously at the government buildings where working life continued as normal. Ministers had everything and they had nothing. 'Keir didn't get to lead the party because of lockdown,' recalled one key member of his court. 'He didn't get to engage. He was having to dispense justice via Zoom and conduct a party overhaul without being able to get in the room with everyone. I don't think you could overstate how hard the positions of lockdown made the management of the political party and it was completely asymmetric because we were not allowed to organise and the Tories were.'

One evening McSweeney walked with Roberts along Whitehall. They passed the Cabinet Office, then Downing Street. 'This is insane,' the pollster said. 'You and I are limited to this, and they're all allowed to be inside together. *This* is the best that we can do – and *they* get to do all of that.'

'Yeah,' McSweeney said. 'Knowing them, that's probably not the only thing they're doing. I bet they've got the beers in.'

It was a joke – an outlandish caricature of what Johnson's opponents imagined him to be. Yet it turned out to be true, though nobody would prove it for another year. On 1 December 2021, the front page of the *Daily Mirror* read: 'BORIS PARTY BROKE COVID RULES. No. 10 hosted boozy bashes while millions endured strict lockdown.' The story, by the paper's political editor Pippa Crerar, had been long in the making. Rumours of illegal gatherings in government buildings had bounced around Westminster for some months. Paul Ovenden, by now returned to the leader's office as Labour's head of attack and rebuttal, had played his part in spreading them. Yet it was Cummings who put them in print. ITV was already in receipt of footage captured inside Downing Street the previous winter, in which Johnson's press secretary Allegra Stratton joked awkwardly about a 'Downing Street Christmas party on Friday night'. Her colleagues bantered about cheese and wine. 'This fictional party was a business meeting and it was not socially distanced,' she said, grinning. Unable to broadcast the clip on the strict orders of cautious lawyers, an ITV executive took it instead to a friend of Cummings. They vowed to make the public aware of its contents. Via the *Mirror*, they did. ITV News broadcast the video six days later.

Cummings went to the press because he knew how Johnson would respond to difficulty. He lied and lied and lied. His spokesman lied, telling the media: 'There was no Christmas party. Covid rules were followed at all times.' The prime minister lied in the Commons, telling the Labour MP Catherine West on 8 December: 'No. The guidance was followed and the rules were followed at all times.' Voters did not believe him. Opinion polls recorded a dramatic collapse in their trust in the Conservative Party, and never again did they overtake Labour. In an instant Starmer ascended to the terrain he knew best: the moral high ground. He dissected every dissembling denial like the barrister he was. The beginning of 2021 had brought despair; the middle the very real prospect of his resignation. By its end, the long and squalid fall of Johnson was in train. Scandal infected everything in British politics – including Starmer himself. Before long the fate of two leaders had been placed in the hands of unaccountable power – a civil servant in the Cabinet Office, and a police officer in Durham.

★

Starmer despised Johnson. In the 2000s they had worked two doors apart on Doughty Street. In his chambers at No. 54, the young barrister worked long hours on cases he hoped would buttress a new architecture of human rights law. In the offices of the *Spectator*, at No. 56, the shambling editor of the house journal of high Toryism mocked and belittled his neighbour's mission as he slept with his staff. In almost everything they were opposites. To his advisers, Starmer often recounted a story from a session of Prime Minister's Questions. 'I'm looking him in the eye. I know he's lying, he knows he's lying, but there's nothing I can do about it.' He felt helpless to resist what Johnson was doing to British politics – electorally and morally. A friend of Starmer later said: 'He always felt that with Boris in place, Labour would end up losing. Despite the sleaze, he thought that by 2024 it would have faded into the background and Labour would struggle to win back the seats in the north and Midlands that it lost in 2019.' That his hate for the prime minister was unrequited illustrated that much too. The worst Johnson ever said to his own team about his opposite number was: 'He's quite boring.' At the dispatch box he mocked him as 'Captain Hindsight', 'a great pointless human bollard', and 'Captain Crasheroonie Snoozefest'. There was method in his rhetorical madness. Firstly, as one of Johnson's closest aides explains, 'it gave the media something to say about Starmer, who at that stage was basically just a blank canvas'. Secondly, the Labour leader hated the mockery. His public service was Johnson's punchline. He could not stand it. In public he was all lawyerly restraint – or quite boring. Passion was never his natural register. In private, he raged. Aides in the leader's office did not disagree with him but were sceptical whether righteous anger had any political value. Simply hating Johnson, or denouncing him as a liar and demagogue – as so many progressives did – would not rebuild the red wall by itself.

That was reflected in what the Labour leader said about Tory scandal. Much of the time it was nothing. Initially this had been a deliberate strategy. To the frustration of junior colleagues, Ben Nunn had calculated that the public had little appetite for partisan attacks on a government whose success during the pandemic would make the difference between life and death. In early 2020, Steve Reed had been alone among the shadow cabinet in monstering his opponent, the housing secretary Robert Jenrick, for unlawfully approving a housing development for the Conservative donor and newspaper tycoon Richard Desmond – sparing him £45 million in tax in the process. That campaign was abruptly curtailed when Reed tweeted that Desmond, who was Jewish, acted as 'the puppet master to the entire Tory cabinet'. In this case column inches were nowhere near proportionate to political impact. Jenrick survived. Johnson seemed impervious to the kind of controversy that would fatally wound an ordinary politician, no matter how hard so many journalists worked to uncover it.

Cummings changed that, too. On Friday 22 May 2020 the *Daily Mirror* and *Guardian* had revealed that he had broken lockdown rules to drive from London to Durham while showing symptoms of Covid.

Johnson again ignored opprobrium from the press and public. His Svengali stayed – at least for a few months longer. But the Labour leadership adjusted its thinking. Nunn had known the story was coming and had prepared an anodyne response for whatever frontbencher was available to approve it. As he prepared to issue the words in the name of Andrew Gwynne, the ever-helpful shadow health minister, he read the *Mirror*'s report. Buried in it was a quote from an eyewitness who had seen Cummings on his travels. 'We were shocked and surprised to see him because the last time we did was earlier in the week in Downing Street,' they said. 'We thought: "He's not supposed to be here during the lockdown." We thought: "What double standards, one rule for him as a senior adviser to the prime minister, and another for the rest of us."'

'That's it,' Nunn thought to himself, hastily rewriting the statement now he knew the kid gloves he had reluctantly worn might come off. 'That's the line.'

It remained the line for the best part of the year. With his videographer wife he rushed to Starmer's home the next morning. If any moment had been made for a fastidious, almost comically punctilious lawyer, it was this. The leader stood before a brick wall and repeated the line – 'One rule for them, and another for the rest of us' – in a clip for social media, subsequently seen by millions. That weekend the era of constructive opposition that Labour had promised ended. Labour stuck to that script throughout the following months – partly because it had little else to say and still lacked the ability to campaign conventionally. Newspapers loved it. The public agreed with the premise. Yet still they voted Tory, in Hartlepool and almost everywhere else.

By the summer of 2021, however, attack came naturally to a party that had spent its first year in a defensive crouch. To Mahmood and McGinn, politics was blood sport. When the Conservative backbencher Lee Anderson publicly foreswore against watching England's successful run in the European Championships as long as its players took the knee before matches, they commissioned a petition demanding he continue his boycott to the final. These individual stunts were well received but did little to shift public opinion. But however sharp their distaste for the antics of the Tory party, the voters Labour most needed remained sympathetic to Johnson – even as the seeds of doubt sown over the first year of his premiership began to germinate. Research commissioned by Deborah Mattinson demonstrated the scale of the challenge. It revealed that voters not only needed to believe whatever attack Labour was mounting – and by 2021, many of them did – but had to have felt the same sort of pain that Starmer was seeking to inflict. Parties in Downing Street ticked both boxes. In Labour's focus groups the same anguished complaints recurred: 'I couldn't go to my mum's funeral.'

Starmer's response betrayed little of his hatred for the prime minister. Mattinson believed that a full-frontal assault on Johnson's wanting morality would achieve little politically. Labour could not mount 'a character assassination, just for its own sake, and think: "Job done." ' Instead Starmer resumed his old constitutional role as national prosecutor: exacting and dispassionate. The Commons was now his courtroom and over several months he built the case that eventually left the jurors of Parliament's privileges committee with no option but to convict Johnson for misleading MPs. On 1 December, the day of the Mirror's first report on parties in Downing Street, he asked Johnson: 'As millions of people were locked down last year, was a Christmas party thrown in Downing Street for dozens of people on 18 December?' He read in full the relevant government guidance, complete with its explicit proscription on Christmas lunches and parties. To that Boris said: 'What I can tell the right honourable and learned gentleman is that all guidance was followed completely in No. 10.' Only when Johnson spoke were there flashes of the fury Starmer expressed in private. He threw his hands in the air in disbelief and slapped his forehead in despair. Tentatively, the lawyer began to play politics. Seven days later, after ITV published the footage that exposed that assurance as a lie, Starmer returned to the theme: 'The prime minister and the government spent the week telling the British public that there was no party and that all guidance was followed completely. Millions of people now think the prime minister was taking them for fools and that they were lied to; they are right, aren't they?' Even as he squirmed Johnson did not deviate from his central – and dishonest – assertion that his staff had acted within the bounds of the law. 'I apologise for the impression that has been given that staff in Downing Street take this less than seriously. I am sickened myself and furious about that, but I repeat what I have said to him: I have been repeatedly assured that the rules were not broken.'

The public did not believe him. As Johnson's ratings tumbled West-minster began to take seriously the prospect that the man who only months earlier had agonised and considered resigning over the impos-sibility of Labour ever winning an election under his leadership could now become prime minister. Starmer was almost alone in refusing to believe. His former PPS Carolyn Harris, whose admiration for her friend was undimmed despite the unseemly circumstances of her sack-ing, texted him with another prophecy: 'You're going to be the next prime minister.'

'Well, we can't be complacent,' Starmer replied.

*

Though his own doubts had not yet dissipated, converts sprung from unlikely places. By now Starmer was speaking regularly to Tony Blair. The self-denying ordinance imposed by his advisers during the previous year's leadership contest was lifted, for now he had new advisers who were prepared to embrace the former prime minister without embarrassment. McGinn's first act upon joining the leader's office had been to seek Blair's advice in a private audience at the offices of his consultancy, with its oil painting of Jerusalem looming over the man who still hoped to bend history to his will. At first Blair had doubted that Starmer would ever do the same. His diagnosis of Labour's lost decade was that 'frankly, we chose the wrong Miliband'. At first he doubted that Starmer would embark on the course correction he believed necessary: a handbrake turn away from the left and towards the glossy vision of modernity his Institute for Global Change sold to foreign governments. 'There were a lot of people talking about whether you really did need to find something new,' Blair recalls. 'Once Keir came in, it was a question of: "Well, let's see what he does. If he moves in the right direction, the Labour Party will be back on the pitch again." But if it didn't do that, then we were going to have to look for something new.'

They found something new in the rejuvenated Keir. That Novem-ber, New Labour's great and good had gathered at the Kentish Town home of Georgia Gould to commemorate the tenth anniversary of the death of her father, Philip – the advertising executive whose insights had been the spur for Labour's transformation in the 1990s. As leader of

Camden Council, she was a rare thing among the Blairite aristocracy: a close friend of Starmer, who mingled awkwardly with a generation who still struggled to accept him as one of their own. Yet Blair offered his benediction, if cautiously. In a speech given in Starmer's presence he expressed his guarded optimism that his successor was at last 'heading in the right direction'. It was hardly effusive. But by Blair's own standards – and compared to his withering criticisms in private – it was a more ringing endorsement than any of his contemporaries had expected. They had long feared that Tony would prefer to undermine the new leadership – perhaps with a new party – than support it. So says a friend of Gordon Brown, who preferred to convey his feelings through barked phone calls from his home in Fife. 'Gordon was deeply worried about the direction that was headed in with Tony . . . he was treating Keir as a bit of an irrelevance when, as far as Gordon was concerned, Keir was doing an incredibly difficult job building us back from scratch and just needed to be helped onto his feet.' Starmer found them as Johnson staggered.

Behind him stood a new shadow cabinet and re-energised staff. In his first meeting with Starmer, Sam White had said: 'Of the things we need to do in the first ninety days, one of them is a reshuffle.' The team assembled haphazardly in the weekend after Hartlepool was a monument to a weakness the leader's intimates no longer felt. McSweeney, once hidebound by his responsibilities as chief of staff to the leader – an almost ambassadorial role that precluded him from expressing his own opinions – spoke of his motives with a new transparency. Addressing the NEC for the first time that November, he mocked the hard left to their faces: 'Winning teams are laser-focused on voters . . . and you're talking about Corbyn instead of what the voters want.' Supporters of the leadership thumped the table with glee. Privately, Starmer wondered why the shadow cabinet failed to show the same enthusiasm.

In the summer of 2021 he had commissioned an assessment of their performance – and that of Labour HQ – by senior staff. 'He asked us to feed in what the fuck was going wrong,' one said. 'And one of the things we fed in was about shadow cabinet ministers who weren't performing, who weren't turning up to meetings with business, or turning up half an hour late and having their camera off. People like that were sacked in the reshuffle. Keir was not messing about.' In covert meetings at Mattinson's home in Muswell Hill that summer, fortified by expensive wines, he played the game of fantasy politics that he had always forsworn – unimaginatively christened 'Operation Deborah's House'. Names were scribbled on fridge magnets White had bought from Amazon. Rachel Reeves and Sir Alan Campbell, Nick Brown's replacement as chief whip, were only initiated into the circle of trust after several weeks of private discussion. Shabana Mahmood was not. Her uncompromising style had alienated White and Mattinson, so much so that they discussed a plan to strip her of responsibility for Labour's campaigns. Mahmood believed her only sin was to have demanded high standards, and confronted Starmer: 'One thing I will not tolerate is being condemned – being charged, convicted and sentenced without the chance to plead my own case. There are two sides to every story, and if I'm butting heads with your staff, the real question is: why?'

The final result was revealing. Mahmood stayed, but Starmer killed his friends. Ed Miliband, unstintingly loyal to the man whose political career he was responsible for, was stripped of his business brief and left with the title of shadow climate secretary – a post that had no equivalent in government. 'Ed was very credible in the environmental world,' says one aide involved in the decision to demote him, bluntly. 'He's not credible with business.' He was replaced by the affable Johnny Reynolds, whose soft Sunderland accent belied the sharpness of his Blairite politics. White, late of the City, told colleagues that Reynolds was one of the few Labour politicians his fellow executives had been relieved to meet. Nick Thomas-Symonds was unceremoniously dumped as shadow home secretary in favour of Yvette Cooper, the former cabinet minister and failed leadership candidate who had returned to relevance as chairwoman of the home affairs select committee. As the last Brownite standing at the summit of Labour politics, her past divided opinion, as did her reputation for indecision. Her detractors delighted in the old joke: 'Does Yvette want a coffee or a tea? She doesn't know, she's called for more research.' Starmer took the decision regardless, abandoning one of his few true allies for a bigger name. 'If you're going to create a government of all the talents,' another adviser said, 'do you leave out someone who's visibly a big fish and a big hitter, and has held cabinet positions and run for the leadership?' Thomas-Symonds, one of Starmer's first and firmest friends in the Commons, later remonstrated with him over the betrayal over festive drinks at a Kentish Town pub. More straightforward was the promotion of David Lammy to shadow foreign secretary. He was a one-man exception to the usual rule that the length of a Labour MP's service was inversely proportional to their enthusiasm for Starmer. After Corbyn's defeat in 2019, the former minister had summoned Starmer to his Finsbury Park home. Starmer went assuming that Lammy would reveal his own intention to run for the leadership, as he invariably threatened to do after Labour lost an election, but his host did the opposite: it had to be Keir.

The leader had no compunction sacking Nandy as foreign secretary – an appointment which stemmed from the early unity phase more than any genuine kinship for a woman known for prolifically briefing and accusing Starmer of failing to speak up on antisemitism. Any lingering hope that the Starmer of 2021 might continue to preach the anti-austerity gospel of his leadership campaign was extinguished by the appointment of Pat McFadden, New Labour's Mr Gradgrind, as Reeves's deputy. Wes Streeting, princeling of the right, became shadow health secretary.

When the reshuffle eventually came, on Monday 29 November, Starmer left his party in no doubt as to where influence now lay: with the people he had very deliberately chosen not to empower the previous year. This was a team he believed might better communicate a new politics to a country finally prepared to listen to Labour. It resembled nothing so much as a reverse takeover by the party's right. Divided from the team that had made him, he turned to anyone who might help him win – whatever that meant for the old vision and whoever was humiliated in the process. None were left more chastened than Angela Rayner, the crowing victor of May's unfinished reshuffle. On the morning of the reshuffle she was speaking on sleaze in politics at the Institute for Government, an intervention long planned and approved by the leader's office. McSweeney told Jack McKenna, her spokesman: 'We're doing a reshuffle this morning.' Bewildered, her team asked for it to be delayed until the conclusion of her speech. They did no such thing. Questioned by journalists, Rayner had little option but to admit her isolation from authority and confess that she had known nothing. She claimed not to 'know the details of any reshuffle' and added, a little sniffily: 'We need some consistency in approaching things as an opposition.' McKenna went further, telling journalists:

'She was not aware of the details of the reshuffle and she was not consulted on the reshuffle.' With that response the leader's office were
none too pleased, and demanded an explanation from the nonplussed
McKenna. Why had they offered such a grudging response? 'Because
you did a reshuffle in the middle of her speech,' McKenna said. In that
awkward moment, the power dynamic that had defined so much of
Labour politics in 2021 was inverted. Whoever now ran the opposition,
it was not Angela Rayner.

His own authority at last secured, Starmer dismantled what little
Johnson retained with a new vigour and moral certainty. Fate, his old
enemy, appeared to align behind him just as the Blairites had. To the
relief of his advisers, that November the Corbynite MP Claudia Webbe
avoided a custodial sentence when she was convicted for harassing a
woman with whom her partner had conducted an affair – sparing the
leader's office the trauma of a by-election in her seat of Leicester East,
whose sectarian politics had toxified to the Conservatives' advantage.
'If there'd been a by-election,' one of its in-house pessimists said, 'we'd
have lost that, 100 per cent, to the Tories. Then we would have lost
Hartlepool in a white working-class seat, narrowly held on in Batley
and Spen – a Muslim seat – and then lost Leicester. There's no way he
stays on in that scenario.'

As 2022 began Starmer was no longer losing MPs but gaining them.
In hindsight, the signs that Christian Wakeford was unhappy sitting as
the Conservative member for Bury South were always there. He owed
his seat to Johnson but had come to dislike his style of government –
the dishonesty, the disregard for rules and convention, the betrayal of
the sacrifices they had demanded of the public – with a similar intensity
to Starmer. Westminster ought to have known that he would soon be
a Labour MP when, confined to crutches by a ruptured cruciate liga-
ment and high on prescription painkillers, he hobbled up to the former
cabinet minister Owen Paterson as his Tory colleagues reluctantly
filed through the division lobbies to exonerate Paterson of lobbying charges. Johnson had ordered his backbenchers to vote through
sweeping changes to Parliament's anti-sleaze regulations as a favour to
a friend. His voters were disgusted, and told their MPs so. The besuited
and balding Wakeford looked every inch the accountant he once was,
but spoke like a football hooligan as he squared up to Paterson.

'Fuck you, you fucking selfish cunt.'

That brief explosion illuminated every division in Johnson's Conservative Party. MPs for its new electorate of working men and women in the north and Midlands could neither understand nor explain the patrician entitlement of its old guard, the gilded sons of true blue shires. With every new revelation of rulebreaking, Wakeford's discomfort soured into disgust. Like his constituents, he could neither believe Johnson's denials nor tolerate his obfuscations. He demanded the prime minister's resignation, then considered his own. Over several months he stole fleeting moments in Commons lifts with Chris Elmore, a curmudgeonly Labour whip who heard Wakeford's counsels of despair with uncharacteristic patience. Their conversations always began with cleansing small talk about professional wrestling, a mutual passion. Alan Howarth, the last Conservative MP to defect directly to the Labour Party in opposition, some twenty-six years earlier, was enlisted to offer avuncular advice. Wakeford agonised. He no longer wanted to compromise himself by serving under Johnson. But nor could he bear the shame of betraying his friends by defecting to the Labour Party. Even once he had met Starmer under cover of darkness on the evening of Tuesday 18 January it was unclear whether he was willing to jump. As he teetered on the precipice the next morning, the leader's office decided to shove negotiations to their conclusion.

In Operation PLP+1, a WhatsApp group convened by Sir Alan Campbell and his enforcers in the Whip's Office, Luke Sullivan told colleagues that the papers had caught wind of a possible defection. 'They don't have his name yet,' he said, 'but can't be long until it's openly speculated.' Elmore replied: 'I was just wondering if I could push, gently.' Sullivan agreed: 'Absolutely should.' As ever, Conor McGinn went further: 'He's going today at 11.30. Either we announce it in a planned fashion or the tabloids do it in a chaotic one. Give him the choice. He's not dealing with a bunch of fucking monkeys and we aren't being fucked around. If it leaks then he gets nothing from us and he's on his own.' Elmore then drew up the terms of the blackmail: 'I'll say "*The Times* are asking us who is crossing, they seem to have it, it's a short list of possibles."' Little more than two hours later Wakeford walked into the chamber of the House of Commons, his anxious face hidden by a Union Jack facemask, 'shaking like a shitting dog'. He took his seat behind Starmer for his first session of Prime Minister's Questions as a Labour MP. His new colleagues cheered rapturously. 'Like so many people up and down the country,' Starmer said, suffused with a new confidence, 'he has concluded that the prime minister and the Conservative Party have shown themselves incapable of offering the leadership and government this country deserves.'

Within a week the Metropolitan Police announced they would investigate allegations that lockdown law had been broken in Downing Street, the very building in which the same laws had been written. Having built his case against Johnson, Starmer came to its inevitable conclusion at PMQs on 26 January. He asked the prime minister whether he believed he was subject to the ministerial code, complete with its prohibition on misleading the Commons. Johnson rambled but eventually answered in the affirmative. 'I think the prime minister said yes, he agrees the code does apply to him,' Starmer said. 'Therefore, if he misled Parliament, *he must resign.*' The new national mood of hostility towards Johnson – still molten and inchoate – began to take shape in Starmer's hands. By 31 January there was no ambiguity in his demands to Downing Street: 'Honesty and decency matter. After months of denials the prime minister is now under criminal investigation for breaking his own lockdown laws. He needs to do the decent thing and resign.'

To some in the shadow cabinet it all sounded hubristic. They worried that enshrining any violation of Covid restrictions as a capital offence – even those made unintentionally – might backfire among voters. 'We needed to carve out a space for inadvertent breaches because that was probably where most of the public were. If you do holier than thou and you're found to have made an inadvertent breach, they're going to treat you like the worst of the criminals . . . I had anxiety about that: pitching yourself as something you might not be, when you don't know what you are.' They were right to be anxious.

★

It began with ninety-six words in the *Sun*. Easily missed, tucked beneath a grainy still from a smartphone video on 2 May 2021, they told a short story about Starmer's own adherence to lockdown law in the days before the Hartlepool by-election, when he had made a brief stop in Durham and visited the office of Mary Kelly Foy, a Labour MP.

> Sir Keir Starmer has a beer indoors with colleagues on the campaign trail – but Labour says its leader did not break Covid rules as it was work.
>
> He was seen mixing with party workers in a constituency office in Durham on Friday night.
>
> Rules state you can meet indoors for work but not socially.
>
> Tory party co-chair Amanda Milling said: 'People will rightly be asking questions.'
>
> A Labour spokesman said last night: 'Keir was in the workplace, meeting a local MP in her constituency office. They paused for dinner as the meeting was in the evening.'

Milling was right. People *did* ask questions. Unfortunately for her party, those people were Ivo Delingpole, the Durham University undergraduate – and son of James, the headbanging right-wing columnist – who shot the thirty-four-second clip of the maskless Starmer sipping on a bottle of San Miguel and Labour activists eating curry around him; and Laurence Fox, the alt-right actor who had swapped a career in cosy crime drama for conspiratorial tweets. For all their undoubted energy this odd couple were no match for a flat denial from the office of the leader of the opposition. The story died a quick and quiet death. Before long, however, it was resurrected.

December 2021 was a bleak month to work in Conservative Campaign Headquarters. Starmer had forced the natural pugilists of British politics into a corner. Labour – and the media – were armed with a seemingly limitless supply of incriminating material leaked from within Downing Street. Ross Kempsell, the head of the Conservative Research Department, had nothing. This was unusual. Every week he held tutorials with Johnson on Labour politics. He had come to work for the prime minister via Guido Fawkes, the muckraking blog whose merciless exposés on political misconduct had ended many a political career. Then, as now, Kempsell spent long days listening to the left-wing podcasts and watching recordings of the fringe meetings Labour's shadow cabinet had forgotten they had ever spoken to. He excavated their words and gave them to the right-wing press. To Kempsell, the

Sun, Daily Mail and *Daily Telegraph* were his 'customers'. Their relationship was symbiotic. The success of the political agenda they prosecuted together would live and die on the quality of his wares. If Kempsell had no reply to Partygate, then all was lost. The scandal had already destroyed their most fundamental assumption about British politics. Until that winter, Johnson had assumed that Starmer would not be his opponent at the next election. 'We were devoting a significant amount of time and effort trying to prepare for a potential Rayner, Nandy, or Streeting leadership,' an adviser to the then prime minister recalls. 'We were more worried about Labour frontbenchers who we thought were genuinely challenging our constituency in the red wall. Ironically, we were quite relaxed about Starmer, because we thought that he was quite easy for Boris.' No longer. Starmer had become a clear and present danger Johnson could no longer afford to ignore. Kempsell and Isaac Levido, the Australian strategist who had won the Tories their majority in 2019, feared Downing Street was incapable of grasping the scale of the danger Johnson now faced. Dominic Cummings, Pippa Crerar, Keir Starmer, the *Daily Mirror*, the *Guardian*, the BBC: all combined in a perfect storm that Kempsell and Levido knew to have lethal potential. Crying conspiracy, as some Tories did, would solve nothing. Kempsell believed that attack was the best form of defence. He remembered the video of Starmer. Desperate, he told his team to get to work.

The result was a dossier of fifty-four pages, compiled over a couple of weeks that Christmas. It reconstructed, to the minute, what Starmer had done that night in Durham. Though it was never released to the public, its contents were soon splashed across the front page of the *Daily Mail*. Johnson's January had been punctuated by the metronomic drip-drip-drip of bad news and undeniable evidence of wrongdoing – an email to Downing Street staff in which they were invited to 'BYOB' to a Christmas party; reports of government advisers drunkenly breaking a child's swing and dancing to a DJ set on the eve of the Duke of Edinburgh's funeral; the Metropolitan Police launching an inquiry and questioning the prime minister himself; Sue Gray, the Civil Service sleazebuster appointed to establish the truth of the affair, ruling that there had been 'failures of leadership and judgement' in No. 10. Kempsell attempted to subject Starmer to the same onslaught. On 15 January, the *Mail*'s front page screamed: 'STARMER THE COVID PARTY

HYPOCRITE'. Two days later: 'STARMER <u>MUST</u> SAY SORRY FOR DRINKS IN LOCKDOWN'. Its breathless reports were followed by the *Sun* and *Telegraph*. Yet the Tories still wanted for a smoking gun. The story lacked a sense of plausibility. Readers were invited to believe a politician whose respect for the letter of the law was so unwavering that he once walked the four miles from Parliament to Kentish Town after testing positive for Covid before a session of Prime Minister's Questions rather than risk infecting his driver was now as cavalier as Johnson. Starmer's spinners repeated their denials. Broadcasters, who always held the power to elevate a story from newsprint to national conversation, remained uninterested. Beergate – as it had since been nicknamed – died its second death on 7 February, when Durham Constabulary issued a terse statement: 'We do not believe an offence has been established in relation to the legislation and guidance in place at that time.'

★

Soon nobody was talking about parties. For that Johnson had Vladimir Putin to thank. As Westminster debated the morality and legality of cheese and wine, the Russian president had been amassing tanks and troops on the Ukrainian border. On 24 February, they made their move. The invasion suspended the normal rules of British politics. Briefly, a new spirit of bipartisanship prevailed. Conservative MPs who had spent the preceding weeks organising to oust Johnson had little option but to suspend hostilities and allow him to live out his Churchillian dreams as leader of the Western alliance. Starmer, equally keen to play statesman, criticised nothing the government did.

In those weeks Starmer had only one confrontation. Eight days before the invasion, eleven Corbynite MPs had put their names to a statement from the Stop the War Coalition – the alliance of anti-imperialist protesters whose marches against New Labour's foreign policy had been the making of its chairman, Jeremy Corbyn – that blamed Putin's expansionism on the British government's 'sabre-rattling' over Ukraine, as well as its support for Kyiv's membership of Nato. 'We refute the idea that Nato is a defensive alliance,' the letter read, 'and believe its record in Afghanistan, Yugoslavia and Libya over the last generation, not to mention the US–British attack on Iraq, clearly proves otherwise.' By 2022 the pronouncements of the Labour left were largely ignored, and until the day of Russia's incursion this howl of indignation against the West was no different. On the day of the invasion, that changed. Diane Abbott, Tahir Ali, Apsana Begum, Richard Burgon, Ian Lavery, John McDonnell, Ian Mearns, Bell Ribeiro-Addy, Mick Whitley, Beth Winter: all were names that by then meant little to the Labour leadership. Over 2021 these left-wingers had been marginalised and in 2022 the leader's office had been determined to consign them to permanent irrelevance. Their support for a statement that contradicted Starmer's claims to lead a party united behind the Western alliance thus posed a big political problem. Johnson never declined an opportunity to paint Starmer as Corbyn in disguise. Here was one such chance.

In the office of the chief whip, just behind the Speaker's chair, Starmer's aides considered their options. For all Labour MPs' misgivings about antisemitism on the left under Corbyn, that debate, still less the word itself, had had limited cut-through among the British public. Cummings had said as much at the time, writing to his interlocutors in the leader's office in April 2019 to report: 'Fascinating – almost nobody has even heard of the antisemitism story! One of the best examples I've seen in twenty years of how SW1 focus is out of kilter with public.' Nobody could say the same for Corbyn's handling of foreign policy. Even Andrew Murray, one of his advisers, later publicly acknowledged Corbyn's failure to repudiate Putin after the attempted assassination of Sergei Skripal had marked the beginning of the end of his leadership – a turning point in Westminster and the country from which he did not recover.

Starmer's team were determined not to make that mistake again. So were members of his shadow cabinet, haunted by history. They had served on the front bench during the Corbyn years, and witnessed first-hand the damage his purported lack of patriotism had done to the party's electoral appeal. Skripal was only one example. Where Theresa May and later Boris Johnson had no problem singing the national anthem, expressing support for the royal family, Corbyn appeared awkward and conflicted. A lifetime of activism also made it impossible to distance himself from the radicalism of his comrades – from John McDonnell, whose support for the IRA came up again and again in focus groups, to the tens of thousands of members who had joined to support Corbyn and whose social media profiles were routinely combed for evidence of the anti-western politics of which they were collectively accused. As unfair as Corbyn felt the criticism was, survivors of his leadership knew it could have been worse. One MP who served in both Corbyn and Starmer's shadow cabinets recalled the discovery that one of the three terrorists who attacked London Bridge in June 2017, killing eight people and injuring dozens more, had joined the Labour Party the previous year. That fact was kept secret and for once never leaked. In a rare act of unity, Corbyn's advisers in the leader's office and his moderate adversaries at party HQ met and resolved it served neither faction's interests for it to be publicised less than a week before a general election. Although police were notified, the National Executive Committee was not: due to a quirk of the rules, the party's governing body only needed to be notified of people whose membership had been discontinued if they were alive. As the assailant in question was shot dead during the attack, that did not apply to this Corbyn-era recruit.

Nobody could accuse Starmer of sharing Corbyn's politics. In fact, those who served him during those years said the response to Skripal in March 2018 and the BBC *Panorama* documentary on antisemitism the following June, brought him to the brink of resigning. Yet Starmer had served all the same – a fact of which Johnson regularly reminded him across the despatch box and to which he had no easy reply. For that reason, many in his office believed the Stop the War letter signed by Labour MPs should be seized as an opportunity to reject once and for all the politics it represented. Those who had signed it could be suspended en masse. What had started as a rallying cry would become the left's suicide note. Said one: 'My view was: kick them out. Just do it. Why not do it? This was purely about: "What takes us closer to government?"' Another adds: 'To have written it in that context was such a political misjudgement, and sent a signal about who the Labour Party is which is so wrong, considering the Labour Party signed Britain into Nato, set up our nuclear deterrent . . . we are not the party of apologists for Putin and dodgy regimes.' Luke Sullivan, who had spent fifteen years of his life playing peacemaker between past leaders and recalcitrant MPs, was reluctant to launch a purge. Deborah Mattinson believed the public were simply uninterested in Labour's civil war at a time of actual war. McSweeney agreed, telling his colleagues:

'The public have forgotten about Corbyn, so don't distract them by reheating the issue.' Sam White, whose private view was that the back-benchers deserved to be expelled, agreed with Conor McGinn that the left should instead be given an ultimatum: withdraw their names or lose the Labour whip, and suffer the same indignity in exile as Jeremy. Sir Alan Campbell, convinced that forcing the left to back down would strengthen Starmer's hand as he held Johnson to account, conveyed the message. One by one those who received the warning resiled from their true beliefs, and one by one their names were drip-fed to the media. Corbyn alone refused. Again the left was divided against itself. Blairites once spoke of confining their factional opponents to a sealed tomb: this time the left had climbed into the crypt voluntarily, and shut the door themselves.

Starmer's authority over the Labour Party was now so secure that his adversaries were unwilling even to put up a fight. For now that suited him. As so often he strove to appear above politics. With the enemy within his own party vanquished, he extended a beneficent hand of friendship to his opponent in Downing Street. Ten days later he told the BBC: 'I'm very clear as the leader of the opposition, leader of the Labour Party, that when it comes to standing up to Russian aggression, and standing in support of Ukraine, it's very important in the United Kingdom and in our politics that we show the world that we're united.' Such solidarity with Johnson – and sure-footedness on questions of foreign policy – would have been unthinkable once. It flattered Starmer that while commentators looked on approvingly, his stance hardly merited coverage. Just as Corbyn had become irrelevant, so too Starmer's instinctive patriotism had become a self-evident fact of his leadership. During those weeks after the invasion, the greatest compliment the media and public could pay the party was their disin-terest. For once, Labour was not the story.

Focus groups were not the only people to note Labour's foreign policy shift. The Kremlin paid heed to it too. That, at least, was the conclusion many in the leader's office drew when Starmer was noti-fied that his personal email account may have been compromised shortly after Russia's invasion began. If only for a fleeting moment, Starmer's fate was once again bound up with Johnson's. Just days after Johnson went on a surprise 'walkabout' in Kyiv with the Ukrain-ian president Volodymyr Zelensky in April 2022, Russian operatives

seeking revenge hacked the email accounts of several British Eurosceptics, among them the former MI6 chief Sir Richard Dearlove,
and leaked 20,000 of the emails online. The correspondence, dated to
2018, displayed little more than the frustration of their authors at the
state of Theresa May's government. Yet the website which published
them purported to show an establishment 'coup' against Theresa
May – betraying the sort of 'hack and smear' tactics the Russians
routinely deployed in an attempt to stoke controversy and destabilise democracies abroad. As MI5 and MI6 investigated, it emerged the
perpetrators had not limited their attack to figures of the right. Paul
Mason, a former BBC journalist and leftist commentator, was also
targeted. While he later publicly confessed to having been hacked in
order to blunt the damage of any subsequent leak, what he was not
authorised to mention was the sophistication of the operation. In
his case, a mutual friend of his and Dearlove had his email compromised to the extent that the Russians were able to masquerade as that
individual and engage in strikingly plausible correspondence with
others. By opening those emails and responding, Mason handed the
Russians the keys to his seemingly secure Proton Mail account. That
may not have mattered, were it not for another detail never reported
at the time: Mason was by then informally advising John Healey, the
shadow defence secretary, on Russia and industrial policy. In fact, he
had been in Ukraine days before the invasion, where military intelligence had implored him to raise the alarm about Putin's imminent
attack with as many politicians as possible. Mason sent briefings not
only to Healey, but also, via intermediaries, George Robertson, the
former Nato secretary general, and Starmer. His account also contained detailed correspondence from Healey, which, according to a
source, had limited intelligence value, but would have given an adversary insight into 'how he thinks' and potentially the evidence needed
to impersonate him digitally. In the event, the Kremlin-linked hackers
captured Mason's emails, but, unlike the earlier leak, declined to publish them. They instead began a higher-stakes attempt to infiltrate the
political establishment, apparently downloading Mason's contacts and
sending fake messages with sophisticated malware to other Labour
figures. The messages appeared strikingly real: one was an invite to
a 4 July reception at the US Embassy; another an invitation to join an
imminent Zoom meeting.

Recipients included Healey, the shadow home secretary Yvette Cooper, and Starmer himself. Shortly after he discovered he had been hacked, Mason notified the intelligence services. They promptly launched an investigation. Within days, senior figures in the leader's office were summoned to the National Cyber Security Centre in Waterloo, where they were brought into a secure room and briefed on what had transpired. One party official present recalls the security services were clear that Labour's cyber defences left much to be desired: 'We really need to improve, and they can help us on that.' Later, Starmer was informed his own 'personal email' account 'may have been compromised' too. While intelligence never found evidence of materials being published online, they could not guarantee the Russians had not plundered sensitive information. As the matter was being investigated, Jill Cuthbertson, his head of office, circulated a note without explanation instructing staff not to email Starmer under any circumstances. In due course, on official advice, the leader changed his email account, the address for which a source described as dangerously obvious. As a final step, he added two-factor authentication – a basic fail-safe in which users are granted access to an account only after presenting two pieces of evidence to a password mechanism – to his Gmail and parliamentary inboxes. As the price of presenting a united front against Russia with Johnson, who granted him extensive access to meetings in which classified intelligence was presented and mounted no real critique of Labour's position on the invasion, it felt like a small concession.

★

The peace did not hold. By 30 March, the Met had issued fines to twenty people found to have broken the law. Johnson was not among them – not yet – but that did not stop Starmer asking the prime minister across the despatch box: 'Why is he still here?' That question was increasingly difficult to answer. On 12 April, when Johnson, his wife, and his chancellor were fined for having gathered to celebrate his fifty-sixth birthday in June 2020 with beer, supermarket sandwiches and cake, it became impossible. Johnson was desperate; Starmer ascendant. It was as if fate itself was heeding the three-stage plan for the Labour leadership of which McSweeney had spoken – first change the Labour Party, then expose the failures of the Conservatives, and

finally set out a vision for Britain. The Labour leader spoke content-
edly of 'moving through the gears'. The Tory leader was assailed
on all sides by his internal critics. His defenestration now seemed
to be a question of when, not if. Local elections loomed and the
Labour campaign, led by Mahmood and McGinn – in whom Starmer
invested so much trust that he did not speak to them once during
its duration – made much of the scandal. Kempsell threw the dice a
final time, and at last got lucky.

On six consecutive front pages before polling day the *Daily Mail* –
aided enthusiastically by Kempsell and Richard Holden, the Tory MP
for North West Durham – swung at Starmer again, and again, and
again. On 28 April: 'POLICE REVIEW OVER STARMER'S LOCK-
DOWN DRINKS'. On 29 April: 'LABOUR'S LOCKDOWN LIES
AND HYPOCRISY'. That story revealed that Rayner, too, had been
in attendance – despite previous denials of her presence. On 30 April:
'POLICE TOLD TO INVESTIGATE LABOUR'S LIES'. On 2 May:
'SHOW US THE PROOF, SIR KEIR'. On 3 May, beside the smirking face of the paper's resident misanthrope, Richard Littlejohn: 'Sir
Keir's Beergate hypocrisy – and why people who live in glass bottles
shouldn't throw mud.' On 4 May, the eve of the locals: 'MAN WHO
JUST CAN'T ANSWER A STRAIGHT QUESTION'. The singular
and almost deranged intensity of the *Mail*'s campaign had the desired
effect. Shadow ministers who had the misfortune to be caught in front
of microphones were asked to account for his behaviour and could
only repeat the denial. For the first time since the story broke the leader's office began to question itself.

On 29 April, after the paper revealed the police had folded to political pressure and initiated a 'review' of its evidence, Starmer's aides
convened on a conference call. It was their first collective discussion
of the facts of a story they had unthinkingly – and in Rayner's case,
mistakenly – denied for the best part of a year. Beforehand, Alex
Barros-Curtis offered his legal advice in a note circulated to attendees:
'The public position can remain that we say there was no breach of
the rules . . . the only relevant exception here is Exception 3 – that the
"gathering is reasonably necessary" for work purposes or for the pro-
vision of voluntary or charitable purposes.' That argument cut to the
quick of the contradiction at the heart of every allegation of lockdown
rulebreaking by Johnson and Starmer alike. Barros-Curtis continued:

'Keir was at work at the time – his "work" is to be a politician and the purpose of the gathering was political activity. The fact he had a drink is irrelevant – the question is what was the purpose of the gathering, or, if there was more than one purpose, the primary purpose.' He offered those guarantees without full knowledge of the evidence. The call began. McGinn asked how the party could be sure that no rules had been broken. Barros-Curtis could not say. Nobody had collated the evidence. This, another shadow cabinet minister reflects, was symptomatic of how the new model leader's office viewed the period of recent history that pre-dated its arrival: 'Their view tended to be that whatever had happened before May 2021 wasn't their problem.' Soon it would be.

Beyond Westminster the public still appeared unmoved. The results of the local elections on 5 May made clear the limits of Fleet Street's influence in the third decade of the twenty-first century, and the mood of the electorate. The Tories lost 485 seats, Labour won 108. Towards Johnson there was fury, at least in London and the south-east, where the crown jewels of Margaret Thatcher's municipal empire, Westminster and Wandsworth, fell to Labour – as did Barnet, whose rejection of Jeremy Corbyn in 2018 had come to symbolise the revulsion of British Jews towards the party that had once been its own, and Dover, ground zero of Britain's immigration debate. Overnight on the BBC, Charlie Falconer spoke glowingly of the victory in Wandsworth, the borough in which he and Tony Blair had lived as young barristers. Towards Starmer there was a new if tentative openness – yet the north-east, north-west and Midlands of England were reluctant to throw their weight behind him. Still, on 6 May the mood at Labour HQ was one of jubilation. Only a year earlier they had lost everywhere. Rayner had threatened to oust Starmer and Starmer had threatened to oust himself. This time they could call themselves winners.

At 2.41 p.m. the *Daily Telegraph* called time on the celebrations. It reported a new statement from the police: 'Following the receipt of significant new information over recent days, Durham Constabulary has reviewed that position and now, following the conclusion of the pre-election period, we can confirm that an investigation into potential breaches of Covid regulations relating to this gathering is now being conducted.' Starmer's destiny no longer lay in the hands of the Corbynites, nor Johnson – the two adversaries who had defined the first two years of his leadership of the Labour Party – but a group of face-less detectives working on an industrial estate just outside Durham. His aides had been given little notice. With unfortunate timing they had learned of the announcement just as Sadiq Khan, the mayor of London, arrived to congratulate exhausted staff for their hard work. Khan knew nothing of their torment as he made small talk with Starmer's inner circle. Altogether more problematic was the leader himself. Sleepless but chipper, he was 319 miles away in Carlisle, hymning his own triumph before activists and the press. Matthew Doyle – who as head of communications was now doomed to spend an indefinite period spinning the fact of a police investigation into a politician who had made so much of Johnson's own brushes with the law – called Steph Driver, Starmer's press secretary, with a simple instruction: leave immediately. As the leader walked into Carlisle station, his hands in his pockets, his face betrayed nothing. Doyle and Driver had hoped he might evade the press pack that had followed him and alight incon-spicuously at an intermediate station to address the breaking news at a BBC studio in the provinces. But already his luck had run out. Pursued onto the train by a gaggle of hacks, soon it was all too clear what he was discussing at his table in first class. At Euston the cameras waited. Starmer passed them without a word and went straight to the second floor of Southside, as he had been damned to do so often at moments of crisis. Upon his arrival he expressed his deepest anxiety immediately. It was not for himself. He sat down, encircled by his advisers.

'Hang on a minute. Before I ask anything, how are the staff? I know that the staff who were with me that night will be worried.'

Within minutes he had settled on his preferred response. For the second May in as many years he contemplated his resignation. 'If I'm found guilty, I will quit.' This time there would be no threat of a Rayner coup. She too was under investigation and had little option but to follow suit.

All but one of his advisers agreed. Doyle thought it unsustainable for Starmer to say anything else. Until the Durham detectives showed their hand, every interview to which the leader consented would con-sist of the same question asked repeatedly: would he resign if fined? Mattinson, knowing full well that Starmer's mind was already made up, urged him to grasp the nettle. Others echoed their thinking, though by now the political wisdom was self-evident and their principal needed no convincing. White stood alone in demanding Starmer take his time. Having endured the financial crisis at the right hand of Alistair Darling, the chancellor who dared to defy Gordon Brown, the leader's chief of staff was not averse to taking calculated risks. Yet for Starmer to subcontract his future to a police force that had already proven itself susceptible to political pressure was in White's view a risk with little upside. He urged Starmer to consult his wife and family. That much he did. Just as he had the previous May, he vanished. 'He disappeared on that Friday,' a shadow cabinet minister said. The only conclusion they reached that afternoon was to say nothing.

Starmer woke early on Saturday 7 May to find the *Daily Mail* taunting him. 'NOW IT'S SLIPPERY STARMER IN CRISIS,' crowed the splash headline. The team that had long prided itself on discovering the discipline that had eluded the Labour leadership in 2020 was now subsumed by panic. McSweeney spent much of the day on the phone to Mahmood, who could barely believe that Starmer had chosen silence over action. White, meanwhile, reached for his extensive Rolodex of contacts from the governments of Blair and Brown. Those greybeards knew only too well what it was to exist at the uncomfortable intersection of policing and politics: in 2006 and 2007 Tony had become the first serving prime minister to be questioned by police investigating allegations that the Labour Party had offered honours to donors, and in 2009 Brown had contended with the prosecution of Labour MPs accused of fiddling their expenses. They warned White that any investigation was bound to inflict political pain, regardless of its outcome. He knew immediately what they meant. However confident Starmer was of his own probity, he was powerless to control his shadow cabinet. White recalled A. J. P. Taylor's explanation of the First World War. From railway timetables that revealed the mobilisation of enemy troops, Europe's great powers had reluctantly concluded that they had no option but to mobilise their own. It did not matter that they did not want war. Their rivals clearly did. Failure to prepare meant inevitable defeat. Another adviser to Starmer said: 'We did know that there would be an inevitable loss of political authority for the period while people were thinking: "What if this does go horribly wrong?"'

Emboldened, the left filled the vacuum. Mocking the leader that had threatened to suspend her all of three months earlier, Diane

Abbott declared: 'If he actually gets a fixed penalty notice, he really has to consider his position.' Colleagues who might have been supportive were not consulted. Emily Thornberry, handed the hospital pass of the shadow attorney-generalship in the November reshuffle, briefly considered volunteering herself as 'the leader of the opposition's lawyer', compiling evidence, and making representations to the police on behalf of the fellow barrister she had first worked alongside in the late 1980s. Wary of the political risk, she decided to stay quiet.

For much of that Saturday, Starmer brooded at home. He was inaccessible to everyone, even McSweeney. Eventually he was convinced to seek the counsel of trusted colleagues: Reeves, Mahmood, McGinn, Falconer, Nick Thomas-Symonds, and David Lammy. To this small circle he made clear that he too was alive to the risk that most preoccupied his advisers.

'Look,' said Thomas-Symonds, over the phone, 'we can talk about this one way or another, but I know exactly what you'll do.' Then the kicker: 'But you do realise that it's going to cause enormous instability in the shadow cabinet.'

'There is no other option,' Starmer said. 'I'm not having you and other people going out on the media trying to defend me in an ambiguous position.'

Falconer hedged his bets. Mahmood and McGinn offered an unvarnished judgement: that Starmer had no option but to offer up his own future. There was no way out, no matter how desperately he sought one in those difficult conversations. Mahmood consoled him with the possibility that, should the worst happen, he had every chance of serving in one of the great offices of state when another Labour leader was elected prime minister.

The old friends who had left the leader's office under dark clouds were recalled to service. Ben Nunn counselled that only a promise to resign could protect Starmer's reputation and extract the poison from a narrative over which he otherwise had no control. Johnson, after all, had neither offered to quit if fined, nor quit when fined. What else would Starmer, the man for whom integrity meant everything, do anyway? Chris Ward, ever protective, disagreed. He was horrified to learn that Starmer had been forced to contemplate the waste of their sacrifices by the right-wing press, and that Blair had advised him to offer his resignation too. Ward saw vultures where others saw well-meaning confidants. He took the opposite view: that the leader's CV contained the ready-made rebuttal. Starmer had been director of public prosecutions. *Obviously* he would respect any ruling by the police. There was the answer. There was no need to create political jeopardy where none needed to exist.

It was no use. By the evening of Sunday 8 May the die was cast. White went to Starmer's home in Kentish Town. In an irony unacknowledged by either man, they shared a couple of beers in the garden. They talked through every possible permutation of the coming week but the conclusion was inescapable. Just as he had said more than forty-eight hours earlier, the leader of the Labour Party would tell the country that he would resign if found guilty. The decision was formalised at a meeting in the leader's office the next morning. Several advisers present insured themselves against another change of heart by briefing *The Times*. At 4 p.m. Starmer said it for himself. Five minutes before he addressed the media at Labour HQ, he texted Ward a single word.

'Sorry.'

To the press he was more expansive. Still asserting his innocence, he made the vow: 'I simply had something to eat while working late in the evening, as any politician would do days before an election, but if the police decide to issue me with a fixed penalty notice, I would, of course, do the right thing and step down.' He left, as so often at times of triumph and despair, for Jenny Chapman's home on Arlington Road. After every local election she invited Labour luminaries to share barbecued meat and war stories. Given the context, 2022's gathering might have resembled a wake. But Starmer arrived in high spirits. Nunn told him: 'That was exactly the right thing to do.' For once the voters agreed. 'If you look at the polling,' said one of the advisers most relieved by Starmer's embrace of the inevitable, 'it was one of those cut-through moments with the public . . . and people did see that as a positive contrast with Johnson.' Another said: 'It was a big turning point for him, doing that, and a real point of distinction between him and Boris and, as it turned out, Sunak as well. You could see his personal ratings transform with people looking at him again at that time.' Gary Neville, the former Manchester United footballer, expressed this logic most succinctly in a tweet sent minutes after Starmer spoke:

'This is a great speech from @Keir_Starmer that restores faith. Over to you liar!'

The next morning, those words of encouragement echoed across the shadow cabinet table. Circling the wagons, Mahmood, McGinn and McSweeney were listed to speak first. Mahmood said: 'He's done the right thing and we're very proud of him.' If only temporarily, the tension that gripped her colleagues dissipated. None showed outward signs of the intoxicating uncertainty and ambition that was to influence their behaviour over the next two months. Every contribution began with three deferential words: 'Thank you, Keir.'

Outside the room, confusion reigned. White, dismayed by what he deemed to be a hysterical reaction from staff in the leader's office, gathered his team and told them, bluntly, that none of them were ready to work in government. Alice Perry, godmother of the moderates on the NEC, called Matt Pound in a state of disbelief. Did they know the risk they had taken? 'Keir was director of public prosecutions,' said Pound. 'Keir knows the law better than we do.'

The law, maybe. But the politics? Nobody could claim to know the politics with any certainty.

*

Also unknown were the immediate consequences of Starmer's potential resignation. As he compiled a one-page contingency plan for the scenario none hoped would come to pass, White was troubled by the realisation that he did not know who would succeed the leader in the interim. Would it be David Evans, as general secretary? Acting alone, Mahmood and McGinn sought to answer that question for themselves. Here was their opportunity to reassert the authority of the Parliamentary Labour Party. The unelected advisers with whom they frequently clashed were deliberately excluded from their discussions. Mahmood met with Sir Alan Campbell and John Cryer, the taciturn Yorkshireman who played shop steward to Labour MPs as PLP chairman, to agree a timetable for the election of Starmer's replacement. All agreed – without ever consulting him – that John Healey, the shadow defence secretary, would be appointed caretaker leader. Their allies on the NEC – Unison's Wendy Nichols, Usdaw's Paddy

Lillis, and Margaret Beckett – were instructed to agree to as truncated a timetable as possible.

Why? That was explained by the absence of McSweeney. Mahmood often joked to his face that his ultimate objective was to install Wes Streeting as leader of the Labour Party. Rayner's aides took that mischievous suggestion rather more seriously. One remarks acidly of McSweeney and his friends from south London: 'They all got together and agreed they had to rebuild the Labour Party that resulted in Wes Streeting becoming prime minister.' Neither Rayner nor Mahmood knew of the Lambeth dinners hosted by Roger Liddle, at which Streeting was ever-present. But Mahmood was anxious that there could be no perception of bias, however misguided those assumptions may have been. Nor was Streeting's vaulting ambition a secret. From the moment he arrived in the Commons in 2015 the words 'future leader' had been appended to his name like a Homeric epithet. His approach to politics was one of hyperactivity. After his appointment as shadow health secretary the previous November he blitzed the newspapers, broadcast studios and gatherings of party donors. To say it all amounted to a leadership campaign, as so many of his colleagues so enviously did, was an exaggeration. For telegenic Blairites such as Streeting such things were merely the stuff of serious politics. When confronted by journalists he said, loyally, that Starmer was secure enough in his position to tolerate 'tall poppies'. Fellow MPs were unconvinced. They chafed at his ambition and briefed jealously that Waheed Alli, the media millionaire and moneyman to the New Labour diaspora, had hosted a fundraiser for Streeting at Alli's Covent Garden apartment. Unlike their leader, they thought tall poppies were best cut down, even as Streeting submitted himself to broadcast rounds in which he attested to Starmer's innocence.

Few believed him. Streeting knew what his colleagues thought. His natural effervescence gave way to depression. To friends he complained: 'All the thanks I got was people basically saying: "Oh, Wes is putting himself out there."' That Starmer's aides had assured him that the leader did not share their suspicions did little to reassure him. Colleagues thought him guilty of a staggering lack of subtlety. When Streeting agreed to be interviewed by the *Financial Times* magazine on a trip to Israel, he thought it might allow him to speak seriously about health policy. Instead his pouting face and sharp suit appeared under the headline: 'Is Wes Streeting the saviour Labour desperately needs?' To many Labour backbenchers the answer was short and unambiguous: no. Shadow cabinet ministers, several of them friendly with Streeting, coalesced into a hastily assembled Stop the Wes Coalition. One said: 'He misread the politics of the PLP. They respect ambition up to a point. They don't expect you to be a dickhead about it . . . He just can't help himself. There's just a streak of immaturity there, which just means that people don't take him seriously, or what he has to say seriously.' Another added: 'It was obvious what Wes was up to.' To one senior official, Streeting's ambitions were not only self-evident, but the fulfilment of a decade-old conspiracy by the Labour right – first set in motion after McSweeney's old boss, Steve Reed, had lost out on a parliamentary seat to Chuka Umunna – to install him as leader one day. Peter Kyle, Streeting's closest friend in politics, even approached shadow cabinet ministers to disavow his leadership bid. And despite the ostentatious displays of loyalty, there *was* a leadership bid. His natural constituency of Blairites, young and old, was divided. Some urged him to seize the prize with both hands, whatever the damage incurred in doing so. Others advised him to bide his time. Enthusiastic support instead came from unlikely quarters. Andrew Gwynne and Lyn Brown, two stalwarts of the soft left who had served on Corbyn's front bench, both offered their support – as did Jess Phillips, whose abortive 2020 campaign Streeting had helped run. If part of his appeal lay in his status as 'heir to Blair', to many to his left, that was precisely the problem. He was a talented communicator: that nobody could deny. But he was also the personification of what Blair had got wrong – first and foremost the disavowal of Labour's own traditions. At a political shadow cabinet meeting the previous year, in a speech sarcastically labelled his 'Rivers of Blood' intervention, he had told colleagues Labour needed to go further than slaying its holy cows on the NHS, privatisation and much else: it needed to force every cow to the marketplace and slaughter them until their knees were covered in blood. That was a mindset many MPs could do without.

As Streeting complained to friends he was 'more talked about than talked to', Peter Mandelson allegedly took it upon himself to canvass the shadow cabinet. One of its members recalled the Prince of Darkness making the case for Wes, declaring over the phone: 'He's brave, he's great on the media, he's got the ideas.' She rejected the entreaty out of hand. Blending the menace and theatricality for which he was famed, Mandelson is said to have deadpanned: 'You are a very cruel woman.' He would later insist the conversation had not happened. For all his belief in Streeting's talents, he told friends, he only shared his true position with a handful of intimates, none of whom served in Starmer's team.

Lisa Nandy also excited the animal instincts of MPs who believed the mere fact of a colleague's appearance on television was tantamount to a leadership bid. Shadow cabinet ministers came to view their meetings as de facto hustings between Streeting, the prodigal son of New Labour, and Nandy, who as shadow levelling-up secretary spoke as if she were governor general of the red wall. 'Shadow cabinet had just become performative,' one of its members complains. 'It had just become those two staking positions: usually Wes staking a sort of Blairite right position regarding what it takes to win, and Lisa sort of staking a more left-of-centre position.'

Neither would have won. It was the shadow cabinet minister who did least who won the most support. Without lifting a finger, Rachel Reeves emerged as the preferred candidate of the PLP's powerbrokers. Mahmood and McGinn separately resolved to convey the message. For once, they decided to do so without consulting the other. But as Mahmood left the shadow chancellor's office, she discovered McGinn arriving to impart the same instructions. Another MP who encouraged Reeves to stand recalls: 'She was grateful, and she definitely wanted to do it in that moment. She definitely wanted it. It was like: thank you so much . . . I'm really going to need you . . . let's stay in touch.' To another party grandee, she was more Delphic, conveying her concern that her past language about those on welfare, and her fiscal conservatism, might make her unelectable before the membership. 'Rachel's view was that the party would never elect her,' recalls this person, who told her: 'You've got to be prepared for every eventuality.' What the grandee could never surmise was whether her doubts were an attempt to throw him off the scent. Still, he suspected she would run. So did Streeting. For the shadow health secretary, this was a nightmarish eventuality. Reeves was an unusual thing in a party often governed by deep and burning hatreds: a true friend. As Blair and Brown had told themselves in 1994, a prize fight between two heavyweights with near-identical politics would divide and then ruin a generation that had hitherto only known unity of purpose. What it might do to their friendship was too ugly to contemplate. One night in the Commons, Streeting forced the question upon her.

'Have you thought about what you're going to do if the worst does happen?'

'Well, I don't think it is going to happen,' she said, outwardly unmoved.

'Well, I don't either. But we do need to think about what happens in that scenario.'

The division bell rang. Reeves made away to cast her vote. They never spoke of it again. Doing so may have been pointless. Streeting was unaware of the hardening resolve among his shadow cabinet colleagues. Starmer's late-onset enthusiasm for a politics that paid no obeisance to the sacred cows of leftism might now be in danger of falling to the wayside under a new leader like Nandy. Only Reeves, whose carefully confected public image as an aspiring central-bank governor hid a burning contempt for the Labour left, was trusted to play the role of 'the anti-Labour Party candidate' who so many in the shadow cabinet wished to carry on Starmer's work. She did not canvass because she did not need to. Her stature did the talking. Labour HQ had made a concerted effort to enhance the shadow chancellor's profile long before the question of the succession arose. At Mahmood's behest they had spent £100 a day on Facebook advertisements designed to establish Reeves in the public consciousness. Her growing influence over Starmer as shadow chancellor – a deliberate strategy instigated by Reeves's chief of staff, Katie Martin – was well known among the PLP.

Still, some were determined to resist the pressure for a coronation. Clive Efford, chairman of the hundred-strong Tribune Group of soft-left MPs – a motley crew of the dispossessed and never-possessed derided by one shadow cabinet minister as the 'Lonely Hearts Club' of Labour politics – told one shadow cabinet minister: 'You guys don't get to decide this, you know.' That iconoclastic view was shared by the shadow mental health minister Rosena Allin-Khan, perhaps the only frontbencher who rivalled Streeting's aptitude for self-promotion, who courted colleagues too. Despite his departure for Manchester, Andy Burnham's spectre haunted the corridors of Westminster. Sadiq Khan was so widely suspected of plotting a job swap with the Corbynite MP Dawn Butler, who spoke openly of her ambition to occupy London's City Hall, that the NEC would later delay his reselection as mayor as punishment. Instability reigned. Labour's whips were so disconcerted by the oppressive atmosphere of mutual suspicion that one of their number was deputed to tell both Reeves and Streeting that only one of them could run.

*

Starmer played no part. If another future was possible for his colleagues, he had no place in it. Those weeks ought to have been a new beginning for his leadership. The public were now willing to vote for him. Johnson was inches from oblivion. His reward was not a victory lap but purgatory. His MPs spoke as if he was already gone. On 14 June, disobliging commentary from five shadow cabinet ministers appeared on the front page of *The Times* under the headline: 'Stop boring voters to death, shadow cabinet tells Starmer.' That much he might have grinned and borne. Politics had never been his game. By now he was inured to the endless chorus of criticism that came with the job of leader of the opposition – the insults and anonymous briefing he consumed voraciously in 2020. But he could never adjust to life in the dock. The mere suggestion of wrongdoing sapped at his sense of self. Outwardly he appeared 'very calm' to aides. Those who looked closer, as he stared vacantly out of windows on long train journeys, detected a deeper discomfort. 'You could tell, as it went on, and we were waiting for the results, and you'd just catch those odd moments on visits, or when you were on the train . . . I could just tell that it was on his mind. I could tell that the thought of being found guilty of having broken the law, which is effectively what it was, really played on his sense of values and character in quite a profound way.'

Nor was his office immune from the contagion of disunity that spread among Labour MPs. The leader's team still resembled the cohort of advisers it had replaced in one respect: they were hopelessly divided against themselves. On one side was McSweeney, on the other, White and Mattinson. As the PLP debated who might lead them, so too did an unhappy class of advisers. Plans were afoot to shift staff from the leader's office to Labour HQ – where they would work for the Irishman and prepare for an election. That was not McSweeney's idea but the recommendation of *Organise to Win*, a review of the party's unwieldy maze of internal structures, commissioned by David

Evans and conducted by Lord Kerslake, the former head of the Civil Service who had tried and failed to impose order on Corbynism in its terminal phase. White disagreed, and made an alternative proposal to Starmer under which the leader's office would remain the nexus of political power. The two proposals were mutually exclusive. Only one man could win. There was no doubt as to where the loyalties of most advisers lay. White had burned his bridges with an outburst in the days after the police announced their investigation. He believed his colleagues had overreacted, raising their voices and squabbling over how they might best respond. 'I'm not putting up with this behaviour,' he told Mattinson, Helene Reardon-Bond and Vidhya Alakeson, who had joined the leader's office to effect introductions between Labour and business. 'I'm going to call them out.' They tried to dissuade him but he ploughed on regardless. Raising his voice, he told staff their behaviour had been 'unacceptable' and chastised them for 'shouting in meetings'. Most damningly, he said: 'In politics, there are really tough days. At No. 10, it's a tough day every day. If you can't cope with this, then you shouldn't be here.' The feeling was mutual. While McSweeney maintained a diplomatic distance from the fray, his admirers began to brief journalists of their dissatisfaction with White and Mattinson, the latter of whom was so destabilised by their viciousness that in weaker moments she wished that Starmer might be found guilty, so that she could walk away.

Relations had deteriorated to such an extent that neither aide was invited when the leader's inner circle met for an awayday at McSweeney's mansion in Cleghorn, a Lanarkshire village the Romans had once fortified, on 8 July. Inside his own citadel he kept Labour's strategy a secret from its head of strategy and the leader's chief of staff.

White had called Mattinson: 'There's this thing going on. Are you going to it?'

Mattinson replied: 'No . . . '

In fleeing his colleagues, McSweeney had isolated himself from the most consequential conversations that happened that day. Mattinson's phone rang. Carol Linforth, the logistical mastermind who had served six leaders at Labour HQ, had heard news from the police yet found the rest of the leader's office were uncontactable. 'I'm hearing that we're going to hear something today,' she said, elliptically. 'Should I start to set up a press conference?'

'I don't know,' said Mattinson. 'Ask the people who've gone to Scotland.' Furious to be marooned in Scotland, Matthew Doyle barked instructions down the phone to Steph Driver.

Soon all the anxiety of the previous weeks dissipated, and every contingency dissolved into memory. The parlour games were over. Reeves would not be leader of the Labour Party, nor Streeting – not yet. That job still belonged to Keir Starmer. Just after 2 p.m. he took to his lectern in Southside, flanked by two Union Jacks.

'I've always said that no rules were broken when I was in Durham,' he said. He clenched his fist. 'The police have now completed their investigation and found there was no case to answer. People said to me I was taking a risk by saying I would step down if I was fined. It was never about that. For me, it was a matter of principle. It shouldn't be controversial to say that those who make the law can't break the law.'

Conservative MPs had finally admitted that much twenty-four hours earlier. Brought low by over fifty ministerial and cabinet resignations over a few days in early July, Johnson had resigned. His time was over. Starmer's was only just beginning.

PART IV: RECKONING

14

Liz

For almost half an hour the plane circled above Aberdeen, waiting to descend through heavy fog. Its passenger still saw the world clearly, unclouded by doubt. It was 6 September 2022. Mary Elizabeth Truss, the new leader of the Conservative Party, was late for her first audience with Queen Elizabeth II.

Twenty-four hours earlier, Tory members had elected Truss to succeed Boris Johnson. Rishi Sunak, her opponent, stood little chance. At the last he had betrayed Johnson and resigned as chancellor. Truss, the foreign secretary, stayed loyal. Under Sunak, taxes had risen. Truss, breezily defiant of mainstream economic opinion, vowed to cut them. Like her heroine Margaret Thatcher, she was a daughter of provincial England. Like Jeremy Corbyn she admonished her colleagues for betraying their values. 'I was elected as a Conservative,' she said, invoking Tony Blair's 1997 victory speech with a flatness that made Keir Starmer's oratory sound lyrical, 'and will govern as a Conservative.'

That work could not begin without constitutional ritual. For new prime ministers, accepting the Queen's invitation to form a government ordinarily meant a short trip from Downing Street to Buckingham Palace. The journey for the Queen's fifteenth premier was longer. Once Truss had navigated the winding roads from Aberdeen to the royal family's retreat at Balmoral, the cause of this departure from precedent became clear. By then ninety-six, the Queen – for so long essentially ageless – suddenly looked like a very old woman. Supported by a stick, she held out a hand for Truss, and said: 'Pace yourself.'

Truss would not heed the advice. Her philosophy, which seemed indivisible from her temperament, did not involve restraint. There was no political or economic challenge she did not meet with whatever argument appealed most to her party's animal instincts: a small state and lower taxes. For years the also-ran of the Tory race for self-advancement, she had become leader after a shameless campaign of self-promotion conducted via newspaper briefings and social media posts. Said one shadow cabinet minister, admiringly: 'She used Instagram to become prime minister.' But events afforded her no respite either. Only two days later she went to the Commons to announce she had written a cheque for £150 billion. As a leadership candidate, she had rejected the premise that the state should intervene to insulate the public from the shock of rising energy bills, which had spiralled since Russia's invasion of Ukraine. On 8 September, as prime minister, she did just that. Subsidisation this large was a painful paradox for Truss, whose premiership was built on the theory that the market could always be trusted.

For Starmer it was all opportunity. His young team had been slow to grasp the politics of inflation, which had seldom troubled Britain in the twenty-first century. That summer his head of policy, the sometimes divisive Stuart Ingham, had reacted sceptically when shadow cabinet ministers suggested they attack the Tories for rising prices. 'Well of course,' Ingham had said, 'inflation's not really the government's fault.' His bewildered colleagues believed the art of opposition was opportunism: they vowed to blame the Conservatives for anything and everything. Soon Starmer condemned without compunction. After Truss had defended her decision to bail out the energy companies without taxing them, Starmer shouted into the din of a restless chamber: 'The prime minister is opposed to windfall taxes. She wants to leave these vast profits on the table with one clear and obvious consequence: the bill will be picked up by working people.' As he began to criticise the Conservatives for their failure to invest in green energy, Starmer did not notice Nadhim Zahawi enter the chamber, just before 12.10 p.m.

Zahawi, caretaker of the constitution as minister for the Cabinet Office, did not swagger as he usually did. With strained solemnity he approached Truss and whispered into her ear. He passed the prime minister a note and crossed the chamber to pass another to Angela Rayner. Impassive, she studied its contents. 'The Queen is unwell and Keir needs to leave the chamber as soon as possible to be briefed.' That short sentence was at once direct and euphemistic. The Queen was dying. Buckingham Palace would tell the BBC of her condition at 12.30 p.m. Simon Case, the cabinet secretary, had resolved to tell Truss and

Starmer before the breaking news notifications on their phones. 'The best thing we can do,' Zahawi told Case, 'is to write something for the PM and leader of the opposition so they don't get caught out cold.'

Starmer complied with his instructions. At once he left the chamber to meet government officials, and then for the leader's office, where he prepared for the worst. Though the unthinkable still went unsaid, the deep state acted as if the monarch was already dead. Case called. Before long Sarah Healey – who as permanent secretary of the culture department was custodian of Operation London Bridge, the decades-old plan for the Queen's passing and state funeral – arrived in Starmer's room. What followed was a private tutorial in the protocols of national mourning. Healey, however, spoke in the conditional tense, declining to say whether the Queen had, in fact, died. Starmer and his advisers sought clarification as gently and gracefully as possible. Healey neither confirmed nor denied but said, suggestively, that she might tell them more at 6 p.m. Having revealed everything but the facts, she left the leader's office with Helene Reardon-Bond, an old friend from the Civil Service as well as Starmer's deputy chief of staff. As they did so they made small talk about their children. Healey glanced at her phone.

'I need to go back up,' she said. Liberated from pretence, she returned to Starmer's office.

'I've been told by the cabinet secretary that I can inform you that Her Majesty the Queen has passed away.'

'Thank you very much,' said Starmer, stolidly. The public still had a few hours to wait. He left Parliament to speak to the nation from the Covent Garden flat of Waheed Alli, whose expensive tastes in interior design provided a more appropriate backdrop for the moment than the fading wallpaper of Norman Shaw North. Having changed into a black suit, with mournful eyes Starmer paid tribute to 'our longest-serving and greatest ever monarch', the woman who transcended the fractious politics of the nation he had begun to imagine leading. 'For the vast majority of us, the late Queen has simply been the Queen. The only Queen. Above all else, our Queen.' Truss, by contrast, spoke in clunking, leaden cliché from the steps of Downing Street just after the news broke at 6.30 p.m.: 'Queen Elizabeth II was the rock on which modern Britain was built.'

Neither leader spoke of the future. Politics as usual would not resume for the best part of three weeks. However fiercely they had been prosecuted only hours earlier, debates over Truss's fiscal policy paled suddenly into insignificance. Those weeks were not about the new prime minister, still less the leader of the opposition. But almost imperceptibly they told a story of a new Labour Party. For a century the left's relationship with royalty had veered between deference and protest. Ramsay MacDonald, Labour's first prime minister, had been so anxious to impress George V at his initial audience that he arrived at Buckingham Palace in white tie hastily hired from Moss Bros. Harold Wilson behaved as if he were the Queen's best friend; his firebrand ministers less so. Tony Benn believed studied disdain to be a mark of socialist pedigree, ostentatiously rejecting invitations to receptions. Barbara Castle, though beloved by the royals, betrayed her discomfort with a half-bow instead of the customary curtsey. Richard Crossman arrived late to meetings of the Privy Council, so that he might keep Her Majesty waiting and assert the superiority of elected politicians. Tony Blair gently admonished her silence after the death of Diana, Princess of Wales. Jeremy Corbyn, like Benn a committed republican, gave her the gift of mouldy jam from his allotment. As a young barrister Starmer had demanded the abolition of the monarchy, a passing fancy he remembered with amusement upon his appointment as Queen's Counsel. Now he would prove that, unlike his immediate predecessor, his Labour Party was no threat to the British establishment, nor uneasy with its traditions. Instead he appeared effortlessly at one with both.

Nothing Labour did in those days of national mourning provoked much comment at all. That was deliberate. Small gestures that blended seamlessly into the grand displays of national ceremony were in fact the product of many months of exacting preparation. At Starmer's insistence the leader's office had worked fastidiously to ensure he did not become the story. Jill Cuthbertson prepared sheets of black-edged notepaper. Its digital team wrote new scripts for Labour's website that would adjust the QC after Sir Keir Starmer to KC. Such close attention to detail was pure Starmer. Low politics never came naturally. Process and formality did. On this, at least, the leader's operation was capable of behaving with a focus and discipline that was often absent from discussions about policy and political strategy. If nothing else, he was capable of looking like a conventional prime minister who led a functional party.

Over 2022, as rumours of the Queen's failing health took root in Westminster, he made subtle overtures to her heir. That February he had made a low-key visit to the Prince's Trust in Southwark, playing table football with the disadvantaged children served by Charles's charity. In public, every move was calculated to endear the leader to the man who would soon be King. In private, Starmer imposed the same discipline on his colleagues. When shadow cabinet ministers met on the morning of 9 September, he told them: 'Right, we're going to do a minute's silence for the Queen.' Said a survivor of the Corbyn years present at the meeting: 'I was thinking: "Blimey, Jeremy wouldn't have done this."' They reflected that more rumbustious members of the last shadow cabinet might have instead agreed that the death was 'an opportunity to get rid of the monarchy'. Whatever he may have thought in his twenties, Starmer said nothing of the sort. For once he had the licence – better still, the obligation – to situate himself above politics. A few hours later he read a speech to a hushed Commons. Written in half an hour by Paul Ovenden and laced with literary allusions by Phil Collins, the former *Times* columnist and speechwriter to Tony Blair, it channelled T. S. Eliot and quoted Philip Larkin:

> In times when nothing stood,
> But worsened, or grew strange,
> There was one constant good:
> She did not change.

Starmer exhibited such impeccable small-c conservatism that it might have looked confected. To a certain extent it was. He had prepared for the Queen's death as if it were a party conference speech. But there was an authenticity, too, in this audition for statesmanship. While much else about his leadership remained inchoate – so much so that it took weekly meetings with Rachel Reeves, Pat McFadden, Shabana Mahmood and Conor McGinn for Starmer to begin to think seriously about political strategy – he believed in nothing as much as duty and public service. Here, at last, was a challenge he could rise to instinctively, without the guiding hand of McSweeney or instructions from the 'quad' of shadow cabinet ministers who took the most difficult decisions for him. Restraint and reticence came naturally. In the eleven days between the Queen's death and funeral, only the dependably businesslike shadow trade secretary Nick Thomas-Symonds was allowed in front of a microphone, appearing on the BBC's *Any Questions?* under strict instructions to say nothing political.

Others in the shadow cabinet reverted to type. Ego's pull was irresistible even in a period of state-enforced solemnity. On 10 September most of the shadow cabinet went to St James's Palace as members of the Accession Council, where Charles was formally proclaimed king. Hugh Dalton, chancellor under Clement Attlee, had described its last meeting in 1952 as a gathering of politicians 'one didn't realise were still alive . . . and some looking quite perky and self-important'. 2022 was much the same. Starmer stood between Tony Blair and Gordon Brown. For the first time it looked like a meeting of equals. Looking up from his conversation with David Cameron, Nick Thomas-Symonds thought to himself: 'There he is: the seventh Labour prime minister with the fifth and sixth.' Once the formalities concluded, the King returned to Buckingham Palace and MPs to Westminster, where Starmer and a select group of party grandees retook their parliamentary oaths to a new sovereign. Harriet Harman, mother of the House, was the first Labour MP to do so. Starmer came next, followed by Thangam Debbonaire, the shadow leader of the Commons; Sir Alan Campbell, the chief whip; Rosie Winterton, Labour's deputy speaker; and the shadow cabinet ministers John Healey, David Lammy, Yvette Cooper and Pat McFadden. Absent from the list, prepared by Campbell, was Angela Rayner. She was furious to learn of her exclusion, and told colleagues: 'I must have been missed.' Thérèse Coffey, Truss's deputy, was there to swear *her* oath. Yet Labour's order of precedence was not a matter of constitutional rules. Rayner's exclusion was intentional. Still sensitive to real and perceived slights to her authority some sixteen months on from Hartlepool, she sought clarity. None was forthcoming. 'I think you should hang around, go into the chamber and see what happens,' advised one aide.

'Oh no,' Rayner said, storming back to her office to retrieve her belongings. 'I'm not staying.'

If ceremony and royal ritual eased Starmer's status anxiety, they only exacerbated Rayner's. She already felt marginalised. The uneasy pretence of partnership the leader's office had contrived after Hartlepool had gone, replaced by mutual suspicion, forced politeness, and bouts of paranoia. Earlier that year, in February, the deputy leader had joined her chief of staff Nick Parrott for pints at the Clarence, a Whitehall pub frequented by parliamentarians and their staff, to bid farewell to her departing spin doctor Jack McKenna. There fellow drinkers overheard her predicting her own political death.

'He's going to sack me,' she said of Starmer.

'But he can't,' one of her companions replied, 'because you're elected.'

'No,' she said. 'He'll do it at the NEC. He'll get them to vote against me . . . he'll do it, just because he wants to.'

With parliamentary business and political campaigning suspended until the Queen's funeral, those concerns – disputes over factionalism, power and influence within the Labour Party – ought to have receded from Rayner's mind too. As shadow deputy prime minister and shadow chancellor of the Duchy of Lancaster she might reasonably have expected that her place in the pageantry that now overtook the usual business of politics was guaranteed. Instead she felt excluded and unloved. Her own overtures to royalty had been rather more colourful than Starmer's. After attending an International Women's Day reception at Clarence House earlier in the year, a jokingly outraged Rayner told friends that Camilla, then Duchess of Cornwall, had told her: 'Oh, you're Angela Rayner. You look much younger in person than you do on TV.' Never anything other than herself, on another occasion, Rayner turned down an invitation from the royals on the grounds that it clashed with an NEC meeting. She had let it be known the invite she truly coveted was to a state dinner, yet none was forthcoming – a fact she warily attributed to the leadership. 'They wouldn't let her do it,' said a friend.

Rayner's public bearing in the days after the Queen's death remained appropriately inscrutable. Behind closed doors, however, she spoke hard truths to the Palace. All but one aspect of the royal succession had been settled immediately: who would now deputise for the King, giving assent to legislation and representing him officially at state functions, if he was abroad or incapacitated? The Regency Acts of 1937 and 1953 decreed that the sovereign's spouse and the next four adult royals in line to the throne would serve as Counsellors of State: Camilla, now Queen, Prince William, Prince Harry, Prince Andrew and Princess Beatrice. The press made much of the inclusion of Harry, brooding in Californian exile and irreconcilably at odds with his immediate family.

But Rayner, who was the opposition's Commons spokeswoman on questions relating to the constitution, was more exercised by Andrew. His desire to play an active role in public life was undimmed by allegations he sexually abused a 17-year-old, his payment of a £12-million settlement to his accuser or the ongoing taint of his long association with Jeffrey Epstein, one of the world's most notorious paedophiles.

Rayner thought that an outrage. 'She was very actively reaching out to the Palace, the upper echelons of the Civil Service,' an adviser recalled, 'and said she thought this was a huge problem, and that the government needed to address this, and that she would offer cross-party support to make sure it happened. That's – to be stereotypical – her working-class view. She's not anti-monarchist, but she doesn't like a paedo.' In those discussions she offered the empathy of a mother who knew what it meant to raise a complicated family. Her message, according to her adviser, was: 'I know how difficult it is to be in a big, dysfunctional family where you've got the black sheep, they're really damaging to the rest of you but they're still in your family.' She nonetheless advocated excluding Andrew from royal duties entirely. That nuclear option proved too much for the Palace and Downing Street to take. The same went for the leaders of both parties in the House of Lords, who had been happy to defer to the Crown and thought ill of the intercession from the lower chamber. Even though the King had made clear to his private secretary, Clive Alderton, that he had no wish to devolve any duties to Andrew, the Palace, Downing Street and the peers entrusted with codifying any solution preferred a more delicate solution. Together with the cabinet secretary, Alderton alighted on a diplomatic fix: the list would be expanded to include Princess Anne and Prince Edward, so that neither Harry nor Andrew would ever be required to act on the King's behalf. Doing so still required new legislation, setting in train an intricate waltz between royalty, government and Parliament. Rayner would be required to deliver a statement on the new settlement on behalf of the opposition. Extending the list to add new Counsellors of State, however strongly she agreed with the intended effect, would require her implicit endorsement of the existing cohort. That proved too much. With negotiations ongoing she walked indignantly into her office and told her team: 'I'm not going to vote to keep that nonce on . . . I can't go back to my constituency and say, yeah, I support that.'

Soon Rayner was summoned for a Zoom meeting with Simon Case. Before their discussion, Rayner's aides warned her that 'it would be far more complicated to remove [Counsellors of State] than to add, and also remove Andrew'. One relayed Whitehall's fears that doing so could have 'legal implications' in the event of 'the US government wanting to extradite Andrew'. Another cautioned that dealing with Andrew would invite questions about Harry – questions his father, anxious to de-dramatise his succession, wished to avoid. Unbowed, Rayner made her point to Case, but emerged from their meeting chastened. 'After that conversation, she went quiet,' an adviser said. 'She never, ever spoke about the royals like that again.' Andrew and Harry remained as Counsellors of State, though Lord True, the minister responsible, re-assured Parliament that the Royal Household had no wish to see them serve. Still, Rayner had lost the argument. The force of her personality had very nearly dislodged the leader of the opposition but it failed to sway the pillars of the British establishment.

★

For McSweeney that was just as well. Despite the anarchic streak in the Irishman's politics – despite the fact he was an Irishman – he had no wish to offend or challenge that establishment. He wanted Sir Keir Starmer's Labour Party to *be* the establishment, to look and sound like good royalists. Labour conference fell only five days after the Queen's funeral. Unlike the Liberal Democrats, the leadership chose not to cancel. There would, however, be two changes. The conference slogan – 'A Fresh Start' – was changed. And delegates would observe a minute's silence and then sing the national anthem. No Labour conference had ever done so before. They sang 'The Red Flag' and 'Jerusalem' at Labour conference. Never the national anthem, with its lyric of deference and divine providence. Those words never had come easily to the sort of person who might stand for election as a Labour Party conference delegate. Not even at the seventy-fifth anniversary service for the dead of the Battle of Britain had Jeremy Corbyn sang the national anthem. When asked during a 2019 election debate whether the monarchy was fit for purpose, he had said: 'Needs a bit of improvement.' That view was rather less unorthodox among the Labour grass roots than the display of patriotism that McSweeney had in mind. In Liverpool, where conference would be singing, objecting to the national anthem was hardly controversial at all.

So it was unsurprising that GMB leader Gary Smith thought it was 'a fucking stupid idea'. He was probably right. McSweeney had only narrowly escaped humiliation by the Corbynites in Brighton a year earlier. At that conference Starmer could not make it through a speech without audible protest from the left. His advisers had fixed and fiddled the election of conference delegates but had no means to exclude their opponents entirely. The most McSweeney had done was confine Unite, his old enemies, to the very back of the conference hall. Now he was proposing to compel an entire hall of activists to sing a national anthem they resented in a city whose football fans met every rendition with a chorus of boos and whistles. McSweeney met Smith to brief him on his plans for conference one Friday that September, over six pints in Glasgow's Horseshoe pub. He showed Smith the branding. Union Jacks were everywhere.

'Fucking hell,' said Smith. 'It looks like Ibrox.' He was a fan of Hibernian, Edinburgh's Catholic club. They were not in the habit of toasting the monarch at Easter Road.

'Gary, you're just going to have to sing the national anthem. And if any of your lot kick off, we're going to boot them out the fucking door.'

'You can fuck off. I've got a better idea for you,' Smith said. He turned to a crowd of burly men – gas workers who paid their dues to the GMB.

'Billy, come over here.'

Billy was the biggest, six foot four.

'This is Billy. He's a Rangers man. This lunatic Irishman wants to sing "God Save the King" in *Liverpool*, at a *Labour* conference. This is a fucking stupid idea.'

Smith turned to McSweeney.

'But if we bring Billy and his Rangers mates down, you can put them across the front row and they'll blast it out for you. Go ahead, Billy.'

Billy obliged. 'GOD SAVE OUR . . .'

After his sixth pint McSweeney took Billy's card. 'Have you got more of you?'

'There's loads of us,' said Billy. 'We'll come to your conference, down to Liverpool.'

'I'll give you a bell tomorrow,' McSweeney insisted, drunk on nothing as much as his own conviction.

He never did. But to each union in turn he later gave the same
warning. Any activist who disrupted the silence would be ejected from
conference and expelled from the Labour Party. There was no guarantee they would abide by their orders. A single voice could destroy
everything – the seemingly spontaneous visits to royal projects, the
speeches, every gesture of condolence Starmer had planned for would
be destroyed by the party he now claimed to control. For the second
year in a row McSweeney gambled everything, including his leader's
dignity, on his belief that he could make the Labour membership do
exactly what he wanted. 'There's a boldness in saying "I'm prepared to
play this high-risk game that could go *really* wrong,"' observes another
aide to Starmer. 'But for Morgan it's all a game of continual high-stakes
poker – but with the sort of skill that makes him think: *I'm going to win
more often than I lose.*'

Sam White had suggested Starmer sing the words into a microphone, like Cliff Richard on a rainy day at Wimbledon. He was ignored.

When conference met on 25 September, Starmer repeated the lines
he had delivered on the day of the Queen's death. He told delegates:
'As we enter a new era, let's commit to honouring the late Queen's
memory. Let's turn our collar up and face the storm, keep alive the
spirit of public service she embodied, and let it drive us towards a
better future.' The minute's silence passed without disruption. They
sang 'God Save the King'.

'Are you going to sing?' asked Hollie Ridley, who watched the chorus
at McSweeney's side.

'No.'

The rest of the Labour Party did.

★

Starmer had travelled to Merseyside with a new confidence. Five
days after the Queen's funeral, Liz Truss ensured that her own reign
would be measured in days, not years. Like Rayner she struggled to be
anything but herself. With the business of public life back underway,
the prime minister moved quickly to reclaim the initiative circumstance had stolen from her. On 23 September her chancellor and

fellow traveller on the rightmost lane of Conservative politics, Kwasi Kwarteng, rose to tell the Commons of their plan for growth. With almost perverse irony it had been christened the 'mini-budget'. That hardly captured the scale of what Truss and Kwarteng had planned. The 45p top rate of income tax was abolished. The basic rate was cut from 20 per cent to 19 per cent. Plans to increase corporation tax were abandoned. Boris Johnson's health and social care levy – an additional rate of National Insurance designed to end the public policy nightmare that no government had dared confront – was cancelled. For the first time since the financial crisis of 2008, City bankers would be allowed to take home bonuses of any sum their bosses pleased.

Both sides of the House were incredulous. Truss and Kwarteng had told nobody of their designs for a new economy: not Conservative MPs, not the watchdogs of the Office for Budget Responsibility, not the markets. It had been exactly fifty years since another chancellor, Anthony Barber, cut so many taxes at once in pursuit of growth. Though a historian, Kwarteng spoke without heed for Barber's unhappy ending: of inflation, crippling strikes, and a run on the pound. Across the despatch box, Rachel Reeves smouldered with indignation as his public school baritone rattled the foundations of the national finances. The shadow chancellor accused him of reading 'a menu without prices'. Colleagues on the opposition front bench found it difficult to understand how a prime minister and chancellor with no mandate from the public could behave so destructively. They watched Truss alternate between knowing smirks and vacant stares. Emily Thornberry, who had shadowed the prime minister in her previous guise as Johnson's trade secretary, called it The Wall. 'It goes up, she switches off, and she's just like: *I actually don't care*,' Thornberry explained to colleagues. But Truss had always known her audience: Conservative MPs, newspaper editors, economists at right-wing think tanks. For a few minutes they revelled in her vision. The pound rose, if only marginally. Chris Philp, the chief secretary to the Treasury, tweeted: 'Great to see sterling strengthening on the back of the new UK Growth Plan.' Within hours it had slumped to a thirty-seven-year low. Truss retreated behind The Wall. 'We'd literally just watched them implode,' a shadow cabinet minister said. 'We had no power over what they chose to do at the budget. And they just did implode.'

By the time Starmer travelled to Liverpool for Labour conference two days later the markets had made clear they had no confidence in Britain's new government. Pension funds teetered on the brink of collapse as investors launched a fire sale of government bonds. Interest rates would soon rise, and with them the mortgage repayments of voters who had relied on the Conservatives to make them rich. Tax cuts for which no voter had asked were a gift to a Labour Party that had so often struggled to be sure of itself on economic policy, paralysed between the competing incentives of redistribution and reassurance. But for once its leader could give a straight answer when the BBC asked him what he would do about the abolition of the 45p rate. 'I do not think the choice to have tax cuts for those that are earning hundreds of thousands of pounds is the right choice when our economy is struggling the way it is, working people are struggling the way they are,' Starmer said on 25 September, the first morning of the first conference at which he might now be taken seriously as a prime minister in waiting. 'That is the wrong choice.'

★

His shadow chancellor had waited a long time for this kind of opportunity. Reeves, like her colleagues, did not expect the Conservative Party to be so careless as to hand it to her on a silver platter. 'It didn't feel inevitable,' another shadow cabinet minister recalls, 'because when you've lost as many elections as we have, you never believe that.' Reeves herself had become wearily accustomed to obscurity in the Labour Party and the country alike. Under Corbyn she had become a pariah, shamed constantly for her judgemental rhetoric on welfare claimants. In the first year of Starmer's leadership she had been a backroom politician, too unpopular to work front of house. With Claire Ainsley, Labour's director of policy, she dreamt up new philosophies for the centre left, convening on Zoom the thinkers and experts in whose ideas the ever-apolitical leader could never feign interest. Along with many others Reeves had initially doubted that Starmer could save their party, and freely confided those doubts to friends as her contemporaries gave up on Labour altogether. Yet in the months since May 2021 she had become the lynchpin of his inner circle, second only in importance to McSweeney. Reeves was one of a handful of politicians whose advice was reliably taken by the leader: it was only after her interventions that Corbyn was not readmitted as a Labour MP. Occasionally she spoke in terms that Starmer never could, telling one interviewer soon after her appointment as shadow chancellor: 'You don't have to be a fucking economist to work out that if less stuff is coming onto shelves, prices will go up.' With Shabana Mahmood, Conor McGinn and Pat McFadden she taught him political strategy at weekly meetings in Camden, where the quartet of seasoned politicians sat patiently as Starmer learned the trade that they knew instinctively. As the summer approached she spoke enthusiastically of her weighty reading list for recess as Starmer confessed to reading Victoria Hislop on the beach. For all the superficial similarity – the sobriety, the nasal tones – as politicians they were unalike. It was that contrast which had led so many MPs to conclude that her coronation as leader would not have been the worst outcome had Starmer been forced to resign over the Durham Constabulary's inquiries.

The public had proven far harder to convince. She longed to be taken as seriously by voters as Gordon Brown, whose photograph had hung on the wall of her university bedroom, had been viewed as chancellor. Yet aides matter-of-factly accepted she played politics on what they called 'hard mode', both as a woman and as a Labour politician. Voters could be just as disdainful of what McSweeney called 'librarian Labour' – the well-meaning academics and wilting daffodils on the front bench – as they could the expropriating radicalism of John McDonnell. Reeves needed to persuade them she was neither.

Deborah Mattinson's focus groups showed how difficult that would be. She knew all too well the difficulty Labour leaders had in convincing the public of their prudence, having told Neil Kinnock's shadow cabinet as much in 1990. More often than not its leaders and their chancellors were at odds, or trapped in uneasy tension: Harold Wilson and James Callaghan, Neil Kinnock and John Smith, Tony Blair and Gordon Brown, Ed Miliband and Ed Balls. 'It became abundantly clear,' an aide to Reeves recalled, 'that this whole project was only going to work if Rachel and Keir were seen as a proper partnership, and that Rachel's profile was elevated as part of that – it became absolutely fundamental to the leader's office.' Katie Martin, a former press officer to Gordon Brown recruited by the shadow chancellor as chief of staff, ensured Reeves and Starmer were seen together. Reeves's speeches and interviews were laced with references to her career as an economist at the Bank of England, just as Sadiq Khan, London's Labour mayor, never ceased to speak of his father's job as a bus driver. 'We wanted to get to the point where people took the piss out of her with Sadiq and the bus.' That would show the electorate, rather than merely tell them, that she was committed to sound money and fiscal rectitude.

At first they made little headway. The same focus groups that said an experienced shadow chancellor would help them trust the Labour Party were unconvinced by Reeves. Although women liked her ('She seems like she really understands things', 'She's like a normal person'), men were harder to please ('She seems alright . . . but, you know, what does she know about the economy? What credentials has she got?'). Inverting Einstein's definition of insanity, her advisers resolved to do the same thing again and again until it yielded a different result. To Reeves it came naturally. Like Brown, her great hero, she jettisoned the economic theory she held dearest and shackled herself to prudence. Her work as a central banker had focused on Japan and its decades of stagnation, which she blamed on under-investment in infrastructure and poor productivity. Under McSweeney's watchful eye she had written pamphlets for Labour Together that demanded stronger rights for trade unions and new taxes on wealth. As shadow chancellor she spoke like a Thatcherite. She narrowed her horizons so that the public might trust her. With McFadden as her deputy she began to say no to almost every request her shadow cabinet colleagues made for new spending. Katie Martin's first act as chief of staff to Reeves had been to do away with the form with which they demanded the party commit to new policies, with each judged on their individual merits. 'It was £2 million here, £20 million here, £200 million here.' On McFadden's first day as shadow chief secretary to the Treasury, he had been the horrified recipient of a spreadsheet – compiled by the despairing Tim Waters, an aide to his predecessor Bridget Phillipson – that detailed every spending commitment Labour had made in eighteen months. Throwaway lines in press releases written to placate campaigners lobbying shadow ministers added up to tens of billions of pounds that voters would not trust Labour to spend.

Reeves inhabited her persona like a method actor. After breakfast

meetings with captains of industry and finance at Franco's, a restaurant on Jermyn Street, she would wrap up leftover pastries in tissue
paper, secreting them away in her handbag. As the markets signalled
their disapproval to Truss and Kwarteng she knew she might finally
take centre stage. In daily conference calls after the mini-budget she
wrote the script for a political morality play that cast the Tories as economic vandals. In some respects it aligned with the conventions of
Labour thinking. Kwarteng was wrong, she said, to have rewarded the
wealthy and corporate interests as working Britons struggled with the
cost of living. In others it was subversive. Reeves began to criticise the
Tories because other taxes were too *high*. For that reason she endorsed
Kwarteng's tax cuts for the lowest earners. This was not what voters
were accustomed to hearing from Labour politicians. Yet as the markets panicked and the pound approached parity with the dollar, they
were willing to listen.

But what would they hear? The leader's office agreed on one thing
only: that they led a changed Labour Party. To what end it had changed
was a more difficult question. Their flagship economic policy was a
case in point. At 2021's Labour conference, a world before Ukraine
and rampant inflation, Reeves had announced a £28-billion-a-year
programme of borrowing to fund investment in renewable energy
infrastructure. With McSweeney preoccupied by the scrappy business
of changing Labour's rulebook, she had pledged to become 'Britain's
first green chancellor'. The author of those lines was Ed Miliband,
who like Reeves was inspired by the lavish fiscal stimulus introduced by
Joe Biden in the wake of the pandemic – and unlike the Blairites now
arrayed around Starmer, Miliband still believed that Labour should
make the case for economic radicalism in an age of global crisis. By
2022, however, Reeves had begun to doubt her past self. Labour had
not explained exactly how it proposed to spend such an enormous sum
of borrowed money. 'A borrowing target on its own is not a policy,'
explains one of her confidants in the shadow cabinet. 'It's a borrowing target.' Whatever it was, the leadership could not even agree on
its name. On 19 September, a week before conference, Deborah Mattinson emailed colleagues: 'There has been a revival of the names
debate (FYI Rachel not v happy). I have adapted a note . . . summing
up where we have got to with the name. My preference remains Green

Prosperity Plan (Keir liked this too . . .) but I would also be content with Climate Prosperity Plan or even Climate Investment Plan.' Mattinson was in a minority of one in the leader's office in truly believing in 'A Fairer, Greener Future', the slogan that had been hastily drafted to replace the insensitive 'A Fresh Start'. She spoke often of the risk the Greens posed to Labour's electoral revival. McSweeney liked to say he worried more about winning over Tories. His allies had come to resent what they saw as Mattinson's tendentious interpretation of polling and focus groups, which always seemed to serve whatever outcome they assumed she desired.

To McSweeney's chagrin she got her way, even if the debate would dog them for another year. The newspapers spoke breathlessly of infighting and they were not wrong. Starmer, however, did not look like the patriarch of a squabbling family when he gave his speech to conference. In the preceding weeks he had slaved over a first draft that expounded on his own political philosophy – his overdue reply to the critics who accused him of standing for nothing. After the mini-budget, it was all deleted. That he was not Liz Truss was all that now needed to be said. By the time he read his second script he was seventeen points ahead in the opinion polls. Quoting Blair, he said Labour was once again 'the political wing of the British people'. He announced a policy whose branding everyone behind him liked – GB Energy, a state-owned electricity company whose name was claimed by everyone from Miliband to Reeves and Gary Smith, who swore it was the product of another night in the pub with McSweeney. He sounded surer of himself than any of the aides in his office felt. With the Tories and markets in freefall, that was all that mattered. Reeves took a train home to London with Deborah Mattinson. Their phones relayed news of an emergency intervention from the Bank of England and a fire sale of government bonds.

'Fucking hell,' the shadow chancellor said.

'That was the Black Wednesday moment,' a shadow cabinet minister says now. 'That was the moment of the Parliament that, as it turned out, was the point of no return.' Truss went to Birmingham for her own conference a week later. Already it was obvious that it would be her first and last as leader. On its opening morning Reeves went to Birmingham, the BBC having relaxed the broadcasting convention that usually precluded opposing parties appearing at each other's conferences. 'The prime minister just doesn't seem to understand the anxiety and the fear,' she said. 'This is a crisis that is made in Downing Street, but ordinary working people are paying the price.'

Britain had made up its mind. But inside the leader's office, they had barely begun to make up theirs.

15

The Van

It was only a van. From afar it looked as if it belonged to a plumber or a painter. Had that been the case, Sue Gray would not have remembered it, parked unobtrusively outside the primary school a hundred yards from her home near Epping Forest. Her husband was a roofer. She knew that tradesmen rose early, just as she did, so she barely noticed it as she began another drive to work. Gray had lived thousands of mornings like this one. At first nothing distinguished this journey in early 2022 from any other she had taken to the Cabinet Office on Whitehall. Her journey that morning would soon pass into Labour legend, the tale embellished in the telling and retelling by her colleagues, as the drive that took her from a long career in anonymous officialdom to Keir Starmer's desk, and the vicious world of party politics.

Gray *had* been anonymous, at least before that winter. Like any other civil servant, she lived a private life. Even her year of birth remained a secret to those who sought it. But few ever had. Sue Gray was a name that only occasionally troubled ministerial memoirs or newspaper reports. For years she had been Whitehall's director of propriety and ethics: the official guardian of standards in government. Her adjudications on what politicians could or should not do had exposed her to the spotlight of media scrutiny only fleetingly, as a supporting player in other people's drama, and its glare had always passed quickly. That suited Gray.

No longer. Her mornings had already changed – even before the van. Gray's work was now an inquiry into a serving prime minister. In December 2021 she had been asked to determine the truth of reports of lockdown parties in Downing Street. Questions to which the answer was Gray were ordinarily rather dull. Had a parliamentary undersecretary of state broken the ministerial code? Could a former special adviser publish their memoirs? Was this *News of the World* kiss-and-tell about a cabinet minister true? Could a director general at the Department for Environment, Food and Rural Affairs sack their private secretary? These were the grubby inquiries that strait-laced civil servants were either too afraid, or self-regarding, to pursue. Instead they asked Gray. Gus O'Donnell, cabinet secretary to Blair, Brown and David Cameron, asked prime ministers of their misbehaving juniors: 'Do you want me to phone them, or do you want Sue Gray to phone them?' But never before had she been asked to decide whether the prime minister might remain in their job. Boris Johnson's future was in her hands. Suddenly an entire nation knew the name and recognised the face. Reporters observed her ordering coffee and tweeted her tastes to tens of thousands of followers. She hated it. Paparazzi gathered outside of the doors to 70 Whitehall, through which she had passed inconspicuously for decades, hoping to catch a glimpse of the woman who might bring down a prime minister. She took to sneaking into the Cabinet Office through the Scotland Office, a hundred metres up the street. To friends she never spoke of 'gatherings in No. 10' or 'compliance with Covid regulations'. It was always 'Fucking Partygate'.

She drove away from home. There it was, in the rear-view mirror, following her: the van. Whoever its driver was had taken their cue from her departure. She drove on. After every familiar turn it remained, as if it were her shadow. By now Gray could see its windows were tinted. 'That's weird,' she thought. Perhaps she was being paranoid. There was nothing unusual about a van driving from Essex to central London. Then she pulled onto the forecourt of a petrol station. So did the van. She knew what that meant.

'I'm being followed.'

Gray drove on. All the way the van followed. Eventually in central London she veered late into a turn it did not expect her to take. Only then did the van disappear, unable to escape the maze of central London's streets. Her commute ended as uneventfully as those before it.

The next morning she swore she saw the van again. After the third morning she began to worry. The van might have belonged to tabloid journalists. No – Conservative Campaign Headquarters had hired a private investigator. Or was it the security services? After a lifetime's anonymity, all she knew was that she was now a marked woman.

On the fourth morning Gray took a different route. She did not turn south to Westminster. Instead she drove west through north London, past Birmingham, between the cities of the industrial north – all places settled by Irish immigrants, like her parents – and into Scotland. After eight hours she reached Cairnryan, a little town at the very edge of the Rhins of Galloway, the double-headed peninsula that juts out towards Ireland. She boarded a ferry to Ulster. An hour later she was in Armagh, in the holiday home whose address was known only to her family. She stayed there for weeks. When she returned she slept in the spare rooms of sympathetic friends. Although banned from speaking to Simon Case until the completion of her inquiry, she did so via intermediaries: first to tell him she suspected she was being followed, then to petition him for a government-funded car. The cabinet secretary had always believed her decision to lead the inquiry a mistake. He thought it constitutionally unwise for any official to preside over an investigation into a sitting prime minister, not to mention career suicide. Upon her appointment, he had told her as much. 'Sue, what have you done?' he called her to say. 'You've got to say you won't do it.' By then it was too late. The intrusion of which Gray later complained was one of the appointment's many inevitable consequences. Although Case ceded to her request, granting her the use of a car, it was obvious the controversy surrounding the report would be impossible to solve. So long as Partygate was part of the political lexicon, Gray's Civil Service career would be the subject of relentless scrutiny. She knew she needed an escape. In the Labour Party, she would find it.

When she arrived she told anyone who would listen about the van.

★

When it came, Gray's report into Partygate unleashed a wave of turbulence upon the Conservative Party. Johnson would not survive it. Yet even as Starmer reaped the benefits, his office was racked by the same instability.

New Labour's gilded sons prided themselves on knowing what perfection looked like, and so Sam White did not think much of his colleagues. Nor did they think much of him. 'I think Sam felt in 2021,' said a sympathetic shadow cabinet minister, 'that there had to be a lot of drastic changes . . . the person who came in to do that was always going to end up with a massive political cost, because the only way you do that is to sack people. Politics is a blood sport. The office is where the problems came.' Many of the staff in the leader's office were scrappy and argumentative. White spoke like the corporate trouble-shooter he was. When he took McSweeney's old job as chief of staff in September 2021 he spoke of it as a 'turnaround mission'. To him, running the Labour Party was no different to running Aviva, the embattled insurer he had joined after leaving government in 2010. His sentences were laden with buzzwords his political staff were unused to hearing. McSweeney's task had been 'storming the citadel', White's was to 'professionalise'. They rolled their eyes as he spoke of ration-alising teams and achieving synergy between HQ and the leader's office, of his strategic 'Baker's Dozen' and 'Delivery Plan', of 'Hero Voter Political Strategy', 'Planning as Strategic Tool', 'Upskilling', 'Barnacle-scraping', and 'Super-charge Fundraising'. Talking as he did, White always knew that he would put noses out of joint. It was never his intention but if wounded pride was the price of a Labour Party capable of winning a general election – the result he had promised Starmer – then he was prepared to pay it. He believed there were only eighteen months to ensure that Starmer could win an election, that transforming the party – still hamstrung by a financial deficit that ran into several millions of pounds – could only be achieved at breakneck pace. Marooned in London far away from his family in North York-shire, he worked seven-day weeks – just as he had as a special adviser at the Treasury during the financial crisis.

Back then, White's boss Alistair Darling had been prepared to weather Gordon Brown's fury because he believed he was right. As Starmer's chief of staff White was similarly defiant. Colleagues were similarly furious. First they were furious when Claire Ainsley, Labour's head of policy, was allowed to work from home in York on a draft of the party's election manifesto when she suggested the time might have come for her to leave to spend more time with her young son. Then they were furious when he attempted to veto the appointment of Stuart Ingham, the aide who had known Starmer longer than any other, as Ainsley's replacement – a decision that was overturned by the leader himself. They were furious when White advised Starmer against announcing his intention to resign on the day Durham

Constabulary announced its investigation, and more furious still when he told them they would not be able to cope with the pressures of government. Mahmood and McGinn were furious when he accused them of bullying advisers on morning conference calls. McGinn was so furious he would text Starmer to tell him that he had gone 'on strike', so unbearable did he find White's style of management. And the rest of the shadow cabinet was furious when Lisa Nandy, ever anxious to preserve her credentials as a woman of the left, defied instructions to avoid picket lines at the height of industrial action that August and was pictured with striking telecoms engineers in her Wigan constituency. She insisted that White had given her permission.

White's detractors were many but they had one thing in common. They questioned his political judgement. After the Corbynite shadow cabinet minister Andy McDonald resigned at conference in 2021, White had proposed that Starmer write a letter of commiseration in reply. As the leader brooded in his hotel suite, demanding the television be turned off so that he did not have to see McDonald's face, Conor McGinn told White to sit down and shut up. They wanted to work for McSweeney, not him. At first the Irishman worked well with White. On big calls – changing the party's rules, disciplining MPs who questioned Nato, barring Corbyn from readmission – they mostly agreed. But McSweeney had removed himself from Westminster to work from party headquarters, itself now relocated from SW1 to Southwark, so that he might prepare for a general election campaign free from the distractions of Parliament – not least MPs themselves. 'He had no regard for politicians,' says another shadow cabinet minister. Inside the bubble of the parliamentary estate they obsessed over passing frenzies that the public never noticed. From his new vantage point across the Thames, McSweeney sought to burst it. By the summer of 2022 he had another by-election victory to his name, a gain from the Conservatives in Wakefield, and told Starmer that more money, staff and resources should drain from Parliament and be pooled in Labour HQ. The leader did not need much convincing. He hated Westminster as much as McSweeney. He had none of the reverence for Parliament exhibited by more romantic Labour MPs, nor their addiction to its clubbish bars and cliquish social scene. To Starmer it was a workplace, and a dysfunctional one at that. 'They make out that it's a great virtue of Keir's,' said a shadow cabinet minister of McSweeney and his friends. 'Like, you know, he hates Parliament so much, and loves being in HQ. Well, you are the leader of the *Parliamentary* Labour Party.'

White disagreed. He wrote Starmer a paper proposing the opposite solution to McSweeney: that the chief of staff run the party – its campaigns, its policy and communications – from Westminster. By then Starmer was no longer ignorant of the rising tide of exasperation towards his chief of staff. One evening in the autumn of 2022, as the leader drained the last of several pints he had shared with one of his advisers, he said: 'I'm aware people are unhappy with Sam.' He counted himself among them. On 11 October, White conceded defeat. He had failed to make the case for his own empowerment in a series of private meetings with the leader and left by mutual agreement. The headlines said he was sacked. Starmer told the shadow cabinet: 'The government's collapse has given us a huge chance. The instability means they could fall at any time.' Misleadingly, he added: 'We've been planning this for a while but the scale of the Tory collapse has brought it forward.' In briefings to journalists, his spin doctors said that policy advisers and communications staff would now answer to David Evans, the general secretary, and work from HQ. Like the statement announcing White's departure, it was close to the truth, but not quite right. As one member of the leader's kitchen cabinet said at the time: 'That's Evans, spelt M-c-S-w-e-e-n-e-y.' White would remain on good terms with Starmer. They would meet for beers long after his departure. As far as both men were concerned they had agreed to part as friends. Yet that was not the narrative that was spun by Starmer's own advisers, who paraded their prize scalp to colleagues and journalists. They briefed that they had ousted White. Starmer read what they said. But he never intervened to stop them.

McSweeney and his acolytes saw themselves as insurgents, even in their own office. That autumn they believed they had won a total victory. As long as Starmer's private office was functional, they could control the party's politics themselves – without interference from small-minded Westminster villagers. Occasionally they spoke of their leader as if he were a useful idiot. Said one, referring to the driverless Docklands Light Railway that wound its way through east London: 'Keir's not driving the train. He thinks he's driving the train, but we've sat him at the front of the DLR.' Another admirer, from the shadow cabinet, adds: 'Morgan was in charge of campaigning . . . he could be in the lead position, power completely unthreatened, and that's exactly what he drove through then. Until we get Sue Gray.'

★

The newspapers first caught wind of Starmer's search for a civil servant to run his office in January 2023. There were limits to what McSweeney could do without his imprimatur. Fevered talk of an imminent general election did not convince Starmer to give him total authority over the Labour Party – quite the opposite. The leader worried that Labour was still unready for the reality of power, however capable his campaign team was of winning it. He wanted a chief of staff who could help him prepare to govern. His insistence confused his political team. In the weeks he initiated his search for a new chief of staff, Labour's poll lead over the Conservatives soared as high as thirty-three points. 'Why did they feel the need to do that?' asked one. 'We had a system that was working.' But Starmer wanted the experience that too few of the advisers around him had. He wanted Sue Gray. 'Like a lot of Keir's decisions,' recalls a member of his inner circle, 'it was quite a gut call, where he thought: "This is who I want." There wasn't a lot of haggling.'

None of the media reports mentioned Gray's name. They wrote of Jonathan Powell, recruited from the US Embassy by Blair and Brown, and of Tom Scholar, sacked by Kwasi Kwarteng as permanent secretary of the Treasury in the weeks before the mini-budget. They wrote of Olly Robbins, chief Brexit negotiator to Theresa May. When *The Times* first revealed Starmer's search for a senior official, Damian McBride's phone buzzed incessantly with calls and texts from civil servants he had known from his past life at Gordon Brown's right hand. 'Is this true?' they asked. 'Who do I need to speak to about throwing my hat in the ring?' But of Gray the papers wrote nothing. Her recruitment sounded plausible only as a conspiracy theory. As Westminster had waited for her verdict on Partygate, Guido Fawkes, the muckraking blog, kept reminding its readers of her familial links to the Labour Party. Liam Conlon, Gray's son, had worked for Tessa Jowell, the late cabinet minister and high priestess of Blairism. He was chairman of the Labour Party Irish Society, and counted among his predecessors Conor McGinn and Matthew Doyle. These attacks on Gray's integrity and impartiality were dismissed as desperate and baseless. It was not that journalists were ever told that she would *not* be Starmer's chief of staff. It was that they never imagined the civil servant who had served in the Cabinet Office as a willing hatchet woman for four Conservative prime ministers would ever have considered the job, so they did not think to ask.

Suggestions that she was somehow a sleeper agent for the Labour Party were considered cheap and nasty by her allies and admirers. To friends, the former Tory chancellor George Osborne insisted: 'There is no way Sue Gray would ever do in a prime minister.' Shadow cabinet ministers old enough to have known her in government had never detected a leftish streak in her politics. 'I did not get any sense whatsoever,' one said, 'that she was Labour, or left of centre. I got the impression that she was straight down the line, pure Civil Service.' Nor was the notion of Gray the fifth columnist borne out by the findings of her report, which described 'failures of leadership and judgement in No. 10 and the Cabinet Office' but stopped short of censuring Johnson himself. Among civil servants who had offered their testimony, rumours persisted that Gray had omitted allegations of sexual encounters in Downing Street. That hardly supported the theory that she was working hand in glove with Starmer's office.

But it was not without truth.

Conlon, a grown man in his thirties, neither spoke nor worked for his mother. But his proximity to the powerbrokers of the Labour Party meant his political ambitions, for a time, became inextricably entwined with her reputation. As his mother became a figure of national notoriety, Conlon received support from the many shadow ministers he knew, as well as texts of consolation from Doyle, who had known Gray in his days as a Downing Street aide to Tony Blair. When he briefly considered seeking selection as the Labour candidate for Peterborough, the leader's office – without his knowledge – discussed a plan to delay the contest until after the publication of Gray's final report to spare him yet more negative publicity (in the end, like most aspiring MPs approached to run, he chose not to stand). They knew when that date would come, because Gray told them. Though her own future in the Labour Party was never discussed, she was communicating with its leadership long before she left the Civil Service. Johnson later told a friend that Michael Gove, Gray's great patron in the Conservative cabinet who had employed her as his principal adviser on devolution and the future of the United Kingdom, had authorised her to meet with Starmer and his aides to discuss his plans for government as early as 2021.

Starmer, more than anyone else around him, was determined that she would lead them. He wanted Gray from the beginning. As director of public prosecutions he had known her from weekly meetings on Whitehall, and admired her drive. She was not like the other mandarins in those meetings, mostly men with Oxbridge degrees and public school ties: her Civil Service career had begun at seventeen, with a posting in a dole office in Cricklewood, and paused for five years while she pulled pints for IRA men in a pub in County Down. So curious was her route to Whitehall – to developing and enforcing the principles of ethics in modern government – that some speculated she must be a spy. That much Gray had always denied. What she never admitted was what she desperately wanted to do for the British state instead, for it would have betrayed the vulnerability and insecurity she never revealed to the ministers she served and sacked. More than anything else she longed to be a permanent secretary, to run a Whitehall department of her own, to prove herself the equal of the posh boys whose dirty work she had conducted without complaint.

Yet when she applied to run Northern Ireland's Civil Service in 2020 she was blackballed by the Democratic Unionist Party. 'Why did I not get the job?' she asked a year later, in an interview with the BBC. For a senior civil servant to complain publicly of an unsuccessful job application was highly unusual. She went on: 'I'm not sure I'll ever quite know . . . but I suspect people may have thought that I perhaps was too much of a challenger, or a disrupter.' When she applied to run the Department for International Trade in 2022, she was blackballed. Kemi Badenoch, its secretary of state, had implored Simon Case to put her on the shortlist, a request he rebuffed on the grounds it was for the appointments commissioner, not him, to decide. Yet Gray still blamed Case, the forty-three-year-old cabinet secretary who had not yet been born when she first went to work, and who personified the Whitehall establishment she believed was arrayed against her. 'She was very let down by the Civil Service,' said a shadow cabinet minister who came to know Gray well. 'She felt she was thrown under the bus.'

Again Gray contemplated escape from the controversy and condescension and celebrity she had never sought. It began, unrevealed to all but three people close to Keir Starmer, in the weeks after Sam White's departure. To McSweeney, Deborah Mattinson and Jill Cuthbertson, the brisk and officious administrator who ran his office, the leader issued simple instructions. *Find me someone who knows their way around government.* 'He asked the three of us to think about what kind of person we wanted,' says one adviser present for the discussion. 'Clearly a big part of the scope would be somebody who knew their way around Whitehall because there was nobody in the team that did – most people in the team had not even worked in government, let alone knowing it well.' McSweeney left the reconnaissance required to draw up a shortlist to Mattinson and Cuthbertson, both survivors of Gordon Brown's Downing Street.

They alighted on names that had fallen out of favour under Boris Johnson, whose rumbustious government was frequently at odds with senior civil servants. Helen MacNamara, once his deputy cabinet secretary, was on the list. Having fled Whitehall to work for the Premier League, she knew Starmer from the executive boxes of the football grounds he much preferred to Parliament. There was Jonathan Slater, too: the former permanent secretary of the Department for Education, sacked to save the skin of Gavin Williamson, the blundering minister responsible for the disastrous grading of pupils whose exams had been cancelled due to Covid. Tom Scholar was highly regarded too, and raised eyebrows with his presence at Yvette Cooper's silver wedding anniversary party. But Gray overshadowed all three. Cuthbertson had worked with her in Brown's No. 10. Helene Reardon-Bond had been a beneficiary of her kindness to women in the Civil Service, repaying Gray with a text expressing solidarity during the Partygate inquiry. And above all, Starmer wanted her.

'He looked at the list,' said one of the advisers involved in Gray's recruitment, 'and said: "She's great."'

To McSweeney, Starmer said: 'I want this to be Sue.' He insisted that there would be no repeat of the power struggle that had ended in White's departure. 'We've moved to a campaign structure now,' he explained. 'But we need somebody who's got government experience.'

Yet despite his enthusiasm Starmer was only too conscious of the political risk. Hiring Gray would legitimise every conspiracy theory the right had advanced during her inquiry, invite allegations that she had breached Civil Service rules by communicating with the opposition, and politicise a post Starmer was determined to fill with a bureaucrat. Johnson himself concluded that it was proof of malign intent, as one of his confidants recalled: 'Boris feels that Sue was not an impartial or objective investigator into the issue . . . he genuinely does believe that what she did was corrupt.' If Labour spinners foresaw that narrative, they had no recourse to warn Starmer. He was unwilling to have his choice circumscribed by right-wing critics who would attack him whatever happened. Furnished with Gray's phone number, provided by Reardon-Bond, he made contact at the end of October 2022. At first she was unpersuaded, and still hoped for promotion within the Civil Service. When her appointment to the Department for International Trade was vetoed in favour of yet another Oxbridge graduate, she knew it would never come.

Talks dragged on over the winter. McSweeney, now the undisputed master of the leader's staff, was consulted on the shortlist and met Gray. They had still not concluded on 1 March, when Sky News published a short story on its website. It ran to only 248 words but its first sentence said all that was necessary. 'Labour leader Sir Keir Starmer is considering recruiting senior civil servant Sue Gray to be his new chief of staff.' Though it read like a fait accompli, Gray had not yet made up her mind. Yet the moment those words were published she knew her four decades in the Civil Service had come to an enforced and abrupt end. In talking to Starmer she had exploded her own neutrality. Gove was dumbfounded, asking Gray why she had chosen to destroy her life's work in the Civil Service. So often the judge, jury and executioner of investigations into misconduct in Whitehall, Gray immediately became the accused. Labour's response to Sky would not survive twenty-four hours: 'The process is ongoing. Nobody has been offered the job.'

Gray no longer had a choice. She called Starmer. He assured her that she was the only candidate he wanted. Just as Doyle had predicted, a blizzard of criticism set in. Gove, her old friend and boss, privately likened the predicted and predictable reaction to 'a *Scooby-Doo* moment for the right' – the villain theatrically unmasked. Officials past and present were just as perplexed: even Gus O'Donnell, the former cabinet secretary after whom Gray had derived her 'deputy GOD' nickname, questioned the appointment, both on the grounds of its implications for Civil Service propriety, and, more ominously, the suitability of his ex-mentee. 'He just had his head in his hands when he heard that Keir had appointed Sue,' recalled a close friend. 'Not [just] because of all the controversy . . . but because she was completely the wrong official.' For years, Gray had carved out a unique role as a troubleshooter and investigator, one which had limited, if any, crossover, with the managerial, strategic and political responsibilities of a chief of staff. Said one person of the reaction among permanent secretaries: 'Oh, Christ, this guy is going to be prime minister, and he's picked the wrong person.' As Starmer awaited the government judgement that would determine when she could start the job, his advisers lost sight of his intentions. Privately they discussed abandoning Gray altogether. It was all too much fuss. In turn she assured Starmer he would have only three or six months to wait. Eric Pickles, the former Tory cabinet minister who ruled on the ethics of such appointments, was an old friend of hers. She told Starmer that she was sure he would back her.

A number of Gray's new colleagues instead feared they would face a long, rudderless year. At first, McSweeney was not among them. Shortly after the news leaked, he had been unusually sensitive when a friend questioned the wisdom of the appointment. 'He couldn't understand why I was negative.' By April, that had given way to scepticism. He confided in the same person: 'It's unprecedented to have somebody like that move out of the Civil Service. Keir will bring her in, but he'll pay a price for doing so.'

In June Starmer learned that he had only three months longer to wait for her. Soon the Labour Party would turn in on itself again, just as McSweeney believed he had forced it to face the voter.

16

'Why us?'

The briefing ran to thousands of words but could have been summed up in four: do as you're told. 'Keir believes the way politics is conducted is broken,' it began. 'Coming late into politics he believes it to be more about posturing than action.' The shadow cabinet knew that the great paradox of their employment under Keir Starmer was that this professional politician did not like politics at all. But never had this confounding truth been expressed to them so bluntly.

They read on. 'Keir has thought a lot about the perils of modern politics. Twenty-four-hour media, social media echo chambers, virtue-signalling all conspire to constrain the space in which politicians can operate and harms serious policy and finding the right solutions for the country . . . Too many previous prime ministers have been blown off course, ending up reacting to events rather than shaping them. Keir wants his administration to be different.'

This meeting certainly was different. Starmer's shadow cabinet had never quite got the measure of him. They were younger, hungrier, obsessed with the minutiae of Labour politics. They knew what they wanted for party and country. In private, they asked one another whether Starmer was any of those things. Every Tuesday morning they met with him, awaiting the election they felt they were destined to win, and still they confessed to knowing nothing of his politics.

Only to trusted friends did they confide their doubts about the man whose government they would lead. They knew what they wanted. They knew what Morgan McSweeney wanted. But what did Keir Starmer want? His office had come to speak of his leadership as a three-stage plan. They pretended it had always been that way, but really the formula had been hastily drawn up in a strategy meeting in 2022. First they had reformed the Labour Party. Second came the exposure of the

Conservatives as unfit to govern. In both of those tasks they had ample assistance from the self-destructive tendencies of the Labour left and Tory right. Jeremy Corbyn was just beginning his third year as an independent MP, abandoned by his few allies in the Labour Party – who feared that any gesture of solidarity would see them suspended too. Liz Truss's forty-nine days in No. 10 had the same effect on her party's standing in the opinion polls as it had on the financial markets.

But the third stage was trickier. It was expressed as a question, and its answer felt impossible to discern from a leader who did not narrate his motives and seemed happiest behind a desk: *If not them, why us?* It demanded Starmer define himself in something other than the negative. It would no longer be enough to *not* be Jeremy Corbyn, or Boris Johnson, or Liz Truss. He admitted as much to *The Times*. 'First stage – change the Labour Party. That was when I took over three years ago, starting straight away. There were plenty of people at that stage shouting from the sidelines saying: "Set out a vision, set out a vision, go further." And I knew that stage one had to be change, change, change, and that we had to ignore the noises until we'd got that change done.'

But as shadow cabinet ministers tasted power they felt the answer slip away. Instead they asked: *If not them, why him?* To journalists they complained that Starmer was incapable of the political artistry that came naturally to his predecessors. This leader, one had once told *The Times*, painted only 'in primary colours'. With friends they were more candid.

A small group went to Alan Milburn, once health secretary and strategist to Tony Blair, and asked how they were supposed to work under a leader who seemed to possess everything a prime minister would need – except a vision.

'He's more of a buyer than a seller,' counselled Milburn, long retired from politics but still revered by the young Blairites who hoped to emulate him. He advised the shadow cabinet as he did his corporate clients: slowly, deliberately, in a soft Geordie burr. When it came to Keir, nobody seemed to know what he was all about. Starmer was not Blair, nor Thatcher – politicians who knew themselves and their projects and who subjected every decision to the logic of their own politics. Milburn recalled his meetings with Blair. However long his agenda was, Blair's was longer. However big his ideas, Blair's were bigger.

Tony Blair was a seller. Keir Starmer was not.

'Look,' said Milburn. 'I don't think he is that person. He doesn't come from politics. He travels relatively light.' McSweeney had sold him his leadership campaign. That he seemed allergic to defining his politics was part of what had drawn the Irishman to him: the hard left was all vision, inflexibly expressed. But now Starmer seemed to be saying nothing. If the shadow cabinet had ideas for the country, Milburn warned that they would first need to ensure their leader would buy them. They were still considering that advice when they met on 23 February 2023, and at last learned that their leader had something to sell.

In sonorous tones the shadow cabinet were reminded that their leader was indeed different. Before them stood Peter Hyman, another apparition from the recent past. Tall and professorial, he addressed the shadow cabinet like schoolchildren. Having left Blair's Downing Street for a second life as the headmaster of an academy school in east London, Hyman had returned to Westminster – landing, as so many old Blairites had, in Starmer's office – to teach the Labour Party a new theory of politics. For more than a decade he had contemplated why the project he had helped shape as a young speechwriter had failed on its own terms – why New Labour's ambition to reshape politics for a new century had ended unfulfilled, dashed on the rocks of petty rivalry between its founding fathers.

He blamed Gordon Brown for destabilising New Labour with his desperate pursuit of the premiership; he blamed Ed Miliband for trashing its achievements, for his 'posturing' as leader. In his headmaster's office Hyman had absorbed the lessons of Charles Handy, the Irish philosopher of management who believed that successful organisations renewed themselves at the peak of their powers, rather than at times of crisis. Hyman had concluded that politics itself was broken: its leaders forever chasing the dopamine rush of tabloid affirmation, too eager to please the media with policies whose implications they had barely considered before announcing them. When he went to work for Starmer, in the summer of 2022, he found the leader agreed with him.

So when Hyman told the shadow cabinet that he had found a 'different way of governing' that morning in February 2023, he spoke for the leader they still struggled to imagine governing at all. Starmer had heard every impatient criticism from his shadow cabinet. He knew they thought he had no politics, stood for nothing. It was to Hyman he turned to prove them wrong. The leader would respond to his doubters in a new language. He would prove his political acumen by reimagining politics entirely. Once, he had spoken in pledges, just as easily made as discarded. Now, as if evangelising to political savages, he took up his five missions.

*

In a party of competing, mutually exclusive world views, Starmer stubbornly resisted the factional taxonomy through which his colleagues understood politics. To his biographer Tom Baldwin, he said of Blairites, Brownites and Corbynites: 'It's a bit like asking people whether they're Protestant or Catholic, I don't care – it's about whether they can do a good job.' When Corbyn's friends had accused him of betraying the left, he had snapped at them: 'There's no such thing as Starmerism and there never will be!' Ed Miliband, who knew Starmer's mind better than others in the shadow cabinet, said: 'He's nobody's -ite.'

Observers who dared to categorise his politics were admonished and upbraided. After the *Guardian*'s Owen Jones condemned the Labour leadership for betraying the left in 2021, Starmer texted him as if he were a hurt and disappointed father. Jones, the leader grumbled, was better than that. By 2022, the criticism was much harder to ignore. The leader who had bristled at suggestions he might tell voters about his difficult childhood now spoke fluently of his youth and private passions on political podcasts; an operation that had once disavowed the grubby business of negative campaigning now knew its enemy, and pursued the Tories under their new leader, the irritable multimillionaire Rishi Sunak, with viciousness and vigour. But to what end? Labour did not want for policy. Under Starmer's watch it had announced hundreds. Yet almost all of them were ignored. As long as the leader's office awaited the arrival of Sue Gray from Whitehall, questions of how it would implement a manifesto would have to wait. Shadow cabinet ministers found it easy enough to speak, but to speak coherently on behalf of a leader whose reasoning remained opaque even to his intimates felt impossible.

Alan Milburn was not alone in his confusion. At the beginning of 2023 Peter Mandelson had written to Starmer at length, urging the leader to think more deeply about the difficult choices that lay ahead, and just how much of the party's agenda could survive in a new era of fiscal restraint. New Labour, Mandelson told anyone who would listen, had been built on detail. It articulated its world view not through the glitzy presentation and spin for which the Prince of Darkness had become known but through iconoclastic policy that challenged the old assumptions of Labour politics. He believed Starmer's Labour had forgotten his golden rule: *detail*. To the extreme irritation of Rachel Reeves, Mandelson had said in a speech to business leaders in Durham that Starmer risked 'sneaking over the finishing line' and would condemn Britain to 'inertia and decline' unless he overhauled his economic policy. Once he had received Mandelson's note, a tracksuit-clad Starmer went to Mandelson's mews house, an old vicarage in Regent's Park, to hear a similar sermon first-hand. After an hour the architect of New Labour bade him farewell, unconvinced his visitor had understood what he meant.

Yet Starmer knew he was lacking something. In his discussions with Deborah Mattinson he confessed that his offer to the public was doomed to fail. However enthusiastic voters were about this individual policy or that individual speech, Starmer knew their faith in mainstream politics had waned. They were all too accustomed to hearing politicians say things they agreed with, only for their words to remain abstract and their lives unchanged. On that much he agreed with them. He had no time for politics or politicians either. Had he been a participant in one of Mattinson's focus groups, he would have spoken just as dismissively or cynically of Westminster and its broken promises. So when she suggested recalling Hyman from his educational exile to Labour politics, Starmer assented enthusiastically. He wanted – *needed* – ideas that would transcend the vicissitudes and passing frenzies of parliamentary politics and media storms. The opinion polls suggested that the Conservatives had trashed their own reputation so spectacularly that he might be prime minister of a broken country for a decade. If Starmer understood anything about politics, it was that he had not yet given any sense of the philosophy that would guide him. He had said as much in his earliest conversations with Hyman. Starmer's advisers knew, too, that their policy meant too little to the voters they needed to win. 'There was a lot of policy,' Hyman said, 'that Labour people, that progressive people, wanted. But there was a bigger question – linked to the voters we were going after – which was: what's the focus, what's the priority? How do you prioritise? How do you get real ambition?'

Yet Starmer detested words like philosophy – words like *vision*. He was allergic to slogans too. Shortly after his arrival, Hyman had set himself the task of identifying Labour's three-word strapline, the equivalent of the 'Take Back Control' or 'Get Brexit Done' which had so elegantly codified the Conservative Party's political and electoral proposition over the preceding years. The leader chafed against it, questioning if that sort of vocabulary did not represent an attempt to solve politics with the same populist rhetoric, the same deceptive simplicity, that had served Johnson, but not the country. From the moment Sunak entered Downing Street in October 2022, promising to rectify what he understatedly described as the 'mistakes' of his predecessor, Starmer and Hyman instead undertook to learn a new language for progressive politics. The next Labour government would not speak of pledges, as Sunak did, or priorities – but *missions*. That was the sort of word Starmer had begun to use in private, inspired in part by his constituent and sometime adviser Mariana Mazzucato, the economist who had argued since 2017 that the modern state should work with the private sector to solve the 'grand challenges' thrown up by a dysfunctional, capitalist economy. Their lodestar was no less lofty than John F. Kennedy's race to the moon. Even as his government contended with war, disease and natural disaster, it might still think the unthinkable and devote its resources to bigger ambitions. Even if it fell short of those ambitions, it might still make progress towards goals that politics ordinarily failed to address. 'The great thing about the moonshot and the moon landing,' said Hyman, 'was all the stuff that was created by trying to land someone on the moon: all the new materials that were created for the first time, to go into astronaut suits and rockets and all the rest of it. The great thing about setting a goal that's really ambitious is that you don't quite know what the other unintended but positive consequences are.' For a while Starmer toyed with borrowing Kennedy's language and speaking of his own moonshots for the British state. But Hyman recalls now: 'We debated that. I liked the moonshot language. But the implication of it, if it's too aligned to Kennedy, is almost that you're getting on with the day job and the real governing, but you've almost got this side thing – this ambitious moonshot – that's slightly detached from people's lives.'

Starmer adjusted his horizons. He turned away from Camelot and looked instead to Berlin, where Olaf Scholz had been swept to power in 2021 with a programme for government codified in four missions to revolutionise the German state's approach to climate change, transport, technology and health. Claire Ainsley, Labour's policy director, had studied Scholz closely. She was not alone in observing parallels between the quiet man from Hamburg and the quiet man from Holborn and St Pancras. Both were mocked for their dullness, plodding presentation and timidity. Both were struggling to return enfeebled parties of the centre left to the head of government after decades on the margins – the SPD as junior coalition partners, Labour as a divided party of opposition. Both eschewed the ideologies championed by critics to their left. Conversations with their German counterparts helped the leader's office – and Starmer himself, who visited the Berlin Wall dressed in a football hooligan's uniform of a Stone Island polo shirt in July 2022 – clarify their thinking.

That Christmas, Hyman and Mattinson drew up a list of five missions. Their brief from Starmer was to set goals that elicited a 'sharp intake of breath' from those who heard them: first the leader himself, and then the country. They were deliberately broad. The detail on which New Labour had been built would come later. All emphasised ends, rather than means. A Labour government would achieve the highest sustained economic growth in the G7; it would make Britain a 'clean energy superpower'; reform the National Health Service to make it 'fit for the future'; make the country's streets safe; and break down the barriers to opportunity at every stage of life. When Starmer read those missions for the first time they elicited not so much a sharp intake of breath but a nervous gulp. For all his dislike of the old labels, there was more than a pang of Blairism in the language – with its almost post-ideological emphasis on outcomes. What mattered to Starmer, like Blair, was *what worked*. His predecessor had used that phrase to differentiate himself from the 'forces of conservatism' on left and right that he had denounced in a 1999 speech written by Hyman. Starmer deployed the same mantra to demonstrate the seriousness he thought sorely lacking from so many of his colleagues. When he launched the missions in a speech at the Manchester headquarters of the Co-op on 23 February, he sold them as a solution to the 'sticking-plaster politics' that had come to frustrate him after eight years in Parliament. It was a cumbersome phrase, much mocked by the commentariat – but, unusually, it was Starmer's own coinage. 'I wish I'd come up with it,' said Hyman. 'It captured the sense of chaos, short-termism, that was embodied by five Conservative prime ministers in seven years. The missions fitted as a perfect antidote: more ambitious, more long term – the opposite to short-term, sticking-plaster politics.'

The muted reception to the speech served only to convince Starmer that he was right. Once he had stewed over every critical word written or tweeted by journalists: no longer. 'Let me give you an example,' he said. 'Zero-carbon British electricity by 2030. A huge goal that will allow us to accelerate to net zero. Make no mistake – this goal would turn Britain into a clean-energy superpower. It puts us ahead of any major economy in the world. *That's the sharp intake of breath.*' None was audible in the room. Instead the press let out a disdainful sigh. The *Guardian* said the missions were neither inspiring nor designed to excite. The *Daily Mail* asked why he had not promised to stop small boats crossing the English Channel. The leader column in *The Times* sniffed: 'Sir Keir clearly hoped to deflect public attention from his lack of policies by talking about the principles that would underpin future policy . . . As a prosecutor, he is more at home dissecting the failings of his opponents than coming up with creative solutions to problems. There is evidence that this is a vulnerability for Labour.' When confronted with these criticisms Starmer was defiant: these were not throwaway commitments to be judged by the next day's newspapers, but a genuine attempt to reimagine politics for the long term. The doubters were not only to be found on Fleet Street. Even after their tutorial from Professor Hyman that same day, the shadow cabinet lived down to Starmer's low expectations of politicians as he explained each of the missions at length in four subsequent speeches. They had been warned in their briefing note: 'Keir has a ruthless streak, and, unusually for a politician in opposition (where pandering to every interest group is seen as essential), he is unafraid to tell people that the missions are a prioritising mechanism and not everything will get top billing.' Hyman's presentation had also made clear that, in time, the missions would be translated into marketable policy – that voters would be sold the how, as well as the what, when Starmer announced his 'first steps' for government just before the election. Still the shadow cabinet moaned to anyone who would listen that it was all half-baked and highfalutin. On one occasion, at a meeting in Canary Wharf to discuss the plans, they unburdened themselves before Starmer himself. Reeves was tight-lipped, but behind the scenes even she too was concerned. Achieving the highest growth in the G7 was a hostage to fortune, inasmuch as it not only required Britain to buck a decade of anaemic output, but also assumed other industrialised nations, among them the US, would fall short of their own targets. Said one party staffer who shared her misgivings: 'What are you going to do if there's runaway growth in Japan? Send in Godzilla?'

As ever, Angela Rayner feared the leader's office were embarked on yet another mission to erode her influence. When told by an adviser that Starmer's new agenda included neither housing nor workers' rights – her two biggest responsibilities – she 'exploded', and queried whether a sixth mission could be added to the list. Assurances that she would be involved in the original five as deputy prime minister eventually placated her.

Others engaged in the sort of playground mockery Starmer loathed. Hyman, the very model of the experienced administrator that had been missing from an operation preoccupied with the rough and tumble of faction fighting, had undoubtedly added intellectual heft to the leader's office. Yet some of his colleagues remained uninterested in ideas. As far as they were concerned, only one mattered: that an unpopular Conservative government should be blamed for the rising cost of living. They considered Hyman's policy proposals with derision. His enthusiasm for education reform endured and so for the education mission he proposed a platform for school leavers to exhibit extracurricular activities and achievements other than basic grades – an idea already in use in the sector. Advisers misinterpreted the idea as a sort of 'LinkedIn for Kids' and cackled at the safeguarding implications. For the health mission, brainstorming sessions covered a plan for a national recipe competition to replace additive-laden ready meals with nutritious alternatives recommended by the government, and the impact of mirrors and techno music on the mental health of gym patrons.

Some in the shadow cabinet thought those ideas – or the mocking interpretations of their advisers – 'bonkers'. But they did not leak them. McSweeney, meanwhile, was cautiously supportive – if doubtful that Starmer's speeches were doing much to bolster his campaign strategy. Hyman was well aware of their opinions. That April, he told a friend: 'People, including the shadow cabinet, don't understand missions. They want retail politics, but actually the public wants long-term plans.' Starmer, he said, was on his side, and had finally begun to engage in 'stocktakes' of policy. Hyman recalled: 'I called it the tip of the sword. There were some people who thought we should go straight to retail pledges. And, indeed, some journalists said this when we launched the missions: "Oh, well, they're not retail enough." Of course, that was never the point. The point was to create an edifice in order for the other pledges – the first steps – to mean something to the public.'

Whatever the point was, much of the Labour Party was still missing it. Shadow cabinet ministers found the missions so broad that each sparked countless debates with the leader's office over new policy. Ambiguity abounded, not the promised clarity. The leader had been comforted by focus groups revealing public enthusiasm for ten-year plans, but polling suggested minimal awareness of the missions among the public. By the early summer, Hyman's colleagues were briefing against him to the newspapers Starmer had made it his business to ignore. In anonymous asides to *The Times*, printed under the ugly headline 'Labour insiders criticise Keir Starmer's "terrible" campaign strategy' on 22 May, they described the missions in terms they knew would wound their author. 'The missions themselves are a good idea,' said one. 'Miliband-style missions and highfalutin' language are not.' Said another: 'We are all annoyed about these missions.' A shadow cabinet minister sought to consign them to irrelevance: 'They've just not captured the public's attention. They're actually not a bad way to think about government but they're a terrible way to campaign.' That much seemed to have been proven by their absence from a council election offensive that ended with Labour as the largest party in local government earlier that month.

Starmer ignored the hue and cry. The missions, unlike anything else he had announced, were the embodiment of his politics. His closest advisers understood those beliefs not in terms of left or right, nor through Blair's binary of old versus new. They instead described Starmer almost like a baby yet to grasp the concept of object permanence. Only when confronted with a problem was he moved to advocate for its solution. 'He comes back from visits incensed,' said Hyman, 'and thinks: this is a mad way of running a country. He came back from a visit to Alder Hey [children's] hospital completely furious that the biggest source of admissions was for tooth extraction – not for more serious procedures, but because families couldn't get a dentist . . . Unlike other leaders I've seen, he's very experiential.'

*

Fittingly, it was experience – not the missions – that truly clarified the vision of politics that Starmer would take to the country. Not for the first time, Boris Johnson would force his hand.

The former prime minister had lingered in Parliament ever since his defenestration from Downing Street. His first attempt to resume his old office after the fall of Truss had ended in failure. He bided his time, chuntering unhelpfully behind Sunak, until 12 June. Johnson had tired of waiting for the verdict of the committee investigating accusations that he had misled MPs by denying lockdown parties had ever been held in No. 10. Describing the inquisition as a 'kangaroo court', he pre-empted their verdict by resigning from the Commons on 12 June. His firmest friends on the back benches soon followed his lead. Nigel Adams and Nadine Dorries, two former ministers who had played bodyguard and cheerleader to Johnson, had believed they would be elevated to the peerage at his behest. When Sunak made clear that he would do no such thing, on 20 July they quit as MPs too.

Dorries protested in idiosyncratic style, delaying her departure for more than a month as she contested her exclusion from the Lords. Adams went immediately. Both he and Johnson knew that resigning left Sunak vulnerable to electoral humiliation. Labour's poll lead still stood at more than twenty points. However unlikely it seemed, that meant it might win Adams's seat of Selby and Ainsty. His corner of North Yorkshire was a microcosm of the England McSweeney had in his sights. Selby was an old mining town, its skyline still dominated by a coal-fired power station, set among rolling hills dotted with villages full of wealthy people. Labour had not won there since Blair's last election victory in 2005; in 2019, Adams had won a majority of 20,137 votes. The by-election he triggered was the ultimate test of McSweeney's conviction that Starmer could and should be capable of beating the Conservatives anywhere. The Irishman had taken to quoting the message written by Tim Berners-Lee, the inventor of the World Wide

Web, for the opening ceremony of the 2012 London Olympics: *This is for everyone*. Was Starmer? He ought to have been in Johnson's old seat of Uxbridge and South Ruislip, at the very least. The far west of London was home to many of Mattinson's hero voters – younger families with mortgages with small-c conservative sensibilities who drove cars to work and had engaged with politics only to express their disgust at Partygate. 57 per cent of Johnson's constituents had voted Leave. In 2019 his majority had stood at just over 7,000 – the sort of number that would easily be overturned if the national polls were correct. All being well, whatever the outcome in Selby, Starmer could count on at least one new MP when voters in both seats went to the polls on 20 July.

Yet all was not well in Uxbridge. There, Labour would be forced to run a campaign against itself. In the weeks before Johnson's resignation, the London mayor Sadiq Khan had announced the extension of the capital's Ultra Low Emission Zone (Ulez) to all thirty-two London boroughs. Drivers whose vehicles did not satisfy modern environmental standards would be charged £12.50 a day to drive within its boundaries. Once confined to the inner city, those liable to pay would now include the tradesmen and shift-workers of suburban London – the very voters in Uxbridge whose finances had been shredded by 10 per cent inflation and ballooning mortgage premiums. Under the tutelage of Greg Hands, the Tory chairman still cursed by McSweeney for defeating the Labour campaign he ran in Hands's Hammersmith seat in 2005, the Conservatives seized the opportunity to fight the by-election as a referendum on Khan and Labour's environmental policies. Danny Beales, the flame-haired Camden councillor selected in place of Ali Milani, the Corbynite who had run Johnson close in 2019, became the unwitting poster boy for Labour's 'war on motorists'. As with Brexit, the voters of Uxbridge were only too happy to be given an outlet for the fury that would later manifest itself in the vigilante vandalism of the towering CCTV cameras erected to enforce the levy.

Starmer had a problem. Mattinson knew it, for voters kept telling her so. Steve Reed, the shadow cabinet minister responsible for the campaign, knew it too. McSweeney knew it, noting with some horror that the Tories had won a council by-election in Cambridge amid protests against a near-identical policy. He thought it obvious that his leader's 'stocktake' of policy had not yet gone far enough. And Pat McFadden, despite busily dousing the party's pledges with political pesticide, had not managed to kill the darlings of every shadow cabinet minister. Labour was still seen as a party willing to make punishing demands of the public in pursuit of its own passions. However much the working man or woman of Uxbridge whose votes it coveted believed in clean air or lower carbon emissions, they were less prepared to make themselves poorer to fulfil the pledges of politicians. Rachel Reeves had realised as much the previous month when she moved to silence critics of her £28-billion-a-year green borrowing pledge – a promise made for another world, unshaken by the war in Ukraine and Liz Truss – by clarifying that she would hit that target only after five years in power. Ulez was different. It lay in the domain of a mayor with his own mandate, who assiduously cultivated his personal brand, and was ever watchful of the Labour members who might one day make him party leader: so watchful, in fact, that Starmer's allies on the National Executive Committee had deliberately delayed his reselection as mayoral candidate as an unspoken punishment for his manoeuvring as Durham Constabulary deliberated over the leader's future.

In the leader's office they debated how they might mitigate the damage to a campaign Starmer ought to be winning by default. Some urged McSweeney to reframe the policy as a means of 'protecting children from asthma'. His own assessment was as simple as it was fatalistic. He told colleagues that voters would say: 'This is adding to my cost of living, and I don't like it.'

Indeed they didn't. Voters hated it. To the Irishman there were no good answers. He could separate his candidate from the electorate and launch a suicidal defence of Ulez. That he never countenanced. He could separate his candidate from his leader, who had previously endorsed Khan's policy. That was not credible. The nuclear option was for Starmer to denounce Khan and pledge to overturn the mayor's policies if elected prime minister, which would elevate a little local difficulty to national prominence. That was too dangerous. 'It would have created a much bigger story about Uxbridge being a Ulez by-election,' recalls one aide in the leader's office. 'That would have made it much harder to do anything to mitigate it. In a very short campaign of five weeks, the split would have been the dominant story.' Having mulled over this uniquely unappetising menu, McSweeney chose to divide the candidate from the mayor. On 4 July, the same day that voters in Cambridge rejected Labour, Beales told a hustings in a draughty church hall that it was 'not the right time' to extend Ulez, and told locals that he had written to Khan to demand the policy be abandoned. Starmer remained silent. When the leader asked whether he agreed with his candidate or his mayor, he said nothing. When the mayor was asked if he would reconsider, he refused. Ambiguity reigned.

Yet when polls closed at 10 p.m. on 20 July, McSweeney briefly dared to dream that Labour had won both seats, and told friends as much. It was not enough. Just as the polls suggested, Starmer had indeed secured one new MP. But his name was Keir Mather, and his seat was Selby and Ainsty.

*

It could have been a crisis. On the morning of 21 July, a smirking Sunak was able to pose, implausibly, as a man of the people as he lauded the new member for Uxbridge, the Conservative councillor Steve Tuckwell, at a greasy spoon. Sounding off to journalists, shadow cabinet ministers demanded the head of Ed Miliband, unfairly blamed for every Labour policy with a green tint. Privately, Rachel Reeves blamed Khan, confessing to friends that she was furious with the mayor's intransigence.

McSweeney was furious too. Just as Mandelson had warned, the leader was burdened like a packhorse with policies the Irishman's voters did not much like. It was as if they had been transported back to 2021, back to Hartlepool. The same siren voices resumed their appeal to McSweeney's better nature. Labour had won Selby. To overturn a majority that massive suggested Starmer would easily win a general election. Uxbridge was a fluke result, a freak result. The plan was working. There was no need to linger on the defeat, as they had warned McSweeney in May 2021.

He ignored them. As the leader's office decamped to Nottingham for the party's National Policy Forum – the gathering of shadow cabinet ministers, trade unions and members at which the basis of its election manifesto would be agreed – McSweeney resolved to make a virtue of his own failure. The forum's first day, Saturday 22 July, had been planned as a catwalk for Keir Mather, the golden boy of Labour's revival. He had been scheduled to give a speech declaring the party on course for a landslide, congratulating Starmer for convincing voters who had never backed Labour before to endorse him as Britain's next prime minister. The script ended up in a leader's office bin.

Delegates were instead treated to an unexpected appearance from Beales. As he took to the stage McSweeney saw an old friend grimacing at him. It was clear what was coming. 'Our relentless focus on the cost of living hammering voters across the country should have been enough to win my home seat,' Beales said, unburdening himself with words written by Paul Ovenden. 'Because – let me be frank – a single policy cut us off at the knees. This isn't complicated. You cannot tell working people you are laser-focused on the cost of living, on the difficulties facing them, on making life easier and then also penalise them simply for driving their car to work.' To Khan's shock, Beales added: 'Ulez is a bad policy. It must be rethought.' Starmer followed. 'We are doing something wrong if policies from the Labour Party end up on every Tory leaflet,' he said.

There it was. No principle was too sacred for Starmer. The radical barrister who had told Gordon Brown's aides that he wished to strengthen environmental law if he was ever elected as a Labour MP stood before the Labour Party and drenched its most ambitious green policy in petrol because he had been told it would help him become prime minister. The leadership candidate who had sold himself to party members as a champion of Labour's internal democracy – of the inviolable right of the grass roots to advocate for progressive policy – abandoned it all summarily. Many with memories of that contest increasingly did not recognise the man before them. Among them was Martin Taylor, the hedge fund millionaire with a social conscience who had funded Starmer's leadership bid and who uncharacteristically let it be known within the party that Starmer was leaving himself vulnerable before Labour's core vote. With leadership forswearing tax and spend economics, and under pressure to pare back its £28-billion pledge, he feared a situation in which Starmer had little to offer the lower-to-middle-income workers it existed to serve. Nobody could accuse Taylor of being a Corbynite. He had after all funded Labour Together when McSweeney was turning it into a vehicle to rout the left. Yet Starmer was unmoved by such talk, sincere or not, still less the criticism of his Ulez reversal. He approached no task with the alacrity he showed when rewriting his own history. Like the hardening of his project after Corbyn's suspension, unhappy accidents like Uxbridge were recast in an instant as strokes of political genius. Only six days earlier Starmer had provoked another bout of infighting when, unintentionally, he had told the BBC's Laura Kuenssberg that a Labour government would not abolish the two-child cap on benefits introduced by the Conservatives.

'If you have more than two children at the moment, you don't get benefits. Would that change under a Labour government?'

'We're not changing that policy,' he said.

As in Uxbridge, there was no plan. He spoke unthinkingly. It was a straight answer to an unexpected question. If anything, it was a mistake. Starmer did not intend to start a fight with his own MPs, who railed against his heartlessness, just as he had not intended to use a by-election defeat as a pretext for another assault on the left. Yet three days later he spoke as if it had always been the plan. 'We are now at the stage of setting out our missions for government,' he told a restive shadow cabinet. 'They are built on the rock of secure and responsible economics. And that's hard . . . "Tough choices" is not a sound bite. We're going to have to take them. Without them, we don't get to the next stage. Tough choices give us the platform and the permission to have a bold, reforming Labour government that can do those things: raising living standards, investing in public services, tackling child poverty. It's vital to us being able to do what we need to do in government and getting over the line. Simply saying we're a bold, reforming government doesn't deliver us a bold reforming government – otherwise we'd have had Labour governments permanently.'

In Nottingham the unions threatened to bring Starmer to heel, to turn back the churning tide of his pernicious revisionism. Once McSweeney had begged them for help. Now he threatened them. 'If we can create a good policy platform,' he told union leaders, 'we will campaign on it.' If they disagreed with Starmer, they would be ignored. 'The alternative is that you could create a bad policy. You could use your votes to get it across the line. But what do you really think will happen then? We're not Bennites. We will take that document, we will throw it in a bin, and I will write the manifesto. That's what will happen.' He meant what he said. Angela Rayner's programme of protections for workers' rights was watered down. When Unite's delegation learned of that betrayal, they arrived at the forum's gala dinner, lifted the wine from its tables, and went home. Their colleagues in the union movement had little choice but to comply. Starmer left Nottingham with his five missions formally adopted as party policy, with his old commitment to a legal right to transgender self-identification abandoned, with the two-child cap firmly in place. Experience bulldozed through his principles – and he hated no experience more than losing. Sincerity had been subjugated to the cold, remorseless logic of victory. That, in reality, was the one mission. The statement issued as the NPF adjourned late on the evening of 23 July defined the person Starmer's advisers now pretended he had always been: 'There are no unfunded spending commitments in this document.'

That night they told themselves that there was no disaster they could not spin into a triumph.

17

Israel

All was quiet in the Negev desert. Its calm would be punctured only by song and dancing. 7 October was Simchat Torah, the festival to celebrate the completion of the year's cycle of readings from the Hebrew Bible. But there were few prayers of exaltation at kibbutz Re'im, a village not far from Israel's border with Gaza. Here Israel's secular youth raved to trance music, celebrating 'love, friends, and infinite freedom'.

At 6.30 a.m., Hamas rockets streaked across a cloudless sky. Paragliders flew overhead, their motors inaudible over heavy bass. Then came the gunfire. Within hours, 364 people were dead: their bodies heaped semi-naked in hot, bloody sand. Forty more were taken hostage. Some were raped. Across the border similar violence was streamed live to a world that watched in horror. What began as a day of joy ended as the blackest in modern Jewish history. Not since the Holocaust had more Jews been murdered in a single day. Later that day, Benjamin Netanyahu sent Israeli troops into Gaza. Before long they would kill many more Palestinians.

That morning Keir Starmer had little sense of what a new outbreak of bloodshed would mean to Britain's Jews, to their Muslim neighbours, or the Labour Party. His relatives had lived much closer to conflict – the relatives of his wife, Victoria, were Polish Jews who had chosen both London and Israel for sanctuary after the Second World War – but he, at least, was safe. More than safe: he was happy. The previous evening had seen Labour secure a new Member of Parliament in Rutherglen, just outside Glasgow, from the Scottish National Party. Statistically it was a small victory. Beforehand, Labour had one MP in Scotland. Now it had two. But when the returning officer announced a Labour majority of more than 10,000 it vindicated the gambles Starmer's critics had

called mad: to sack Richard Leonard, the misfiring leader of Scottish
Labour, and to spend money campaigning in a country whose working class had abandoned the party that was made for them. Now those
voters were coming home in such numbers that McSweeney, whose
mansion was only a few miles away, told his colleagues that they might
soon have forty MPs north of the border.

Starmer would soon be prime minister. He knew it as he spoke in
Rutherglen: flapping his arms like a flightless bird, the happy voice
creeping up half an octave. 'They said that we couldn't change the
Labour Party, and we did it. They said that we couldn't win in the south
of England and the north of England, and we did it. They said: "You'll
never beat the SNP in Scotland," and Rutherglen, you did it. You blew
the doors off!' It had been a good week and a better weekend awaited.
On the night of 6 October his staff gathered in the bar of Liverpool's
Pullman Hotel, protected by its own impenetrable ring of steel, as they
toasted the birthday of his spin doctor Steph Driver. They laughed at
a *Times* profile of McSweeney, illustrated by the faces of the Labour
leader and his chief strategist looming over the Palace of Westminster.
It was knowing laughter. However ridiculous it might have seemed,
that night Starmer and the Irishman were the coming men of British
politics. Their party conference, which would begin on the morning
of 7 October, was the gathering of a government in waiting. When the
leader arrived in Liverpool he was applauded as if he had already won.

Before long the jubilation faded. The television screens studding the
walls of the convention centre were windows to hell. Young men and
women scrambled vainly for cover in the desert. Dead bodies were
strewn across tarmac. An eighty-five-year-old woman, aged only two
when the Nazis began the Holocaust, sat stoically in a golf buggy
commandeered by Islamist terrorists. Many of the murdered, who
eventually numbered 1,180, embodied an Israel the Labour Party knew
well – an Israel it could support without embarrassment or equivocation. They were peace activists, kibbutzniks, proud 'leftists' in a country
where the Hebrew translation of the word had long since become a
term of derision. These dead had once given progressives hope that
another country might live: a Jewish state capable of transcending its
troubled birth and violent adolescence. Starmer and his team understood that dream, implausible though it increasingly seemed under
Netanyahu. They knew the Israel that progressive Jews had sought to

build. They were the extended Starmer family. They were the factory foremen who had taught the teenaged McSweeney to work on their kibbutz. They were the young, left-wing Zionists whose east London youth movements were eulogised in essays by Wes Streeting; the feminists whose toil and visions of equality inspired admiration in Rachel Reeves, who fondly recalled Harold Wilson greeting Golda Meir with a spontaneous kiss.

Starmer did not yet understand that the Israel he knew lay in ruins. At 9.51 a.m., after speaking to David Lammy, he posted the sort of pro forma tweet that wrote itself: 'I utterly condemn the ongoing attacks on Israel and her citizens. There is no justification for this act of terror which is being perpetrated by those who seek to undermine any chance for future peace in the region. Israel has a right to defend herself.' It was only after calling Merav Michaeli, the leader of the country's Labor Party, that he realised this was no ordinary incident. He opened by offering his condolences for what then, from his safe distance, appeared to be another deadly skirmish in a long war. Wailing sirens were audible from Michaeli's bomb shelter. She could not say how many people were dead. 'All of a sudden, in that call,' said one of Starmer's aides present for the conversation, 'he woke up. You could see him thinking: *Oh shit, I need to speak to Vic . . . hang on, are the family safe? This is a full-scale attack, almost like 9/11. It's not just the exchange of rockets across the border. It's real. What else is going to happen?* You could see that kicking in. There was a clear sense of worry.' Starmer spoke with the Israeli president, Isaac Herzog, too. David Lammy, the shadow foreign secretary, was told to leave Liverpool for a hastily arranged vigil in London. Starmer knew then that Labour were gathering in the long shadow of an outrage.

★

Only one week a year was ever about the Labour Party. By convention, conference obliged news broadcasters to clear their schedules of sniping government spokespeople and forced ministers to clear their diaries of announcements, so that the eyes of the public might be trained on the opposition alone. 2023 was Starmer's fourth autumn as leader but the first occasion on which he expected to address the country on his own terms. In 2020, the year of Covid, he had spoken from a lectern in an empty room; 2021 had been one long, deliberately secretive rearguard against the Corbynites; 2022 had come uncomfortably soon after the death of the Queen. This time he expected to stride into the limelight as a leader who at last demanded the respect the media could barely bring itself to give. Yet events had intervened again, and the events of 7 October posed their own challenge to Labour. To speak in Westminster's language of optics and political tests seemed almost crass. But within hours of the attack, that was what the leader's office was doing. McSweeney came very quickly to his own understanding of what the attack meant for Starmer. The leader's reaction to the slaughter of civilians in the world's only Jewish state would test his theory of change.

The word 'antisemitism' was still incomprehensible to much of the public – as Dominic Cummings had told Jeremy Corbyn's team, for years most voters scarcely noticed the allegations levelled against the Labour Party – but Starmer himself had made it synonymous with his party's moral and political condition. Given his enthusiastic service in Jeremy Corbyn's shadow cabinet, Starmer was well aware that many of Britain's Jews were only superficially persuaded by his promise to tear antisemitism out 'at the roots' of the Labour Party. Then there was foreign policy. Would the Labour Party stand squarely with its allies in Israel and the United States? Starmer's predecessor had rejected the premise of that question. He accepted its parameters as immovable.

'They said that we couldn't change the Labour Party, and we did it.' Conference would measure the truth of that statement on a much greater scale than a single by-election. To this Labour leadership it was not the festival of democracy enshrined in the party's constitution, but a media spectacle first and foremost. Those who did not share Starmer's assessment of the politics of the Middle East, still less the Atlantic alliance, had come to Liverpool in their thousands: though diminished in numbers, the Corbynites remained a visible part of the Labour membership. Many believed, just as sincerely, that Israel was an apartheid state. They condemned what Hamas had done, too, but would not blind themselves to the suffering inflicted on Gazans by right-wing Israeli governments for the sake of politeness. McSweeney was determined this would not be their day. In another era, Corbynite delegates may have used such an attack to condemn Hamas and Israel in equal measure. At 9.49 a.m., with the carnage still unfolding, he messaged colleagues to confirm there was 'no way anyone can put this on the conference agenda'. They assured him that it was too late to do so – and that Luke Akehurst, the moderate stalwart whose day job as a pro-Israel lobbyist made him a hate figure to large parts of the left, would be chairing that part of the day's proceedings. 'Keep him there,' he decreed. 'We need a strong chair.' If marginalising members was straightforward, MPs belonged to a different category. The bodies of the dead were not yet buried as Apsana Begum and Afzal Khan posed for pictures with the Palestine Solidarity Campaign (PSC) in the conference centre. Factionalism briefly threatened the mood of sobriety. The leader's office and party whips were immediately inundated with angry messages demanding they be disciplined, if not suspended. For once, they sought to de-escalate: 'I don't see a rule breach here,' said Alex Barros-Curtis, the party's head of legal who had overseen Corbyn's suspension, over WhatsApp. 'PSC is a legitimate organisation,' echoed Luke Sullivan, the political secretary. An apology from Khan was deemed sufficient. Meanwhile old friends did their bit to calm the mood. Said Jill Cuthbertson: 'Just bumped into Luciana [Berger, the Jewish former Labour MP]. She's doing quite a bit of media on the situation. Could someone send her the lines on Apsana and the photo.' One of the aides involved in the conversation recalled: 'Even then, there was nothing illegitimate with calling for a free Palestine.' McSweeney agreed that amplifying the leadership's critics would not help. It was better to drown them out. He resolved he had to demonstrate the truth of what his leader had said in Rutherglen: that Labour *had* changed, that its massed members felt the same revulsion towards the terrorists as he did.

In 2018, the same conference hall that Starmer was about to address in Liverpool had been a sea of Palestinian flags. No gesture would make McSweeney's point as powerfully as the sight of the same room observing a minute's silence for the Israeli dead. He tabled his proposal with Starmer. The leader agreed on the same basis as he had assented to the rule changes in 2021: if McSweeney could be sure that it would work, he would do as he was told. But the Irishman could not be sure. This was not a test of Starmer, nor the shadow cabinet, but of hundreds of grass-roots and trade union delegates. The lonely voice of a single protester would be enough to turn sixty seconds into a permanent shame, and undermine three years of hard work. He had known as much when he had staged a minute's silence for the Queen. This, however, was a more profound test: of Labour's compassion towards a devastated community in no mood to give Labour the benefit of the doubt – not its constitutional propriety or decorum. McSweeney brooded as conference proceeded before an uninterested media pre-occupied not with speeches from shadow cabinet ministers but a rising death toll.

On Monday 9 October he woke in a foul mood. 'This isn't okay,' he thought to himself. The veil of ambiguity and confusion that had shrouded the events of the preceding Saturday had not yet been lifted. What was by then obvious, however, was that the number of dead, maimed and abducted would exceed the casualties of any terror attack since the carnage of 9/11. Had conference coincided with an assault on any other of Britain's allies – be it 9/11, the 2015 attacks in Paris, or the 2004 Madrid train bombing – McSweeney knew he would not be agonising over a minute's silence, the most perfunctory form of public sympathy it was possible to demonstrate. 'We felt, morally,' said a Labour official who was party to this moral debate, 'that if it had happened in Paris, we would have done it.' Why, McSweeney asked himself, should Israel be any different? Why, given the expressions of condolences issued in council chambers and places of worship across the country, should the annual conference of Britain's aspiring govern-ment be any different? He chided himself for allowing the party's recent past to limit his ambition – his humanity – in the present. To colleagues he said: 'We just have to do this.' He gathered his closest lieutenants in the windowless green room behind the conference stage: Marianna McFadden, his deputy; and Hollie Ridley and Teddy Ryan, the married couple who had paved the way for his ambush on the left in 2021. All agreed that a silence should be held. But they too asked the same ques-tion as Starmer: would it be respected?

They had purged the membership and wielded the Labour rulebook like a cudgel so that rooms full of activists would do as the leadership wanted. Yet McSweeney could not say with any certainty what this room would do, and nor could they. 'I don't know,' he said. 'I gen-uinely don't know. But we're going to do it.' They eyed each other warily, contemplating the stakes. Loyal apparatchiks from Labour's regional offices were instructed to corral their delegates into the con-ference hall at the designated hour of 5 p.m. This itself was a risk. The bigger the crowd, the greater the danger that a minority might dissent. McSweeney and his inner circle took the opposite view: that the basic principles of crowd psychology dictated larger numbers raised the social stigma any protester would have to incur. As so often, they made their plans in secret – so that the left had no time to organise a counterprotest. Arguably their prudence had become paranoia. Their view of the Corbynites was if anything unrealistically low. No sensible person on the left wanted to make themselves the villains of an already miserable story. In reality, John McDonnell and James Schneider were in constant communication with the leader's office, anxious to avert a catastrophe that would have discredited both the leadership and its critics.

Yet everything was choreographed to intimidate the left. McSweeney did not ask Starmer to announce the silence. He turned instead to Angela Rayner, a woman who retained in the eyes of the left and the unions a degree of the credibility that the leader had made such a virtue of burning. If the members' tribune in the shadow cabinet could stand in silence for Israel, so could the conference hall. Rayner required no convincing. Years earlier, she had told the Jewish donor Trevor Chinn of her willingness to expel 100,000 activists if it brought an end to accusations of antisemitism against Labour. Her resolve was undimmed, and she instantly agreed. McSweeney explained the plan. If a single person disrupted the silence, Rayner would announce a pause. Bouncers would remove the offending activist from the room, march them to a shredder, destroy their conference pass, and expel them from the building. Rayner would then begin the silence again, and again, until a minute had passed in total silence. Just as McSweeney had done in 2021, when the Labour membership had been forced to vote on emasculating itself, he engineered a seating plan that would leave observers in no doubt as to what the leadership believed. Margaret Hodge, Ruth Smeeth and Luciana Berger, who as Jewish MPs under Corbyn had borne the brunt of misogyny and racism, were positioned on the front row. Behind them were activists from the Jewish Labour Movement and Labour Friends of Israel – lionised by McSweeney as the 'soldiers' who had kept up the fight against Corbyn.

Five o'clock arrived. McSweeney was so nervous that he swore he could feel his bones shake. What came next did little to calm him. Rayner took to the podium and looked straight at a broken autocue.

She was left to deliver an improvised statement in a metre redolent
of John Prescott: jumbled, but somehow more than the sum of its
parts. 'I would be grateful now to remember all the victims and sympathy with their bereaved if you could join us in a moment's silence,'
she said, head hanging in reverence. At this juncture she realised that
she had no way of calculating how long a 'moment' was. She timed a
minute with her phone. It passed without a word. There was no need
for the bully pulpit. As the room emptied, one watching staffer turned
to a colleague: 'Tomorrow, we're going to arrange a standing ovation
for Margaret Thatcher.' Not for the first time, McSweeney's almost
millenarian fear of the left amounted to nothing. That the show of
mourning was unanimously respected was no surprise to a press that
by then believed in McSweeney rather more than he was willing to
believe in himself.

*

Despite themselves, left and right declined to politicise events.
Ordinarily the leader's office might have leapt at the opportunity to
censure Corbynite MPs such as John McDonnell and Bell Ribeiro-
Addy, who shared a platform with the Palestinian ambassador as he
accused Israel of war crimes. Starmer's enforcers resolved that was
unnecessary. So long as they condemned any off-colour remarks,
shadow ministers would be allowed to appear alongside him too.
'I think re Palestinian Ambo we shouldn't boycott events he's doing,'
said Luke Sullivan, Starmer's political secretary, in 'I&P', a WhatsApp
group hastily convened to coordinate the leader's response to the
conflict. 'We need to ensure that any Labour frontbencher if on a
platform with him robustly challenges any unacceptable comments
e.g. whataboutery.' One aide recalled: 'The Labour Party, when
there's these big issues in Israel and Gaza – the politics of whatever's
happened comes hurtling towards us very quickly. We weren't going
to make it about us.' Besides, the Labour left shared Starmer's revulsion at civilian deaths – if not their geopolitical analysis. The leader
himself focused his attention on the shell-shocked Jewish members
whose approval he had made the litmus test of his leadership. So did
his shadow cabinet. On the conference fringe they sought out candles
of remembrance before they reached for warm white wine, and

queued out of doors for vigils held to honour the dead rather than
boozy receptions. Rachel Reeves and Lisa Nandy wept as nearly 1,000
mourners recited the words of *Kel Maleh Rachamim*, the centuries-
old prayer of remembrance first recited for Jewish victims of the
Crusades, at a gathering held by the Labour Friends of Israel. Starmer
sidled up to Louise Ellman, the former MP who had resigned from
Labour after fifty-five years of membership in protest at Corbyn's
handling of antisemitism. Silently, many in the room contemplated
how Corbyn might have responded had he been leader that day.
Cutting a lonely figure on the streets of Liverpool, he answered
that question for them. Corbyn was asked by Channel 4 News if he
condemned Hamas. Using the same formulation he had barked at
countless interviewers who had asked him about antisemitism, he
condemned 'all attacks'. Starmer strove to appear his exact opposite.

Shortly after the shadow cabinet had left, suturing the old wounds,
Ellman approached Michael Rubin, the vigil's organiser, to offer a word
of wisdom. She remembered the intifadas; the Lebanon Wars; the decades of violence in Gaza. Wearily, she warned Rubin that this moment
of uncomplicated solidarity with Israel would not last forever.

*

Ellman was right. Within twenty-four hours her party's mood began to
darken. Politics returned, and with it the sharp old dividing lines. For
that, two men were responsible. The first was Benjamin Netanyahu,
whose military response would kill tens of thousands of Palestinian
civilians, many of them children, and raze Gaza to rubble. The second
was Keir Starmer.

The leader was tired by the early hours of Wednesday 11 October.
But before he left Liverpool one last obligation remained. His final
morning at conference obliged him to run the gauntlet of makeshift
broadcast studios dotted through the hall. BBC Radio Four, Five Live,
Times Radio: each interview passed without incident, the boilerplate
lines delivered effortlessly. Less than twenty-four hours earlier Starmer
had shrugged off a protester who climbed onto the conference stage
and interrupted a well-received speech with a brief rainstorm of glit-
ter, shouting to his adoring audience: 'Protest or power? That's why
we've changed!' His final engagement was with LBC. By 8.33 a.m.

he was live on air with Nick Ferrari, the veteran host of the station's breakfast programme.

Ferrari, who knew how to ask a difficult question of a politician, began with an appeal to reason. Surely, despite the success of conference, Starmer would understand the need to discuss the mounting crisis in Gaza?

'Absolutely,' the leader said.

Ferrari ventured a deceptively simple question. Two days had passed since the Israel Defense Forces had announced a 'total blockade' of the Gaza Strip. Its electricity and water had been shut off; supplies of food halted. Ireland's Taoiseach had warned Netanyahu of the need for a proportionate response. But what, Ferrari asked Starmer, did 'proportionate' mean?

Starmer demurred. Events were evolving on the ground but his response was frozen in amber. He ignored the question entirely, repeating his support for Israel's right to self-defence.

'I'm very clear. Israel does have that right, must have that right, to defend herself, and Hamas bears responsibility.'

Ferrari clarified his line of inquiry. 'A siege is appropriate? Cutting off power, cutting off water, Sir Keir?'

'Well I think Israel does have that right, it is an ongoing situation. Obviously everything should be done within international law but I don't want to step away from the sort of core principles that Israel has a right to defend herself and Hamas bears responsibility for these terrorist acts . . .'

The conversation rattled on, both men unaware of the significance of what Starmer had said. In the moment, he would later insist, he had not meant to give carte blanche to as violent an assault as Netanyahu thought necessary. Yet to many listeners, his words amounted to an endorsement of war crime: the collective punishment of the Palestinian people for the crimes of Hamas. Soon, the brief exchange – amounting to no more than thirty seconds – had been wrenched from its context and distributed through social media and then via encrypted messaging networks to hundreds of thousands of British Muslims.

As LBC's clip of the exchange set social media ablaze, his advisers realised he had a problem. 'I'm getting a few MPs pinging me about this,' McSweeney messaged I&P. Harjeet Sahota, head of external relations in the leader's office, agreed: 'I am also getting very upset

Muslim and other stakeholders,' she messaged. Starmer, always his own harshest critic, was hearing similar. He blamed himself. Appearing comfortable before the media was a constant struggle. If the offence was misexpression, he was a serial offender. To his team Starmer was apologetic. He had not intended to cheer on IDF brutality. As a human rights barrister he would never do so. Fatigued, he had failed to keep up with Ferrari's breakneck pace. When he uttered the words 'Israel does have that right', he told staff, he was answering the previous question – defending the Jewish state's right to self-defence within international law. Aides never doubted his intentions – only those who questioned them. When Luke Sullivan, Starmer's political secretary, discovered that Sayeeda Warsi, the Muslim peer, had posted a clip of the LBC interview and asked if the leader had given the IDF carte blanche, he said he would get a mutual friend to speak to her: 'It's beneath her and just not true,' he wrote.

The problem, as Starmer would be told again and again in the ensuing weeks, was that too many people did not believe his protestations. Starmer seemed to have picked a side. Matthew Doyle, his director of communications, was alive to that perception. Still, he continued to believe it could be easily resolved. He asked LBC to delete its posts promoting the clip. That seemed a reasonable solution. He was certain people would see reason, assuring colleagues: '[Keir] said . . . last night and on various interviews this morning that Israel needs to act in accordance with international law.' As for Warsi, he instinctively dismissed the idea that she, or anybody else, should be given private assurances or clarifications. 'Sorry but we have to stick with what Keir has said publicly. It looks awful if it looks like we're trimming our message to different audiences privately.' Stuart Ingham, the leader's head of policy, was just as defensive. The day after the attack, colleagues had proposed that Starmer respond to the death of Nathanel Young, a twenty-year-old British Jew serving in the IDF, by saying he supported Israel's right to 'protect its citizens in line with international law'. Ingham had argued for the last five words to be removed, if not for reasons of principle, then for reasons of perception. 'Is the "in line with international law" bit necessary? It is an addition to what we said this morning and yesterday and the difference will be noticed and be seen as the subject of internal discussion of whether the initial response was unbalanced,' he said.

'Good point,' said Doyle, who duly excised the words.

As the pressure intensified over LBC, Ingham resolved not to give any ground. He told colleagues there should be no clarification: 'Keir did not say that Israel has a right to cut off water. He said Israel has a right to defend themselves and go after hostages but everything must be done in accordance with international law.' The idea that Israel may have committed war crimes was similarly out of the question. Ingham: 'As soon as we assert Israel has broken international law the main news line is us criticising Israel whilst they are in live hostage negotiations with terrorists.' As one adviser present for those discussions recalled: 'We wanted LBC to delete it, because it took what he'd said out of context . . . [Starmer] was down about it because he was very clear in his mind what he had meant, and that it came across wrongly . . . it felt ridiculous to assume he had meant anything else.' That, it transpired, was a minority view.

LBC did not oblige. The station went only so far as to update the online article accompanying Starmer's interview with an exculpatory line of text. It added his caveat: 'Obviously everything should be done within international law.'

In the analogue age, when print and television news still retained its supremacy over the anarchy of social media, those words might have amounted to a perfectly reasonable compromise between a politician and broadcaster. Starmer himself could hardly complain. His comments had been reported in full, with the context his own phrasing had occluded. In 2023 it would not be enough. LBC dealt not in continuous prose but viral content, tailored for the confines of the smartphone screen and short attention spans. The offending sentences may have been ignored by newspaper reporters and other broadcasters but still rang out of Twitter feeds, TikTok algorithms and WhatsApp groups, the clarifying context buried on a website few if any viewers knew existed.

Shabana Mahmood, the only Muslim in the shadow cabinet, called Doyle to tell him what her constituents believed they were hearing: the leader of the Labour Party giving succour to war crimes.

'You need to sort this out,' she said.

'That's not what he said.'

On that point the leader's office was initially agreed. But as they returned from Liverpool to Westminster they began to reckon with their own helplessness. Starmer's intended meaning was obvious only to himself. Said one of his closest advisers: 'It was going like the clappers around TikTok and WhatsApp.' Owen Jones and Warsi led a chorus of righteous indignation. That need not have mattered. Shadow cabinet ministers would submit themselves for interviews that evening, and the next morning. All that was needed was the straightforward explan-ation that Keir Starmer did not believe that Israel had the right to shut off Gaza's supplies of electricity and water.

Doyle did not want to give it. What was the point of repeating himself? He told colleagues: 'Keir has referenced international law in every single one of these broadcast interviews.' McSweeney, ever bull-ish, agreed. He said that if anybody should apologise for indifference towards Palestinians, it was the perpetrators of the attack. 'We can be stronger,' he messaged colleagues. 'If Hamas are worried about lives being lost they should return every hostage they've captured and do it today. We need to make it more about them.'

Said one aide in the leader's office: 'Keir had been flawless all week. He was tired. Everyone's going home. People had worked really hard . . . the view that was taken was from a traditional comms point of view: if we go out and try and clarify this, it makes it worse, or it makes it a bigger story.'

Emily Thornberry was unaware of the debate in the leader's office when she was instructed to appear on the BBC's *Newsnight* programme back in London that evening. Despite her demotion to the margins of the shadow cabinet, Starmer's aides trusted the shadow attorney gen-eral to impart whatever message they wished to be heard. Yet nobody had decided what that message was.

That left her to improvise. Her own conversations with lawyers and diplomats had convinced her that Israel would shut off power and water only to facilitate a brief raid to free its hostages. And so the only point she clarified was the one that Starmer had not intended to make. Said an aide: 'There was just a sort of gap in the staffing cover, and nobody briefed her before she went on and did it. Having just heard what Keir said, she thought she was doing the right thing by kind of not distancing herself from what he had said.'

As Thornberry sat beneath the studio lights of New Broadcasting House, Victoria Derbyshire, *Newsnight*'s host, asked the same question Ferrari had posed to Starmer.

'Whatever actions are taken by a democracy,' Thornberry said, 'has to be done in accordance with international law. And we have heard tonight from the president of the United States and he has been on the phone to Netanyahu and both of them have agreed that democracies need to act in accordance with international law.'

Derbyshire interrupted. 'Pause there, if I may. Do you think cutting off food, water and electricity is within international law?'

'I think that Israel has an absolute right to defend itself against terrorism.'

'That's not the question I asked.'

'It is an answer to the question that you've asked. And I think it's an appropriate one at this time.'

★

Within hours the Labour Party was asking another question of its leadership: did they understand those words had provoked a crisis of confidence among British Muslims? In Gaza, destruction soon reigned. Israel's counteroffensive proved as grimly modern a spectacle as the attacks it had endured. The bombs that fell, the wounds that were inflicted on young and helpless bodies – every day horrifying scenes were beamed from smartphone cameras in Palestine to smartphone screens in Bradford, Birmingham, Leicester and east London. To speak of Labour's 'Muslim voters' was grossly simplistic. Britain's Islamic communities were a large and complicated family, divided by geography, class, age and religious observance. Yet what united them as the war began was the pull of *ummah* – the sympathy with their fellow Muslims in Palestine. That magnetic force had dragged them away from the Labour Party during the invasion of Iraq some twenty years earlier. In 2021 it had very nearly lost the Labour Party a by-election in Batley, and its leader. Now it returned, unleashing currents of despair and disgust that Starmer would struggle to control.

Councillors began to resign: among them Amna Abdullatif, the first Arab Muslim woman elected in Manchester, and Mona Ahmed, a Labour councillor in Kensington and Chelsea. Others joined imams, doctors and other professionals – pillars of a community that voted as reliably for the Labour Party as the white working class had in decades past – in signing an open letter that told Starmer: 'Your consistent defence of Israel's actions, often with limited regard for the humanitarian plight of the Palestinians, has left many members of the Muslim community feeling unheard and unrepresented.' To their mind the Labour Party had indeed changed. Where under Jeremy Corbyn it had been alive to injustice, sympathetic to the plight of the Palestinians, unafraid to take the side of the oppressed in international conflict, its new leadership stood behind the aggressor. It had done what Corbyn would never have done – *could* never have done – and sided with Israel. That was not the impression Starmer had intended to give. But with his words still unclarified, it became the truth.

On the evening of Monday 16 October, Sue Gray – who watched her new colleagues argue over the LBC interview with a dispassionate, sceptical eye – convened Labour's leaders in local government on a Zoom call. At her side was David Lammy, the shadow foreign secretary. As a campaigning backbencher he had been a voluble critic of Israeli governments and the conduct of their troops in Palestine. Realpolitik required him to soften his often strident rhetoric. Labour's councillors were in no mood to moderate theirs. They lived among the people who were most outraged by Starmer's language – they *were* the people most outraged by Starmer's language. Furious, they told Gray and Lammy of collapsing support for the Labour Party in towns and cities with large Muslim communities. If Starmer did not apologise, their councillors would resign. Labour would lose control of town halls it had ruled for years. Having rebuilt the red wall of the white working class, another pillar of Starmer's support in the country began to buckle. To the left it appeared that the leadership did not care. Their nemesis Lee Harpin, a former tabloid reporter who prowled the corridors of Westminster for the *Jewish News* and hated Corbynites as they hated him, quoted an anonymous Labour source celebrating the resignation of Muslim councillors. 'Shaking off the fleas.'

The shadow cabinet met the following morning. It had been a long ten days since 7 October. By now Shabana Mahmood, so often hard and unflinching when the Labour Party went to war with itself, felt miserable and conflicted. The whole moral architecture of her political career was collapsing. She knew the pain the Jewish community was feeling – how desperately it wanted for friends in a party it had only just begun to forgive. That was why she had fought on their behalf over her lonely years on the NEC. Suddenly she felt the same loneliness again. Her spirit was crushed beneath the weight of the words she felt she might have at last outgrown: *the only Muslim in the shadow cabinet*. They brought with them a perspective and responsibility her colleagues could not understand. However horrified they were on 7 October, every subsequent day had inflicted new horror on another people – Mahmood's people. Visibly emotional, she told Starmer that his words had caused enormous offence to British Muslims: to her constituents and fellow worshippers in Birmingham, who had addressed her at Friday prayers with disgust and disbelief. Only the clarification that the Labour Party did not endorse the collective punishment of the Palestinians – that it did not blame them for the attacks on Israel, and thought them deserving of food, water and medicine – would begin to calm tensions. Those who heard her speech saw a politician torn apart by two loyalties in their own violent conflict: to a political project she had worked so hard to build, and the people she represented. Solidarity, Mahmood said, was not a zero-sum game between supporting British Jews through their generational trauma and showing the minimum of empathy with Palestinians.

She was not alone. Wes Streeting, just as loyal to a leader who had promoted him to heights commensurate with his own ambition, expressed his own reservations. Uniquely among the constituencies represented around the shadow cabinet table, his east London seat of Ilford North was home to Muslims and Jews in large numbers. He had watched one community turn their backs on the Labour Party and knew that another was about to follow. Weighing his words carefully, he warned that Starmer appeared cold and uncaring. 'Our Muslim communities are frightened,' Streeting said. 'We've got to put our arms around them in the same way.' He denounced the religious extremists who served in Netanyahu's government. He warned, too, that Israel's political mainstream now spoke of Palestinian civilians as legitimate targets, as the country's president Isaac Herzog had done when he said: 'It is an entire nation out there that is responsible. It is not true this rhetoric about civilians not being aware, not involved. It's absolutely not true. They could have risen up.' To Streeting that was tantamount to collective blame laying the moral foundations for collective punishment. 'I think we've got to be really careful about how

Israel conducts this war.' Louise Haigh, the shadow transport secretary, asked why Labour had not shown an emotional connection with
suffering Palestinians.

Starmer's advisers looked on impassively. McSweeney had always
embraced the possibility that Labour might lose millions of voters
who had been willing to support the party under Corbyn. The old
electoral coalition of urban progressives, public sector workers and
ethnic minorities had never been enough to win power. In his view the
hard left was always quick to claim entire communities as their own,
in service of a politics he and many of its members did not share. He
was equally wary of the Muslim groups suddenly dictating to Starmer.
Many had issued similar demands of him at the start of his leadership. As far as he was concerned, they had not had his best interests at
heart then and did not now. When the Labour Muslim Network had
called for the leader to apologise for his remarks on LBC three days
earlier, McSweeney had messaged colleagues: 'LMN are not an affiliated organisation and are not good faith actors.' Even then, a number
of colleagues had sought to soften his thinking. Harjeet Sahota, in
the leader's office, had warned: 'the sentiment is v strong across other
Muslim stakeholders too – on this point they are actually reflecting
how the community feels following LBC'. If the White House could
show humanity, she later added, so could Starmer: 'I think the nuance/
empathy is missing from our lines. We can be empathetic and our position be the same. Which has been nicely done in Biden's.' Vidhya
Alakeson, Starmer's director of external relations, agreed. 'They aren't
affiliated and haven't always been good faith, I agree. But we shouldn't
let that blind us to the fact that there is anger in the Muslim community over what has been said. We can try and manage by responding
proactively but we will be forced to deal with their statement otherwise. I would suggest we speak to Shabana or someone like that if
we want to gauge community sentiment from a more trusted source.'
David Lammy soon reached a similar view. 'We need to ensure our
lines are evolving to reflect how debate and sentiment is moving –
especially to hold the PLP together,' he privately told the leader's
office over WhatsApp. 'That means more empathy as noted above,
reflecting the awful scenes people are seeing on their TVs and being
clear on humanitarian issues.' He added pointedly: 'It won't work to
simply blame Hamas and mention self-defence. Emily T just got a real

roasting on *Newsnight* because she just kept repeating self-defence line and had nowhere to go.'

His intervention meant that, by the time the shadow cabinet convened, nobody could pretend calls for clarification were confined to the fringe. Those who spoke up during the discussion made the allegation of bad faith even harder to make. Shabana Mahmood was not the hard left. Wes Streeting was the very antithesis of the hard left. Liz Kendall, Jess Phillips and Helen Hayes – three other shadow ministers who demanded Starmer denounce Netanyahu and apologise for his LBC interview when the Parliamentary Labour Party met on the evening of the 14th – were not the hard left either. If the leader's office had been prepared to ignore councillors resigning, it could not pretend that its loyal lieutenants were giving voice to the ulterior motives they still suspected among the Corbynites.

Yet Starmer and his team were not for turning. Still the offending line held. The next day at Prime Minister's Questions, Starmer did not take the opportunity to acknowledge what he had said in Liverpool, nor apologise. In his exchanges with Rishi Sunak he called for an investigation into an explosion at Gaza's Baptist Hospital, and hundreds of deaths initially blamed on Israel. He asked what the government was doing to expedite the delivery of 'medicines, food, fuel and water' into the Gaza Strip. Fumbling for balance, he recounted his conversations with the families of British–Israeli hostages, and asked the prime minister to agree that Hamas would not have committed its attacks if it truly cared for Palestinian life. His tone was sober and lawyerly, the phrasing as precise as it had been in 2020 and its days of 'constructive opposition'. For his critics it was not enough. Nor was the mealy-mouthed, unrepentant explanation his spokesman offered to the lobby journalists huddled in the Commons press gallery, who minutes later asked the question Starmer steadfastly refused to address: had he not endorsed everything that Israel was now accused of doing? 'If you listen to the tape, it was one of those things where there were overlapping questions and answers based on what had been being said before.' It took another two days for Starmer himself to confront his own mistakes. On Friday 20 October he told the BBC: 'I know that LBC clip has been widely shared and caused real concern and distress in some Muslim communities, so let me be clear about what I was saying and what I wasn't saying. I *was* saying that Israel has the right to

self-defence, and when I said "that right", I meant it was that right to
self-defence. I was not saying that Israel had the right to cut off water,
food, fuel or medicines.'

It was not the apology the shadow cabinet had wanted to hear. At
best it offered some belated context. At worst it was a complaint that
Muslims who were offended had not listened hard enough. In the following days there seemed to be limits to his empathy. On 21 October,
Starmer told Labour councillors: 'This is a terrifying and distressing
time for everyone – Israeli, Palestinian, Muslim and Jew.' He added that
it was 'important that people hear directly what our position is'. Yet
they *had* heard him explain that position in those words to LBC, whose
widely understood meaning was still disputed by the leader's office.
Critics of the leadership began to speak of 'gaslighting'.

Now Starmer faced another test. Calls for an immediate ceasefire, first aired fleetingly in the Commons by the SNP on 18 October,
became ever louder as Israel's bombardment of Gaza intensified. But
so too did Starmer's resolve. That word – ceasefire – posed questions
of semantics and principle, just as his interview on LBC had. Still a
lawyer as much as a politician, he was more than mindful of the long
list of human rights cases against Israel. The kitchen cabinet whose
advice on the war he most valued was not composed of MPs but old
friends from the bar like Philippe Sands and Richard Hermer, Jewish
jurists committed to nothing more than the sanctity and inviolability
of international law. Both had signed a letter to the *Financial Times* ten
days after 7 October, urging Israel to abide by the laws of war – even if,
as Jews, they were shaken to their 'core' by events.

For once their former colleague begged to differ. This was not a
problem to be solved with clever arguments in a chambers conference room, but an audition to run a nuclear power. As Britain's next
prime minister his first obligation was to live in the geopolitical reality
that existed, not the statute book. He wanted to be taken seriously,
not least in Washington DC. He feared that calling for something that
would not happen, no matter how noisily the Labour Party demanded
it, would compromise his ability to talk to all sides. Keir Starmer was
nothing if not *serious*. He would not be blown from his moorings
by public controversy or internal pressure. At Gray's behest he was
now in daily discussions with his advisers and senior members of the
shadow cabinet, analysing the conflict and its domestic implications as

if he were already in Downing Street. He denied himself the sweetest luxury of opposition: to speak without responsibility, to advocate for the impossible. Nor did he take lightly his promises to the Jewish community, many of whom felt threatened by weekly pro-Palestinian marches in London, whose peaceful attendees were overshadowed by protesters glorifying Hamas. If anything, the louder they chanted, the stiffer Starmer's resolve became. In those early weeks, he was also fortified by polling which drew a reassuring distinction between noise and signal. Despite the objections on the streets and in the shadow cabinet, by 27 October, Labour Together had conducted private research which showed his support among members had swelled to 81 per cent – a gentle increase since the spring, attributed mostly to those who had supported Lisa Nandy's leadership bid in 2020 and had until then remained sceptical. Its report included an intriguing detail. Members had expressed their support despite, rather than because of, his stance on Israel. On that matter, they were ambivalent: a little less than half thought he had handled the events since 7 October well, with 40 per cent saying he had done poorly. A slender majority thought he had been 'too supportive' of the Jewish state. Yet when it came to it, of 1,101 members polled, 67 per cent said they would vote for Starmer if the leadership contest was rerun, leaving Nandy and Long-Bailey in the teens. Nothing gave the leader's office succour like the belief its position was less damaging than its critics claimed. Tony Blair could not help but admire Starmer's clarity of mind, even as it plunged the Labour Party into instability. The former prime minister observed events closely from his central London office, its waiting room wall adorned with an oil painting of Jerusalem. Initially, Blair said, Starmer had been 'somewhat to the left . . . pretty vaguely'. That changed. 'He was thinking about government,' Blair says now. 'We could see that over Gaza, for example, which was really difficult for him. But he was approaching it as if he were prime minister, which you could agree or disagree with, but his mindset had completely altered. He was no longer thinking in terms of vague progressive thoughts. He was thinking: "Okay, I'm going to be governing the country. Where do I stand on these things?" '

Starmer refused to blink. To Wes Streeting he said: 'I need you to know, I am not going to call for a ceasefire at this stage.' He was unmoved even by the coordinated intervention on 27 October of Sadiq

Khan, the mayor of London, Andy Burnham, the mayor of Greater Manchester, and Anas Sarwar, the leader of Scottish Labour. In a testy phone conversation, Starmer had pleaded with Khan not to defy him. But the mayor was not for turning, and nor was the leader. In conversations with aides Starmer was unambiguous: he did not do 'fudgy' leadership, and nor would he change his mind. On the last day of October, with twenty-three Muslim Labour councillors having resigned and sixty MPs demanding a ceasefire, he told Chatham House that the rebels were 'not correct'. Now he had picked his side.

*

Mahmood sank into despair. Starmer sounded like a robot. His advisers were worse. She knew his intransigence would have consequences, because she would be forced to face them. Her childhood trips into central Birmingham with her Pakistani father had been soundtracked by racist abuse. Now, at forty-three, she was bullied again. Friends and neighbours became tormentors, their rage rising with every intervention from Starmer or the IDF. They picketed her home and called her an apologist for genocide. Everywhere was angry: her doorstep, her street, her constituency office, the halal butcher frequented by her elderly parents. As they waited in its queue on 2 November they heard a woman curse the name of Liz Kendall, their daughter's colleague in the shadow cabinet. When Kendall had been asked by Sky News whether the Labour Party would condemn the alleged Israeli use of white phosphorus, an incendiary prohibited by international law, she demurred – unlike Conservative ministers. 'I think it would be unwise when we are not on the ground to comment,' Kendall said. Hours later, the words of the shadow work and pensions secretary were the stuff of furious conversation on the streets of suburban Birmingham. Mahmood's parents listened nervously.

'That Liz Kendall. She basically said white phosphorus is okay. Did you watch the clip? I'll send it to you.'

Starmer inhabited another planet. Mahmood knew the leader's office neither heard nor understood the conversations she had no choice but to listen to. Nor was she invited to theirs. There was no place at the daily crisis meetings for the only Muslim in the shadow cabinet. She had not been asked for her opinion when Starmer tried and failed to assuage concerns about his words on LBC. She had ascended to the commanding heights of Labour politics, run its election campaigns, saved Starmer in Batley, won promotion to the post of shadow justice secretary, yet still they refused to respect her. To her old friend and deputy Conor McGinn, the Irish Catholic from South Armagh, she had often complained: 'Even though we're insiders, we'll always be outsiders.' Mahmood did not want sympathy. She wanted her arguments – on the merits of a ceasefire, on the need for the concerns of Muslims to be treated as legitimately as the pain of British Jews – to be taken as seriously as Starmer took himself. They were not. Mahmood diagnosed in the leader's office a debilitating case of double standards, suspecting privately that they believed that opposition to Israel's actions was driven by antisemitism, that their appeals for justice were hard-left protests by another name, that they were uninterested in how their actions appeared to British Muslims. It was, she concluded, as one-sided as the approach of the British governments who had defended the interests of Ulster Protestants while ignoring Catholics. She was not entirely wrong. Dining with friends, one senior adviser to Starmer airily remarked that Muslims had taken 'the Corbyn Palestine pill'.

The leader himself was neither a storyteller nor a winner of hearts and minds. His enforcers had deliberately marginalised the politicians who might have done so for him. But that was hardly enough. 'If you're going to support Israel over Gaza,' said Andrew Murray, a former adviser to Corbyn who had watched his own project self-combust over questions of war and peace, 'you need left cover . . . You need a Clare Short, who gave Tony Blair quite important support at the outbreak of the Iraq War, or a Robin Cook. Keir had denuded himself of anyone plausible on the left who could give him that support.' Mahmood, though not of the left, might have been that person. But Starmer gave no shadow cabinet minister licence to stray from his hard line. Nor did she wish to sacrifice the job she had coveted for years on the altar of Gaza. Her resignation would help nobody. Instead she made her case to Starmer directly.

They met alone and in secret in Parliament, away from colleagues and advisers, in the office of Thangam Debbonaire, the shadow leader of the House of Commons. Mahmood appealed to her leader's self-interest, rather than the emotions hidden beneath his armour of professionalism. Outsourcing Britain's foreign policy to the US would not work in the country's interests, she argued. Labour risked aligning itself with the far-right ministers in Netanyahu's government. Starmer was still unmoved. She urged him to lift his ban on Labour MPs attending – and, by virtue of their presence, moderating – pro-Palestinian demonstrations. He looked baffled. By now Mahmood was tearful, overcome with the weight of her responsibility to Muslims not just in her native Birmingham, but across Britain.

Starmer extended a consoling arm halfway around her shoulder. Then, as if taken aback by his own tenderness, he froze.

*

Sue Gray, beginning her third month as Starmer's chief of staff, had been observing the leader and his advisers at a degree's remove: watching, learning.

On her first day in the office – the day that once looked as if it would never arrive – she had told her new colleagues: 'You had my back. I'll always have yours.' But what struck her now, three months in, was that the men she worked with appeared only to watch their own. In meetings she wondered aloud why so few women and elected politicians were allowed into the inner sanctum of the Labour Party. The boys beside Starmer reciprocated her scepticism. They had quickly come to question not only her methods, but her character too. Weeks after arrival, Gray had pointedly asked that the leader remove a reference in his conference speech to No. 10 staff leaving cleaners to mop up sick during the Partygate affair – a reference to a finding which had appeared in her own inquiry. At first, Starmer's aides were perplexed. In time, they sensed her intervention was designed not to spare her former subjects' blushes, but to avoid repeating a claim she herself knew to be untrue. Unbeknown to them, Simon Case had privately reached the same conclusion about that detail months earlier. In the event, Starmer referred only to cleaners scrubbing 'mess off the walls'. Gray was unapologetic. Her message: she was far more concerned by the mess the boys seemed to be making now. She even chided staff at headquarters for expecting their rubbish to be cleared by the cleaners.

Gray took it upon herself to step out of the shadows and clean up. Mahmood's phone rang. It was Sue, asking to meet. 'I'm going to do the relationships for Keir,' Gray said.

The first thing she did was give the shadow justice secretary a hug.

PART V: RESOLUTION

18

Palestine

In the weeks and months after 7 October, Sue Gray found herself in rooms full of young men who advised Keir Starmer. She made it her business to educate them in the facts of life and government. They did not take kindly to her lessons.

The chief of staff posed questions to which they believed they knew the answers. She introduced their leader to people he knew already. At all hours of the day she sent messages that made them roll their eyes. Take her WhatsApp to colleagues in the leader's office at 5.51 p.m. on New Year's Eve, just after US helicopters sank boats belonging to Houthi militants in the Red Sea. 'Not sure military action can always wait for Parliament to be recalled,' Gray wrote. 'Where not possible to wait would expect govt to come to House as soon as it can to explain. But would be good to know whether we ever said anything previously on recall in similar circs.'

How the boys laughed. Did Gray know nothing of the party she had joined? Starmer had once campaigned for a parliamentary vote before every military intervention overseas, before abandoning that promise and each of the other Ten Pledges he made to the Labour membership. They knew this, for they had been at his side as he tore it all up. As a new age of conflict took its toll on Starmer, they began to wonder whether the woman who now controlled the Labour Party really understood it.

*

Every morning at 8.30 a.m. from 11 October onwards, at Gray's instruction, the leader held a conference call on the conflict in the Middle East. These were not the calls to which his advisers had become accustomed – conversations among themselves, with elected politicians excluded. Gray, who had watched those conversations lead Starmer down blind alleys and into crisis in the wake of his LBC interview, made sure of two things when the calls began in the subsequent days. Firstly, shadow cabinet ministers were invited into the rooms that had for so long been closed to them. Secondly, Sue Gray would have the final word on what that room decided.

The presence of elected public servants was a more radical measure than it may have sounded. Starmer had never been one for the company of his fellow politicians. 'We would ask him to spend ten minutes on the phone with this MP or that,' one of his advisers said. 'Just ring them. Just pretend you're listening. He wouldn't do it. "Why should I do that?" It's something he never understood the point of.' Nor did his inner team do much to disguise their view that Labour MPs were mostly a nuisance. 'They don't understand Parliament,' said one shadow cabinet minister, 'and they don't want to. They've got no regard for politicians. No: they *don't care* about politicians.' The disdain shadow cabinet ministers sensed from within the leader's office invited an equal and opposite reaction. MPs wrote them off as aloof and condescending.

Gray noticed that immediately. She sought out the dispossessed and never-possessed, threw maternal arms around them, sent sympathetic texts and flowers. And so every morning, David Lammy, Lisa Nandy, Yvette Cooper and Angela Rayner were at the other end of the line as Starmer digested developments from Gaza, finally enjoying the dignity and respect that their titles of shadow foreign secretary, shadow international development minister, and shadow home secretary implied. Where Starmer's speechwriters had once written jokes at Andy Burnham's expense as a rebuke for his disloyalty, she hugged the mayor of Greater Manchester close. Now the rest of Starmer's advisers were left watching and learning, just as Gray had, as their new master changed the way the Labour Party worked. Much of this was to Starmer's satisfaction. He was a man of formalities and structure. When a crisis struck, as it had in Gaza, the leader wanted serious discussions fortified by expert opinion. Gray watched his advisers run his life on WhatsApp instead, with decisions taken without heed for their impact on the politicians who would be forced to account for them.

In taking control she showed Starmer how his government might work – how *their* government might work, with the chief of staff as its centrifugal force, listening and absorbing the information that others had been wont to ignore. But, more subtly, Gray sought the change that her predecessor had tried and failed to effect. Gray saw the team Morgan McSweeney had built in Starmer's office as a boys' club and cartel. She saw herself in turn – as she had said in her only ever interview with the BBC two years earlier, in which she bemoaned her failure to be appointed as head of Northern Ireland's Civil Service – as a challenger, and a disrupter.

'She was definitely trying to do . . . well, what Sue does. She courts the politicians,' said one aide present throughout the fractious discussions on Israel she chaired. 'She became the biggest internal voice: "We need to basically do whatever the MPs say, and the mayors say."' Yet Gray did not realise that Starmer did not want to hear them.

★

By November, the slow trickle of dissent against the leadership became a hard rain. Their old assumptions offered no shelter. Just as the Corbynites rediscovered their voice and began to speak with the moral clarity that Starmer had beaten out of them, MPs who had learned loyalty relapsed into doubt.

There was no escape from protest. Starmer's call for a 'humanitarian pause' in hostilities on 25 October – to allow the safe passage of food, medicine, water and hostages before Netanyahu's assault on Hamas resumed – did little to reassure the growing ranks of rebels in the Parliamentary Labour Party that he understood them, or the voters whose furious missives now filled their inboxes, whose protests filled the streets outside their constituency offices. By the following day, a quarter of Labour MPs had called for a permanent ceasefire. From every angle came criticism. When Starmer went to Chatham House on 31 October to give a long and overdue speech explaining his opposition to a ceasefire, he was met by furious picketers – among them his old adversary James Schneider, from Corbyn's office, and his biographer Oliver Eagleton, son of the Marxist philosopher and critic Terry – who brandished banners stained with bloody hands and chased his car. They chanted: 'Keir Starmer, shame on you, Palestinians are humans too!'

The location of his speech had been kept secret, so as to avoid exactly the scenes that unfolded. But it leaked from inside party headquarters anyway, and there they were: the exiled activist left, returning to the relevance Starmer had stolen from them, telling the Labour Party what to do. 'Ceasefire now! Ceasefire now!' The leader's reflex was to ignore such demonstrations as the 'politics of noisy performance', but that line no longer rang true. Minutes before he spoke, the shadow minister Alex Cunningham – a name that seldom troubled Labour's whips or political correspondents – defied Starmer to demand the very thing he was about to dismiss, 'an immediate ceasefire'. A fortnight later, when MPs came to vote on an SNP motion demanding a ceasefire on 15 November, eleven frontbenchers resigned rather than incur the wrath of constituents outraged by the Israeli onslaught on Gaza. Jess Phillips gave up a seat on the front bench in the hope that it would save her seat in Parliament.

By and large the dissenters were not predisposed to cause trouble for Starmer. Accepting as much was a psychological challenge for the leader's office. Shadow cabinet ministers never knew how bluntly some in the leader's office could speak of such issues in private, but assumed they thought so anyway. As one explained: 'They see Palestinian activism as a creature of the hard left.' Ironically, what was left of the hard left in the Commons if anything became more compliant. After the former shadow cabinet minister Andy McDonald was suspended for using the controversial phrase 'between the river and the sea' at a pro-Palestinian rally on 28 October, the career rebel John McDonnell began sharing the text of his speeches with the chief whip in advance of their delivery – so anxious was he to avoid the same fate. MPs who lived in the mainstream of Labour politics offered no such courtesies. In the hours before the vote on 15 November, Starmer spent thirty minutes with a backbencher to whom he had once been close. His visitor explained that their Muslim constituents were angry.

'It's gesture politics,' Starmer said of a ceasefire. 'Israel won't accept it. Hamas won't accept it. It's grandstanding.'

Vainly the leader tried to convince the MPs of what they acknowledged was a 'perfectly cogent intellectual argument' for a humanitarian pause instead. The rebels struggled to understand his intransigence. 'What the UK government was saying was irrelevant,' said one of their number, recalling a circuitous conversation with Starmer. 'What we in the UK opposition were saying was even more irrelevant. For us, calling for a ceasefire was first and foremost a domestic political problem. A political response could have saved us a lot of pain.'

Starmer did not want to grandstand. Gesture politics – all politics – was beneath him. The conflict was nothing less than his audition for statesmanship. Gray played on-call therapist to the disgruntled and discontented, but the flowers, hugs and dinner invitations to wounded shadow cabinet ministers would not themselves change Starmer's mind. She heard their complaints, but the leader did not listen to them. He had made his decision. When Washington's stance softened, so would Labour's. However consultative a leader he appeared to be on those morning calls, he jealously guarded his primacy in determining the party's position. He was not yet prime minister but already he acted as *primus inter pares*. Only he would decide when Labour said what so many of its MPs and members wished it to say. This too required some adjustment of his team's expectations. The Starmer they had come to know was a delegator. He devolved his political thinking and campaigns to McSweeney; he devolved his economics to Rachel Reeves. But on Israel he took personal responsibility. If a decision was to be made, he needed to be present and involved – hence Gray's meetings. Yet in his absence, no breakthrough would ever be reached. And as the war ground on, he stopped attending.

'It became frustrating,' said one adviser present for every summit, 'because if Keir wasn't there, there wasn't going to be a decision. Sue would often promise that they were somehow going to make a decision in these meetings, and that wasn't happening – I think because Keir clocked that if he wasn't there, decisions weren't going to be made . . . or shouldn't have been made.'

Politics never weakened his resolve. Nor did expertise. Gray recruited an ensemble cast of wise men and women to dispense counsel to Starmer – Jonathan Powell, former chief of staff to Tony Blair; Cathy Ashton, the New Labour minister who had graduated from the House of Lords to become the EU's first high representative for foreign affairs; Daniel Levy, the IDF veteran, former peace negotiator and son of Michael Levy, Blair's chief fundraiser – but even they failed to convince him that he was wrong. Nor was he swayed by Philippe Sands or Richard Hermer, two Jewish friends from the bar who knew more than almost any British lawyer about war crimes, the International Court of

Justice and the West Bank. Together this advisory council was exactly what Starmer valued – what his chief of staff knew he needed. After only two months at his side Gray intuitively understood his impatience and contempt for those who did not know their subject matter. All had deep and meaningful experience from government, the law, or their own service in the Middle East. Yet Starmer stood his ground.

Gray herself came to be regarded by colleagues as a less than helpful presence. Her admirers diagnosed in her critics petty jealousy. She had certainly challenged their monopoly on advice to Starmer. In conversation with disaffected shadow ministers she made frequent reference to her texts to 'Keir'. Yet those doubters were less concerned by her embrace of outside experts than the quality of her own insight. Gray shared old speeches and columns from White House officials such as Jake Sullivan, President Biden's national security adviser, which the supposedly lackadaisical lads in the leader's office had in fact read weeks earlier. In one meeting she uttered the truism: 'The Americans are historically very close to Israel.' This, said a nonplussed attendee, had the ring of a lesson in 'GCSE History' that none present needed. Others resented the breathless newspaper briefings that suggested she had revolutionised their way of working. Starmer's star chamber, after all, was mostly made up of people he knew already. 'She always brought people that she knew, or people she knew Keir really liked,' said one adviser in the leader's office. 'It made her look like she'd brought them into the room – but we were talking to them already.' Indeed, Starmer had already resolved to make Hermer, the human rights barrister, his attorney general.

The experts kept talking, yet nothing changed. Nearly two months had passed since 7 October but aides suspected that Starmer still inhabited those horrifying moments – that he still felt the fear for his wife's family. He had always understood, as viscerally as intellectually, that the Jewish state had lived its own 9/11. He resolved not to waver in his loyalty to Israel or the United States. His moral position soon assumed its own political significance. Starmer felt instinctively that Britain's interests, and his own, were best served by hewing close to whatever line was set by the Americans. His commitment was singleminded and masochistic. Calling for a ceasefire would ease his pain at home. But what would it mean unless the US did the same? All it would have demonstrated was opportunism – *gesture politics*. All of his speeches about Nato and Ernest Bevin would have been exposed as empty words. Clever, caveated positions designed to satisfy the hostile electorates of Labour MPs would invite more questions than answers from the international leaders he was increasingly sure he would soon take his place beside. When he called for a ceasefire, a humanitarian pause, or a cessation in hostilities, on what basis was he doing so? Israel had struck pragmatic peace agreements with Egypt and Jordan not in pursuit of pacifism or human rights per se, nor in response to international pressure – but out of clear-eyed self-interest. Any deal Netanyahu struck on Gaza needed to satisfy the same base criteria. Starmer wanted to play his part, to be in the room. He refused to speak in any language but that of geopolitical reality. Before conversations with foreign leaders, he told his advisers: 'I want a clear position because I'm talking to international partners, I want to be credible.' As a source close to him recalls: 'Keir was very much: "No fudgy language." He thought that would lead him into more questions.'

★

By turns those who worked with Starmer that autumn saw a diplomat, a lawyer, and a bureaucrat. They seldom saw a politician. But those who looked closest saw the man. His was a proud refusal. As the weeks passed and the death toll rose, his colleagues realised that Labour's position was not really about the Americans, nor international law. It was all about Keir Starmer.

Starmer hated weakness. He had been pushed around enough. He had not taken orders from Len McCluskey or Jeremy Corbyn. McSweeney had always intellectualised the demands of the left as exercises in blackmail and power politics: 'unity' was a weasel word that concealed their entitlement and desire for control. Starmer was less interested in the Darwinian struggle that waged between this faction or that. Instead he hated looking like a fool. 'I don't think Keir ever wanted to look like he's weak, or that he's been forced into doing anything,' said one of his senior advisers. 'That's one of the things that pushes his buttons. He never wants to look or *seem* weak.' To Starmer, weakness meant admitting fault – that others had known better.

Starmer refused. By the end of November he had grown irritable. Advocates of a ceasefire were all around him. He dismissed them as tacticians, not strategists, even as his shadow cabinet joined their ranks. Mahmood, who was not invited to the daily calls, had been lobbying him since mid-October, a struggle with which newspapers were made especially familiar. Privately she concluded that the US would not care if Britain deviated from its position. That Starmer ignored her was no surprise, not least to the shadow justice secretary, who never felt her words were valued. Her friends accused the leadership of unconscious bias. Starmer's resistance to David Lammy, his shadow foreign secretary, was harder to explain. Lammy watched anxiously as European powers began to use the word Starmer refused to utter. Spain's centre-left government called for a humanitarian ceasefire on 25 October; the French president Emmanuel Macron did the same on 11 November, challenging the Israelis to stop killing babies and children. 'David would much rather have been in the French position – maybe even a bit further, like Spain – rather than where the United States were.' Nandy, who had once led Labour Friends of Palestine and otherwise needed no excuse to question Starmer's judgement, occupied a similar place. As shadow home secretary, Yvette Cooper was ever mindful of the dangers to community cohesion in England's inner cities. Only John Healey, the shadow defence secretary, was consistently on message. 'In those morning meetings, David would say: "People should back a ceasefire." Lisa would say: "Totally agree." Yvette would say: "Totally agree." Almost all of the politicians agreed in the room.'

Starmer heard those arguments, but he did not listen. To MPs he could only say tough luck. 'The PLP just want a ceasefire,' one aide says of the leader's assessment of his restive flock. 'They don't care what it is. But by saying it, it stops their emails.' The inboxes and constituencies of MPs, who believed they were being treated 'like paralegals' by their lawyer leader, mattered less to Starmer than the corridors of power in Washington, Jerusalem and Doha through which he one day hoped to walk.

He asked the same question of himself – and colleagues – again and again: if Labour calls for a ceasefire, what will it achieve? None of their answers satisfied him, despite Gray's best efforts. This was his conclusion. There had been no mistake, increasingly keen though the chief of staff was to highlight the errors of her male colleagues. That Starmer had not called for a ceasefire was not the fault of her bêtes noires Matthew Doyle, who as head of communications was blamed for the LBC debacle, nor Luke Sullivan, who failed to prevent front-bench resignations as political secretary, nor Stuart Ingham, whose work as head of policy had not yet cracked the two-state solution – nor any of the other men she privately derided as lazy, louche, and incapable of dressing properly. 'She said they were casual,' a shadow cabinet minister said, 'she didn't feel they had attention to detail. She didn't feel that the way they presented themselves was professional.'

The boys knew what Gray said. 'I'm sure Sue thought people like us were the blockers,' said one. 'The reality is we weren't: *Keir* was being the blocker because he wasn't going to say yes to it, and we just knew that.' Another said: 'People would get annoyed and say: "You just need to tell him." What they weren't understanding was that this was his well-reasoned view.'

They found an unlikely ally in Angela Rayner, sympathetic as she was to her agonised and exasperated colleagues. Her loyal lieutenant Wajid Khan knew full well the corrosive effect that Starmer's pride was inflicting on Labour's relationship with British Muslims. She saw, too, the case for reassessment of the party line – but had no opportunity to make it, as her staff were among the only advisers not invited to daily discussions on Gaza. Yet despite her misgivings and bruised ego she understood the competing demands on Starmer better than others in the shadow cabinet. So too the realpolitik of a troubled region. Among her friends she counted the chief rabbi Ephraim Mirvis, Lord Michael Levy and Sir Trevor Chinn, three of the leading lights of British Jewry. In the weeks after 7 October she had been given the brief of liaising with ambassadors from the Gulf, joking to one MP that the Saudi envoy was seeking her hand in marriage. Over private lunches and dinners at Harrods she told him: 'You need to stop chopping people's heads off.' Endowed with a nuanced understanding of the politics at play, Rayner did not exploit the instability within Labour to her own ends. To shadow ministers who came complaining about Starmer and demanding a ceasefire, she said: 'No, we've got a spotlight on this – he's looking at the bigger picture.'

In Westminster there was stalemate. Resolution and release would

only come from Washington. Anxious to prove their influence and relevance abroad, the leader's office sought an invitation to the White
House. That idea had long pre-dated 7 October but the war injected it
with a new urgency. Merely telling the Labour Party that Atlanticism
offered a faster track to peace than protest had failed to convince. Pictures of the leader of the opposition shaking hands with the president
in the Oval Office would make the same point all the more powerfully:
that Starmer was a world leader in waiting to whom the Americans
were willing to listen. To the leadership's surprise, the White House
was unbothered by the diplomatic sensitivities of a visit from an
opposition leader. Sunak was clearly living on borrowed time. Yet the
most the Biden administration could offer was the vague promise of
a meeting in the event that Starmer happened to find himself in DC,
with no further specifics. Said an aide involved in those fruitless negotiations: 'We told the Americans quite a few times a year: "You have to
tell us yes. You have to give us a day." We can't just go across and say:
"Keir's visiting the United States of America and doesn't have a meeting with the president yet."' While in public Starmer was unfailingly
discreet on questions of Biden's health, his advisers openly speculated
that his infirmity and senility were the real barrier to a meeting. 'It
wasn't necessarily that they didn't want to meet Keir – they don't really
care – but it may have been about protecting Biden, not overloading
his day with meetings with people he didn't necessarily need to meet.'
In a presidential election year the risks of unintended consequences
were probably too high to countenance. 'He might have just got his
name wrong.'

Three of Starmer's intimates tried and failed to secure a meeting
and with it their boss's affirmation: Jill Cuthbertson, the head of office
who had worked for Gordon Brown and Ed Miliband; Doyle, who was
better placed than any other adviser to cash in Tony Blair's months
of assurances that he would help engineer a meeting with Biden;
and Lammy, who constantly made 'big' claims of his friendship with
Barack Obama, despite the froideur between the former president and
his successor. The shadow foreign secretary said repeatedly: 'I'll get
this done.' He did not. Nor did Gray, whose text correspondence with
Jake Sullivan could not break the impasse either.

*

It would be months before Starmer moved. In the meantime his position only hardened, and while the transatlantic rationale behind it may have crystallised, it became no easier to sell. 'The geostrategic element,' says a shadow cabinet minister, 'was very important to him. Where were the other western countries?' As an intellectual position it was defensible. As a political proposition, however, it came across merely as a hollow imitation of its recent past: a nation that moved on the world stage only in lockstep with Washington. The image of Tony Blair as George W. Bush's poodle still lingered in folk memory. Two questions hung heavy over Starmer. How might he explain that his opposition to a ceasefire amounted to more than deference to the Americans? And if a ceasefire was gesture politics, what was Labour's alternative vision for peace in the Middle East?

Looming in the wings of the party's psychodrama were the two giants of its last foreign misadventure, waiting expectantly for their invitation to take centre stage. Blair and Gordon Brown still believed they could save not only Starmer but the world. From his desk in his Institute for Global Change, Blair spent the early days of the conflict waging his own campaign of diplomacy. As much as anything else the outbreak of violence – and the destruction of Gaza – upended the new Middle East he had strived to build. As an author of the 2020 Abraham Accords, the peace treaties designed to normalise relations between Israel and its Arab neighbours in the Gulf, he had come to believe that the region might move on from mortal tension over Palestine to a new era of cooperation in trade and diplomacy, and unity against Iran. Underpinning it all was the premature conclusion that the Palestinian conflict had been contained and frozen – that stasis punctuated by occasional if manageable eruptions of violence was a status quo tolerable to the Gulf's great powers. Blair had sat quiet and inconspicuous in the White House Rose Garden as Donald Trump had announced the first agreements between Israel, Bahrain and the United Arab Emirates, satisfied that the ultimate prize was now within reach: a deal between Israel and Saudi Arabia. He counted the leaders of both states as his confidants, taking money from Mohammed bin Salman even after the 2018 murder of the dissident journalist Jamal Khashoggi, cleaving close to Netanyahu even as his war machine was condemned by the world's progressives. Blair ignored the opprobrium. He had grown more dismissive of media noise with age. If breaking bread with strongmen was the price of peace, so be it. Yet 7 October was a watershed for his new world. Palestine and its people could no longer be ignored, not least by Arab leaders whose people felt the pain of their neighbours. Blair sought to drag Netanyahu back from the brink, and save Starmer from the electoral fate that had befallen New Labour after the Iraq War – when Muslim voters had deserted their party too.

It was not that Blair disagreed with Starmer. The doubts he so volubly expressed to friends in 2020 and 2021 had subsided. The old master had come to admire his apprentice, and commended his realism – not least because he arranged many of the meetings the shadow cabinet now found itself having with envoys from the Gulf. Yet Blair knew Starmer lacked his powers of storytelling, or the appetite for masochism he had demonstrated in the months and weeks before the invasion of Iraq. Keir, by contrast, preferred to withdraw. Even in private he seldom expressed positions that seemed self-evident to him with the necessary clarity or emphasis. In public, the press made a great sport of coaxing 'lines' out of the leader, alive to any minute deviation from what had been said before. Trying and failing to speak to two audiences at once, the shadow cabinet bemoaned the inconsistency of Labour's message, too: 'One day they'd come out and say: "You're really bad, Netanyahu." The next they'd be placing a story in the *Jewish Chronicle* saying they weren't going to recognise the Palestinian state. It all just looked like overcorrecting from event to event.' Blair agreed that this would not be enough. 'He [Blair] thought we were in the right place,' said one Starmer aide, 'but that we had to do a better job of communicating the place we were in as a party . . . and that Keir should be more out there . . . He was probably right.'

In a private memo to the leader's office on 15 October, Blair set out the case for Israeli restraint with greater clarity than Starmer would be able to muster for weeks if not months. Recommending a strategy to minimise civilian casualties, establish 'safe zones' secure from Israeli bombardment, pauses in fighting and safe transportation for Palestinians fleeing violence, and the free passage of aid from Egypt, he wrote: 'We fully support Israel's right to defend itself against what was a savage attack of total inhumanity and brutality . . . However, there is no doubt about the scale of this humanitarian catastrophe unfolding in Gaza.' Even if Starmer remained unwilling to utter the word 'ceasefire', Blair urged him to explain his alternative. This very Blairite problem of war abroad demanded the most Blairite solution of all: spin. As if moving in equal and opposite reaction to his old adversary, Gordon Brown let it be known that he was a man with a plan. He had assiduously avoided culpability for Blair's foreign policy as chancellor, but now the great clunking fist of legend slammed a blueprint for peace onto Starmer's desk. Aides in the leader's office were well accustomed to Brown's long, rambling missives on any subject at any time of day: from the education of girls in the developing world to the elimination of child poverty, invariably via more devolution to Scotland. One of Starmer's first acts as leader was to commission a review of the constitution by Brown, which reported in 2022, proposing the abolition of the House of Lords and a new era of devolution in England. When the shadow cabinet questioned its length, Brown's next draft was several pages longer. When he read that aides in the leader's office questioned its political value, he called a friend to ask of one of Starmer's spin doctors: 'Who is Paul Ovenden, and why does he hate Scotland?' On another occasion, when it was reported that the Lords may not be abolished by Starmer after all, he called a shadow cabinet minister and opened their conversation with the barked greeting: 'WHAT'S GOING ON?' Brown lacked Blair's glimmering ego but his Calvinist's work ethic and intellectual self-belief more than compensated. In the enormous type and eclectic combination of fonts necessitated by his failing eyesight he hammered out the lines he believed Starmer *must* take on Israel with the same manic certitude. Like the man, the plan Brown proposed was fiddly and complex, inspired by the American statesman John Kerry's 2014 framework for a series of land swaps between Israel and the Palestinian Authority in the West Bank. Brown urged Starmer's office to adopt it as their cause, and campaign for it internationally. His proposals were received with a polite mixture of gratitude and bewilderment by the leader's office.

The advice of both men was gratefully received but tacitly rejected by Starmer. Brown's vision was a non-starter. To have hawked the former prime minister's late-night missives to negotiators risked exposing him as a rank amateur. As an aide explains: 'We weren't a government. He couldn't say: "We're not going to do a running commentary on this whole situation, but by the way, here's my peace plan!"' Blair's prescription for storytelling was at once easier to accept and harder to swallow. As the war dragged on, it became more difficult for Starmer to tell any one story about its causes and effects. Indeed, it was not so much a war but a series of overlapping conflicts, each with its own challenges to the progressive world view. There was Hamas versus Israel; Israel versus Hamas; Israel and the US versus Iran. There was the illegal occupation of the West Bank by Israeli settlers, the erosion of the rights of Muslim worshippers at Jerusalem's Al-Aqsa Mosque. There was Hezbollah's war on Israel's northern borders with Lebanon and Syria and Houthi drone attacks on Israel and the Red Sea. Netanyahu's detractors on the left viewed the Jewish state he led as the last remaining – and most egregious – example of what Lenin had called the highest stage of capitalism: imperialism. Supporters of Palestine in Britain's Muslim community saw it as the ultimate expression of western attitudes to their people's lives: disinterest at best, genocide at worst. Israel's supporters regarded it just as many had in 1948, 1967 and 1973: a miracle, the last and only hope of the Jewish people after two millennia of deadly persecution, and the only true democracy in the Middle East. The phase of the conflict that began with massacres in border villages on 7 October spread not just through Israel and Palestine, but across the world. Soon it was everything, everywhere, all at once. That was the real explanation for Starmer's reluctance to offer a single, grand unified theory of its beginning and end; of his refusal to pick a perpetrator and a victim. If he had adopted the narrative many of his MPs and the activist left had urged him to tell, he knew condemnations of ultra-Zionist violence in the West Bank and mass deaths in Gaza would come easily. But he suspected he would be found wanting if Iran's proxies fired sophisticated missiles towards the homes of Jewish civilians the following day, or Hamas made good on its threat to conduct another 7 October. All of which explained why, instead of appealing to hearts and minds, the leader continued to present his diffident and reluctant self to the House of Commons. No story was better than the wrong story. Less would have to be more.

Advisers regretted his reluctance. They believed Starmer to be far more compelling than either he or his critics gave him credit for when he did explain his thinking. 'When it was still a bit touch and go on Gaza, Keir went to shadow cabinet,' said one. 'I said: "You're going to have to talk them through why this is your position." He did it, and there wasn't a bit of dissent. People might not have agreed with him, but they completely understood his argument. It was perfectly rational. He had his best success in persuading people when he said it, and he took people through point by point. We could never win on this topic, but we did have a nuanced, different position to the Tories. It was perfectly intellectually sound: caring and compassionate. You'd have people say some fucking wild things like: Keir doesn't care about Muslim lives. Nothing could be further from the truth. But he's also a realist about how you *do* achieve things, and how you get things done.' Yet Starmer offered his barristerial best only on rare occasions.

★

Despite Labour's unchanging lead in the opinion polls, Keir Starmer staggered into the new year bearing the heavy burden of his own reputation. Within the shadow cabinet, in newspapers and on the airwaves, they no longer spoke of the strong-willed and ruthless leader who had emerged from the ashes of Hartlepool in 2021 and conquered all before him. They spoke once more of a man of chronic indecision.

Gaza had come first. Then that old, familiar number: £28 billion. What had started life in 2021 as the party's flagship economic policy had become another albatross of the leadership's own making. Rishi Sunak had failed in every one of his vain attempts to close the yawning gap that still separated the Conservatives from Labour in the opinion polls. The prime minister made five pledges to the public that went unfulfilled. In his conference speech of 2023 he claimed, implausibly, to offer the electorate a radical break from fourteen years of Conservative failure. None of it worked. But he still had 'The £28 Billion'.

McSweeney called that number a 'zombie policy'. It refused to die, and hobbled menacingly behind his campaign. Even Rachel Reeves, who had announced that she would borrow that amount of money for every year of a Labour government to fund Britain's green transition, had come to view it as mad. Pat McFadden, by now entrusted with leading Labour's election campaign, was viciously sceptical too. Of the lugubrious Scotsman who ran the rule over Starmer's plans for government, Wes Streeting told an audience of friends: 'If you say "spending" three times, Pat appears with a scythe.' The policy – and as far as Labour's threadbare offer on the economy was concerned, it was *the* policy – amounted to little more than a large number which the Conservative Party could repeat ad nauseam, like a spell to summon the ghosts of profligacy that haunted voters' memories of Labour government. Nobody referred to the Green Prosperity Plan, the name devised after long and torturous discussions in the leader's office in 2022. Nobody spoke of what it would fund, for Labour had not yet decided. Nobody appeared to have noticed that Reeves had already downgraded the borrowing target from £28 billion per year to £28 billion by the end of the fifth year of Labour's first term. Instead they spoke only of the number, and nothing else.

By January 2024 the number was a problem. It was a bigger problem than Ed Miliband, the climate evangelist who – resented though he was by the likes of Peter Mandelson – had first warned more than a year earlier of the dangers of borrowing such gargantuan sums in a new era of high interest rates. It was a bigger problem than Angela Rayner, who emerged as the policy's great champion the moment she realised her own package of reforms to workers' rights would be culled by McFadden next. It was a bigger problem than the debatable popularity of the net-zero agenda it existed to enact, too. For that reason Reeves, McFadden and McSweeney resolved to delete the number from Labour's lexicon entirely. Over four months from September 2023 they trawled through every one of the green policies to which Starmer was notionally committed and discovered nothing that dissuaded them from their view that the £28 billion could never be mentioned again. Its advocates were isolated. Miliband, though alive to the risks, had become attached to the figure: a symbol, he believed, of Labour's commitment to environmentalism. Mattinson, as much its intellectual godmother as Reeves, was so convinced of its electoral power that she had proposed Starmer embark on a nationwide bus tour to spread the gospel of green investment to the public.

That never happened, for Starmer did not really care for the number either. McSweeney, frustrated by its long afterlife, took it upon himself to ask the leader whether he truly believed in the policy. He did not. The green agenda mattered to Starmer, but not the number. He was perfectly happy to sell each environmental policy on its own terms, without the forbidding price tag. He was happy, too, to delegate the small print of policy and politics to those who cared for such things with the intensity he could never summon. 'Most of the time,' said one adviser involved, 'Keir gives a lot of responsibility and agency to individuals, and expects them to get on with it.' Yet in public he continued to read words that implied the precise opposite. His aides had discussed junking the number in his first speech of the year, at a factory in Bristol on 4 January. They decided to wait, to kill it instead under the cover of the budget in March. Starmer offered a lukewarm endorsement to his own economic policy in his first interview of 2024 the following day, telling LBC that the £28 billion was 'subject to our fiscal rules . . . it's a confident ambition'. Two days later he used his next public appearance, on Sky News, to offer a far more enthusiastic endorsement that matched his true feelings: 'It's absolutely clear to me that the Tories are trying to weaponise this issue, the £28 billion . . . it's a fight I want to have, if we can have a fight going into the election between an incoming Labour government that wants to invest in the future long-term strategy that will lower our bills and give us energy independence, versus stagnation, more of the same under this government.'

The only fight that raged was within his own office. Gray again loomed over the politicians whose will she was supposed to enact. Even she referred to the policy by its price, not its content, but her own assessment of the politics sharply contradicted the agreed consensus. U-turning on the figure would imply weakness, and they all knew that Starmer hated that. She warned, too, that Reeves had not yet said which green policies she would be prepared to accept instead. On and on it went, the inevitable obvious to all in Westminster, as Starmer continued to defend a policy that not even he supported. Darren Jones, his shadow chief secretary to the Treasury – who wielded the axe on public spending with as much relish as McFadden – all but buried it on 2 February. 'The number that we will get to, if we are in government, will be subject to two things . . . it will be subject to the state of the economy . . . it will also be subject to a case-by-case business case that, if I'm the chief secretary to the Treasury in the next Labour government, I will have to sign off.' But when Starmer was asked by Times Radio on 6 February, he disinterred the number again: 'Start with the five missions . . . because you can only understand the investment argument by understanding that we want to have clean power by 2030. We're going to need investment. That's where the £28 billion comes in. That investment is *desperately needed* for that mission and I've been unwavering.' Within twenty-four hours both the *Guardian* and the *Sun* reported – correctly – that the £28 billion was not so desperately needed at all, and would be ditched the following day. Finally, it was.

The leaked news shocked nobody but Gray, who again moved to impose her authority on events. Reprising the role she had played for prime ministers past, she confiscated the phones – or, in her words, invited them to share them for inspection – of advisers suspected of the fatal leak. It was, said one of those targeted, a 'fucking mental' decision. Staff complained to the GMB, their trade union, who in turn lodged a complaint with Labour's general secretary. Some wept under interrogation. News of her leak inquiry itself leaked to *The Times* on 13 February, a hostile act that caused a minor explosion in Westminster. It was not the U-turn that had called Starmer's authority into question, but the civil war that had begun among his advisers. In pursuing the culprits so aggressively, Gray let it be known that the lads in the leader's office – who, in reality, amounted to a large group of men and women loyal to McSweeney above all – were on notice. They, in turn, told her that they would not be subdued without a fight.

In her early days as chief of staff, Gray – who posed smiling for a publicity photo on her first morning in post – had asked Matthew Doyle for advice on handling the media. 'My advice,' said Doyle, 'is that you keep a fucking lower profile.' It was too late for that now.

★

In those weeks it seemed as if the entire intellectual architecture of Starmerism was collapsing. Yes, all the available data suggested Keir would soon be prime minister – with Labour's effortless capture of two Conservative seats in by-elections in Kingswood and Wellingborough on 15 February the latest evidence. But the world that awaited him was ever more unstable.

Two days later he flew to Germany, to play statesman at the Munich Security Conference. His meeting with President Biden had not materialised but talks with Antony Blinken, the US secretary of state, were an enticing substitute. Starmer expected to talk about Israel. Yet Blinken was preoccupied less with what Britain could do to mend a broken Middle East than its role in repairing a fractured Europe. He warned Starmer that the greatest favour he could do for America was not mimic its rhetoric on Gaza but unite with the EU. 'Please build close relationships with Europe,' Blinken said. His message, recalls an adviser present, was: 'Brexit's a disaster . . . we can't have

Britain and Europe divided. Europe and Britain need to be aligned, not competitors . . . don't do the deregulation, "Europe is our enemy" thing, you need to come back.' To that, Starmer – speaking like the Remainer he had once been – said: 'That's naturally where we are.'

Starmer had not yet told the British public – and would not tell them even as he campaigned in the general election – that he had designs on a much tighter partnership with Europe than his cautious words implied. Starmer *would*, in time, speak of a security pact with the EU as a bulwark against Russian and Chinese expansionism, but aides explain that his true intentions went much further: 'It's not just about tanks and guns, it's actually about economic security . . . you don't create a new single market, but you ensure that this treaty gives us some sort of access to get around it. It sounds like the customs union, but isn't quite the customs union – it's something new.' To the voters Starmer denied any suggestion that Britain would ever rejoin a customs union with Brussels. Behind closed doors, he had begun to advocate for something else entirely.

Doublespeak came naturally to the leader abroad. In Westminster it had outlived its usefulness. Unlike Blinken, his backbenchers wished only to talk about Gaza, where 1 million displaced Palestinians had crammed into a tiny expanse of land near Rafah – the next target for Israel's troops. Netanyahu's belief that Yahya Sinwar, Hamas's chief, might be hiding among them had garnered precious little sympathy after months of civilian deaths. The SNP had warned of a bloodbath, vowing to table another motion before the Commons demanding a full ceasefire within days. If a vote was held, potentially dozens of Labour MPs would support it. Gray believed saying nothing was untenable. She asked three equally frustrated members of the shadow cabinet – Lammy, Cooper and Nandy – to convey that to Starmer. Away from the male aides she saw as an impediment to progress, they advised that he soften his stance in an op-ed in that weekend's *Observer*. They made a clear demand: that he call for an immediate humanitarian ceasefire. Doing so would serve as the basis of the party's position in Parliament, and give wavering MPs something to cling on to. With Starmer's mind on the world leaders he was about to meet in Munich, he agreed to Gray's plan, asking Doyle, his communications director, to finalise a draft.

Doyle was ambivalent. He took to 'ME op-ed', a WhatsApp group of trusted colleagues, to seek views on the text. Gray was not among them. The 'main thing', he said, 'is the addition of immediate humanitarian ceasefire line . . . I have said post 28bn etc I find it difficult to see what the headline is other than Starmer backs down on ceasefire call etc . . . But we obviously have to move at some point.' He appealed to staff for a 'sense check', asking if there was some other way of communicating the same sentiment – something, anything, that avoided the specific words to which Starmer's critics were seeking to bind him. 'Feel free to tell me I'm worrying unnecessarily / it has to be done.' Mark Simpson, the hawkish head of international policy, was equally ambivalent: 'I think it's where the vast majority of others are now, it's a snappier way of what we have been saying but I totally understand your concerns,' he said. Stuart Ingham, the leader's headstrong and bookish policy chief, was less forgiving. He was everything Gray disliked in politics: an Oxford PhD graduate who made little secret of his disdain for the smaller minds of parliamentarians. But as Starmer's 'golden boy', a loud and proud Leicester City fan who was now the sole survivor of his original team, he could claim to know the leader's mind better than anyone. He noted that, in the proposed piece, Starmer would acknowledge Israel's right to conduct targeted operations to rescue hostages, asking: 'I don't understand how this sentence doesn't totally undermine the argument for a ceasefire?' Doyle replied: 'How else do we say Israel can still get hostages and deal with rocket attacks? I don't have an answer.' Said Ingham: 'The article is just completely contradictory. If there are still going to be targeted military operations then there will not be a ceasefire. If the view is that we still need to be able to say that Israel has a right to conduct military operations then we are not calling for a ceasefire and we just need to drop the whole thing.' He added: 'To be honest it is not even close to being publishable and I can't edit into a form that is.'

Doyle was sympathetic, if wary of frustrating Starmer's wishes. He conceded he needed 'a view on immediate humanitarian ceasefire', but still did not 'understand where we are on that, and to be honest that's really the bit that matters most'. For once, Ingham confessed he did not know either. 'Is Keir asking us to make an op-ed with the words immediate humanitarian ceasefire work, or is he asking us to give a view on whether it is a good idea?' he asked. Said Doyle: 'He wants to see an op-ed with the words immediate humanitarian ceasefire. He

thinks Rafah has to be the thing that has changed the calculation.' That
was clear enough. Ingham stated: 'I think seeing it written down makes
it clear we shouldn't be making the case it is a position change but that
our position has always been that we will call for a ceasefire on both
sides once the conditions had changed and now they have.' Still scepticism prevailed. Ditto the desire to preserve Starmer's integrity. There
was no easy way of explaining why the prospect of civilian deaths in
one part of Gaza was the game-changer the article claimed it to be.
'On the Rafah point,' Simpson had asked, 'it does beg the question,
"so were you wrong?"' No answers were forthcoming. If Starmer's
own team could not explain his position, Doyle and others resolved,
then an elaborate op-ed articulating it was premature. The article was
shelved, although Starmer could not remain above the fray indefinitely.
He resolved a more measured course: when the SNP tabled its motion,
he would produce a concise amendment which stopped short of an
intellectual disquisition, but still contained those three elusive words:
immediate humanitarian ceasefire.

On 21 February, the SNP duly submitted its motion before the Commons. By then, the patience of Labour MPs had worn perilously thin.
Angela Rayner told friends that Starmer's intransigence was risking the
lives of his colleagues – that 'someone pro-Palestinian and anti-Israel
who is pissed off at Labour's position will stab and kill an MP'. Shabana
Mahmood, who had buttressed Starmer at his lowest ebb, had resolved
to resign rather than tell her constituents that she had voted against
an end to the violence inflicted against their fellow Muslims. Resentfully, she often spoke of Starmer's supposed kismet – the Turkish word
for destiny – and marvelled at how apparently catastrophic events
always conspired to rebound to his advantage. With a vote on a ceasefire looming, his luck appeared to have evaporated. She and dozens of
other MPs, many of them shadow ministers, told themselves they had
no choice but to defy their leader and vote with the SNP for 'an immediate and total ceasefire'.

Unbeknown to them, the line was about to collapse. In a tightly
worded motion, Starmer suddenly spoke of an 'immediate humanitarian ceasefire', with the added caveat that Israel 'cannot be expected
to cease fighting if Hamas continues with violence and that Israelis
have the right to the assurance that the horror of 7 October cannot
happen again'. In the world of semantics the Labour Party inhabited,

that language was still measured and ambiguous. Yet it represented a shift – and something MPs could take to their constituents. The question nobody had foreseen was whether Starmer's MPs would have the opportunity to endorse it. While Starmer sought to amend the SNP's motion with his own language, the convention of opposition-day debates in the Commons dictated that the Speaker could not select it for a vote. Starmer disagreed. In that scenario, Labour MPs had two options. The first was to break the whip and vote with the SNP which he did not want them to do. It would cut them off from advancement to higher office in a future Labour government – and bring about the departure of the only Muslim in the shadow cabinet. The second was to vote against the SNP, which would imply they opposed *any* ceasefire – exposing them, they feared, to violence and intimidation outside their own homes. That, in a liberal democracy, was intolerable. In the hours before the vote he made that case to Lindsay Hoyle, the bluff Lancastrian Speaker. He then made another point. If Hoyle did not select Labour's amendment, then the first act of a Labour government would be to whip its MPs to elect a new Speaker after the election they were expected to win.

Hoyle did as he was told. MPs had their vote on Labour's motion. For all the noise the Speaker's decision created, the party's motion passed unanimously. Kismet – destiny – still favoured the leader when all looked lost.

*

That destiny was victory. The spoils would be a divided country. That much became painfully clear a fortnight later.

Ordinarily a by-election in Rochdale, the old mill town in Greater Manchester, would have posed no difficulty to a Labour Party leading the Conservatives by twenty points in the opinion polls. Especially with a candidate like Azhar Ali, a bear of a man who worked to foster good relations between Muslims and Jews. When the old warhorse Sir Tony Lloyd died on 17 January, they had moved to hold a by-election quickly, so that a speedy campaign would not be derailed by discussion of the conflict. There would be no risk of that with Azhar Ali. So dependable a servant of the Labour Party was Starmer's man in Rochdale that he had once joined fellow councillors from the north-west to redecorate Angela Rayner's home. George Galloway, unbowed by his failure in Batley three years earlier, had come to town to quote the Quran and sow division. But no matter how loudly he shouted, how furiously he railed against Starmer's equivocation on a ceasefire and support for Israel, how many times he accused the Labour leader of facilitating genocide, the Labour leadership were sure he would not win.

Yet their destiny had become division. On 11 February, the *Mail on Sunday* revealed that Ali had told a meeting of Labour activists in the days after Hamas's bloody incursion into Israel: 'The Egyptians are saying that they warned Israel ten days earlier . . . Americans warned them a day before there's something happening . . . they deliberately took the security off, they allowed . . . that massacre that gives them the green light to do whatever they bloody want.' For eight hours Morgan McSweeney and Pat McFadden debated whether he could remain Labour's candidate. Reluctantly, they allowed him to apologise. The following day, the *Daily Mail* published the next passage of Ali's rambling monologue – that 'people in the media from certain Jewish quarters' were seeking to silence pro-Palestinian Labour MPs. Only then did they pull the plug. Starmer and his advisers had dithered again, as so often on the Palestinian question. But the leader called it 'tough and decisive action'. Ali remained on the ballot in name only, running a lonely campaign from the boot of his car.

Less than three weeks later, George Galloway was once again returned to Parliament. 'Keir Starmer, this is for Gaza,' he said. 'You will pay a high price for the role that you have played in enabling, encouraging and covering for the catastrophe presently going on in occupied Gaza, in the Gaza Strip . . . Labour is on notice that they have lost the confidence of millions of their voters who have loyally and traditionally voted for them generation after generation.'

'I regret we had to withdraw our candidate, and apologise to voters in Rochdale,' said Starmer. 'I took that decision. It was the right decision.' At Labour HQ, his staff longed for the same sense of certainty.

19

Victory

'I want to start by saying Happy International Women's Day to all of the brilliant women that work for the Labour Party. I hope that you'll indulge me for a few minutes whilst I get my soapbox out. Recently, I've become increasingly agitated by the number of stories that I've seen about this campaign, and the Labour Party itself, being run by men with women's voices ignored.' It was 8 March 2024 and Hollie Ridley, McSweeney's deputy and the most powerful woman in Labour HQ, was addressing hundreds of party staff. Her message was intended for one alone.

If Keir Starmer's Labour Party really was under the control of a boys' club, then Ridley was one of the boys. Morgan McSweeney trusted maybe half a dozen people with the truth of his intentions for party and country, and the smiling thirty-five-year-old from Dagenham was one of them. Nothing in the Labour Party moved without her licence: not a pound from its bank accounts, nor an activist from one constituency to another.

Starmer may have led the party in Westminster, but the party the voters saw on the streets – knocking on doors, pushing leaflets through letter boxes – was led by Ridley. She *was* the Labour Party, the only employer she had ever known except an east London branch of McDonald's: the daughter of a lorry driver, a daughter of deep England, rewriting the rules of British elections from a new-build estate in Essex. But to read of the Labour Party in *The Times*, the *Financial Times*, the *Daily Mail*, the *Guardian* and every other newspaper that had written of its patriarchal management in the weeks before Ridley's speech was to read of a world where she did not exist at all.

Ridley went on, each word a rebuttal to received wisdom. 'So many brilliant women are responsible for ensuring that the Labour Party delivers at the highest level: Marianna, Carol, Jill, Helene, Vidhya, Steph, Sophie, Deborah, Rachael, Gail, Amy, Sheila, Gillian, Tammi, Angela.' She spoke of six more women under her management: Emma, Charlotte, Kate, Jo, Hailey, Pearl. 'At every level, the Labour Party has the most extraordinarily talented and committed women and as an organisation we are so much stronger for it. If those women aren't visible to you, then you may want to ask yourselves why. You don't get more women in the room by erasing the ones already there.' One name was deliberately omitted from Ridley's list of political heroines: Sue.

*

Keir Starmer made hundreds of speeches in 2024, a year that resembled nothing so much as purgatory for his party. So too his shadow cabinet. An election year was now upon them. But only Rishi Sunak knew precisely when – 'the second half of the year' was the sole clue the prime minister offered to an opposition. Condemned to months of nervous agitation, all the Labour Party could do was talk. Starmer spoke of his intentions endlessly. Every speech and interview purported to offer greater clarity than before. Each was analysed to death – even those that really said nothing. Yet none told the truth about the party that waited impatiently to run the country. Only Ridley's words did, and they were neither noticed nor reported outside of Labour HQ.

That spring, Starmer's advisers stood on the brink of a historic victory, as great as any won since 1997 or even 1945. Yet they turned their backs to their new horizon – on the almost tangible prospect of the first Labour government in fourteen years – and turned on each other. Experience and history already inured them to self-belief. No word was dirtier than complacency, no cliché of electoral strategy as well worn as the old Roy Jenkins line about the hyper-cautious Tony Blair 'carrying a priceless Ming vase across a highly polished floor' in the months and years before the 1997 landslide. Labour knew how to lose and, even as every by-election swung in their favour, Starmer's aides struggled to accept that they might have learned to win. Doubt came naturally, not least because they now doubted each other.

Ridley had not only spoken for the Labour women who felt excluded from their own success story – but the other advisers who feared Gray's presence might now change its ending. Said one leading campaign adviser of Gray that January: 'I definitely worry about the effect it's going to have on our ability to win the next election.' Said another: 'Why have we hired someone who's never won a campaign before we've won? It feels like bringing someone in before we've won is tempting fate.' The counsels of despair were sincere, even if the polls suggested they were detached from electoral reality. To outsiders they might have sounded absurd. But the advisers who would run Labour's winning campaign convinced themselves of impending disaster.

Official denials could not obscure the fault line that split Starmer's aspirant government in two. On one side was McSweeney, the other Gray. Neither had instigated the battle for supremacy that was now fought in their name. Their roles had been designed as mutually exclusive. The Irishman would win Starmer his election, and Gray would prepare what the leader would do once it had been won. In reality the demarcation between campaigning and preparing for government was not so clean. The chief of staff was no longer a civil servant, but a politician too. Listening to the MPs the old guard in the leader's office ignored – not least on Gaza – was a political decision. Questioning the wisdom of abandoning the £28 billion was a political decision, too.

Gray, to the mounting horror of McSweeney's loyal acolytes, was more than an office manager or transition planner. She was a challenge to their authority and assumptions. They wanted to plaster Labour's election leaflets with the Union Jack: she asked them why. They wanted to attack the Conservatives for anything and everything, and maintained a team of a dozen advisers to spend their days doing just that: her back still raw with the scars of media hostility, she wondered aloud why 'attack' was necessary at all. McSweeney's people subordinated everything to the brute logic of winning votes. That end justified almost any means, no matter how alienating it was to the Labour Party. Gray conceived of politics as a web of human relationships, with herself at its centre, bestowing on the party's poor and needy politicians the attention her colleagues withheld. As one of Gray's more powerful critics recalled: 'Morgan didn't go around saying: "Keir said this." He didn't throw that relationship around at all . . . Sue would say, in meetings, things like: "Well, Keir texts me all the time, actually." ' The two philosophies were mutually exclusive. Cruelly, some likened her to Dolores Umbridge, the psychotic headmistress from the *Harry Potter* novels who concealed her malign intentions behind a sickly smile and wardrobe of pastels. As one of Starmer's closest female aides passed Gray on her way to the lavatories in Labour HQ, the chief of staff said, 'Oh, us women need to stick together, don't we?'

The handful of shadow cabinet ministers with meaningful influence over the campaign accused Gray of undoing decisions that had been made for good reason. 'Leaders can pick their staff, and they trust their staff because they pick them,' said one. 'They haven't necessarily picked their politicians, and politicians, by their nature, are of varying quality and insight. So it's fine to *say* we have to have politicians involved in everything. But sometimes there's a reason why they're not.'

Just as the irresistible force of polling day ought to have united them, Starmer's advisers existed in a state of conscious tension with one another. At a time when they could have been speaking of almost anything else – Labour's manifesto, another round of local elections in May, and the general election, whenever it came – the leader's office mostly debated the existence of 'the lads' the newspapers now criticised on an almost daily basis. The conflict between the boys and their great adversary consumed everything. For some in the shadow cabinet this was merely a belated recognition of the obvious: that their democratic socialist party now ran on blokeish feudalism. For the aides who took McSweeney as their guide, it was its own kind of sexist nonsense. 'She tried to create this idea of the boys' club,' said one of Labour's leading woman officials. 'Obviously, it was a dig at Morgan and Matthew Doyle. She made women invisible.'

On occasion they suspected Gray was wilfully blind to the work of female colleagues. In the days after the suspension of Azhar Ali, a letter to voters in the name of Andy Burnham that endorsed the now disgraced candidate landed on doormats in Rochdale. Given that it was signed off and posted well before Ali's self-destruction, this mishap could not have been helped. Burnham, understandably livid by the implication that he supported a babbling conspiracy theorist, complained to Gray. She in turn asked the office of Labour's general secretary, David Evans, for the name of whoever managed the party's regional director in the north-west, who had given Burnham short shrift. 'Hollie Ridley,' came the reply. To that Gray said: 'Who's Hollie Ridley?'

It was a question even professional chroniclers of British politics would have struggled to answer correctly at the time, but Gray's response echoed mockingly through Labour HQ – cited as evidence that she neither understood the party she had joined, nor cared to learn about it. The mismatch between the mood in headquarters, whose discontent only occasionally made itself public, and the country, which took every opportunity to demonstrate its readiness for a Labour government, created an oppressive sense of unreality. Even as those he trusted most came to loathe her, Starmer himself never wavered in his admiration for the woman he expended so much political capital in recruiting. He seemed oblivious to the enmity that now infected everyone and everything. But that was Starmer, forever uninterested in the politics of politics itself. Questions of strategy and leadership his team thought existential were seen by the leader as human resources. Gray, says Nick Boles, the former Conservative minister she recruited to help run Labour's preparations for government, was nothing less than Starmer's 'vicar on earth'. She turned the rest of the advisers he most trusted into nonconformists.

*

Starmer did not bridge the divide. Some still doubt he ever noticed it. That task fell instead to Waheed Alli, who bestrode the growing chasm at the heart of the Labour Party like nobody else.

Baron Alli of Norbury – though to Labour people, it was always just Waheed – defied easy description, even by those who could not escape him. He was a self-made millionaire devoted to Labour politics; the son of a Guyanese car mechanic who had taken ermine and a seat in the Lords at thirty-four; a conviction Blairite who believed in Keir Starmer's project. For decades he had lavished his wealth upon the Labour Party. McSweeney and Gray would be equally receptive. The Irishman needed Alli's money, and the money Alli could extract from the rich men and women he knew so well. Gray, burdened with a blank page still waiting to be filled with a plan for government, needed his address book of luminaries from business and politics.

Always anxious to avoid the camera, Alli had made his fortune behind it. He was a banker first – a self-taught City boy. Then show business became his business. *The Big Breakfast*, the estates of Agatha Christie, Enid Blyton and Beatrix Potter: at one time or another Waheed owned the rights to many of Britain's youthful memories. Like so many of the people who now found themselves running Keir Starmer's Labour Party – like Hollie Ridley and Morgan McSweeney – he had learned his politics at the lap of Margaret McDonagh, Blair's general secretary. At her direction Alli spent his riches on New Labour and its heirs, funding their doomed campaigns to stop Brexit and win the party leadership. His own generation had been happy to take his money. They went to his parties and planned their campaigns from his Kent mansion. But they never embraced Alli as anything more than a friendly millionaire. 'Puffed up, peacockish, full of himself,' recalled one survivor of Blair's governments. 'Skilful, sinuous . . . prepared to throw his own money around. He never questions anything politically. No political views.'

Under Starmer, that changed. In 2023 he made Alli his head of election fundraising. That title underplayed his influence. In Keir Starmer's Labour Party, Alli was everywhere, and everywhere was Alli. When circumstances demanded the leader address the nation – another outbreak of Covid in December 2021, the death of the Queen in September 2022 – he spoke from behind a desk in Alli's Covent Garden penthouse. When he needed new suits and spectacles, Alli bought them – at a cost of some £16,000. When McSweeney and his inner circle met to plan Labour's general election campaign, they did so at another of Alli's homes: a Soho town house on Meard Street. Those present felt Alli's presence more keenly than Starmer's. There was McSweeney, of course, with his deputy Marianna McFadden; her husband, Pat, and his fellow shadow cabinet minister Jonathan Ashworth; Spencer Livermore, who had worked for Gordon Brown and Ed Miliband; Deborah Mattinson; Peter Hyman. Their strategy meetings were unlike those they had known before. Pat, Ashworth, Hyman, Mattinson and Livermore had belonged to the original boys' clubs: those led by Blair and Brown respectively. They had only known leaders to whom politics and strategy were everything. Blair and Brown had been authors of their own electoral destinies, and wrote the script they acted out in front of the electorate. Starmer was content to rely on ghostwriters. 'It was a bit weird at first,' said one frequent attendee, 'because we were used to, in our Blair–Brown meetings, watching Tony and Gordon thrash out the strategy. But, literally, Keir was like: "Right, you guys get on with it." '

Thanks to the hospitality of Alli, they could. When Gray wanted to dine with Tony Blair, and when Labour's donors wished to socialise in private, they did so behind the closed doors of Alli's empire. With the chief of staff he advised on who Starmer might appoint to ministerial rank, the boards of government departments and other public offices. He drew up plans to supply the shadow cabinet with advisers employed on secondment from Labour Together, now reborn as a think tank. Its reserves of donated cash meant it could recruit policy experts on the generous salaries the party could not pay. Alli helped direct them to shadow ministers in need. He also ensured they could carry out their work without breaching the strict electoral law that restricted spending. Waheed had at last become indispensable to the leadership of the Labour Party even if – like so many others – he was privately critical of the leader himself. 'He doesn't understand, command or control,' Alli complained to one friend in 2023. He sought to command and control the Labour Party himself. Those who worked with him watched him relish the new sensation of power, rather than mere proximity to it.

'There are four people in charge of everything,' Alli said to one junior official as he passed their desk in Labour HQ. 'Morgan, Pat, Sue, and me.' Others believed he had designs on a ministerial role for himself in due course, potentially a plum post in the Department for Culture, Media and Sport.

Whatever his higher ambitions, Alli remained in charge of Labour's money. Starmer needed more of that than ever. As McSweeney had warned the NEC and shadow cabinet in November 2023, the Tories had nearly doubled the legal spending limit for national election campaigns from £19.5 million to £35 million. 'This means we need to be ready for the election,' he told shadow ministers. 'They still think they can win it – because you don't spend £35 million on a lost cause unless you're Chelsea.' On one occasion, he gave the same speech to business leaders, not realising that one of them, Jonathan Goldstein, owned the football club in question. Alli was entrusted with courting people like him in order to amass Labour's own war chest. Much of it would come from Gary Lubner, a South African businessman who had become bored by his own wealth and approached Rachel Reeves at a dinner to volunteer his riches to the service of progressive causes and refugee rights. The pair struck up a friendship. He had become close to Starmer too, hosting a breakfast at his home in October 2023 for the leader, left-leaning think-tankers and migration experts. Lord Sainsbury, the supermarket tycoon who had abandoned Labour under Corbyn, returned to the fold – donating money and office space for government access talks. So too his daughter, Fran Perrin, who gave generously. Trevor Chinn and Martin Taylor continued to bankroll Labour Together, whose expensive hires bolstered the teams of shadow cabinet ministers.

Nothing, however, rivalled Alli's proximity to power, or fundraising prowess. 'It was like watching a hurricane happen,' said one Labour official. 'I referred a donor who told me he wanted to give fifty or a hundred grand. I had a chat with Waheed, who said: "Well, I'll take him out for lunch." After that, he spent a lot more than he was planning to give.' Alli had become the judge, jury and executioner of Labour's reputation. That same official recalls a man determined to avoid the rows over dodgy donors and political favours that proved part of Blair's undoing as prime minister. 'His threshold for scandal and what was permissible was just so much lower than anyone else's.'

As the rest of Starmer's advisers critiqued each other's decisions, at times Alli alone decided what was acceptable. After he took it upon himself to buy the leader a new wardrobe, it was suggested that he might instead donate his money to Labour HQ, which in turn could have bought Starmer his suits. He refused. 'Waheed would not have allowed any other donor to give directly but made an exception for himself,' an adviser to the leadership said. 'That was a mistake. Keir was advised against taking Waheed's money personally, but Waheed insisted. And Sue, because of her extremely close relationship with Waheed, went along with it.'

When his role was later the subject of intense media scrutiny, Labour insisted that Alli had never wielded any influence over policy. That was not true. In late 2023, Angela Rayner had planned to announce new measures to ban overseas cash finding its way into British politics. By Starmer's own logic it was an utterly uncontroversial policy. Labour defined itself in opposition to Tory sleaze. Rayner's proscription on dirty money from shady oligarchs would slot easily into a manifesto whose offer to progressives was otherwise constrained by the lack of money a Labour government would have to spend. On 17 November,

Rayner's adviser Kate Robson had emailed the leader's office to inform them of her intentions. 'The strategic aim of the policy is to close loopholes in UK donation law which currently allow dodgy money to enter our politics – primarily through the Tory party – via shell companies or companies with no connection to the UK,' Robson wrote. 'This policy will provide us with a robust defence to the Tories' attack on our donations by laying out with full transparency the robustness of our donation due diligence, and inviting the Tories to close loopholes which allow foreign money into UK democracy.' She attached proposals to change legislation to require any individual donor to be a registered voter in the UK. Any companies which donated would also have to be beneficially owned by those 'based' in Britain or on the electoral roll. And parties would be compelled to conduct greater due diligence on proposed contributions. However often they had been at odds before, here was a Rayner policy that none of Starmer's advisers could argue with – their attack and rebuttal unit, after all, had uncovered countless examples of such 'dodgy money' landing in Tory accounts before. Just as pertinently, Starmer himself was committed to the concept: Rayner's team reported that it had originated in a 'high-level meeting in March in which Keir and Angela agreed to a series of recommendations relating to elections'. Robson went on: 'We are looking to announce this on Dec 14th in an event with Chatham House where Ange will make a speech. We want to speak about how a Labour government will protect democracy across the world, celebrate our strong rules on clean donations, and put forward a clean marker in the sand for the Conservatives to clean up their donations. To flag from the outset, Angela wants to do this event with Gordon Brown, and we have already been in touch with his office to secure the date.'

The leader's office did not object. 'I'm coming to this cold,' said its head of domestic policy, Olivia Bailey, on 21 November, 'but it all sounds sensible to me.' Six days later, Robson confirmed that McSweeney was 'happy, as long as we don't come across as anti-donor. He says the message needs to be that people should be able to contribute, to give back. Any voter/anyone with a genuine connection to Britain have a democratic right to donate and engage in vibrant democracy – be that doctors, nurses, or businesspeople. This policy is about [preventing] people who don't have skin in the game from funnelling money in British democracy, this is about clamping down on shell companies.'

Rayner's team knew, too, that Labour had itself turned down £2.7 million in donations from foreign donors. Brown duly arranged his flights from Scotland to London, and booked a hotel.

Then even the deputy leader of the Labour Party and a former prime minister learned they answered to Alli. The policy was abandoned. 'With a week to go,' claimed a party official privy to the fraught discussions, 'Morgan pulled it . . . it turned out Waheed told Morgan to pull it, and so he did.' The reason for the intervention by Alli, who himself had interests in the Cayman Islands, was never made clear.

On other occasions it seemed as if Alli took a closer interest in what the Labour Party said and did than its own leader. Almost exactly three months on from the speech Rayner never gave, on 11 March 2024, the *Guardian* reported that Frank Hester – the Conservative Party's biggest individual donor – had told colleagues at his healthcare technology company that the sight of Diane Abbott on television made him want 'to hate all black women'. Hester went on: 'I think she should be shot.' He made Tory donors seem so boorish and bigoted that the Labour Party would later quote his comments in emails soliciting donations from its members. Starmer's advisers knew of its political power, for the attack and rebuttal had ensured his words were reported.

The leader himself was awestruck by their work. Alli, aggrieved by the message he feared the exposé might send to Labour's own plutocrats, made his displeasure abundantly clear. He feared the story risked a journalistic open season on all political donors, regardless of their party allegiance. That morning staff at HQ noticed something strange. Nobody could find a single copy of the *Guardian*. Some swore they had seen a colleague hiding the paper away, to spare them Alli's wrath in case he saw it.

As the election drew closer, one person sought to limit the peer's influence. When he demanded sight of a housing pledge due to be included in the manifesto, Stuart Ingham, Starmer's head of policy, said no. Alli was not used to hearing that word. What followed was a compromise which satisfied neither man. Alli would see the same documents as other shadow cabinet ministers, if not the manifesto text. Privately, he resolved that, when the time came, Ingham would be replaced. All he needed was the chief of staff's signature.

★

They lived in fear of Gray, too. As the election loomed, they feared its aftermath, when Sue would be master of every lad's destiny. Rumours abounded that she would sack those she disliked: Matthew Doyle, who she blamed for any minor failure of communications; Stuart Ingham, the head of policy she and Alli deemed insufficiently serious; and Luke Sullivan, the political director whose deep knowledge of the parliamentary party did not seem to interest or impress her. Those of whom she spoke most highly were people with 'policy grounding', more often than not Conservative ministers and career officials she had known in Whitehall.

One, the former housing minister Nick Boles, came to Labour HQ to formally advise her on preparations for government. In 2022, Boles had been a lonely Tory supporter of Starmer, tweeting his praise and securing in return a message from the leader. 'He was incredibly grateful, and did I want to come in for a chat?' Boles recalls. 'Then I started very informally lobbing in a few ideas, mainly to Deborah [Mattinson] and to Claire Ainsley . . . about the whole process of policy development in opposition, and how to avoid committing to too many things too early – but equally, how do you generate enough stuff to talk about?' Gray's appointment brought Boles into the fold. 'I sent Keir a message: "I think that was the best single decision you've made as leader of the opposition." To which he replied: "Very pleased to hear that."' The regular presence of Michael Gove's closest friend at the heart of Labour's operation in an election year was enough to make some advisers paranoid – even though Boles had voted for Blair in 1997 and, if anything, was living proof that their strategy of pursuing Tory voters above all others was working. Gray's pursuit of outside expertise was nonetheless interpreted as a threat to the delicate balance of power in Starmer's court.

McSweeney, as much as his friends were wont to hyperventilate, was never at risk. 'It's like they've sworn a blood oath to each other,' said one of his intimates, 'like they made a pact around a kitchen table – Morgan has delivered on every fucking step of that pact, and Keir will back him till the end.' The Irishman nonetheless wondered what role he would play in a Labour government run by Sue Gray. For once, the arch strategist lacked a strategy for himself. In one low moment, he confided in a friend that he might reject a role in Gray's No. 10 altogether. Why not take a break and return to some kind of

advisory role later on in the political cycle? By then, he reasoned, his
skills would be in greater demand anyway. 'It's going to be awful, it's
going to be chaos,' he said. 'I can go in a year. I don't want to be there
when that crash happens.' To that, his confidante had some news: 'Get
a grip.' McSweeney reluctantly did, using Josh Simons, who ran the
new model Labour Together, to broker meetings with the *éminences
grises* of past Labour governments from whom he sought advice on the
shape of a future role: old hands such as Sally Morgan, the lynchpin of
Blair's political office, and Alan Milburn. McSweeney told them he was
not so much interested in titles as learning about life in government.
He did not need to state the obvious: in time, with or without Gray, he
would need to control the politics of a Labour government just as he
had a Labour opposition.

The worries lingered in the back of McSweeney's mind, yet they
would only be aired much closer to polling day with the principal
himself. He knew Starmer would dismiss any complaint – even from
him – as evidence of destructive personality politics: 'Keir would have
said, "Look, you've got to get on with Sue,"' a friend familiar with his
predicament recalled. To so much as name the problems risked vindicating the 'boys' club' narrative which Gray had constructed. It would
seem as though the problem was his, not hers. And so he said nothing.
To even close friends, that diffidence was evidence of the Irishman's
'odd' relationship with the leader. Mutual interest had been their adhe-
sive back in 2019, but their half a decade at the summit of the party
had somehow not given way to intimacy, nor candour. As one of his
sources of counsel, Peter Mandelson looked on in dismay. He saw a
pattern similar to his own experience under New Labour, when, in an
attempt to prise him away from Blair, Gordon Brown had toxified his
name – constantly briefing that the Prince of Darkness was seeking to
destroy any rival sources of influence, Brown included. The intention,
as Brown saw it then, was to create a situation where Mandelson could
not so much as express an opinion on Brown without leaving himself
open to that accusation. Blair had confirmed as much when he visited
Mandelson's home in Clerkenwell in the late 1990s to deliver a decree:
'You've got to get on with Gordon. If you don't, I'm sorry, I'd have to
choose Gordon.' McSweeney did not want a situation where Starmer
was forced to choose.

He had a simple, if temporary, solution to his bind. He ignored it.

From January, he thought and spoke almost exclusively of the election. In public and in private he was tediously insistent that it would come in May.

As evidence he pointed to the government's decision to increase election spending limits and the rushed passage of legislation giving effect to the 2p cut in National Insurance announced by Jeremy Hunt, the chancellor, the previous October. Denials from well-connected Tories such as George Osborne did not dissuade him. 'A little birdy has told me that the various work programmes required to get ready for a general election have that date singled out – 14 November,' Osborne had said on 11 January. On a May polling day, he added, authoritatively: 'It's a non-starter. He's more than twenty points behind in the opinion polls. He's not going to have a spring election.' Nor was he dissuaded by Sunak's own words a week earlier: 'So, my working assumption is we'll have a general election in the second half of this year. And in the meantime I've got lots that I want to get on with.'

McSweeney nonetheless told anyone who would listen – in Labour HQ and the press corps – that Sunak would head to the country on 2 May, the same day as the local elections. He had been saying the same since the spring of 2022, when, in the aftermath of that year's local elections, he gave precisely that day and month to the party's NEC. On 23 January he again warned them that the date in question was 'exactly a hundred days away', adding: 'Opinion polls can move very quickly. Do not underestimate the chaos inside the Tory party, which is broken and divided. The PM may not be in control of events, and may have to call an election to pre-empt a leadership challenge.' Like a conspiracy theorist he marshalled every shred of evidence, however tenuous, in service of an argument that only he appeared to believe. Citing the timing of the budget for early March as opposed to its usual date in late March, increased Tory spending on digital advertisements and leaflets, expedited candidate selections and the cancellation of a House of Lords recess to rush through legislation that would allow the deportation of asylum seekers to Rwanda, McSweeney declared: 'The evidence all points to a 2 May polling day . . . 26 March is the last day on which a 2 May general election can be called and the likely date for calling it would be 17 or 18 March.'

He was wrong. Perhaps he knew he was wrong. But his frenzied prophecies served two aims. The first was to belittle Sunak as a bottler, just as Osborne and David Cameron had done when Gordon Brown shirked the opportunity to hold an early election in the autumn of 2007. The second was to accelerate Labour preparations for polling day, and to wield the 2 May date as a cudgel with which he could beat his internal opponents into submission. In strategy meetings they pored over the endless possibilities, all outside of Labour's control. One attendee recalls the long list: 'What if he launches on a Monday? What if he launches on a Tuesday, after cabinet? What if he launches on a Wednesday, before PMQs? What if he launches at midday? What if he launches at 6 p.m.? What if it's May 2? What if it's launched the day after the local elections? What if he doesn't go until December? . . . What if he opens up by conceding defeat? What if he launched it on the runway, with the first aeroplane off to Rwanda behind him, and GB News covering it like it was the moon landing? We'd sit and go through it. Does Keir go to this place, or does Keir go to that place? What does Keir say when he goes to Scotland? And we rewrote the grid, and we rewrote the grid, and we rewrote the grid.'

★

As Labour awaited Sunak's decision, its campaign machine sat idling – and the aides grew impatient. If McSweeney had a theory of elections it was this: a winning campaign was more than the sum of its parts, a losing campaign amounted to less than the sum of its parts. All of its components would have to work in perfect harmony: its candidates, communications, political attacks, digital advertising, and its voter targeting. If every section of the orchestra perfected its part of the score, the orchestra would swell, the crescendo resonating throughout the room, drowning out mistakes and achieving transcendence for its conductor.

By 2024, McSweeney's players had rehearsed themselves to death. Ridley had taken a sledgehammer to the methods Labour employed when it sent activists and leaflets to voters' doors. She ignored the old demographic categories the party had used to sort the electorate using data from Experian, the credit rating agency, as well as Deborah Mattinson's much-maligned hero voters. Instead she laser-targeted the party's marketing through direct mail and social media to ever more specific subsections of voters. Did they read red-top tabloids, or the *Guardian*? Did they not engage with the news at all, preferring Facebook and TikTok? Did they care for young children, or their parents? Which neighbourhood of a particular constituency did they call home? Ridley sought to transcend the analysis of ages and incomes that had tended to guide parties in approaching one group of voters or another. As a source familiar with the campaign's approach explains: 'You can't just put everybody in an economic bracket and conclude that's the way they think.' David Nelson, a Brisbane-born strategist with shaggy ginger hair who had delivered an election victory for the unshowy Labor leader Anthony Albanese in Australia two years previously, was recruited by McSweeney to refine the party's thinking. Nelson bemoaned the perennial habit of progressive parties 'to punch themselves in the dick'.

It was an approach perfected in victory after victory at by-elections: Wakefield, Stretford and Urmston, Chester, Selby and Ainsty, Mid-Bedfordshire, Kingswood, Wellingborough. Canvassing was no longer conducted via the antiquated Get Out the Vote system pioneered by Ian Mikardo, a long-dead left-winger, in 1945: where constituencies were deluged with activists and individual households approached again and again unless or until they confirmed how they would vote on polling day. Ridley's troops instead pursued voters using Contact Creator, an app that removed addresses once voters had been canvassed, and removed whole streets, neighbourhoods or even constituencies. Canvassers were instructed not merely to knock on doors and ask how a given member of the public would vote, but instead guide them along a 'persuasion pathway'. Rather than ask whether a household intended to back Labour before returning before polling day, activists sought to strike up personal relationships. First they would ask what issues motivated a given voter – not which party they planned to support. Phone numbers and email addresses would be sought to facilitate follow-up conversations. 'They would say, you know, my kids are at school, the NHS is a mess, or whatever – even something as small as: "My cat Barry's just had an operation." That information would go onto a piece of card that would be fed into our system, then, after a certain amount of time, you'd receive a letter from the candidate: "Thank you for taking the time to speak to us . . . PS. I hope your cat Barry's okay." Then the candidate would call you a couple of weeks later, and there'd be another follow-up letter. It was almost trying to trigger this Pavlovian response when they looked down the ballot paper: that's the guy who rang me. That's the guy who sent me that letter. Like it's triggering something warm inside them about this being a decent person that they can trust.' It worked. Since the local elections in 2022, the party had been fortified by data showing that, for every 1 per cent it increased its local contact rate, Labour increased its vote share by 0.17 per cent – translating to one vote for every six conversations. Yet voters whose phone numbers and emails had personally received multiple contacts from Starmer's candidates were 86 per cent more likely to vote Labour.

But who were those candidates? For two years, the impish Matthew Faulding, a friend and protégé of McSweeney and regular attendee of Roger Liddle's supper clubs, had worked at the Irishman's instruction to ensure they were anything but left wing. With his ageless face and boyish giggle, Faulding did not look much like a hatchet man. That, however, was the role he had come to play for McSweeney. With his salary paid by Waheed Alli, he had spent 2021 working to influence the outcome of the election for Len McCluskey's successor as Unite general secretary – disseminating criticism of the union's leadership so that McCluskey's heir-designate, Howard Beckett, did not win power and with it a bully pulpit to monster Starmer. Once that work was done, from late 2021 Faulding was set to work ensuring that Labour selected a slate of prospective MPs who could be relied upon to serve in government – especially a government with a slender parliamentary majority. At McSweeney's instruction he did not seek to parachute individual candidates into individual constituencies, but draw up shortlists strong enough so that any winner would be acceptable to the party leadership.

In July 2022, McSweeney had explained Faulding's work to the NEC. 'Being a Labour candidate says something about our party,' he said. 'A Labour rosette must be a mark of quality and an expression of what we stand for.' He went on, citing the cases of Imran Ahmad Khan, the Wakefield MP convicted of child sex abuse, and Chris Pincher, the minister whose drunken groping set in train Boris Johnson's then-recent downfall. 'The Tories didn't put safeguards in place. It was morally wrong, and it was politically disastrous – it brought down a prime minister. Rightly. I don't want to be sitting here in a few years' time with a Labour PM in trouble, knowing we have let him down.' Conscious of criticism that he was embarked on a factional purge, he added: 'Our approach to selections has not just been about stopping bad people. It is about opening up opportunities for members of all backgrounds to be candidates. Our mission has to be to put candidates forward for election who truly reflect the nation we represent. Increasing diversity and improving quality go hand in hand.'

Definitions of diversity varied. However keen they were to deny that their drive for quality amounted to a factional purge, that the Corbynites were the losers of the new regime could not be disputed. Of the hundreds of candidates selected in winnable seats, no more than five could have objectively been described as left-wingers by the standards of the Labour Party. Sam Tarry, the on-off partner of Angela Rayner, went as far as to refer his own party to the Metropolitan Police when he was deselected in his seat of Ilford South, alleging that its leadership had manipulated the software it used to tally votes and issued ballots in the name of dead members. With every selection came a new complaint of spurious exclusion: would-be candidates barred from longlists for liking social media posts from Nicola Sturgeon, the leader of the SNP, or retweeting the Green Party. Often the reality was more complex. One hopeful was blocked from standing after a trawl of their social media accounts by Faulding's colleague Megan McCann revealed they had once posted about 'Hitler fucking a seal', while another, who had stood in a high-profile contest in 2019, had regularly used the N-word online. Another accused Labour HQ of racism when they were excluded from a longlist, despite having revealed publicly that they had advised a Somalian warlord. Faulding was also a regular recipient of explicit photographs forwarded by whistleblowers. Trade unions aligned with the Corbynite left were quick to complain when their anointed candidates were excluded from longlists and shortlists; and just as quick to abandon the cause when Faulding revealed that he had seen a picture of said candidate's erect penis.

Those who did succeed included many councillors, corporate lobbyists, and luminaries from other walks of public life: doctors, scientists, and fourteen members of the armed forces. Labour officials also vetted at least one high-profile newspaper columnist, and Greg Jackson, the founder of Octopus Energy. With the exception of Douglas Alexander, the former cabinet minister and bagman to Gordon Brown, New Labour's exiled royalty were notably excluded. Ed Balls, the former shadow chancellor and intellectual architect of Brown's economic policy, had been interested in standing in Wakefield in its by-election of 2022. He had wanted to know that he was wanted, for Starmer to call and reassure him that his return to Parliament would not upset the balance of the shadow cabinet. Brown, still his proudest admirer, had made representations on his behalf. Yet Starmer never called. Focus groups suggested the voters of West Yorkshire saw Balls as a celebrity, the man from *Strictly Come Dancing*, and not the economist and politician who once wielded so much influence over Labour politics. For Starmer's office this was retribution. For years Blairites and Brownites, never unsure of themselves, had called their leader a loser. They had not cared who heard them. Now, with victory as good as guaranteed, others returned. David Miliband, eleven years out of Parliament but still lauded as Labour's lost leader, made clear he wished to stand. His appeals were ignored. There would be no special favours.

The chosen were primed early, locked into contracts that required them to commit to canvassing in neighbouring constituencies if their own seats were either too safe or too unrealistic a target. Those who declined, or otherwise erred with even minor indiscretions or unauthorised comments to the media, were called and upbraided: first by Faulding, then by McSweeney, who every week emailed candidates with a league table of their contacts with voters. None were immune to this totalitarian discipline. The father of one influential adviser to Starmer, fighting a vain campaign in one of the party's most unwinnable seats, was banned from accessing party data and had his public liability insurance withdrawn when he ignored instructions. Election addresses from candidates were written by February, ready for posting. Their first video messages to voters welcoming Sunak's decision to go to the country were recorded then, too. With the opinion polls still unmoving, all Labour could do was prepare for an election they had resolved to fight unlike any other before. In 2010, 2015, 2017 and 2019, broadsheet pundits had asked whether campaigns were now won and lost on social media. By 2024, there was no debate – at least in Labour HQ. 'Morgan's great insight,' said one pollster, 'is that digital is now comms, and comms is elite stakeholder management.' Starmer spent many hours courting the editors and proprietors of newspapers but his inner team occupied another plane of reality. Ridley and Tom Lillywhite, Labour's head of digital, wasted no time worrying about the broadsheet leader columns that may or may not endorse their candidate for prime minister. Instead they poured their resources into YouTube advertisements. 'I have never seen something so effective in getting a name out there,' said a leading adviser to the campaign. Fred Thomas, Labour's candidate for Plymouth Moor View, was eating in an Indian restaurant whose television was playing a YouTube playlist of Bollywood music when he was suddenly confronted with his own campaign video. Mike Tapp, the former Royal Marine standing in Dover, found himself followed down the street by children who recognised him from the advertisements that played between their favourite streams, the adviser recalled, 'like the fucking Pied Piper. He literally just had people following him because they recognised him.'

★

17 March, the day McSweeney had long insisted would mark the beginning of the campaign, passed without incident. There would be no general election on 2 May. The near-annihilation of the Conservatives in the local elections that went ahead the same day only solidified Westminster's consensus that Sunak would wait as long as possible before reckoning with the inevitable. Having lost 474 councillors and finished a distant third behind Labour and the Liberal Democrats, Tory MPs were preoccupied less by the question of whether Sunak could win a general election than whether he should be ousted before he could call one. They had lost everywhere. The two mayoralties Sunak had made a bellwether of his credibility gave the most damning and succinct account of his ruin. In the West Midlands, an energetic campaign from Akhmed Yakoob, a solicitor who – through the windows of his Lamborghini – accused Starmer of facilitating genocide, was not enough to prevent Labour unseating the well-regarded Andy Street by 1,508 votes. In the Tees Valley, home to Hartlepool – ground zero of the old Starmerism – the Tory Ben Houchen clung on, his share of the vote falling from 73 per cent to 54 per cent, but the swing against the Tories suggested Labour would win every one of their seats in the north-east of England. In Sunak's own manor of North Yorkshire, voters elected a Labour mayor, too.

The Voter of whom McSweeney, Ridley and their circle so reverently spoke was returning home. Everything Starmer said had been written to convince the older men who had voted for Brexit and Boris

Johnson, who had aged into mortgage-free retirement and loathed the Labour Party of Jeremy Corbyn; the self-respecting working mothers, struggling with the rising cost of living, who had voted Conservative in the past and felt badly let down by scandal and misrule under Johnson, Truss and Sunak. Starmer's march through the town halls of Tory England convinced the Irishman that they were listening. In switching directly from the Tories to Labour, these voters effectively counted double. Their defection insulated Labour against the loss of votes to its left, which McSweeney had always accepted as the price of change.

For Starmer it was all sweetly cathartic. When the same councils had been contested three years earlier, the electorate had rejected the Labour Party with such force that he considered resigning. Now the same voters – as well as electors in Blackpool South, where Labour easily won another by-election in a Tory seat – had told him he would soon be prime minister. The leader strained to appear humble but on Sunday 5 May he positively gloated in the pages of the *Observer*: 'Rishi Sunak might have been too scared to put his name on the ballot this week, but voters sent him a clear message in the local elections anyway. Across the country, people turned out to vote for change – from the manufacturing heartlands of Derby to industrial Redditch and Thurrock in Essex. In Aldershot, home of the British army, Labour won Rushmoor borough council, ending twenty-four years of Tory rule.' Of such unlikely gains from the Conservatives he was especially proud: 'When I set about changing the Labour Party, it was change with a purpose: putting the Labour Party back in the service of working people. Not just Labour voters, not just former Labour voters, not just 2019 switchers. No, my changed party is for anyone who loves this country, aspires for themselves and their family, and knows we can all do better than this.' This was a selective definition of 'anyone', wilfully blind to quickening currents of opinion his advisers were still failing to grasp. He did not mention, even obliquely, that Labour's share of the vote in wards where more than one in five residents identified as Muslim had fallen by 21 per cent. That seemed like a small caveat. Then, at least, the discontent was concentrated in areas where Labour otherwise weighed its votes. Even swings of that scale would not cost Starmer parliamentary seats. So went the logic and in those heady days it was irresistible. If this dress rehearsal for a general election had taught the Labour

leadership anything it was that they knew how to win votes from the
Conservative Party. Those were the votes that mattered most of all.

In one vital respect, the reality of McSweeney's strategy broke from
the rhetoric. In an address to parliamentary candidates shortly before
the locals, McSweeney had again invoked his favourite quote from Tim
Berners-Lee's appearance at the 2012 Olympics. Thanks to the collapse
of the Tory vote, 'this is for everyone' was no longer mere ambition
but psephological reality. What might have seemed vaulting ambition
was by the spring a mere acknowledgement of the changing electoral
map: in every region and nation, Labour had a poll lead. There were
no longer no-go areas for the party so roundly repudiated at the previous election.

McSweeney's approach to targeting was subtler. He never had any
intention to spread his resource equally across the country. Despite
Starmer's privately stated desire to eclipse even Tony Blair's 1997 landslide, 'everyone' was an indulgence he could not afford. He preferred
another watchword: 'efficiency': not just when it came to the distribution of resource, but voters too.

When the election came, he reasoned, the polls would tighten. He
was sure of that. Money, too, would have to be rationed, subject to
spending rules. And voters were far more volatile, far less bound by
party allegiance, than they had ever been. That meant Starmer would
have to reckon with the sorts of unforeseen events and vicissitudes of
public opinion that had destabilised Theresa May's seemingly unassailable campaign in 2017.

Above all, first past the post did not reward parties for gaining a
single vote more than necessary on a constituency level. There was no
prize for losing a seat by a more flattering margin either. The opposite was true: as McSweeney had told colleagues, even if people 'just
stopped' in areas in which Labour was destined for defeat, it would
be better than trying to gather extra votes. 'It's in those places that we
send out the data leaflet that ends up on Guido Fawkes [the muckraking right-wing blog], it's in those places that we get into legal troubles,
in those places where they're overusing the contact database system
and they're not doing anything.'

For that reason, there was no incentive to throw bad money after
good, still less good money after good. If data suggested that a seat

initially deemed marginal but just about winnable was regrettably lost – or for that matter a dead-cert victory – he was determined to ensure not a penny reached it in advertising or leaflets. After he forbade activists from canvassing in safe areas, the general committee of the Constituency Labour Party in Stockton, in the Tees Valley, passed a motion condemning him personally. He wore it as a badge of honour. 'I think they never forgave me,' he joked to friends. The underlying point he sought to make in a more conciliatory note to the CLP was that Britain's system prized efficiency. He had tired of podcasts in which Democratic Party activists had bemoaned Hillary Clinton's 2016 defeat, on the grounds that she had lost the electoral college but won the popular vote. 'Well,' he told activists, 'that was the system.' In a similar way, Britain's map of 650 seats demanded the party spread its support as strategically as possible.

The core question, then, was where to prioritise from the outset. To that, McSweeney had a simple answer: dozens of Leave-voting constituencies in England where Labour not only stood to gain votes, but Tories were poised to lose even more. The ideal dynamic was what McSweeney called the crocodile effect. The higher a constituency's Leave vote in 2016, the higher the swing to Labour – and the swing away from the Tories. It was the latter that would fall most precipitously. The effect, when rendered on a bar chart, resembled a crocodile's jaws preparing to consume its prey. He would welcome either motion. But when both took place at once, it would reduce the threshold for a majority and grant Starmer victories in seats which seemed deluged by votes for Johnson back in 2019; the sort that people said would stay Tory and lock Labour out of power for a decade.

After every round of local elections, he had presented the latest version of the 'crocodile' bar chart to the NEC and shadow cabinet, updating members on Labour's progress in pushing its vote up, while depressing the Tory vote as much as possible. In 2022, he had told the NEC that, among 804 wards that voted 50 per cent Leave, Labour increased its vote share by 5.8 per cent – while doing the same by only 1.9 per cent in Remain wards. The following year, the margin improved even more. If upsetting liberal strongholds was the price of demonstrating Starmer's credentials on the economy, law and order, and foreign policy in Leave territory, that was not even just the price of doing business – but a trend to be embraced. The Tories, for their part, were doing their self-destructive best at keeping their own vote below the waterline.

None of this gave way to complacency. At one meeting in 2024, McSweeney presented a slideshow revealing the latest positive improvement to the crocodile, asking the room what that meant in practice. Click. The next slide revealed a blank page. 'Nothing.' But at least Labour knew the terms on which it had to succeed.

As McSweeney prepared for the contest to come, Starmer was making his own luck. In the last week of April, Sunak's team briefed that he had just enjoyed one of his best weeks in office. Inflation had fallen to within a fraction of the Bank of England target rate. The prime minister had announced he would increase spending on defence to 2.5 per cent. For once, he looked as though he had rediscovered his mojo. Then, on 27 April, Dan Poulter, a Tory MP whose Central Suffolk constituency was the sort Labour now not wholly implausibly thought it might win, announced he was defecting. In a parting shot, the part-time NHS doctor said he could no longer look his colleagues in the health service in the eye and ask them to vote for Sunak.

At home in Lanarkshire, McSweeney turned to his wife, relishing darkly the prospect of the defection ruining the prime minister's Saturday. 'I just love the idea of Sunak now going home, saying: "Do you know what, I've had a good week."' Starmer would have recognised that little flash of sadism. For both men, politics was as much about competition as persuasion.

Poulter was not the last Conservative MP to defect. Sunak endured another bad day at Labour's hands eleven days later, when Natalie Elphicke of Dover crossed the floor at Prime Minister's Questions on 8 May. This stretched the bounds of plausibility and taste even for a leadership that now revelled in offending its own members and parliamentarians. Elphicke, the ex-wife and sometime character reference of Charlie, the disgraced MP for the same constituency, was considered distastefully right wing even by her fellow Tories. She spoke of little else but stopping the small boats of migrants that crossed the Channel and landed on the beaches of her Kent seat. If Labour politicians spoke of Elphicke at all, it was to criticise her, as Rachel Reeves did when she had told her to 'fuck off' after criticising the England footballer Marcus Rashford's political activism.

But after covert conversations with Sue Gray – keen to outdo McSweeney with a show of explosive political theatrics – and John Healey, the shadow defence secretary she had known in her past life as a housing expert, Elphicke agreed to defect and endorse Starmer's migration policy. Alan Campbell, the chief whip, cautioned that their new recruit would unsettle and upset the rest of the Parliamentary Labour Party. He was overruled. Even McSweeney, who occasionally exhibited a playground bully's appetite for inflicting pain on his Tory adversaries, was ambivalent.

MPs of colour in particular found the welcome Elphicke received from their leader nauseating. The palaeoconservatives of the Tory right now seemed more palatable to Starmer than anyone who had so much as once nodded in the direction of the Labour left. One shadow minister moaned to the *Guardian*: 'Are we welcoming Farage next week?' The one person who looked least uncomfortable was Starmer, who said in the chamber: 'What is the point of this failed government staggering on when the Tory MP for Dover, on the front line of the small-boats crisis, says the prime minister cannot be trusted with our borders?' His MPs asked what the point of the Labour Party was if it was prepared to go this far in pursuit of victory.

*

Sunak would not go long. Before the local elections he had already resolved to call a general election for 4 July – still, just about, the 'second half of the year'. His decision to do so on 24 May wrong-footed much of Westminster but not the Labour leadership.

In one of their long discussions at Waheed Alli's house on Meard Street months previously, Jonathan Ashworth had explained the coun-terintuitive case for Sunak going to the country much earlier than he needed to. 'If he's going to have a July election,' he said, 'it'll be that week when he calls it.' It would spare him the grisly backdrop of another summer of small boats crossing the English Channel, for one. 'We thought the best window of good news for the government was that week,' another attendee said. 'We were ready for that week.' When several of Sunak's confidants chose to bet on a July election, it had the effect of shortening the odds of an early poll. McSweeney spotted the shift and intuited what it meant. To his surprise, though, he discovered that the Conservatives had not bought advertising on news websites and billboards for the first week of the campaign. Labour snapped them up instead. By then Starmer's kitchen cabinet had alighted on a slogan, too. The thirteen formulations Starmer had cycled through in opposition – from 'New Management' to 'Security, Prosperity, Respect' via 'A Fairer, Greener Future' – gave way to a single word. The scope of Labour's offer to the country had narrowed with the electorate's wants and needs. Starmer would simply promise *Change*.

Wednesday 22 May proved to be a long day. Speculation that Downing Street was planning a major announcement began early. Yet even at Prime Minister's Questions, Sunak would not be drawn. Watching from the gallery were the bereaved families of the Manchester Arena bombing, in London to mark the seventh anniversary of the attack and discuss legislation that would force concert venues to improve their security measures. As they watched, the prime minister promised that it would pass before Parliament's summer recess. Yet he knew – the entire chamber knew – that a general election made that impossible.

'Speculation is rife,' growled Stephen Flynn, the Commons leader of the Scottish National Party, 'so I think the public deserve a clear answer to a simple question. Does the prime minister intend to call a summer general election, or is he *feart*?'

Sunak grinned. 'There is, Mr Speaker – spoiler alert! – there is going to be a general election in the second half of this year.'

He turned to Starmer. 'At that moment, the British people will in fact see the truth about the honourable gentleman opposite me, because that will be the choice at the next election, Mr Speaker – a party that is not able to say to the country what they would do, a party that would put at risk our hard-earned economic stability, or the Conservatives that are delivering a secure future for our United Kingdom.'

The leader of the Labour Party allowed himself to smirk. He knew the truth, careful though he was to pretend otherwise. Barring a miracle or a catastrophe, within six weeks he would be prime minister. The chamber emptied and Starmer crossed the river, making for Southwark and Labour HQ. He sought out McSweeney and Gray. Here, at last, he could be honest.

'We're ready,' he said. 'And this is going to be good.'

When Sunak called the election only a few hours after Prime Minister's Questions, it already looked lost. Just after 5 p.m. he strode onto a Downing Street overshadowed by black clouds.

'In the last five years our country has fought through the most challenging time since the Second World War,' he said. 'As I stand here as your prime minister, I can't help but reflect that my first proper introduction to you was just over four years ago. I stood behind one of the podiums upstairs in the building behind me.'

He went on, warning darkly of a dangerous world. 'Now I cannot and will not claim that we have got everything right. No government should. But I am proud of what we have achieved together, the bold actions we have taken, and I'm confident about what we can do in the future.'

It began to rain. Then it poured. Sodden, Sunak's suit hung heavy on his tiny frame. He gripped his lectern, as if struggling to bear the burden that grew with every agonising second.

'On 5 July, either Keir Starmer or I will be prime minister. He has shown time and time again that he will take the easy way out and do anything to get power.'

Into every pause burst an old, familiar song. Speakers on Whitehall, hurriedly positioned in the gates of No. 10 by the anti-Brexit campaigner Steve Bray, played the anthem that had heralded Labour's last landslide.

'*Walk your path . . . wear your shoes . . .*'

Sunak persevered, as if temporarily deaf. 'If he was happy to abandon all the promises he made to become Labour leader once he got the job, how can you know that he won't do exactly the same thing if he were to become prime minister?'

'*. . . talk like that, I'll be an angel and . . .*'

By now the prime minister was dripping. 'If you don't have the conviction to stick to anything you say, if you don't have the courage to tell people what you want to do, and if you don't have a plan, how can you possibly be trusted to lead our country, especially at this most uncertain of times?'

'*. . . thiiiiiiings . . . can only get better!*'

As Sunak finished his speech and retreated, oblivious to the laughter echoing across Westminster, Starmer stepped out onto a stage nearby.

Dry between two Union Flags, he smiled. Once the applause of activists subsided, he promised to be a different kind – a better kind – of prime minister.

'I am well aware of the cynicism people hold towards politicians at the moment,' he said, clenching his right fist and leaning physically into his own argument. 'But I came into politics late, having served our country as leader of the Crown Prosecution Service. And I helped the Police Service of Northern Ireland to gain the consent of all communities.'

The smile was gone, replaced by a face that betrayed no emotion. 'Service of our country is the reason – and the *only* reason – that I am standing here now, asking for your vote.'

He eyeballed the camera. 'I believe that with patience, determination and that commitment to service there is so much pride and potential we can unlock across our country. So – here it is – the future of the country, in your hands. On 4 July you have the choice. And together, we can stop the chaos. We can turn the page. We can start to rebuild Britain, and we can change our country.'

*

The next morning Starmer went to Gillingham, as McSweeney had long planned. Behind him on the pitch at Priestfield, the home ground of the town's undistinguished football team, activists waved placards that had been stashed in the nearby garage of a local party official, ready for the allotted day. Labour's chosen launch site was a measure of their expectations. In Gillingham, the Tories were defending a majority of 15,119. But for Labour, winning well would not only mean a reconstruction of the red wall felled by Boris Johnson in 2019. Labour would return, too, to seats it had lost under Blair and Brown – to unfashionable corners of counties like Kent, whose grey Medway towns like Gillingham would be the new heartland of Starmerism. And so the campaign began as it would continue, its words and imagery ruthlessly repetitive, for six weeks: with the leader of the opposition clutching a microphone at a lower-league football stadium, promising that a Labour government would end the chaos. There would, however, be one last burst of chaos under a Labour opposition.

On Tuesday 28 May, with Starmer's tour of the country proceeding smoothly, he declared in an interview with the *Daily Telegraph* that he found it easy to be ruthless. Later that day one of his advisers spoke to *The Times*. Starmer's response to the fallout from this briefing would undermine his earlier claim entirely.

The conversation between said adviser and *The Times* turned to the confirmation of Labour's candidates by the NEC, due exactly a week later. For months rumours had circulated that the leader's office would use that meeting to dispense summary justice to their project's enemies and liabilities: the Corbynites who might in time rebel against a Labour government, and the alleged bullies and sex pests who might disgrace it. They would be barred from standing, their vacancies – and in many cases enviably safe seats – filled by candidates from central casting. That speculation was misplaced. But the future of one left-winger remained deliberately unresolved. What, asked *The Times*, would happen to Diane Abbott?

For thirteen months the first black woman ever elected to the House of Commons had sat, like her old friend Jeremy Corbyn, as an independent MP. In April 2023 she had written a letter to the *Observer* that suggested Jews did not experience racism but mere prejudice akin to the teasing of children with ginger hair. Her words were hastily retracted, their publication blamed on a clerical error, but still Abbott lost the Labour whip. For more than a year she was exiled, despite her apology – and Starmer's surreal willingness to laud her in public. On 13 March, two days after the publication of Frank Hester's racist rant, the leader had praised Abbott as a 'trailblazer' at Prime Minister's Questions. He challenged Sunak to return Hester's millions, so egregious was his offence against Abbott – who stood forty-six times in the hope of contributing to a discussion that was largely about her, only to be ignored by the Speaker. Yet even then Starmer refused to return Abbott to Labour membership. If suspended, of course, she would not be eligible for selection as a candidate.

'Diane,' Starmer had said to her that day in the Commons chamber, 'let me know if there's anything I can do for you.'

'You can restore the whip,' she said.

'I said let me know if there's anything I can do for you.'

'Restore the whip.'

In public, questions about her future were met with procedural waffle and pro forma lines about the independence of Labour's disciplinary process from Starmer and the shadow cabinet. They said an investigation into her letter was still ongoing when it had, in fact, concluded in December 2023 with a formal warning about her conduct and a mandatory course of anti-racism training. She accepted both sanctions but persisted in her public criticism of the Labour leadership. That partly explained Starmer's refusal to lift her suspension despite the conclusion of inquiries into her case. Her 33,000 majority in Hackney North and Stoke Newington was also coveted by friends of the leadership. Luke Akehurst, the Corbynite scourge and McSweeney enforcer who had warmed to the idea of continuing his service to the leadership in Parliament, was one potential replacement. So too Torsten Bell, the economist who had worked for Ed Miliband. To Abbott's ongoing distress, everything was clouded with ambiguity. But with the campaign now underway and the final deadline fast approaching, Starmer's aides felt empowered to speak with greater candour.

'Diane will not be a candidate,' the adviser – one of the few people who could say such things authoritatively – told *The Times*. She was, they said, a trailblazer. Starmer wanted to see Abbott retire from politics 'with dignity'. The previous Friday, 24 May, he had claimed the 'process' over her future would end 'reasonably soon'. The process, his adviser explained, was this: Abbott would be restored to the whip and allowed to end her thirty-seven years in Parliament as a Labour MP. Given her advancing years and failing health, the adviser insisted that it was in Abbott's interests – and the interests of her constituents – to take that offer. 'But it's up to Diane.' Perhaps 'the people around her', imagined in the leader's office as a claque of hot-headed Corbynites who had made Abbott a pawn in their own factional campaign against Starmer, were dripping poison into her ear: pushing her to take one last defiant stand against the leader who had humiliated her.

That, the aide said, would be a fatal mistake. In that scenario, Abbott would not be allowed to stand. With the source's express agreement, just after 6 p.m. that evening – having received no denial from Labour HQ – *The Times* published the story that would overshadow Starmer's campaign for the best part of a week. The headline read: 'Diane Abbott to be banned from standing for Labour.' It expressed, indelicately and unambiguously, the ultimate position of Starmer's team. They hoped Abbott would retire of her own volition. If she did not, their intention was to make the decision for her. Statements deferring to the primacy of the NEC meant nothing: by then it was their politburo, the majority of its members content to do as they were told.

Still unreported was the fact that earlier that day, Abbott's suspension had been lifted after she had a meeting with Luke Sullivan, Starmer's political director. For months Sue Gray and the whips had been conducting clandestine negotiations with Shami Chakrabarti, the Labour peer, former shadow cabinet minister and close friend of Abbott. Whether it was intended as a precursor to a dignified retirement remains a matter of some debate. Abbott herself now says she had no intention of agreeing to a deal that felt like blackmail. Some friends gently suggested she bow out gracefully, others urged her to resist. But in spelling out so coldly the terms of her departure, and allowing them to be published in *The Times*, the adviser in Starmer's inner circle had denied her a choice. The source's colleagues reacted furiously, disputing in their own briefings that Abbott had been banned. In reality they were quibbling over which aspect of the deal to emphasise. Nobody expected her to stand. They merely hoped the situation could be resolved amicably first.

29 May was all about Abbott. At 7.34 a.m. she texted Joe Pike of the BBC and said: 'Although the whip has been restored, I am banned from standing as a Labour candidate.' Two hours later, at 9.54 a.m., came a plaintive follow-up: 'Naturally I am delighted to have the Labour whip restored and to be a member of the PLP. Thank you to all those who supported me along the way. I will be campaigning for a Labour victory. But I am very dismayed that numerous reports suggest I have been barred as a candidate.' One source familiar with the negotiations over Abbott's future claimed at this juncture that she had decided to remain a Labour MP so as to generate extra publicity for her upcoming memoir. Starmer, surrounded by student nurses in Worcester, strained to sound as if he was offering a denial. Asked by the BBC to give a simple yes or no answer to the question of whether Abbott had been banned, he said: 'No, that's not true. No decision has been taken to bar Diane Abbott. The process that we were going through ended with the restoration of the whip the other day, so she's a member of the Parliamentary Labour Party and no decision has been taken barring her.' Who, then, would be the Labour candidate in Hackney North? Here his words betrayed the essential truth of what his adviser had said: the leadership hoped, however it may have happened, that it would

not be Abbott. 'It's ultimately a decision for the National Executive Committee on all candidates,' Starmer said. 'There will be a decision in due course, but they haven't taken that decision, though. Stories this morning were wrong, factually inaccurate. She has not been banned or barred from standing.' However emphatic it sounded, its implied meaning hung on the omission of the word 'yet'.

His words convinced nobody, not least the left – who believed, with some justification, that Abbott was seen by the leadership as a Corbynite nuisance first and a 'trailblazer' second. As Jess Barnard, a left-wing member of the NEC, said that day: 'It is clear for everyone to see that they are running the clock down to the general election and they are using the NEC as cover to run an alternative candidate.' The abiding mood across the Labour Party was deep discomfort. Momentum condemned Starmer as 'appalling, vindictive and cruel'. John McTernan, the former adviser to Tony Blair, said whoever was responsible for the suggestion she had been banned from standing should 'hang their head in shame . . . It's not for the Labour Party to ban a woman with Diane Abbott's record to stand for the Labour Party if that's what she wishes to do.' Ed Balls added: 'She has been a pioneering Labour woman MP going back over forty years. On what basis could they possibly say, "but we've now decided you can't stand" other than because of totally factional reasons?' On that morning's broadcast round, even a squirming Wes Streeting said he was 'not particularly' comfortable with Abbott's treatment.

Growing suspicions of a purge only deepened that evening, when two more candidates of the left were summarily blocked from standing in seats that had been theirs for years. Lloyd Russell-Moyle, Corbynite MP for Brighton Kemptown since 2017, was suspended after a complaint of sexual harassment. In Chingford and Woodford Green, the leftist economist Faiza Shaheen was summoned onto a Zoom call with three members of the NEC, confronted with a list of posts she had liked on Twitter, and told she would not be allowed to stand. The purge appeared to have begun, with Abbott – the best-known survivor of the party Starmer insisted he had changed out of existence – its ultimate victim.

It fell to Angela Rayner to try to save Abbott with an intervention one figure on the campaign acidly described as 'stupid, duplicitous, or a bit of both'. Only a handful knew Starmer was by then looking for an off-ramp, and had himself sanctioned it. To the *Guardian*, on the morning of 30 May, the deputy leader proclaimed: 'If Diane wanted to stand again, I don't see any reason why she can't.' She denied that there was any concerted campaign against candidates of the left. Hours later, Russell-Moyle's vacant seat was filled by Starmer's old adviser Chris Ward.

Several other fellow travellers and favourites of the leadership – including Mark Ferguson, ever useful to McSweeney as Unison's political officer, and Josh Simons of Labour Together – were imposed as candidates elsewhere by the NEC. Yet another power play proscribed by the Ten Pledges of 2020 was now accepted practice for Keir Starmer's changed Labour Party. As this chosen few were announced as Labour candidates, Abbott stood on the steps of Hackney Town Hall, thronged by supporters. Her cry of defiance bled into deafening cheers: 'By any means possible . . . I WILL BE THE CANDIDATE FOR HACKNEY NORTH AND STOKE NEWINGTON!' The heavy implication was that she would run against the Labour Party if needs must. Barely two miles away in Finsbury Park, Jeremy Corbyn was asked at the launch of his own campaign against Starmer whether Abbott, too, was the victim of a purge of left-wingers and freethinkers. 'It looks like it,' he said.

But Abbott survived. Having concluded that a national debate on the finer points of his party's rulebook and accusations of racism were not the soundtrack of a winning campaign, Starmer said in Scotland on 31 May: 'Diane Abbott was elected in . . . in . . . 1987, the first black woman MP. She's been a trailblazer. She has . . . carved a path for other people to come into politics and public life. The whip has obviously been restored to her now, and she's free to go forward as a Labour candidate.' This disavowal of the ruthlessness with which the leadership usually approached the left was in its own way ruthless. Abbott remained highly unpopular with the voters Labour was pursuing and some in the party believed such voters would approve of her exile, unlike the Labour aristocracy and commentariat. But they could no longer afford distraction. As a senior campaign official explains: 'It wasn't a problem with the voters, but it was clouding our messaging.'

Together this seventy-two hours of bitter briefing, howling headlines and contradictory statements became a Rorschach test for the Labour Party. To some it proved the enduring power of Rayner in spite

of attempts to emasculate her. To others, particularly on the left, it was
a welcome reminder that the right of the party was not yet omnipotent. For those closest to Starmer himself, it had yanked back the
curtain on the dysfunctionality that still reigned over Labour's commanding heights despite the likelihood of victory. Starmer had been
wrong-footed twice: first by his own aides, and then by Abbott. Even
advisers loyal to his leadership questioned his political agility.

Said one of the Abbott debacle: 'Keir's instinct was to see her go . . .
[but] Keir doesn't lead, and everyone circles around each other. *The
Times* was semi-right in saying Diane would be barred. That was when
HQ understood from the chief whip that she was agreeing to stand
down . . . she changed her mind and conveniently blamed the *Times*
"briefing". The decision-making process was too iterative, because it
was separate from the overall MP retirement strategy, which was managed by Morgan. The Diane part of it was managed by Luke, Sue, and
the chief whip. It wasn't integrated.'

However unsatisfactory his inner circle found the process and outcome, Starmer's surrender to Abbott at least allowed the campaign
to move on. Holed up with Pat McFadden in a windowless room at
Labour HQ they called 'The Cell', McSweeney did not agonise over
the mistakes of that first week. Parties that lingered over mistakes and
distracted themselves by apportioning blame were parties that blew up
their own election campaigns. However intense his dislike of the Corbynites, he thought it best to move on. The first week of the campaign
had been one great rolling disaster for the Labour Party. The second
was more representative of what was to come. Abbott's survival alone
had not rewritten McSweeney's script, in which Keir Starmer acted
out the process of change with ever-decreasing degrees of subtlety.
On 3 June he went to Bury, flanked by the fourteen military veterans
selected as Labour candidates, and said without hesitation that he was
willing to use nuclear weapons. As with so many of his campaign
announcements, Starmer had in fact said such a thing before. Two
months earlier the same vow had splashed the usually hostile *Daily
Mail*, a coup that so delighted McSweeney that he had spent much of
12 April waving a copy of the newspaper in the faces of colleagues and
declaring: 'If I could marry a front page, it would be this one.'

But as far as the election result was concerned, Starmer's speech
paled in significance to another made in Westminster that same

morning. Grinning wildly, Nigel Farage had skipped onto a stage at Church House next to Westminster Abbey, sacked the leader of Reform UK, appointed himself, and announced his candidacy in the faded Essex resort town of Clacton. Making clear his mission was to bury the Conservatives for good, he barked: 'They are split down the middle on policy, and frankly right now they don't stand for a damn thing! So our aim in this election is to get many, many millions of votes. I'm talking far more votes than Ukip got back in 2015.' If parties of the radical right could sweep the board on the continent, as they had done in the previous month's elections to the European Parliament, then so could he. 'I promise you,' he said, 'something is happening out there.'

Indeed it was. Farage was right about what he would do to the Tory vote. From that moment all Sunak could do was await the blood-bath. Only the leader of the Labour Party gave them fleeting hope. Isaac Levido, the bearded Australian at the helm of the Conservative campaign, thought the mere fact of an election in July – before the economy and opinion polls had had time to recover – was mad. But he also believed Starmer was Labour's great liability. Its leader's mis-firing performance in the first head-to-head debates with Sunak on 4 June suggested Levido's judgement was something more than self-delusion. The Tories had demanded six debates, one for each week of the campaign.

Starmer, who had spent many long afternoons in a hired television studio in south London under the supervision of Paul Ovenden and Stuart Ingham, preparing for the clashes to come, agreed to only two. The reason for the difference became clear in Salford that evening. Had it not been for Waheed Alli, who again protested against anything that might be inferred by wealthy donors as an attack on their integrity, Starmer would have spoken aggressively and at length about Sunak's work for a hedge fund blamed for the collapse of the Royal Bank of Scotland during the 2008 financial crisis.

Gray shared Alli's instincts. In December she had told advisers to the shadow cabinet she did not believe in political attack. One recalls: 'A month into her new role, she tore into the proposed attack stories about the Tory government's misuse of taxpayers' money, and demanded they be struck out of the plan for Christmas. Expensive corporate awaydays – gone. A personal-chauffeur contract for a minister – gone.

Civil Service waste – gone. She kept saying: "We should not be criticising the Tories for exactly the same things we'll be doing in government ourselves." It smacked of political naivete, and complacency about the level of public anger at the Tories.'

And so Sunak's professional past was mentioned only in passing at the debate, almost apologetically, and instead it was Sunak who seized the initiative. Again and again he suggested that Labour had a secret plan to hike taxes to the tune of £2,000 for every working family in Britain.

For a man reckoning with political death, Sunak was unnaturally buoyant. 'Labour will raise your taxes! It's in their DNA! Your work, your car, your pension: Labour. Will. Tax. It!'

Starmer struggled. However much he had improved as a public speaker since 2020, he was a performer who relied almost exclusively on the scripted word. Improvisation was beyond him. Save for a passing cry of 'absolute garbage', he did not rebut the accusation, nor the £2,000 number the Tories had instructed Treasury civil servants to calculate by selectively interpreting Labour policy. Instead he babbled unintelligibly about the process by which Sunak had come up with it.

He left the stage depressed, and glowered in the green room. His wife tried and failed to rally his spirits. Always his harshest critic, always wounded by failure, Starmer knew instinctively that he injected the only viable attack the Conservatives had left with disruptive energy. Once more it fell to his advisers to right his wrongs. As the debate ended, Paul Ovenden hastily wrote a new script: Labour had no plans to raise taxes by £2,000, and Sunak had lied. It worked. Rachel Reeves spent the following day repeating ad nauseam Labour's opposition to any rise in income tax, National Insurance or VAT. BBC reporters spent it reading the contents of a letter from the Treasury to Darren Jones, in which they disavowed Sunak's numbers. Starmer, however, had read that letter before the debate, but had not seen fit to mention it.

It would not matter. Precious little Starmer said those weeks did. Yet, all but unsaid outside tiny circles of trust within Labour HQ, the old question recurred: why can't he just get it right the first time?

★

Those fleeting doubts were too treacherous to entertain for long. For one thing, the voter research overseen by David Nelson – Labour's own Australian pollster – showed voters increasingly trusted Starmer. Nor, after the blow inflicted during the debate, was Sunak able to press the advantage. 'They landed the tax attack successfully,' said another senior official. 'We had to get out of that quite quickly. So we put pressure on them very fast.' Sunak was in no position to fight. He hit hard, flailing wildly – McSweeney's favourite analogy was that of the punch-drunk boxer on the ropes, swinging desperately in the hope of redemption – but succeeded only in knocking himself out.

For every mistake Starmer made, he was outbid spectacularly by his opponent. Forty-eight hours on from the debate, on 6 June, both men went to Normandy to mark the eightieth anniversary of the D-Day landings. That morning the few dozen remaining British centenarians met with the King for a memorial service; that afternoon the leaders of the western world convened on Omaha Beach, where the Americans had begun the liberation of Europe. As an opposition leader, Starmer, by rights, ought not to have been there. Only after the wily intercession of David Lammy, who spied a political opportunity, did the French extend an invitation. Starmer shook hands with the president of Ukraine and looked as if he were already prime minister. By then Sunak had already left, early and unannounced, for an interview with ITV in London – his first opportunity to respond to Labour's claims of dishonesty. For a leader whose campaign had begun with a promise to reintroduce national service, it was a suicidal misjudgement. For that McSweeney's circle took credit. 'Sunak had to leave D-Day,' one said, 'to go on ITV and say he wasn't a liar.'

So catastrophic was the backlash that some wondered whether Sunak would still be leader of the Conservative Party on 4 July. At 7.45 a.m. the following morning he apologised: 'The last thing I want is for the commemorations to be overshadowed by politics . . . After the conclusion of the British event in Normandy, I returned back to the UK. On reflection, it was a mistake not to stay in France longer – and I apologise.' He was reduced to denials that no Conservative leader had ever had to make before: 'I care deeply about veterans.' On neither count was it convincing. Sunak's mistake overshadowed everything, so much so that Labour's manifesto already seemed surplus to requirements. Abbott and the debate increasingly looked like exceptions that proved the rule of the campaign. Sunak could not fulfil any obligation without making yet another mistake. For Starmer, the routine passed without incident. Even his critics conspired to prove whatever point McSweeney wished to make on any given day. Even Unite's refusal on 7 June to endorse the manifesto was neither a humiliation nor a crisis, as it might have been in 2020 or 2021. After all those angry hours on the phone with Len McCluskey and Howard Beckett, it now felt like the sweetest victory of all.

Events seemed to follow an unwritten but irresistible rule. Any Labour announcement of any significance would fall on the same day as another calamity for the Conservatives. 13 June, the day of Labour's manifesto launch, was not dominated by analysis of the threadbare policy offer contained within its 142 pages, behind a cover that paid homage to Tony Blair's manifesto in 1997. By then Starmer had almost become redundant as Sunak sought to prove the old adage that elections were lost by governments rather than won by oppositions. Tory spokespeople were forced to spend the day condemning their colleagues for betting on the election date rather than critiquing Labour's policies after Sunak's closest parliamentary aide, Craig Williams, had been exposed by the *Guardian* the previous evening.

How voters felt about it all was proved at 8 p.m., when *The Times* published a YouGov poll that showed Reform UK ahead of the Conservatives for the first time. Britain, like the Labour Party, had not fallen in love with Keir Starmer: on 12 June he had been irritated when his robotic tribute to his father's profession of toolmaker was met with gales of laughter from the audience of a Sky News debate in Grimsby. What mattered more was that those same people had come to loathe the Conservative Party, so much so that it now languished in third place on 18 per cent of the vote. The question that had weighed so heavily on the leader's office in 2023 – *why us?* – receded entirely from view. Paul Ovenden's attack team may have landed 150 stories about Conservative misdeeds in the newspapers over the course of the campaign, forcing Sunak to disown several of his own candidates, but the die was cast.

*

Sue Gray sat far away from McSweeney, at the end of a long corridor at the opposite end of Labour HQ. There, with Nick Boles and Waheed

Alli, she planned for what would come after the victory. 'I used to sit in Keir's office,' said Boles, 'and work on this ever-evolving architecture for the delivery of the missions, on appointments to No. 10, the structures in No. 10.' He sought counsel from Jonathan Powell, who, like Gray, had left the Civil Service to work for a Labour leader heading for a landslide victory.

There was a strange unreality to their discussions. As was noted by some of the nonplussed staff Boles strode past most mornings, here was a former Conservative minister drawing up the blueprint for the first Labour government in a generation, his work a mystery to the people running its campaign. He admits now that this incongruous sight led to 'the odd raised eyebrow' in an office that by then was high on tribalism. 'I couldn't quite believe it,' he said. 'There I was: fifty-eight years old, a failed politician, and I was producing all the organograms on PowerPoint. Fuck knows – I literally must be the least well-qualified person to do PowerPoint slides . . . but because it was all quite secret squirrel, I had to do them myself.'

So stark was the divide between Gray and McSweeney that the staff assigned to lead Labour's preparations for government worked from a separate building – an office block a short walk away in Waterloo, decorated, incongruously, with scenes from *Alice in Wonderland*. Even Gray herself was an infrequent visitor. Key decisions on how Labour would spend its first hundred days in government were taken late, as Boles freely admits: 'We suddenly realised that there wasn't going to be much time before we delivered a King's Speech – we were trying to work out what legislation was ready. It was really the first time that anybody had started thinking about that stuff, quite rightly, and obviously the snap election had made that more acute.'

He nonetheless insists that they were prepared. 'I gained confidence from the process that Sue went through and led Keir through on the missions, delivery, and the structures of the centre. Because, bluntly, it was a far more elaborate process than I ever went through when I was doing a similar job in opposition for the Tories.' Starmer himself watched from afar, content, as ever, to delegate the mechanics of leadership to other people. 'He had this sort of interrogative process – a sort of iterative process – that I thought was very impressive,' Boles adds. 'He was genuinely engaging with the material that was sent to him . . . we ended up, not only in a relatively short space of time but with relatively little of his time, deciding some quite complicated things. We ended up with a much better set of proposals than they had been right at the start.'

Other advisers beg to differ. One, in Rayner's team, said policies so often cited as evidence of their intention to hit the ground running – in the case of her brief, a pledge to build 1.5 million homes a year – were made with an alarming lack of consultation before or after they were announced. Said another official: 'There was no grid for the first hundred days, the one thing [Gray] was expected to be working on while everyone else was busy on the campaign. There was barely a single story about how the culture of government was being changed. And of course, a total lack of foresight or awareness about the criticism that would be coming down the pipe over crony appointments, wealthy donors, freebies . . . all the stuff she assumed would be OK because the Tories had done the same thing.'

But the campaign was anything but complicated, and nor, draining though it was, was the leader's life in those six weeks. In planes, trains and hired cars he travelled from town to town, from pitch to pitch, repeating the same lines about his changed Labour Party. In fleeting moments his advisers watched him lost in thought, staring silently through windows, reckoning with the change that awaited him. Every Sunday he returned not to Kentish Town but Alli's Covent Garden penthouse, given freely to the Starmer family to protect his children from waiting journalists as his son sat his GCSEs. All he could do was wait.

*

As June ground on, nothing rescued Sunak. By the end of the month he no longer spoke of winning, but pleaded with voters to spare the country the fate of a Labour supermajority. That was what the polls suggested Britain would get, and from The Cell it appeared those polls were right. Tony Blair wrote to Hollie Ridley in his barely legible script, praising her as the 'field marshal' of Labour's ground forces. As polling day approached it had come to resemble an unstoppable, all-conquering army.

They dared to dream of victory in seats that other parties considered their birthright: Dundee, the spiritual capital of the SNP's campaign for

Scottish independence, Folkestone and Hythe, a true-blue citadel of
Toryism on the Kent coast. Activists who dared deviate from the plan
were banished like heretics during the Spanish Inquisition. 'Members
in Sevenoaks spoke to 600-odd people one Saturday,' another campaign
source recalls. 'We told them that wasn't good enough. There were
winnable seats all around them. And yet they're in fucking Sevenoaks.
They refused to comply. So we just shut everything off.'

The faintest hints of discontent were heard mostly in the seats
with large numbers of British Muslims. McSweeney had argued they
were safe regardless of discontent towards Labour's position on Gaza.
Labour candidates were in more danger than he had initially foreseen.
In Leicester South, the shadow cabinet minister Jon Ashworth – who
spent much of the campaign evangelising for Starmer in broadcast studios, and playing up to his role as campaign mascot by shredding copies
of the Tory manifesto for giggling journalists – was chased through
the streets by demonstrators who accused Labour of facilitating genocide in Gaza, on one occasion seeking refuge in a vicarage. Voters told
him that Starmer was a puppet of the Israeli government. In Dewsbury and Batley, Heather Iqbal – a former aide to Rachel Reeves – was
stalked by a car whose loudhailer declared that, as the wife of a white
man, she was not a true Muslim. Despite their majorities stretching
comfortably into the tens of thousands, the Birmingham seats of Shabana Mahmood and Jess Phillips were deluged with Labour activists.
Wes Streeting, who had privately dismissed the independent campaign
against him as a 'crank bingo' of disaffected left-wingers who had quit
the Labour Party, began to fear for his own seat. In Islington North,
thousands of activists travelled hundreds of miles to knock doors on
behalf of Jeremy Corbyn.

In the New Labour years, Peter Mandelson had breezily declared
that the white working class 'had nowhere else to go'. Two decades on,
they were returning to Labour. But Muslim voters – and voters of the
left – were finding a new outlet for the politics that Starmer so publicly
denounced.

*

Come the week of the election those seats felt a world away from
Labour HQ. McSweeney and David Nelson took the view that to talk

about Labour's problems with Muslim voters would only encourage their critics on the left. Said a colleague familiar with their thinking: 'It was always understood to be a problem . . . but it was clearly not in anyone's interests to talk about it. And that was the problem.'

Tentatively, they began to embrace their own victory instead. Blair paid a royal visit, signing copies of the manifesto and praising the leader he had once doubted so profoundly. 'Labour has changed,' he said, 'from the point of extinction. That's down to Keir's leadership. But it's also down to all of you.' Starmer and the shadow cabinet thought that too generous. They believed it was really down to one man. On the evening of 3 July, Pat McFadden gathered the few staff that had been spared canvassing duties in marginal seats and remained in Southwark. 'You know,' he said, 'it's not fair to single people out. But the Labour Party is so lucky to have had Morgan directing this campaign.'

On election day, 4 July, Ridley's army of activists spoke to 1 million voters. That morning the *Sun* endorsed the Labour Party for the first time since 2005. But as his party's reach grew beyond recognition, Starmer's world shrunk. That evening he retreated, with his immediate family and closest aides, to Waheed Alli's penthouse. Caterers had been hired for the occasion. McSweeney awaited 10 p.m. and with it the exit poll at HQ. As the hour approached he stood almost inconspicuous amid the throng. Over the Thames, Starmer held his wife and children tightly. The first of Big Ben's chimes rang out. The BBC reported the first proof that another future really was possible.

LAB   CON

410   131

'And as Big Ben strikes ten, the exit poll is predicting a Labour landslide,' said Laura Kuenssberg, her voice barely audible at Labour HQ as the party took leave of its senses.

'Sir Keir Starmer will become prime minister with a majority of around 170 seats,' said Clive Myrie.

McSweeney grabbed Ridley. He punched the air, screaming. The head of press Sophie Nazemi, a couple of metres in front of him, wept with joy.

Kuenssberg went on, each toll of the bell reverberating through the crowd. 'The exit poll predicts that Labour will have captured 410 seats,

adding 209. It suggests the Conservatives will have lost 241 MPs, landing on 131.'

The Irishman gave Ridley a kiss. Then he kissed her husband too.

In Covent Garden, a deathly hush fell over the room.

'Well,' said Matthew Doyle, with the same bone-dry detachment
known to the nation's journalists. 'We've won, then.'

★

At Labour HQ, the chimes never stopped. With every declaration over-
joyed officials fought over the bell that was stationed by Ridley's field
team, rung to herald the arrival of each MP. With every Labour gain it
rang. It rang when Fred Thomas unseated Johnny Mercer, the most pugi-
listic of any Tory minister, in Plymouth Moor View. It rang for minutes
when Liv Bailey, Starmer's head of domestic policy, won in Reading
West. It rang when Jacob Rees-Mogg lost in North East Somerset, and
when Penny Mordaunt, the favourite for the Conservative leadership,
fell in Portsmouth North. It rang over and over again when Liz Truss,
the prime minister they all had to thank, lost in South West Norfolk – a
seat to which Labour had devoted neither attention nor resources.

As dawn approached, faint shadows were cast over their celebrations. Turnout was low. Labour's mandate would be gossamer-thin.
Thangam Debbonaire, the shadow culture secretary, lost badly to the
Greens. Ashworth lost to a pro-Gaza independent, as did three other
Labour candidates. Corbyn won. Wes Streeting barely won, with a
majority of little more than 500. Jess Phillips was booed and barracked
as she railed against the intimidation she had suffered at the hands of
George Galloway's activists. Shabana Mahmood, returned by a slender
margin of only 3,000 votes, said much the same. Clutching a leather
folder, once more looking like the lawyer he remained, Keir Starmer
stood smiling as he learned that his own majority had been cut to 9,000
by the left-wing journalist Andrew Feinstein.

But they allowed themselves to forget it all. From Alli's penthouse Starmer's inner circle walked through central London and
over the Thames to Tate Modern, where celebrations began in earnest. The leader arrived at around 3.30 a.m. The crowd rose up to
meet him. He roamed the gallery's cold halls as they echoed with
disbelieving and delighted cries of a changed Labour Party. 'What a

team,' Starmer said, like a grinning robot, as he clutched the hands of exhausted staff.

McSweeney could not speak. He laughed instead.

At 5 a.m., the man who would soon be prime minister spoke. His voice cracked.

'We did it!'

His right hand, so often a clenched fist, now cut through the air as if slicing a joint of meat. Behind him fluttered crosses of St Andrew, as if in tribute to the thirty-six MPs he had won in Scotland.

'You campaigned for it! You fought for it! You voted for it! And now it has arrived. Change begins now!'

They cheered again.

'And it feels good, I have to be honest. Four and a half years of work changing the party. This is what it is for.'

*

Seven hours later, the sun shone on Downing Street. Along its pavement stood everyone who meant something to Keir Starmer. His car arrived from Buckingham Palace and he stepped out, Vic at his side, as only the fourth leader of the Labour Party to have ever won a parliamentary majority.

At every step he reached out to touch the past he was leaving behind. The lawyers he had known so well: Patrick Stevens, Parvais Jabbar. Old friends from Kentish Town, like Martin Plaut. The political thugs who had remade his party, like Matt Pound. Those who had spent long years exposing his opponents for lawbreaking and corruption: Paul Ovenden, like a cat burglar in a black polo-neck jumper, and his deputy Megan McCann. The Jewish activists he had addressed with his first words as leader, four years earlier: Mike Katz, Adam Langleben. Ben Nunn and the boys who had pulled him back from the brink after Hartlepool. Carolyn Harris, who had told him nine years earlier that she would make him leader of the Labour Party, her hair dyed an electric purple. His own children, besuited and awkward. Vic's father, Bernard, with tears in his eyes.

One man was missing.

Starmer smiled again. The shoulders, tensed for four years, now relaxed. In a new burden of responsibility he had found his release from the politics he despised. 'I have just returned from Buckingham Palace, where I accepted an invitation from His Majesty the King to form the next government of this great nation.'

He paid tribute to Sunak, and then began to bury him.

The rhythm of his speech began to slow, as if unconsciously resisting what would come next. 'So . . . with respect . . . and humility . . . I invite you all . . . to join this government . . . of service . . . in the mission . . . of national . . . renewal. Our work is urgent . . . and we begin it . . . today.'

With that he turned away from the cameras that had pursued him for six weeks. He held his wife tightly and waved the campaign good-bye. He walked through the black door of No. 10, and into government, into another future, into the office he had vowed to make his own nine years earlier.

The civil servants applauded him, as they applauded every new inhabitant of Downing Street. McSweeney stood, in the only good suit he owned, between Waheed Alli and Starmer's speechwriter Alan Lockey, clapping bashfully. For once he looked like just another adviser.

The Irishman watched his candidate take his first steps into government. Starmer walked on and stopped. The first thing he did as prime minister was shake Morgan McSweeney's hand.

Epilogue: 100 Days

With the general election won there was only one place left for Morgan McSweeney to go. In 2021, as his colleagues plumbed grim depths of despair after Hartlepool, he had scrawled four words on a whiteboard: 'CHANGE LABOUR. CHANGE BRITAIN.' The first half of the mantra was now fulfilled, but it would be for others to begin the work of government. That weekend the Irishman left Westminster for the old country. He had missed his son's birthday, and Cork's hurlers were playing Limerick in the semi-final of the All-Ireland Championship. That was where he needed to be. On Sunday 7 July, as Keir Starmer prepared to fly to Washington to address Britain's Nato allies as prime minister, McSweeney was in Dublin, watching the game. Cork won.

In Downing Street, victory felt more elusive. Two days earlier, on the morning Starmer had gone to accept the King's invitation to form the first Labour government in fourteen years, McSweeney had arrived at the Cabinet Office to accept his appointment as the prime minister's head of strategy. After two hours of sleep he was fortified with coffee and a bacon sandwich by civil servants and told that he would take shelter with Starmer in the event of a nuclear strike on Britain. Beside McSweeney was Tom Lillywhite, the Camden boy who had run Labour's digital campaign. The Irishman gestured to his colleague and asked: 'What about him?' No such luck. Even now, with the election over, the new prime minister wanted McSweeney closer than the rest. When Armageddon came, Starmer would need McSweeney to explain it.

*

It came quickly. Labour had a long time to prepare for government. However distrustful its leadership had been of opinion polls, their lead over the Conservatives had endured for nearly two years. But on 5 July, as they each came to Downing Street to be formally appointed, new ministers still struggled to believe that power now belonged to them. With every arrival in the Cabinet Room the same phrases pricked the ears of officials. 'I can't believe we're here,' several said, as if office could still be snatched away. From others: 'We weren't supposed to get here in one term.' Senior civil servants in Downing Street and the Cabinet Office had dismissed Labour's old line of 'no complacency' as a verbal antidote against tempting fate. But no – many in this new cabinet really seemed to have believed it.

Overnight their lives had changed more profoundly than some were willing to accept. McSweeney embraced Labour's new ministers as they left their meetings with Starmer and Simon Case, the cabinet secretary – each smile a little vindication of two long decades of hard and often dirty work. The sight of Liz Kendall emerging from the Cabinet Room as work and pensions secretary made him happiest: here they were, nine years on from the leadership election they had together lost so conclusively to Jeremy Corbyn, running a Labour government at last. After a little while McSweeney's phone rang.

'What's happening?' asked his old friend Steve Reed, as he had so many times in Lambeth.

'We've just won the general election,' said McSweeney. 'Where are you, Steve, anyway? Shouldn't you be in Downing Street?'

Reed was still at home, in a pair of Hawaiian shorts. For so many of the cabinet, government would demand sharp adjustment to a new way of working and living. So too the new staff in Downing Street. That evening more than a dozen filed into the room to listen to Starmer take a congratulatory call from President Biden. There was no reason why they should have done. Those who wished to listen could easily have dialled in from their own offices. Starmer, said one person present, was clearly irritated that his first act of diplomacy had become a spectator sport. Not for the first time, he said nothing.

Only a handful had felt the burdens of ministerial office and the awesome responsibilities of power before. That, of course, was why their leader had hired Sue Gray.

★

The election had not put an end to the tension that made Starmer's inner circle such an unhappy place for so much of 2024. Instead it had made that tension manageable. For McSweeney's campaigners it was a welcome reprieve. On 17 April, little more than a month before Rishi Sunak went to the country, Starmer had for the first time acknowledged the prevailing narrative now attached to his advisers by the press: that Gray was locked in mortal combat with the boys' club. In a speech at Labour HQ he vowed to sack anyone, 'whoever they are', whom he caught criticising their colleagues to the newspapers. 'I know why they brief against people in this room,' he said. 'They do it because they don't like the change we've brought to this party, and they do it to damage everything we've worked for.' Starmer insisted there was no such thing as 'the boys' or 'the lads'. To speak in such terms was 'an insult to the brilliant women . . . who do brilliant work every day'.

There was no point pretending that the leader's court was not divided. Division was how they had come to understand themselves. They were either with Sue or they were not. Gray herself knew it acutely. To a succession of colleagues she read a long list of advisers she suspected of briefing and leaking against her, headed by McSweeney and Matthew Doyle. Neither of them ever did so – their interactions were a study in fastidious courtesy – but Gray felt alone and besieged. The election did not so much release this barely functional team from division as formalise it. For the duration of the campaign there would at least be a contractual basis for the split. McSweeney would win the election. Gray would prepare for what came afterwards. Each had their strengths and expertise. Undistracted by any battle for supremacy, they might finally do their jobs as well as Starmer told himself they could. The transition to government, when it came, would surely be seamless.

Labour's preparations for government gave every appearance of methodical planning and discipline. There were the official access talks, mediated by the Civil Service, which had begun in February. Starmer and Gray met the cabinet secretary at the London office of Waheed Alli and a property made available by David Sainsbury, another multi-millionaire donor; the likely cabinet met senior officials from the departments they would one day run. While the election campaign was run from party headquarters in Southwark, where Gray did most

of her work, a team of policy officials and external consultants sec-
onded from the private sector worked from a satellite office set aside
for preparing for government, a short walk away in Waterloo. Alli, despite the concerns of colleagues wary of the conflict of interests that
might arise from his other role corralling corporate money behind the
Labour Party, busied himself vetting appointees for ministerial office
and other government posts. He kept a chart with empty slots for every
position in every government department. They called it Operation
Integrity. The impression was of frenetic activity on several fronts.

In the week before polling day staff who had been busy on the campaign came abruptly to the opposite conclusion. Labour's preparations
for government primarily existed in Sue Gray's mind. 'She quickly
became a bottleneck,' complains one senior party staffer whose work
cut across both her domain and that of McSweeney. 'She held a lot
of information, very simply, and wouldn't share.' If the chief of staff
looked busy, then her colleagues concluded she was busy doing nothing. Said one, who worked with her at close quarters: 'She loved the
fact that she was the gatekeeper, and she loved it at a personal level.
Basically, it was pretty narcissistic and bizarre behaviour.' On the evening of the first election debate, on 4 June, Gray neither accompanied
Starmer to Salford nor joined a team of advisers working on media
responses from a room in HQ. Instead she sat apart from harried colleagues, drinking wine.

Mounting bafflement at her behaviour was not confined to her own
party, either. As access talks between individual departments and their
new ministers proceeded at pace, civil servants grilling the chief of
staff were increasingly concerned that they had made no headway on
the biggest questions that would face a Starmer administration. One
senior official recalls now: 'We were putting a lot of information in,
as is perfectly normal. How do you form the government? What's the
role of the prime minister constitutionally? What does the prime minister's diary look like? How does Downing Street work? How is No.
10 set up? How are we going to do mission-led government? We were
doing bucketloads of work, and it felt like it was all going into a black
hole. Certainly, as we got into the election period, we said: we really
should be talking about cabinet appointments. We really should be
talking about a plan for the first hundred days and the first fortnight.

We were constantly being told: "Oh yeah, yeah, we'll come on to that." And it never happened.'

These were questions to which any number of Starmer's advisers had coherent and developed answers. Yet the civil servants with whom they would soon be working – most notably Simon Case – were never given the opportunity to put them to anyone but Gray. Whitehall expected to meet not only the chief of staff but the other advisers who together formed the backbone of Starmer's operation in opposition and would in time surely do so in government: Stuart Ingham, the policy chief, communications director Matthew Doyle, and head of office Jill Cuthbertson. They never did. Even McSweeney was excluded from deputations to the Cabinet Office. That senior official adds: 'Normally, during access talks, you would expect to sit down with the key figures who were going to form the senior leadership team of Downing Street, to start forming relationships and talking about issues. But it was quite odd. Despite lots of pushing, Sue always kept it to herself.'

None of this was known to Starmer's team until it was too late. Despite their reservations, they had trusted Gray. She did not trust them. The leader himself may have dismissed the briefings against the men in his team as media noise, but neither he nor the newspapers knew just how destabilising it was. Gray trained her crosshairs on Doyle, Ingham, and Luke Sullivan, Starmer's political director. When Doyle first read reports that Gray wished to sack him – in the reliably hostile *Mail on Sunday*, with the hashtag #JustStopDoyle, months before the election – he asked her whether it was true. She claimed it was not. Still, talk persisted that he was doomed. Ditto Ingham, who refused to give Alli sight of policy papers. The rumours *were* true. Gray was convinced of neither man's competence. She repeatedly told Starmer to sack them both. He refused, asking her to reserve judgement until Christmas. Sullivan, meanwhile, was blamed without evidence for every unhelpful leak.

Come the week of the election, none knew whether they would have jobs in a Labour government. Senior civil servants tried in vain to establish who exactly would be working for the prime minister and received no clarity from Gray. Said one: 'We were trying to work out why, despite endless invitations and prompting, we weren't getting a sense of who this team was going to be. But then, what was Sue saying to us about all of this? I think she thought they weren't very good. I think she thought that they didn't know how government worked. She thought they weren't disciplined enough, ordered enough, and experienced enough. Certainly in the last week or so, it was pretty obvious to us that she was in the process of trying to persuade Keir that Stuart couldn't be head of the policy unit and Matthew shouldn't be director of comms.'

The Irishman alone knew he was safe. From Starmer he had extracted the assurance that he would answer only to the prime minister, not Gray, as the head of a political strategy unit. She would have oversight of everything else. The separation of powers that had proven so dysfunctional in opposition would be hardwired into the structures of the new government. However grateful personally he was for a cordon sanitaire around Gray, McSweeney knew it would be a disaster for Downing Street. He scrawled the organogram on a whiteboard for the benefit of his intimates in The Cell, the windowless meeting room in Labour HQ where he toiled with Pat McFadden. 'This,' he said, gesturing wildly at the proposed power structure, 'is nuts.' At this point McSweeney's confidants warned that the frosted glass separating them from a room of staffers that hung on his every word only obscured half of his scribblings.

They need not have worried. Most of their colleagues agreed. It was indeed 'nuts', they thought, that only days from power they did not know which jobs – if any – they would do in No. 10. Only at 4 p.m. on polling day were Matthew Doyle and his deputies, Steph Driver and Sophie Nazemi, told they would work for the prime minister. Only then did they discover that the grid of announcements for Starmer's first days and weeks in office was empty. They assumed it had been Gray's responsibility. Gray was adamant that it belonged to Doyle and McSweeney. For that reason Doyle's planning for the first hundred days began that evening. He hastily planned a Downing Street press conference and tour of the four nations of the United Kingdom. Others were not so lucky. Hours before the exit poll told them they had won, Gray told several staff that they were sacked. Some, like Sullivan, would wait weeks before they knew for sure.

Aspiring ministers were forced to endure a Damoclean existence at Gray's pleasure too. On 5 July it appeared that Starmer would make good on the easiest promise any opposition leader can make: to *do politics differently*. The appointments of two ministers from outside the Labour family suggested his words amounted to more than a slogan. James Timpson, the penal reformer whose family chain of cobblers employed ex-convicts and made him an acceptable face of *noblesse oblige* capitalism to the centre left, became the prisons minister. Patrick Vallance, chief scientific adviser during the pandemic – who, secretly, had advised Gray and Labour Together on their preparations for government – joined the government as a junior minister too. It would be weeks, however, before every post was filled. That afternoon Gray had surprised officials who expected a fully formed plan for appointments by wondering aloud of one former cabinet minister she thought might like a job: 'Does anyone have Jacqui Smith's number?' Of Alan Campbell, the despairing chief whip, one Downing Street adviser said: 'Sue made Alan lose the will to live.'

He was not alone. Emily Thornberry, the longest-serving member of the shadow cabinet, learned that she would not be attorney general when she watched Richard Hermer, Starmer's friend from the bar, stride up Downing Street on television. Thornberry did not know that her leader had concluded six months earlier that Hermer would have the job, but she did expect to be given another position in government. To Gray she had sent a list of potential alternatives – including a junior role at the Home Office working on the fraud policy she had drawn up in opposition – and in return she was given assurances that the prime minister would consider them. He never did, because Gray never showed him the list. Indeed, Starmer appeared disinterested in most ministerial appointments full stop, leaving Gray and Campbell to make calls that were customarily made by the prime minister. Instead, smarting, Thornberry announced that she would play no part in a Labour government, and was encouraged instead to stand for the chairmanship of Parliament's foreign affairs committee with the tacit support of Downing Street – though her election, when it came, was very nearly scotched by Angela Rayner's covert organising for the Corbynite candidate, Dan Carden.

On 8 July, after Thornberry revealed she was 'saddened and surprised' to have been overlooked for ministerial office, she spoke to Starmer. To her shock, he seemed to have no idea that she had been willing to serve below cabinet rank. 'I'm so pleased we've been able to sort this out,' he said.

Across Whitehall and Downing Street, Starmer's people began to ask the same question of the prime minister: did Gray tell this guy anything?

*

In his first days as prime minister Starmer appeared at ease with power. Unlike his cabinet he was never overawed by his new surroundings. He relaxed perceptibly. So often in opposition he had looked tense, frustrated, wound up. Now he spoke fluently, as if running the country was the easiest thing in the world. In opposition he had often left the Commons chamber in a state of sweary agitation. Johnson's schoolboy jokes, Truss's incompetence, Sunak's evasions: all had mortally offended the dignity of a man who told himself that he could do it better. In victory, Parliament at last felt like home. Starmer was surrounded by proof that his jealous pride had not been misplaced. He said as much to Deborah Mattinson, newly departed as his director of strategy, shortly after the election. Over tea in No. 10 he told her that the number of new Labour MPs must be seen to be believed. With boyish enthusiasm he urged her to come in for Prime Minister's Questions. 'Just listen to the noise.'

For his advisers, the noise was unbearable. Office was supposed to bring an end to the battle of wills and clashes of personality that had so unsettled the leadership of the Labour Party. Within days it had exposed them anew. McSweeney and his strategy team arrived in Downing Street with the expectation that they had licence to think boldly and creatively about the challenges they would face as a social democratic government that had won a mandate in an era of rising populism. Even his friends had questioned whether he cared for government. They wondered aloud whether he would come to Downing Street at all. One confidant had told *The Times* in October: 'Morgan would be happier winning the third congressional district in Kentucky for some obscure Democrat than trying to pass a budget.' Those who knew Starmer best knew the leader would be invigorated by victory. Those who knew McSweeney best wondered whether he might be bored, or silently self-aware that the demands of statecraft might be beyond him.

As they speculated, McSweeney was thinking deeply about power. He sought advice most days from the elders of New Labour: Peter

Mandelson, Alan Milburn, Sally Morgan. One confidence was more surprising. Over dinner at the south London home of a mutual friend, specially convened so the two men could talk freely, McSweeney met Michael Gove – then still serving in Sunak's cabinet.

'You do know,' said Gove, by way of introduction, 'I'm going to have to say all sorts of terrible things about Keir during the campaign.'

'That's okay,' said McSweeney.

As they ate, Gove offered him a crash course in government. Notionally the two men were rivals. But they shared a dislike of the conservatism and caution they had diagnosed in Britain's ruling class. Gove told McSweeney how ministers succeeded, the 'revealed preferences' of the individual permanent secretaries with whom Labour would soon be working, and the impediments they might face to radical policy. McSweeney spoke, as he would more widely as polling day approached, of his desire to lead an 'insurgent govern-ment'. To the rest of the table the subtext was clear: even if Starmer was a model technocrat, the Irishman would infuse his administra-tion with the confrontational, iconoclastic politics he had pursued in opposition.

Starmer would not have been opposed to such conversations. Polit-ics, after all, was what he had appointed McSweeney to do. Theirs was an unspoken understanding: McSweeney had licence to go to lengths the leader never would, provided he produced results.

In government, he discovered that Gray was not of the same mind.

★

McSweeney, never one for luxury, chose as the office he would share with his deputy Paul Ovenden one of No. 10's less salubrious rooms. It was, according to another colleague who squeezed inside its grubby walls in their first week in the job, 'disgusting'. They were some distance away from the prime minister and when political director Vidhya Alakeson and her deputy Henna Shah were present it made for a tight squeeze. Before long they moved, at Ovenden's suggestion, to a roomier office elsewhere in the building – itself a little further away from Starmer. A fortnight later this mundane logistical decision would be briefed to the *Sun* and cited as evidence that Gray was seeking to marginalise McSweeney.

That story was not quite right. Gray's supporters, for their part, suggest McSweeney could have sat as close to the prime minister as he wanted. That he chose to work at a degree's remove suggested to them that he still conceived of his project as something distinct and independent from the government led by Keir Starmer. The whole truth of his arrival in No. 10, wherever he sat, was altogether more extraordinary. Wherever it was they worked, Gray appeared to have no intention of allowing McSweeney and his team to do anything of consequence. In his negotiations with Starmer, the Irishman had agreed that he and other staff in his team would be employed by the Labour Party and not the British state – having heeded Tony Blair's warning that severing ties with the political team at party head-quarters would be a mistake. This, as Simon Case knew, was hardly unusual. Under Conservative governments, senior party staff came and went from Downing Street as a matter of course. McSweeney had been appointed by the prime minister to head up the polit-ical strategy of the government. Whatever the small print of his contractual arrangement, officials had every expectation that they would and should deal with him as they would any other adviser to Starmer.

Gray begged to differ. In their first full week in post, McSweeney received a visit from Darren Tierney, head of propriety and ethics at the Cabinet Office. His job had once been Gray's and soon it was clear to her political colleagues that he was acting under her instructions. Shifting miserably, Tierney told McSweeney that under no circum-stances would he be given access to government papers without a minister or special adviser present. Nor, as an employee of the Labour Party, would he be given a No. 10 email address. Gray, speaking as if her hands were tied, said repeatedly: 'We've got to be really careful.' So careful, in fact, that she forbade the political team from using Downing Street's teabags.

Not for the first time, Gray's motives – beyond the acquisition of power for its own sake – were impossible for her colleagues to divine. Cabinet ministers found themselves irritated by her propensity to promise the world and deliver nothing. The Labour Party had been under the collective impression that it had poached a master admin-istrator from the deep state. Instead, disorganisation reigned. Even advisers in Downing Street who had been disinclined to believe their more fatalistic colleagues grew alarmed by 'the amount of stuff she was just doing through her mobile phone, texting people directly, not getting a proper readout . . . it was just remarkable, this mismatch. All of the reasons we thought she'd be good – systems, process – having been a bit chaotic in opposition at times, we thought: here's Sue, she's the propriety and ethics person, the thorough person. And yet that didn't end up being our experience of working with her.'

It took only nine days for such questions to be asked publicly. On 14 July, *The Times* revealed that Gray had alienated Downing Street colleagues and cabinet ministers with an energetic lobbying campaign for £310 million in government funding for the renovation of Casement Park, a derelict Gaelic games stadium in west Belfast that had been improbably earmarked as a host venue for football's 2028 European Championships. The project, long controversial, was opposed by local residents and – privately – the Gaelic Athletic Association to whom it belonged. Reluctant though they were to say it publicly, almost everyone in Northern Ireland beyond Sinn Féin was opposed. The stadium was too expensive and there was too little time to make it fit for 2028. But to the confusion and concern of colleagues, Gray pushed hard for the money. To *The Times*, alarmed colleagues and ministers on Whitehall and in Stormont confided their concerns that she was seeking to subvert the cabinet. Later, on a visit to Belfast, Starmer described the allegations as 'nonsense', before siding with those who disagreed with Gray. Sympathetic colleagues insisted the briefings were born of anti-Irish prejudice and that her only motivation was paying due respect to a devolved government that had made the stadium its passion project.

In the immediate term the leak succeeded only in darkening the atmosphere of resentment and suspicion that cast a heavy pall over Downing Street. Gray commissioned a leak inquiry, which failed to identify the culprit. Those who had already taken against her could now cite concrete evidence that her idiosyncratic style was disrupting the business of government.

The seemingly untrammelled power of the chief of staff made for a sharp contrast with the troubles of the man who had bent an entire opposition to his will. McSweeney took his own emasculation up with Simon Case. The cabinet secretary struggled to believe what he heard. In turn he instructed Tierney to clarify that the prime minister's head of strategy was, in fact, allowed access to government papers and tea-bags. Wearily, Case said: 'Can you go and tell them how things actually work, please?'

In those first hundred days nothing seemed to work. The timing of his victory meant Starmer spent much of his first weeks in office abroad. Then, on 29 July, the murder of three girls in Southport by Axel Rudakubana, the seventeen-year-old son of Rwandan refugees, sparked race riots across the country. The prime minister rejected entreaties from cabinet ministers to address the political motivation behind the violence – namely rising dissatisfaction with high levels of immigration – and set to work as he had done when England's cities last rioted in 2011. Trials were held within days of arrests and those found guilty were given long prison sentences. 'He was adamant,' said a senior official, 'that this had to be treated as a criminal justice prob-lem. There were a lot of other people who wanted to talk about the root causes – but he was adamant. "We're not getting into excuses, these people are breaking the law, we need a criminal justice response, and it needs to be tough and it needs to be swift." That was revealing for us about the kind of man he is.'

Less than twenty-four hours after the killings, Starmer went to Southport, briefly, and laid a wreath. As the father of a young daugh-ter he had been badly shaken by events. Upon his return to London, his advisers discussed a second trip to thank the emergency services and meet victims in hospital. Police liaison officers warned an advance party from No. 10 that the families were not ready. Gray, fortified by conversations with Merseyside's chief constable and Steve Rotheram, its mayor, urged Starmer to visit. Late on 1 August, hours before his scheduled departure, his team were still divided. Unusually, they told him so. When Starmer's inner circle met in Downing Street that night, Steph Driver, his deputy communications chief, told him that she felt a visit would be too risky – but that colleagues had been unable to agree on a plan. Gray pushed and pushed. She trusted Labour's mayors more than its adviser class. Starmer relented. Even national tragedy had become subsumed by office politics.

The visit went ahead without controversy. Come the end of the first hundred days, Starmer's apparently decisive response to the killings was one of the few successes for which he won meaningful praise. Yet in other respects the new government sought to contrive an image of helplessness. In the hours before the full and horrifying details of the Southport attack became clear, Rachel Reeves had given a gloomy speech in which she claimed to have discovered a £22-billion black hole in the public finances. Masochistically, the chancellor said she had no option but to abandon one of New Labour's proudest innovations – the winter fuel allowance for pensioners. If Reeves had conceived of the plan before the election, neither she, Starmer nor Gray had conveyed the details to officials overseeing the transition in No. 10. It was bad enough that it seriously unnerved Starmer's new MPs, unused to public opprobrium, and reinvigorated a parliamentary left that was supposed to have been consigned to irrelevance by the arrival of 200 leadership loyalists. Soon the public would draw an unedifying contrast between the meanness of this new Labour Treasury and the largesse which ministers were enjoying privately.

*

Nobody knew why Waheed Alli had been given a pass to Downing Street. Not even Alli was sure. Unrestricted access to the corridors of power is usually given only to special advisers and civil servants. But in the days after Starmer's victory, Gray made sure he could come and go as he pleased. Those who knew of the arrangement were surprised and discomfited. Yes, Alli was a Labour peer of nearly three decades' standing. He had become close to – and valued by – the prime minister and his family. Sceptical though others were of his contributions, there was no question that he had been central to Gray's preparations for government, such as they could be said to have existed. After a fortnight he returned the pass, having used it to attend a handful of meetings and organise a party for election volunteers and donors in No. 10's rose garden.

Those were the facts, many of which were arguably defensible. Yet those who had already believed Alli blurred the lines between his role as Starmer's fundraiser-in-chief and political counsellor were uneasy. He had, after all, donated £500,000 to the prime minister personally. Absurd though it may have sounded to the leadership of the Labour Party – most of whom had known Alli for years – there was only one way in which his special treatment was likely to be perceived. Starmer, the man who had promised zero tolerance on any hint of impropriety, was vulnerable to accusations that he had given special favours to his most generous donor.

So it proved. On 25 August, the splash headline on the front page of the *Sunday Times* read: 'No. 10 pass for Labour donor who gave £500,000.' When the paper's inquiries were received by Downing Street earlier that week, Gray instructed the press office to say nothing. The crucial, mitigating detail – that Alli's pass had been temporary, and, indeed, had since been returned – was never published. Starmer's spinners were expressly forbidden from saying who had authorised the pass in the first place. 'It's a mystery,' a Downing Street adviser said at the time, 'to everyone apart from Waheed and the person who gave it to him.'

Over the subsequent days and weeks the prime minister and cabinet were deluged with accusations of cronyism as the scale of Alli's generosity attracted serious scrutiny for the first time. The following Sunday, the same newspaper revealed he had bought thousands of pounds' worth of designer dresses for Victoria Starmer – the receipt of which was declared late by her husband. He had gifted Angela Rayner a free stay at his New York penthouse with her sometime partner, Sam Tarry, whose presence was not declared under Parliament's stringent anti-sleaze rules either. Bridget Phillipson, the education secretary, had hosted a fortieth birthday party funded by £10,000 of Alli's money, too. Taken together with countless other corporate freebies, not least the football and concert tickets so often enjoyed by Starmer, Labour's self-styled government of service was hoisted on its own petard.

In opposition, Alli had been advised against donating to the prime minister personally. When it came to the reputational damage other donors might inflict he was always fastidious, hyper-cautious. 'I used to get quite pissed off with him,' said another Labour staffer entrusted with raising money from wealthy businesspeople. 'His appetite for risk just didn't exist. We turned down multiple seven-figure donations. If he thought there was any whiff to the money, he would not touch it.' Yet those who know Alli best concluded he longed to be indispensable to a Labour leader who paid him the respect his contemporaries never had. Said one veteran of the Blair and Brown governments of his treatment: 'Waheed was used terribly.' But Starmer was always grateful, and Alli was only too happy to be useful. Sue made him feel special.

Alli ignored officials at Labour HQ – among them the ever-vigilant Jill Cuthbertson – who suggested he donate money for the Starmers' suits, dresses and glasses to the party instead, to avoid the unedifying and unavoidable declarations in parliamentary registers that revealed a millionaire donor was clothing the leader of the opposition. To one he snapped: 'I'll do what I want with my money.'

However spurious they thought some of the accusations, most of Starmer's advisers saw the need to respond quickly and decisively. Yet the prime minister was seldom there to advise. When he was not abroad he was busy. When he was accessible he was defensive, as he always was when his wife and children found themselves under the unforgiving glare of the British media. Gray's own hostility to the newspapers that by now devoted daily coverage to her clashes with colleagues was no help either. In meetings she railed against 'scumbag journalists'. Even discussions on matters entirely unrelated to the media invariably began or ended with soliloquies in which the chief of staff said, to nobody in particular, that the stories about her were unfair.

She drew sustenance from her ever-decreasing circle of trust. At one meeting an adviser peered over Gray's shoulder as she texted. 'If you stay strong,' Waheed Alli had written, his words sprinkled with heart emojis, 'you will win.'

*

Nobody – not even the prime minister – seemed capable of gripping events. Generation after generation of Downing Street advisers and the leaders they serve have left government and complained that the administrative centre of the British government is curiously underpowered. Most seek to redress it. Gray, her colleagues contend, did not.

The first sign was her pathological aversion to the concept of the deputy. 'I don't believe in deputy titles,' she told other advisers to the prime minister who quickly found themselves overburdened by the demands of government. That much had already been proven by her hostility to Angela Rayner during access talks. Civil servants expected, given her title, to make good on proposals by Rayner's team to set up a dedicated office for the deputy prime minister. Gray refused.

'Sue was busy taking Angela off lists,' said an official. 'Angela had made clear she was expecting an office for the deputy prime minister, and we were working that up. And then Sue said: "No, no. We're not going to do that."'

For good measure, she denied Rayner a seat on the National Security Council, too. Once in government, Gray's colleagues began to suspect, once again, that she was seeking to concentrate power in her hands alone. 'She refused to have a deputy chief of staff,' a senior aide to Starmer recalls. 'Why would you not want a deputy chief of staff? Why wouldn't you want other people sharing the load with you? Why wouldn't you want to build up the team?'

Gray did, in fact, have designs on team-building. As August ground on there remained a gaping vacancy at the heart of the prime minister's Downing Street team. More important than any other civil servant in No. 10 is the principal private secretary to the prime minister: second only in significance to the cabinet secretary, together with the private secretary to the monarch it forms one corner of the 'golden triangle' of officials who oversee the British constitution's centres of power. Indeed, that significance appeared lost on Starmer. When Gray proposed to appoint Dan Gieve, a career civil servant alongside whom she had worked closely under the Tory minister Francis Maude, Starmer agreed to appoint him without an interview. McSweeney interviewed Gieve with Gray and raised no objections. It was on the strength of these two recommendations and not on his own judgement that the prime minister proposed to appoint the civil servant who would run Downing Street on his behalf.

Case was again alarmed by her intentions. During access talks he had told Gray that the incumbent PPS, Elizabeth Perelman, would leave after the election. Together with Whitehall's permanent secretaries he had compiled a longlist of the Civil Service's rising stars. Gieve, the head of the government's Office for Investment and a former chief of staff to the lobbyist Roland Rudd, was – in the words of another official involved in the process – 'not anywhere near it'. Case told Gray and Starmer in no uncertain terms that Gieve could not be appointed and insisted the prime minister see a broader range of candidates. The process had been all wrong. Special advisers were prohibited from appointing civil servants, for one. Secondly, Gieve could not match the qualifications of the civil servants earmarked for promotion by their Whitehall seniors. Thirdly, his primary qualification appeared to be his friendship with Gray.

New Labour grandees made their displeasure similarly clear to Starmer and McSweeney. In the Brexit years Gieve had clashed with Alastair Campbell and Peter Mandelson, both of whom had their own hotlines to Downing Street, as Rudd had sought to wrest control of the campaign for a second referendum out of their hands. Having showed only passing interest in the appointment, the prime minister found himself confronted with furious complaints: Gieve was too disorganised. Gieve was too close to senior Tories. Gieve was unqualified. His many friends and admirers in Westminster watched in dismay as his reputation was traduced, and blamed Gray.

On Thursday 29 August, when the row made its way to the front page of *The Times*, Gray reluctantly told Case that she had decided to 'pause' the recruitment process. By this juncture Gieve had already been informed he had the job and was due to start the following day.

'Isn't Dan supposed to be starting tomorrow?' Case asked Starmer's team. 'Has anybody told Dan that he's not starting tomorrow?'

'Oh no,' said Gray. 'I've texted him, but I haven't spoken to him.'

This, one confidant to the prime minister recalls now, was the moment 'the scales fell from Keir's eyes'. Starmer hated briefing and bitching. He had reflexively ignored every hostile headline about his chief of staff, the reports of feuds that bore little resemblance to the constructive working relationship she appeared to have with McSweeney. 'Sue and Morgan went out of their way to look collegiate and cooperative,' said one Downing Street adviser who worked with both closely.

But now Starmer knew it wasn't working.

★

Ask any politician or civil servant who has worked with Sue Gray to name her strengths and on one point there is unanimity. A government colleague puts it like this: 'She is one of the most effective relationship-builders I've ever come across, brilliant at winning people's trust and confidence, incredibly good at building a sympathetic environment, and making people feel that she's on their side.' It was that skillset, for so long lacking in Starmer's hard-nosed inner team, that had so enamoured Gray to the shadow cabinet in opposition. In Downing Street she worked herself ragged, as she had always done in her fifty years in public service. The advisers to whom she was closest recall walking past her desk – an ever more lonely place as the first hundred days went from bad to worse – and reminding her to eat, such was her dedication to the job which she kept reading she was making such a mess of. Yet to others in government, she seemed allergic to the candour that colleagues had always valued.

The row that proved to be her ultimate undoing began within days of Labour taking office. Under the Conservatives, even the lowliest cabinet ministers had come to rely on sprawling teams of special advisers. Gray, for years the overseer of ministerial staffing at the Cabinet Office, would not have that again. There was no reason for secretaries of state to appoint teams of five or six advisers when a decade ago they had made do with two or three. She imposed strict limits on who could be hired. Several nonplussed ministers, including the justice secretary Shabana Mahmood, found they could not appoint the policy specialists they had intended to.

Those who were hired were presented with contracts that concealed an unwelcome surprise. Not only were many expected to take considerable pay cuts – which some, proud to at last be working for a Labour government, were reluctantly willing to do – they expressly ruled out the prospect of future increases. Furious, most spads refused to sign their contracts. Before long, the first Labour government in more than a decade faced the unique indignity of its own advisers – corralled by two aides to the deputy prime minister – unionising for better pay and conditions. To their faces, Gray always denied oversight. She, however, was the only political appointee on the Civil Service committee that decided their pay.

What ensued appeared to undermine Gray's analysis of the politics of the Starmer court: that the boys were in charge, and that only she would pay women the respect they were owed. Before long, two of Downing Street's leading female advisers discovered they were receiving much lower salaries than men of the same rank. They inquired with officials responsible for human resources, who told them, suggestively, that their hands were tied by the remuneration committee.

That, of course, was code for Gray. Knowing she was responsible, they sought help from the chief of staff. Having heard their complaints of gender discrimination Gray paused, apparently upset. It looked as if she was welling up. She took a deep breath. She was, she said, so grateful that they had told her. They had her full support in pursuing justice.

Her claims of solidarity convinced nobody. Having made no progress by 18 September, Gray's critics opted for a nuclear strike. Less than a week before Labour's first conference in government, five advisers briefed the BBC's political editor, Chris Mason, and its chief political correspondent, Henry Zeffman, that the chief of staff herself had asked for and been awarded a salary of £170,000. Not only was that several multiples of the wages offered to junior advisers but it exceeded Starmer's own pay by £3,000. Their article, pushed out to millions of readers via the corporation's breaking news app, contained briefing against Gray that was by a considerable distance the most bilious to have been committed to text. 'It was suggested that she might want to go for a few thousand pounds less than the prime minister to avoid this very story,' one source told the BBC. 'She declined.' Said another: 'It speaks to the dysfunctional way No. 10 is being run – no political judgement, an increasingly grand Sue who considers herself to be the deputy prime minister, hence the salary and no other voice for the prime minister to hear.' For another the bitter row over pay was itself a symptom of Gray's uselessness. 'If you ever see any evidence of our preparations for government,' the spad said, 'please let me know.' Starmer tried in vain to kill the story. At his instruction, Case made eleventh-hour calls to Mason and Tim Davie, the BBC's director general. Once the political editor had clarified just how many complaints the BBC had received, it was no use.

It was an ironic intervention. By then some in the cabinet had reached the incorrect conclusion that Case himself was responsible for much of the briefing against Gray, who took the same view. Clashes of personality were easier to understand than the inconvenient truth: that for too many people in Downing Street and ministerial offices the structures of government had simply failed to function.

Gray decided not to attend conference in Liverpool but her presence was still felt. Everybody spoke endlessly of Sue. In their meetings with newspaper editors, several ministers blamed Case for the slew of

negative publicity. These claims were duly reported. One representative headline, in the *Guardian*, read: 'Head of the Civil Service under
pressure to quit amid "anger" over leaks.'

The cabinet secretary addressed those stories bluntly.

'Keir,' he told Starmer, 'you know this isn't true.'

★

What had Labour achieved in its first hundred days? That milestone,
14 October, cast a shadow over Downing Street. At the last meeting of
the cabinet before party conference, McSweeney had furnished each
minister with a list of their achievements. It was worthy, unglamorous stuff: a taskforce on this, a review of that. Yet all the public had
seen and heard was more of the same. Accusations of impropriety.
The grubby intersection of money and power. Feuding in Downing
Street. Far from turning the page, as Starmer had promised to do in
the speech he gave on the day the election was finally called, he had
lost control of his own narrative.

His denials achieved nothing. On 15 September, three days before
the leak of Gray's pay, he had told reporters: 'I'm not going to talk
behind her back and I'm not going to talk about individual members of
staff, whether it's Sue Gray or any other member of staff. All I can say
about the stories is most of them are wildly wrong.' On 19 September,
asked again about the briefing he so disdained as a symptom of politics
at its worst, he told the BBC that he was 'completely in control' of his
own staff. Informed observers begged to differ.

McSweeney watched and waited. He strove to maintain the public
air of harmony that he and Gray had perfected when in the company
of colleagues. His friends thought this unsustainable. At the end of
August, as the row over Dan Gieve raged back in Westminster, he had
flown to the Democratic National Convention in Chicago. There he
bumped into Alastair Campbell.

'I don't know what the facts are,' Campbell said, 'but this has got to
be resolved one way or another because it's clearly affecting the cap-
acity of the operation.' He conveyed a similar message to Gray.

Campbell's New Labour contemporaries were similarly horrified. Some tried and failed to convince Tony Blair to deliver the *coup
de grâce*.

'It might be an idea,' said a friend of Blair, 'if you just phone Keir. Ask to talk to him, and ask how things are going organisationally in No. 10, and just . . .'

Blair refused. 'Oh, he knows I'm here. I can't start phoning him up, starting to interfere. He knows I'll talk to him whenever he wants me to.'

Starmer was not one to seek advice at moments of acute difficulty. Like a High Court judge he sat aloof, listening quietly to the arguments that raged beneath him. From his Delphic silence Gray's opponents could only take hope. They had been here before. The wait was always agonising. But release always came.

There was no pretence now. McSweeney and Gray, however desperate both were to maintain some sense of civility, were conscripted onto opposite sides of a Darwinian war for survival. In Liverpool, one cabinet minister had told the *Guardian*: 'One or both of them will have to go. It's not going to be Morgan.' They were right. Though she retained a handful of admirers in cabinet, the chief of staff was friendless and outgunned. Every morning began with another round of vicious, anonymous and highly personal attacks on her character. Journalists knocked on her relatives' doors. Starmer had once offered her refuge from a media determined to malign her: advisers to the prime minister who had hired her, and the cabinet that had once loved her, now subjected her to new levels of pain and distress.

With every day her isolation deepened. Starmer had always professed to hate the briefing, bitching and leaking to newspapers that many in Westminster accept as part of its laws of political war. Of attacks on Ed Miliband, one of his few true friends in the cabinet, he would say to friends: 'If I knew who it was, I would sack them.' Indeed, he had said the very same to staff at Labour HQ all but three months before the assault on Gray began. Yet friends of the chief of staff claim this was a cheque he was never willing to cash for her. One relays the revealing story of Gray discovering that a sympathetic adviser had witnessed the name of a special adviser pop up on a journalist's phone as the row over spad pay raged. The accompanying message was full of anti-Sue invective. There it was: evidence, at last, of who might be responsible. Gray is said to have confronted Starmer with the name of the adviser in question. Nothing happened. Nobody was sacked.

To another friend Gray confided that she could not ask Matthew

Doyle to stop the briefings. 'He hates me,' she said. In reality, the head
of communications – whose frustratingly straight bat some hacks likened to a cynical Test batsman playing for a draw – was now spending
much of his time offering forceful but fruitless denials to the journalists that circled like vultures around Downing Street.

McSweeney showed no outward signs of worry during his own stay
on Merseyside. Unlike Gray, he had his own people and his own project. Where Gray's politics were emotional, his could appear coldly
transactional. On the evening of Tuesday 24 September he gave a
forty-five-minute speech on Labour's victory to a party thrown by
Gary Lubner. He did not mention Starmer once.

Release finally came after conference. On leaving Liverpool the
prime minister went to the United Nations General Assembly in New
York, with Gray at his side. It would be the last trip they made together.
Blair might not have intervened, but others had. One by one the advisers he trusted most spoke hard truths about the mess his government
had become. From within No. 10 came Jill Cuthbertson and Vidhya
Alakeson. From the Treasury, his old adviser Ben Nunn. At least one
of the trio threatened to resign if Gray was not removed. All offered
the blunt and unvarnished verdict that she could not remain as chief
of staff.

Starmer offered no guarantees. He returned from America and
went to Chequers. He paced endlessly through its long corridors, and
then it was done.

*

On Tuesday 1 October, McSweeney picked up the phone to a friend.
His colleagues knew what that meant. Unlike Starmer, he was always
seeking counsel. When big decisions loomed he disappeared to call
what looked to outsiders to be a hundred people in quick succession.
He was a conversational prospector, panning constantly for nuggets
of insight to make his own. Today he needed advice.

Starmer wanted rid of Gray. He told one senior figure in Downing Street that week: 'I'd spent all my time pacing around Chequers,
trying to work out what to do. I just decided it wasn't sustainable.'
Empowered by her absence, Gray's critics had spoken truthfully to
him. 'What was clear,' another adviser said, 'was that an awful lot of

people had been in his ear during conference saying: *She's got to go. She's the problem.'*

It was a big call. Helpfully, he had already alighted on a solution. He wanted McSweeney to replace her.

'I'm not sure this is a great idea,' said the voice at the end of the line. 'You're in charge of the project. You don't want to desert the project to become the chief paper pusher.'

'Well,' McSweeney said. 'There's no way that will happen.'

'You don't know that job. There's an awful lot of paper being pushed around.'

McSweeney had been chief of staff once before. The administrative demands of running the office of the leader of the opposition had never suited his strengths. Could he really run a government? His friend instead suggested a shortlist of three: a serving minister, a permanent secretary, and a former Downing Street staffer.

Of this triumvirate it was the minister that most excited McSweeney. He told colleagues in Downing Street that Spencer Livermore, the old adviser to Gordon Brown who had helped run the election campaign and had since landed at the Treasury, was the solution.

'It's fine,' he said. 'Spencer can do it.'

Yet each of the colleagues he trusted imparted the same uncomplicated message: *it has to be you*. For four years there had always been someone else to blame. First the Corbynites. Then whichever aide supposedly stood in McSweeney's way: Sam White, Deborah Mattinson, and the rest. Then Gray. There would be nowhere left to hide now.

But by Thursday his mind was made up. Ahead of the election McSweeney had railed against *deliverism*: the idea that leaders of the centre left could wave statistics at voters who felt their lives were darker and meaner and expect to be congratulated at elections. He spoke of running an insurgent government. He had installed trusted lieutenants in the most troublesome government departments as an insurance policy against Gray's obstructions and Whitehall's groupthink. One June evening at Southwark's Libertine pub, near Labour HQ, it had been agreed that Matt Pound would go to the Treasury. Damian McBride, the once notorious but ever astute adviser to Gordon Brown and subsequently Emily Thornberry, would become a special adviser at the Home Office. Oliver Longworth, from Paul Ovenden's attack and rebuttal unit, would go to the Department for Environment, Food and Rural Affairs.

They were no substitute for the control only a chief of staff could exercise. For nearly a hundred days McSweeney had been little more than a bystander as his colleagues failed to govern themselves. He finally agreed. It had to be him.

The Irishman called the same friends in the state of boyish excitement that tended to take hold of him when the fates conspired in his favour.

'Okay,' one said, still unconvinced that it was sensible. 'Just make it work.'

Starmer informed Gray of his decision the same day. Her own intimates were furious. This, they told her, was the Labour leader at his abject, amoral worse. In courting her so persistently in 2022 he destroyed the only career she had known since leaving school at sixteen. Now it was for nothing. There was nobody Starmer would not sacrifice in the name of self-preservation. They urged her not to trust a single word he said. In that spirit, she enlisted Dave Penman, the general secretary of the FDA union for civil servants, to oversee the delicate negotiations over her departure.

Case was informed the following morning, when Starmer came asking for help. Amid the maelstrom of claim and counterclaim about his difficult relationship with Gray, Case had confirmed that he too would step down in short order only days earlier. He, at least, could say he was doing so because of well-publicised struggles with his health. Gray, who loathed him, had nothing.

'I'm asking Sue to step down,' the prime minister said. 'We'll be appointing a new chief of staff, and I want to appoint a new PPS.'

'Please tell me you're appointing Morgan as chief of staff,' said Case. 'Yes.'

In sacking Gray himself, Starmer had spared the cabinet secretary the constitutional nightmare of issuing an ultimatum, as desperate spads had asked him to do. Civil servants who heard similar entreaties from inside Downing Street could not understand the fearful reticence of Starmer's own employees. Nor, in truth, had they ever understood why McSweeney had not been made his chief of staff in the first place.

'You guys have all known Keir for a really long time,' said one official to a member of the prime minister's inner circle. 'Why aren't *you* going to him?'

*

The truthful answer to that question was one Starmer's aides dared not acknowledge aloud, and seldom did even when alone with one another. For a long time they had feared he would pick Gray. His reasoning was almost always opaque. They knew his real life – his true self – was not the work they shared with him. Their political project was predicated on this unpolitical leader doing as he was told. What if he refused?

In his weaker moments, even McSweeney would confide to friends that he knew neither what Starmer thought, nor whose advice he had taken. Hotheads in what was then the leader of the opposition's office had been minded to drive Gray out of her post as early as January, when the 'boys' club' briefings first proliferated in the press. McSweeney's circle concluded it would not work. As one explains: 'The way Sue had spun it, long before the election, was: "This is the lads. This is the boys who don't like their power being challenged." And it put Morgan in a very, very defensive position.'

Gray's allies in government offer an alternative explanation. To even close colleagues and observers there has always been something unknowable about the compact between Starmer and McSweeney. None call it a friendship. Nor does anyone claim that the two men were bound together by a shared world view. Initially, at least, Starmer's relationship with Gray was 'one of mutual respect', said a government supporter of Gray. 'But respect and love are two different things. He fucking loves those boys around him. He sees them like his babies. It's actually quite weird.' As for McSweeney: 'I think there might be some potential fear in that.' Starmer had always subcontracted the finer – and darker – arts of politics to the Irishman. That was the transaction that made him prime minister. Had he come to fear its power?

All that remained now was to escort Gray out of the door. She had already left for Northern Ireland, always her place of refuge when Westminster turned against her, and her resignation was announced on Sunday 6 October. The Civil Service tried and failed to kill off the new role that had been invented to spare her humiliation – that of the Prime Minister's Envoy to the Nations and Regions, a backhanded acknowledgement that she had at least tried to rebuild relations between the Labour leadership and the mayors it so often disdained – before it was announced, unexpectedly, that morning. In a necessary acknowledgement that he was not much of an administrator either, the two women who had kept the show of Starmerism on the road when others about them panicked – Cuthbertson and Alakeson – were appointed as McSweeney's deputies. They would do much of the work he knew he could not.

Gray put her name to a long statement. 'It has been an honour to take on the role of chief of staff, and to play my part in the delivery of a Labour government. Throughout my career my first interest has always been public service. However, in recent weeks it has become clear to me that intense commentary around my position risked becoming a distraction to the government's vital work of change. It is for that reason I have chosen to stand aside, and I look forward to continuing to support the prime minister in my new role.' What she felt most keenly went unsaid. Starmer was not the man she had once so admired. Gray once believed him to be a man of integrity. Privately, she now concluded that he was encumbered by indecision – and would never confront the 'boys' who did not have his interests at heart. Worse still, he had connived to destroy her with Case. To friends she confided her ultimate regret was not sacking the cabinet secretary on day one.

If the intention of a negotiated exit was to permit her one last moment of dignity, it went unfulfilled. Her secretary was forced to clear his desk with its new inhabitant already seated. She studiously refused to make eye contact, as if Gray had never existed. In the first, longer message Downing Street sent to journalists, one sentence stood out: 'Morgan McSweeney moves to chief of staff having served in No. 10 as chief adviser to the prime minister.'

There was much the prime minister did not understand about politics. But there the two of them were, again. There was no emotion, just the same wordless understanding. The old contract had been renewed.

Acknowledgements

2024 was a long year in British politics, as we learned the hard way. Having been commissioned to deliver a manuscript within six weeks of the general election, on 20 May we reassured our agent, Victoria Hobbs of AM Heath, that Rishi Sunak would not call a snap poll. Within forty-eight hours of our leisurely lunch, he had done exactly that.

The months that followed were spent telling the story of a campaign and political project approaching its moment of resolution far sooner than anyone could have anticipated – both for *The Times* and *Sunday Times*, and this book. Certain commodities were placed under sudden strain: our own time, the availability and candour of our sources, and our ability to think with clarity and perspective about the events unfolding around us. If readers judge us to have overcome those challenges, we only did so with the selfless support of a great many people to whom we are unendingly grateful.

Victoria has championed us ever since making our first book happen in 2020. Without her guidance and generosity, you would not be reading its sequel. Will Hammond, our editor at The Bodley Head, has been just as indispensable. Without his wisdom and judicious editing, we would be lesser writers and this a lesser book. Whenever events or our own literary pretensions threatened to complicate a section of text, he reminded us of the bigger prize: a coherent, compelling story. David Milner's peerless copy-editing weeded out more infelicities and inaccuracies than we knew existed. Graeme Hall and the team at Penguin Random House resolved the remaining ambiguities with pace and precision.

With our editors having gone above and beyond, any errors are ours alone. Without their work this would have been a much longer book, such was the volume of interviews and source material we

amassed over the course of the year. Those who spent hundreds of
hours painstakingly transcribing our conversations have our eternal
thanks: Lucinda Dodd, Harry Duell, Billy Maguire, Isobel Mosley and
Lucy Reade. Martin Alfonsin Larsen deserves a special mention for his
industry and his fine research.

It is customary to thank friends and family for their forbearance
for the author's antisocial tendencies during a process such as this and
none know this better than Patrick Maguire's. To much-appreciated
fellow travellers in Southport, London and beyond: thank you, to
Des, Jenny, Tom, Michael, Billy and Lily in particular. In Ireland, Anto
Greene, Paul Kelly and Sile Markey's hospitality was much too kind,
as were tolerant colleagues and bosses at *The Times*, most of all Tony
Gallagher, Steven Swinford and the best lobby team in Westminster,
Neil Tweedie and Roland Watson. Nobody, though, has so selflessly
put up with quite so many words in as unpredictable an order as Paula,
for whom any more would be inadequate: the dues are still unpaid and
the kindness undeserved.

For Gabriel Pogrund, this journey started with Tim Shipman, who
took a chance on a breathless graduate when writing his own book in
2016 and who has supported this project from the outset. He is also
grateful to Ben Taylor, Krissi Murison and Lindsay McIntosh at the
Sunday Times, and to his loving family: David, Melanie, Adam, Ellie,
Matthew. Above all, he thanks Beatrice, his wife and best friend. The
more words one commits, the more diluted the sentiment. Let these
pages record that this book could not, would not, have happened without her support.

The authors are grateful to Henry Zeffman, who subjected the text
to an indispensable close edit and made too many revisions to be enu-
merated here, save to say that each was readily received and instantly
improved the manuscript. So too Matt Chorley, who bigged us up and
spared our blushes with an even closer reading. Will Lloyd opened his
notebook and shared invaluable insight on one of the protagonists.
Nathan Boroda, the sage of Bury, was a much-valued sounding board
in this book's infancy too.

Our previous book amounted to a post-mortem of a project which
had run its course. That Starmer's is potentially only at the end of
the beginning means fewer sources have been able to speak on the
record in this instance. The ever-patient Julian Lovick and his team at

the UnHerd Club ensured we were able to meet many of them with total discretion and endless supplies of Diet Coke.

Most of all we are grateful to all those who have contributed: from former advisers to the Starmer leadership, like Peter Hyman and Nick Boles, and titans of Labour history, like Tony Blair and Neil Kinnock, who were quoted on the record, to the sources, far greater in number, who at their own request and for their own employment prospects were not, but sacrificed many hours of their time, and shared their emails and WhatsApp messages for the sake of posterity.

Many years after our first project began, the authors are above all grateful to each other.

Patrick Maguire and Gabriel Pogrund
London, December 2024

Index